Primary Education in Portuguese Goa

By the same Author

- The Development of Teacher Education in Portuguese GOA (1841-1961)

About the Author

Ricardo Cabral, presently a faculty with the Goa State Council of Educational Research and Training, is the author of the book. *The Development of Teacher Education in Portuguese Goa*. After completing his M.A. (English) through the Bombay University, he got into the teaching profession. He then obtained his M.Phil. (English) through Goa University and finally did his P.D. in Education through the University of Pune.

For many years he has been contributing a number of articles and write-ups to the local newspapers and magazines. He has also presented research papers at different Seminars at the State and National levels.

He is currently working on his third book titled *Impact of Portuguese Education in Goa*.

Primary Education in Portuguese Goa

An Historical Perspective

Ricardo Cabral

CONCEPT PUBLISHING COMPANY PVT. LTD.,
NEW DELHI-110059

ISBN-13: 978-81-8069-957-3

First Published 2013

Published and Printed by

Concept Since 1974

Concept Publishing Company Pvt. Ltd.
A/15-16, Commercial Block, Mohan Garden
New Delhi-110059 (India)
T: 25351460, 25351794, *F*: 091-11-25357109
E: publishing@conceptpub.com, W: www.conceptpub.com
Editorial Office: H-13, Bali Nagar, New Delhi-110 015, India.

Cataloging in Publication Data--*Courtesy:* D.K. Agencies (P) Ltd. <docinfo@dkagencies.com>

Cabral, Ricardo.
Primary education in Portuguese Goa : an historical perspective / Ricardo Cabral.
p. cm.
Includes bibliographical references (p.) and index.
ISBN 9788180699573

1. Education, Primary—India—Goa (State)—History—19th century. 2. Education, Primary—India—Goa (State)—History—20th century. 3. Education and state—India Goa (State)—History—19th century. 4. Education and state India—Goa (State) History—20th century. I. Title.

DDC 372.95478 23

Dedicated

To My Late Parents, Antonio
and
Maria Severina who were

To Me The Greatest Educationists

9. "Colegio de Reis Magos" (College of the Magi Kings) in 1555.
10. "Academia Franciscana" at Bacaim in 1560.
11. "Colegio de S. Nome de Jesus" (College of the Holy Name of Jesus) in 1560.
12. "Colegio Dominican de N. Sra. de Monte" (Dominican College of Our Lady of the Mount) in 1564.
13. "Colegio de Todos os Santos" (College of all saints) at Margao, Salcette in 1574.
14. "Colegio de Chaul" (College of Chaul) in 1580.
15. "Colegio Academico de S.Tomas de Aquino" (Academic College of St. Thomas Aquinas) in 1584 at Panaji and then transferred to Panelim in 1597.
16. "Seminario de S. Hieronimo" (Seminary of St. Jeronimo) in 1595.
17. "Colegio de S. Paulo" (College of St. Paul) in Diu in 1601.
18. "Hospicio de Jesuitas" (Hospicio of the Jesuits) at Parel in 1600.
19. "Colegio dos Agustinianos" (College of the Augustinians) at Goa.
20. "Colegio de S. Boaventura" (College of St. Bonaventura) at Panelim in 1602.
21. "Seminario de Neura" (Seminary of Neura) in 162[illegible].
22. "Colegio de Madre de Deus" (College of the Mother of God) of the Capuchins at Daugim and transferred to Pilar in 1633.
23. "Colegio de Nossa Senhora de Santana" (College of Our Lady of Santana) at Bandra in 1640.
24. "Colegio de Carmelitas Descalcos" (College of the Descalced Carmelites) at Goa.
25. "Colegio de Congregacao do Oratorio" (College of the Oratorian congregation) in 1702.
26. "Hospicio de S. Francisco Xavier" (Hospice of St. Francis Xavier) at Colaba, Bombay in 171[illegible].
27. "Colegio de Chorao" in 1759.
28. "Colegio dos Vincentinos" (College of the Vincentinians) in 1781.
29. "Escola Souza de Mazagao" (Souza School at Mazagaon) in Bombay in 1795.
30. "Escola dos Barretos" (School of the Barretos) at Cavel, Bombay in 1787.
31. "Seminario de S.Antonio" (Seminary of St. Anthony) in Daman in 1887.

Preface

Call it instruction, education or human resource development everybody today is agreed upon its universal importance and omnipotent influence on human development and rightly so because many of our present-day problems can be easily laid at the doorstep of faulty educational policies.

Goa was extremely fortunate to start the educational journey at almost the same time as most of the European countries because the new philosophies and methodologies that were being periodically thrown up in Europe would get transplanted and tried out in Goa for their efficacy and effectiveness. This was one of the major reasons why Goa was on the right track of human development as education was taking roots albeit in a foreign language. And when I say education I mean education and not literacy or instruction or acquisition of qualifications. No doubt the rulers as superiority-complexed colonizers would have their own agenda. But in any circumstance and in any period the fundas in any education system would be the same.

Generally speaking if today Goa has a school-going culture, if Goa is known for its communal harmony, if there are schools in Goa today within a radius of every two kilometres, if Goans are perceived as hospitable and cultured, if today most of the Goan children are third generation learners unlike many of their counterparts in the rest of the country and if Goans have a better quality of life then it is largely due to education in which field the Portuguese, like it or not gave us a healthy headstart.

Even the devil they say should be given his due. It has been my humble attempt to give credit where it is due only with reference to education. *Te poder mele ani te undde kabar zale* so goes the saying in our Konkani language but in this case the fruits are still being reaped. If Goa today is considered an almost fully literate State of the Union of India it is because education all over Goa had started almost a century before that in many other parts of India. Education cannot happen overnight. We have seen that in spite of the country's best efforts for the past sixty odd years after Independence half the population in India is still illiterate forget about being educated. Education spread in Goa both by design (Portuguese) and by default (English). It goes, however, to the credit of the Portuguese for laying the foundation for education in Goa.

Some though will fault me and question me regarding the enrolment and retention figures. I agree with them that education in Goa did have two major drawbacks: it was in a foreign language and it was seemingly not widespread. Simplistically put the rulers of course were Portuguese and hence understandably they were bound to promote their own language and culture. We must also not forget that attempts were made at promoting the local languages especially Marathi. In fact the first Marathi school was established in 1843 in Panjim by Joaquim Garcez Mourao. But did the nationalists do any better? In spite of shouting hoarse against denationalization some of them on their part opened English medium—another foreign language-schools which today paradoxically place us at par with the prevailing global scenario.

As regards their second criticism the fault is more ours than theirs. In spite of their best efforts—enrolling children was even made compulsory besides making use of inducements like free canteen facilities, free books, etc.,—simple folks were reluctant to send their children to school as the importance of education had not yet dawned on them and ordinary people thought attending school was a waste of time exactly as the situation existed a few years ago in India. In spite of that comparatively speaking as per the observation of Dr.Panduranga Sinai Varde in his book *History of Education in Goa* there were "approximately 50 per cent children out of the total population in the age group of 7-13 attending Primary schools in Goa in the academic year 1960-61" whereas it was only in 1991— a whole three decades later—that the literacy level in the rest of the country rose from 18.33 per cent in 1951 to 52.19 per cent. We need to appreciate the fact that when India's literacy level was below 10 per cent around 1931, Goa already had much earlier a well-established educational system in place.

Coming to the work presented here I have attempted basically three main tasks: (1) collection, translation and compilation in chronological order of the legislation like decrees, notifications and orders from time to time almost verbatim to show the gradual evolution of Primary education in Goa, (2) a brief commentary wherever possible either to draw parallels or to show the differences, and (3) presentation of some major findings from the collected data.

The idea is simply to make the historical data available in one place in the English language to researchers, research students and other readers in the hope it would help those interested to take up specific areas like curriculum, syllabus, textbooks, teaching methods, recruitment and service matters of teachers, the learning process, the administrative aspects, etc., for further research studies. History is a record of the past which helps us to discern the present and to plan the future.

The second reason is to bring out the salient features of the system of education adopted by the Portuguese-based on the French system—at the Primary level because with the entry of the English medium schools unfortunately the baby was thrown out along with the bath water. Lastly I wish to acknowledge the contribution of some of the broadminded Portuguese Governors and other officials to the noble cause of education—Western type of course—in this part of the world the effect of which has remained even till this day in more ways than one, both obvious and not so obvious.

I would like to conclude by placing on record my gratitude to all those who helped me in bringing out this volume starting with my wife who always gave me the freedom to indulge in my academic pursuits, my friends who constantly egged me on, my publishers who undertook the task of bringing my work to fruition and the sponsor. Mr. Donato D'Costa, for his financial and moral support.

Candolim, Goa
January 2012

set-up was the Director of Studies, in the colonies there would be a Commissioner of Studies. At the Provincial Level there would be the Schools' Inspector and at the Parish Level would be the quasi-judicial official called the "Regedor".

Earlier the interference of the State in matters educational was not only minimal but also negligible. But with the promulgation of the "Plano de Estudos" the whole gamut of areas and activities under education like the syllabus, the textbooks, the methods, the monitoring, the reporting, the code of conduct for teachers, the pecuniary benefits, etc., were now clearly delineated and directed.

The New Method

Under the "New Method" of Verney certain stipulations pertaining to Primary education which was initially called Lower education ("Escolas Menores, = minor schools) were introduced as follows:

- The teachers' interview should be conducted by a Jury headed in the Dominions (read colonies) by the Commissioner of Studies and comprising of two more members appointed by the President of the Royal Censor Board
- At the end of the academic year the teachers had to send to the Board the consolidated and individual results of the students along with their remarks regarding progress and attendance so that the Board could issue the appropriate Certificate.
- The syllabus would consist of General rules of Portuguese Orthography, the required Syntax so that the students know to write correctly, the four simple operations in Arithmetic, and Catechism and Civility as these could help the students in character formation.
- The Commissioners (in the Dominions) had to visit the schools without notice at least once a month and get the irregularities corrected on the spot.
- Private tuitions home schooling was allowed provided the students submit themselves to be examined officially before being admitted to a higher Class.
- No officially appointed teacher, however, could give private tuitions. If found he would be fined 100 "cruzados" the first time and double of that the second time and could even get a punishment transfer to Angola.

Contents

List of Tables

"Ratio Studiorum" there were at least three difficult stages which the student had to go through before being given the ecclesiastical duties. Initially the students had to register themselves in the Gymnasium, then admit themselves in the Faculty of Arts and then take up Theology only if the vocation of the student for priesthood was doubly certain.

In keeping strictly with the Biblical principle of "many are called but few are chosen" most of the entrants used to fall by the wayside for some reason or the other. Many of them had by that time already cultivated a love for academics though and hence sought ways and means to put their education to good use. Some of the more enterprising ones took up instruction of young boys in the neighbourhood or village either in their own house or in verandahs or even in the open or worked as home tutors.

Pombaline Initiatives

However, the march of the powerful Religious Orders was halted in midstream by the daring Marquis de Pombal when first in 1759 with his Royal Instructions issued on the 5th of March he expelled the Jesuits from Portugal and all its colonies and then in 1836 dealt the same blow also to the remaining Religious Orders. When he showed the door to the Jesuits he declared that he was against their antiquated, narrow, stifling education methods. In fact when he expelled them from the territory of Goeam he expressed his vision in these words: "let there be an institution in the City of Goa for the children and the clerics both natives of the East, a proper language of the land in the Churches and the Missions, the Latin language to initiate the aspirants into priesthood, subjects of Rhetoric, Logic, Morals, History and Ecclesiastic Studies, History of the conquest of the East, the progress achieved in that part of the world, of men who made it possible and the drawbacks".

It would not be out of place to take a cursory glance at the many reforms in the educational sector that the liberal-minded and far-sighted Marquis de Pombal initiated both in Portugal and the colonies which had a profound effect on the educational scenario in Goeam.

Portugal was in the throes of a family strife among the Royals. Lack of stability invariably makes progress and development take a back seat. This was the state of affairs in Portugal and hence destiny ordained that an iron man should burst onto the scene. Cometh the hour, cometh the man and voila! That man of the moment happened to be Sebastiao de Melo, popularly known as Marquis de Pombal.

I
Background

The Occupation of Goeam

The Portuguese captured Goveam or Goeam (it appears that the Portuguese routinely converted 'eam' into 'a' as in Kolveam-Colva, Nagveam-Nagoa, Mapxeam-Mapusa, Vernneam-Verna and Goveam into Gova and then Goa etc.) and called it Goa in 1510 A.D. Goeam—when the Arabs shifted their base of operations from "Vhoddlem Goeam" they brought along with them also the place name albeit in a shortened form and gave it to their new settlement—was a part of the village of Ela included in the present taluka of Tiswadi which was made up of besides Ela the isles of Divar, Chorao, Cumbharjua and Jua. In keeping with the topography the Portuguese had no hesitation in naming the whole area in their lingo as Ilhas (islands). The village of Ela was connected to the former capital, Gopakapattana or Govapuri on the banks of the river Zuari locally called "Vhoddlem Goeam" (great Goa) for obvious historical reasons and probably to distinguish it from the name of the new settlement.

However, the prized catch for the Portuguese was by now internationally well known entrepot of Goeam which was located on the banks of the river Mandovi discovered and developed by the Arab traders after Gopakapattana was found to be unsuitable. As per their habit the Portuguese soon rechristened Goveam as Goa. Thus Gopakapattana or "Vhoddlem Goeam" came to be called Goa Velha (Goa of old) by the Portuguese though it actually meant "large/big Goeam" in the local language and the other Goeam, the entrepot was called in full form as "Cidade de Goa" (City of Goa) and later on came to be addressed as "Velha Goa" (Old Goa) probably to distinguish it from Nova Goa (Pangim/Panaji) which was the new capital. As the Portuguese kept on extending the boundaries more by default than by design the name Goa too came to be extended to the whole territory occupied by the Portuguese.

Tiswadi and the isles were earlier a part of the large Bahamani kingdom which had been carved out of the former Vijayanagar Empire. The entrepot was a major conduit for trade and commerce. Initially it started as a landing point for the small Arab traders who had been doing sea trade for a long time along the West coast of India. In Goa itself they already had a number of landing points named by them like Anjuna (Hanjunem), Arabo, Hannkanne, etc., along the Chapora river (this itself is said to be a corruption of the word Shahapur). Along the Mandovi river there were landing points at Ponnje, Verem, Goeam, Banastari, etc.

The island of Tiswadi which was the first area that the Portuguese appropriated measures about 198 sq. km which incidentally is the second smallest taluka of Goa at present. On the face of it the main objective of the Portuguese did not appear to be imperialistic as occupation of large areas of land would necessitate engagement of more human resources which in the case of the Portuguese were limited in number at least at that point in time. Hence, they tried to adhere to their main intention of only trade and commerce for which reason the idea was to capture coastal spots favourable for the construction of "feitorias" (trading posts) and for the conduct of trade operations.

However, our focus is not on the intentions explicit or implicit in the military actions of the Portuguese but on the subsequent cultural developments which followed in the wake of a major change in the lives of the people living in the hinterland first in the proximity of Goeam and then in the other areas which came to be annexed by the Portuguese one after another in due course of time. The historical event or events that led to the capture of Goa by the Portuguese has been well-documented in the history books which need not be repeated here.

For the record the complete annexation and subsequent creation of a State called Goa was completed only by the end of the eighteenth century. After the Portuguese had captured the Province ofTiswadi from the Muslims, the Provinces of Bardez and Salcette were also ceded to them during the time of D.Garcia de Sa by the ruler Adil Khan in 1548 though he regretted doing it and then tried unsuccessfully to retrieve the said Provinces in 1558. In coalition with two other rulers he made a final attempt and laid siege to Goeam in 1570 but did not succeed in capturing it. Later on the Province of Ponda was conquered in 1763 but was finally annexed to Goa only in 1791 along with the Provinces of Canacona, Zambaulim and the village of Cabo de Rama. The total Province of

Bicholim was conquered only in 1781 and the Province of Pernem was added in 1788. The Province of Sattari was reconquered for the last time in 1782. So it is seen that only at the fag end of the eighteeth century the boundaries of present day Goa were finally and firmly established.

Location and Geographical Features

The Province of Tiswadi is itself an island with the Zuari river on one side and the Mandovi river on the other with the two connected by the Kumbharjua canal. This topography must have appealed to the Portuguese immensely if not initially at least in the later stages as security concerns would be minimized by the natural barriers.

Most of the provinces consist of low lying water logged areas easily getting inundated during the monsoon. However, bringing to bear their genius the people living in the area had tamed the natural forces and reaped a bountiful harvest. They converted the land into fields and grew two crops of paddy during the year. In between the paddy crops some of these fields were converted into salt pans for the production of salt which was a roaring trade in those hoary days. During winter the particular strain of paddy that was grown having tall and sturdy stalks was called *korgutt* which was supposed to be resistant to the onslaught of the floods as the crop was raised in spite of the fields being almost submerged.

The waterbodies were used for transportation and fishing activities. Across many of the water bodies sluice gates had been installed both to control the ebb and flow of the water into the paddy fields and to farm the fish and in some places to produce salt.

As the land was mostly waterlogged and given to cultivation the population was sparse. In 1823 the population count was said to be around 2,60,000. According to 1900 figures the total population of Goa was 4,75,513 and in 1910 it was 4,86,756 showing a slight increase of 11,232 which became 4,69,496 showing a deficit of 17,258. In 2001 the population figures of Tiswadi taluka alone were around 1,59,409. But in the previous census the figures are in the region of 1,31,941. It is seen from the figures that the decadal growth of the population could be both positive as well as negative. Hence, it appears that population growth in those early years generally remained constant given the regular outbreaks of plague and pestilence. In later years probably due to strides in medicine population not only stabilized but took an increasing trend. Between 1900 and 2001 the growth in the population in the taluka of Tiswadi from 47,551 was around 1,11,858, which means within a period of 100 years the population of Tiswadi had more or less doubled. Taking that as a cue and going back every 100 years would give us population figures of 24,000, 12,000, 6,000 and 3,000 for 1800, 1700, 1600 and 1500 respectively in the taluka of Tiswadi. Hence, based on this premise the total population in Tiswadi in the year 1510 must have been around 2,000 to 3000 souls though historians like J.A.J. da Costa would have us believe that there were more than 20,000 natives in Tiswadi around the end of the sixteenth century not counting the merchants and the *reinois*. However, when Rev. Denis de Kloguen visited Goa around 1862 he wrote in his book *An Historical Sketch of Goa* that there were only about 3,200 inhabitants in the City of Goa and in the whole of Tiswadi it was 48,847 which means in the sixteenth century the population in the whole of Tiswadi must have been not more than 6,000.

The habitations themselves must have been sparse and scattered. The people belonged mostly to the farming community as Tiswadi comes under the coastal plains. These people lived in small groups close to their fields which they cultivated with clockwork regularity as allotted to them by the village commune. Showing extraordinary ingenuity these simple folks had reclaimed many of the lands from the sea or from the marshy lands around the rivers.

However, the entrepot of Goeam must have had a larger proportion of the population due to the brisk business activity because of which it had become a cosmopolitan place and this feature might have inflated the population figures to some extent but may not be in the region of 20,000 natives.

In 1510, the area that came under the suzerainty of the Portuguese comprised of Tiswadi, Choddneam, Divadde, Junvo and Vanxim. Later on in 1543 two more provinces, Bardez and Salcette were annexed by the Portuguese and the name Goa which was initially used to refer to Goeam was extended to cover all the three provinces. This then was the first blank page made available to the Missionaries—in obedience to the papal bulls—who had accompanied the Portuguese military expedition by Afonso de Albuquerque, the conqueror of Goa with lot of help from the locals like Timmayya and Mhalu Pai.

The Missionaries and their Colleges

The Portuguese missionaries were familiar with a particular system of education. All education everywhere started with religious instruction. There was no Primary and Secondary education. There was only Superior education what we call today Higher education which was required to prepare candidates to perform ecclesiastical duties. Hence, in the beginning there were colleges rather than schools though in these colleges there was also elementary education which naturally formed the basis of higher education. However this elementary education was not a stage but an integral part of the Superior education that facilitated the study of Superior or Higher education. Initially elementary stage was considered as only a preparation for the higher level.

The Missionaries naturally imported the same concept into Goa and established colleges. The European system of education thus came to be established in Goa by the Missionaries from the middle of the sixteenth century itself and flourished during the first-half of the seventeenth century. In fact some of them dreamt of a European type of Renaissance in the field of letters and arts for which they even competed with one another.

The first such institution of course was the "Seminario de Santa Fe" and its metamorphosis, the "Colegio de S. Paulo", which is said to have existed from 1556 to 1610. The Franciscans had established the "Colegio de Reis Magos" (College of the Three Magi/Kings) in 1555 at Verem and the Seminary of S. Jeronimo or Hieronimo in 1595 in Guirim. These were followed by a host of many others so much so that the second half of the sixteenth century can be called the Golden Age of Higher Education in Goa looking at the number of institutions that came to be established in a small area—a veritable educational hub—which comprised of three present-day talukas, Tiswadi, Salcette and Bardez. The following is the complete list of the institutions founded in and outside Goa in chronological order of their founding:

1. "Colegio de Onze mil Virgens" (College of 11 thousand Virgins) in Daman in 1501.
2. "Orfanologico de Sta. Luz de Agacaim" (orphanage of St. Lucia of Agacaim) in Daman in 1534.
3. "Seminario de S. Fe" (Seminary of the Holy Faith) in Goa (today's Old Goa) in 1541.
4. "Casa de Catacumenos" (House of Catachumens) in Goa in 1543 later on transferred to Betim in 1762.
5. "Seminario de Bacaim" (Seminary of Bassein) in 1546 at Bassein.
6. "Seminario de Thana" (Seminary of Thane) in 1551 at Thane.
7. "Colegio de S. Paulo" (College of St.Paul) in 1556 at Goa.
8. "Colegio de Monte Poinsur" (College of Mount Poinsur) in 1548.

9. "Colegio de Reis Magos" (College of the Magi Kings) in 1555.
10. "Academia Franciscana" at Bacaim in 1560.
11. "Colegio de S. Nome de Jesus" (College of the Holy Name of Jesus) in 1560.
12. "Colegio Dominican de N. Sra. de Monte" (Dominican College of Our Lady of the Mount) in 1564.
13. "Colegio de Todos os Santos" (College of all saints) at Margao, Salcette in 1574.
14. "Colegio de Chaul" (College of Chaul) in 1580.
15. "Colegio Academico de S.Tomas de Aquino" (Academic College of St. Thomas Aquinas) in 1584 at Panaji and then transferred to Panelim in 1597.
16. "Seminario de S. Hieronimo" (Seminary of St. Jeronimo) in 1595.
17. "Colegio de S. Paulo" (College of St. Paul) in Diu in 1601.
18. "Hospicio de Jesuitas" (Hospicio of the Jesuits) at Parel in 1600.
19. "Colegio dos Agustinianos" (College of the Augustinians) at Goa.
20. "Colegio de S. Boaventura" (College of St. Bonaventure) at Panelim in 1602.
21. "Seminario de Neura" (Seminary of Neura) in 1622.
22. "Colegio de Madre de Deus" (College of the Mother of God) of the Capuchins at Daugim and transferred to Pilar in 1633.
23. "Colegio de Nossa Senhora de Santana" (College of Our Lady of Santana) at Bandra in 1640.
24. "Colegio de Carmelitas Descalcos" (College of the Descalced Carmelites) at Goa.
25. "Colegio de Congregacao do Oratorio" (College of the Oratorian congregation) in 1702.
26. "Hospicio de S. Francisco Xavier" (Hospice of St. Francis Xavier) at Colaba, Bombay in 1718.
27. "Colegio de Chorao" in 1759.
28. "Colegio dos Vincentinos" (College of the Vincentinians) in 1781.
29. "Escola Souza de Mazagao" (Souza School at Mazagaon) in Bombay in 1795.
30. "Escola dos Barretos" (School of the Barretos) at Cavel, Bombay in 1787.
31. "Seminario de S.Antonio" (Seminary of St. Anthony) in Daman in 1887.

It is seen that most of the above institutions were located in a radius of ten to 12 kilometres. The fact that around 20 to 25 of these institutions were located in Goa meant that these institutions thrived solely because there was sufficient enrolment. Each institution must have been frequented by forty to fifty students if not more both day-scholars and boarders. Hence, multiplying the number of institutions with the average number of students one can safely say that around a thousand students must have been enrolled in all these institutions out of which half of them might have been either dropping out or passing out.

Though the prime motive of the institutions was to get as many candidates as possible for priesthood/missionary work the selection process was extremely tough as different conditions like good health, family background, monetary capacity and even caste factors were strictly taken into consideration. For this reason many of the aspiring candidates either were forced to quit or gave up voluntarily. But the knowledge they had gained remained with them which some of them might have tried to disseminate to others around them and thus also contributed their humble mite to human development in Goa.

II
The Early Years (1510 to 1808)

The Parish Schools

Though in the beginning Superior education held sway, the Missionaries realized that without the active co-operation of the locals they could not succeed in their twin objectives: proselytisation and enculturation. Hence, again drawing upon the European trends the Missionaries established the song schools in the different Parishes (area coming under the jurisdiction of a certain Church). But the Missionaries faced a very big hurdle. The song schools would train the children to sing for Church services. But they could not be just humming the tune. They had to express themselves in words. Hence, they had to be taught the language. The language of liturgy at that time was Latin. Secondly the children had to be instructed in catechism. Again the problem was of language. Latin is not an easy language to learn. Besides, the idea was not to make the children proficient in that classical language. To tide over this difficulty oral instruction was used with the children being totally ignorant of the morphology, syntax and semantics of the language.

Hence the Missionaries were on the horns of a dilemma. Latin was as much a foreign language to them as it was for the locals. Portuguese too was a foreign language for the locals. And Konkani was a foreign language for the Missionaries. Some progressive Orders like the bold Franciscans argued that it was better to learn the language of the natives rather than teach them Portuguese. Hence, the first Konkani school was established in Reis Magos (Verem). Other missionaries thought otherwise and were keen to impose not only their religion but also their presumed superior culture on the people of Goeam. This dichotomy succeeded in splitting much later the clergy into two well-defined camps, local and foreign and almost started the first war of independence in Goeam called the Pinto revolt.

This setting up of the Parish schools, however, unconsciously laid the foundation for learning and education in Goa as those who were found to be showing keen interest and some proficiency were picked up and admitted into the many colleges abounding in Goeam.

From a very narrow and limited perspective the King, Dom Joao III himself had written that schools should be opened for the Christians in all the villages where the children could be instructed in the catechism of the church. Accordingly from 1542 onwards Parish schools had been consistently and continuously established in the three provinces of Ilhas (Tiswadi today), Salcette and Bardez.

Initially the priests themselves taught the singing and the catechism to the children. But gradually the baton had to be passed on to a *mestre* (master)—locally called *mestri*—because the priest had other more pressing matters to attend to. But with the appointment of the *mestre* the question of payment arose. This necessitated the roping in of the village associations like the "Communidades" or the "Confrarias" who started paying the *mestres* from their own funds. This also necessitated giving the "school" a more secular outlook as some of the components might have raised objections and the teaching of singing alone would appear incongruous as singing also involved at least reading if not writing. Accordingly the *mestre* was expected to teach besides music and singing, Reading, Writing and Counting. But this had to be done in the Latin language. This was how the Parish schools came to be established.

As stated earlier, Latin was generally used for religious purposes and Portuguese for other needs. Because of the good work, (read the spreading of the Iberian culture) that was being done on the education front by these Parish schools the then Governor, Dom Manuel de Portugal, gave Government recognition to these schools in 1830 as he was interested in spreading education in Goa. However, it was seen that the *mestres* were not paying much attention to the academic aspects as they were not competent enough and thus limited themselves to the teaching of the "Primeiras letras" (first letters literally but meaning rudiments of the language) only. This forced the Baron of Candal, to issue a circular that the services of those *mestres* who were teaching only music and singing and failed to take up Reading, Writing and Counting should be dismissed from service. This raised a big hue and cry especially in Salcette and the controversial circular had to be withdrawn. However, the opening of new schools and the appointment of fresh teachers was thereafter strictly monitored.

Since initially education was the monopoly of the Religious Orders schools came to be established in churches and chapels. The Order of the King which the Governor, Dom Manuel de Portugal, issued in 1542 stated that "religious instruction should be given to all children in Goa wherever there are Christians". This provided the leagl basis for the founding of the Parish schools in Goa. Catechism was usually taught by the priest at least in the initial period and music was taught by a music teacher called *mestre*. These schools were maintained from the funds of either the "Communidades" or the "Irmandades". As time progressed after a few decades the three Rs too came to be taught as it would facilitate religious instruction. However, this type of instruction was prevalent only in the three talukas of Tiswadi, Bardez and Salcette.

Because the population in these three provinces was overwhelmingly Christian, we can safely say that most people by the end of the eighteenth century knew perhaps to read and write to some extent. But unfortunately for the rulers it was not the Portuguese language which the priests were promoting in the Parish schools. They were teaching them the Latin language. This was necessitated by the fact that all the prayers and religious services were always conducted in Latin. Latin was a difficult language to learn being one of the Classical languages and, hence, interest in the language was minimal and even if learnt was quickly forgotten after a few years barring the prayers which had to be recited day in and day out. Hence, very little literacy progress was achieved in spite of there being at least one school in every Parish which numbered not less than fifty. Most prayers were learnt by heart without understanding and repeated on occasions.

It is ironical that though instruction was started, it never really made any significant contribution to the overall progress except the teaching of Music. Since Music is a universal language whether taught in the Western style or the Eastern style singing and playing the musical instruments caught the imagination of the natives and a long standing tradition came to be built the rewards of which are being reaped even today. As interest in Music grew by leaps and bounds, conversely interest in academics declined to such an extent that the Parish schools got almost converted exclusively into Music Classes.

Attempt at Reforms of Parish Schools

However, an attempt was made after the introduction of Pombal's reforms in 1772 and after the expulsion of the Religious Orders from Goa in

1836 to bring in some reforms in the Parish schools and to revive interest in the learning of the three Rs. The Baron of Candal issued a circular dated 8th January, 1840 to the Administrators under whose jurisdiction the "Communidades" were functioning—many of the Parish schools were funded by these local agrarian institutions which goes to show that financially they were on a sound footing and were duly respected by the Portuguese—stating that the Music teachers should abstain from teaching the children to read and write because they were neither qualified nor competent enough to teach as they had not passed any examination and at the same time it would be better if they had not to teach except the ones who knew to read and write correctly so that the students did not acquire the wrong pronunciation or wrong orthography which the incapable *mestres* made them to learn. Further he also instructed the Administrators not to allow anybody to start a school (*casa de ensino* = house of instruction) without a proper licence of the respective Provincial Council which order was expected to be scrupulously followed.

However, the Provincial Council of Salcette opposed the above-mentioned circular saying that "the licences to open such schools had been given under the Decree No. 6, dated 29th of March, 1832 and this right was also upheld by the Constitution of 1838, under Article 29 which stated that "the suspension of the Church schools and the *mestres* either authorized or qualified, far from having a salutary effect, on the contrary would result in grave injustice to education and the progress of the children would suffer as they would not be able to study in the public schools located at Margao since they were poor, of tender age and reluctant to get separated from their parents". Hence, a strong plea was made before the Government that the Parish schools, however, imperfect they might have been be allowed to continue as they were serving some worthy purpose in spite of lack of qualified teachers.

The Governor bowing to the pressure of the Provincial Council of Salcette allowed the Church schools to continue. However he suggested to the "Camara" to open more schools and allow the Music schools to continue but only with a qualified teacher so that the children are taught properly and correctly.

Teachers without Schools

Actually it is said that soon after the conquest of Goa "Albuquerque decided to establish schools for the spread of Portuguese language and culture mainly to prepare the natives to discharge official or public functions". Though Albuquerque lived in Goa for a very short while from 1510 to 1515, he is said to have established the first Western style Primary School in Goa for the orphans in 1514. It is said that he wrote to the King, Dom Manuel on the first of April, 1512 that he was going to instruct the natives. He did not seem to be very enthusiastic about opening many schools though as a promoter of the Portuguese culture that must have been one of the methods uppermost in his mind. He might have been discouraged by the fact that the culture he encountered in Goa was not totally illiterate and ignorant. Writing was already in existence. An iron-tipped pen was used to write on pages of *brassus flabeliformis* as recorded by the traveler Letourneau. The Portuguese started following the same practice till the Governor Matias de Albuquerque had to substitute these metal plates in 1593 with paper.

It appears that instruction did spread through some means or the other as Cunha Rivara much later wrote that by 1541 there were already in India (read Goa) Indian "Professors" (teachers were given the lofty title of "Professors"). It may also be mentioned here that the first Western style Primary School in India was established in Cochin by Antonio Galvao in 1508 which was in keeping with the Portuguese subjugation philosophy. The Portuguese presence in any part of the world was typified by these three signifiers: forts, churches and schools.

However, Albuquerque is said to have met with very limited success as he is credited with the opening of only one school that was in Old Goa. One of the reasons for his limited success was because education generally was in the hands of the Missionaries who exercised a sort of monopoly not only in Europe but also in some other parts of the world like Goa. Therefore, when D. Joao III wrote to the then Governor in Goa in 1545 that efforts should be made to establish schools in all the Parishes of Goa it was the priests who established these rudimentary schools which taught the village kids the three Rs and Singing. These schools were to be maintained from the funds of the "Communidades" (village communities) or from the Church organizations like the "Fabricas" or "Irmandades".

It is really interesting to trace the origin and spread of Primary education in Goa. If today Goa manifests some healthy indicators all round one of the major reasons is the early spread of elementary education in Goa thanks to the Portuguese though this education might have had a limited scope since it was Western styled and largely elitist yet some of it might have percolated to the ground level as it invariably does. If it suffered from lack of universal access and retention the reasons are not far to find. To start with education was never valued at that time as it is now. The masses were poor and could not be bothered. It was a foreign education which was always looked at with suspicion. It was linked to the Christian religion. Before the declaration of the Republic in Portugal Hindus were discriminated against.The upper Classes deliberately discouraged the others from attending schools as keeping the masses ignorant was always to their advantage. However, credit must be given to some of the Portuguese for having persevered with the school system in spite of the myriad difficulties.

In the sixteenth and seventeeth centuries education was the sole preserve of the Religious Orders. They had established a total monopoly over this sphere of life in the whole of Europe and they did the same in Goeam. In certain countries they translated this academic power into political power. The Jesuits for example because of their proximity to the political powers exercised a tremendous influence throughout Europe. They were the first ones to develop a particular teaching method called the "Ratio Studiorum". Since the prime purpose of the Missionaries was training of candidates for ecclesiastical duties they limited themselves to higher education.

The same contemporary scene prevalent in Europe was transplanted lock, stock and barrel in Goeam and the Jesuits who were the first to seize the opportunity, firmly established themselves in Goeam putting up the first college called the College of Holy Faith which in due course of time got converted into a sprawling campus and was addressed as St. Paul's University as it had virtually become a University due to the universal collection of its students. The Jesuits were followed in no time by the other Religious Orders like the Franciscans, Dominicans, Theatines, Carmelites, etc., with the result that they started vying with one another in establishing quality institutions so as to attract as many students as possible. They not only offered undergraduate courses but also awarded Ph.D. degrees. It has been recorded by the French traveller, Pyrard that there were around 5,000 students in St. Paul's itself at the time of his visit.

So it is not difficult to imagine that in the sixteenth and the seventeenth century—the Golden period—the Portuguese flag was really flying high both politically, culturally and territorially in the whole of Asia. Though the institutions established by the Religious were primarily supposed to cater to those wishing to aspire for the priesthood it is understood that at least half of the students if not more enrolled in these institutions would discontinue or told to discontinue either after completing the course or even midway. Besides as the teaching learning method was based on the

"Ratio Studiorum" there were at least three difficult stages which the student had to go through before being given the ecclesiastical duties. Initially the students had to register themselves in the Gymnasium, then admit themselves in the Faculty of Arts and then take up Theology only if the vocation of the student for priesthood was doubly certain.

In keeping strictly with the Biblical principle of "many are called but few are chosen" most of the entrants used to fall by the wayside for some reason or the other. Many of them had by that time already cultivated a love for academics though and hence sought ways and means to put their education to good use. Some of the more enterprising ones took up instruction of young boys in the neighbourhood or village either in their own house or in verandahs or even in the open or worked as home tutors.

Pombaline Initiatives

However, the march of the powerful Religious Orders was halted in midstream by the daring Marquis de Pombal when first in 1759 with his Royal Instructions issued on the 5th of March he expelled the Jesuits from Portugal and all its colonies and then in 1836 dealt the same blow also to the remaining Religious Orders. When he showed the door to the Jesuits he declared that he was against their antiquated, narrow, stifling education methods. In fact when he expelled them from the territory of Goeam he expressed his vision in these words; "let there be an institution in the City of Goa for the children and the clerics both natives of the East, a proper language of the land in the Churches and the Missions, the Latin language to initiate the aspirants into priesthood, subjects of Rhetoric, Logic, Morals, History and Ecclesiastic Studies, History of the conquest of the East, the progress achieved in that part of the world, of men who made it possible and the drawbacks".

It would not be out of place to take a cursory glance at the many reforms in the educational sector that the liberal-minded and far-sighted Marquis de Pombal initiated both in Portugal and the colonies which had a profound effect on the educational scenario in Goeam.

Portugal was in the throes of a family strife among the Royals. Lack of stability invariably makes progress and development take a back seat. This was the state of affairs in Portugal and hence destiny ordained that an iron man should burst onto the scene. Cometh the hour, cometh the man and voila ! That man of the moment happened to be Sebasteao de Melo, popularly known as Marquis de Pombal.

The change in the educational fortunes began when on the 28th of June 1759 the King of Portugal issued a long-winded Royal proclamation which primarily showed the existing school system—mostly in the hands of the Jesuits—in very poor light and then laid down a detailed programme both at the elementary education level and the higher/superior education level detailing the functions, responsibilities, syllabi and the methodology that the various educational institutions needed to adopt. It was a comprehensive piece of legislation which aimed at bringing education under a well-defined system. This comprehensive arrangement for the promotion of education came to be called the "Plano de Estudos" whose main author was the Marquis de Pombal. The Royal proclamation read as follows:

"I, the King make it known to those who will receive this proclamation that having understood that the course of Sciences depends upon the happiness of the Monarchy; preserving thus by these means Religion and Justice in all its purity and equality and for these reasons the same Sciences always made the object more worthy of the care of the previous Kings who with their Royal patronage established and encouraged learning, having promulgated the most just laws so that the subjects under their care could make a lot of progress which would benefit the Church; on the other hand the country having understood that the study of the Humanities is the basis of all the Sciences which we see in this kingdom has greatly declined with the schools having been entrusted to the Religious Order of the Jesuits, because of the vague and tedious Method used by them with an inflexible tenacity in the schools both in the kingdom and in the Dominions with which they would argue against the evidence of solid facts and change them into defects; there was the bias of using only one method for a long period of eight or even nine years without learning even the odds and ends of Grammar; bereft of the true notions of the Latin and Greek languages as they could speak and write without wasting time with the same facility and purity used by all the other nations of Europe which have abolished the pernicious method for which the same Religious are the cause of the almost total decadence of the two said languages which they have never ceded either to the invincible force of the great men of all the civilized nations or to the praiseworthy and fervent zeal of the many variants of the excellent erudition which have been clamouring loudly in this kingdom against the Method, against the bad taste and the ruining of learning, like the demonstrations of many and great Latin and Rhetorics which had flourished before this same method in Portugal, till the time when the same learning had been snatched away from the hands of Diogo de Teive and from others equally learned and erudite teachers.

Wishing not to restore the same studies which they cannot stop from falling into the impending ruin totally, but still reviving that previous brightness which had made the Portuguese so knowledgeable in the world of letters before the said Religious Order introduced the teaching with sinister motives and unhappy results, which soon after their principles had been exposed and met with the disapproval of men more learned and prudent in these useful disciplines, which adorned the sixteenth and the seventeeth centuries, which they understood and they would locate immediately the mistakes in the Method, the future and necessary ruin of the indispensable teachings, as it happened for example with the University of Coimbra, opposing the opening of the College of Arts, having been ordered by the same Religious Order in the year 1555; the Cortes which the King, Dom Sebastiao convened in the year 1562 sanctioning then already to it the powers against the acquisition of landed properties, and against the teachings of the said Religious; the Nobility and the people of the city of Porto in the agreement which they had signed on the 22nd of November of 1630, against the schools which the same Religious Order had opened in that year in the said city having imposed severe penalties on those who sent their children to study in these schools.

And lastly even when anybody used the Method of the said Religious, it never gave any kind of confidence to them in the teaching or education of the children and the youth, after having shown so hollow an experience, by the decisive facts and exclusive of all the "tergiversacao" and the interpretation, being the doctrine which the organization of the said Religious congregations made to be given to the students of their classes and schools, wickedly leading them to the ruin not so much of the Arts and the Sciences but of the Monarchy and the Religion, which we, our Kingdom and the Dominions I must sustain with my Royal and flawless protection, I am constrained to deprive entirely and absolutely the same Religious Order in all my Kingdoms and Dominions of the teachings of which I had ordered to be suspended, for which, on the day of the publication of this in advance, if they have, as effectively by closing all the Classes and the schools, with which so pernicious and disastrous effects they had made them opposed to the ends of instruction and of edification of my faithful subjects, abolishing till the memory of the same Classes, as never had existed in my kingdom and Dominions."

In this lengthy proclamation issued on the 28th of June, 1759 in which all the schools following the Jesuit method were shut down and a new regime was started.The King made out his defence for the expulsion of the Jesuits and the shutting down of their schools. Since the schools using the Jesuit method of instruction were ordered to be closed down, new ones naturally had to be opened to take the place of the former. Along with the setting up of new schools the Royal Decree also made provisions for the appointment of a Director of Studies and teachers to teach Latin Grammar, Greek and Rhetoric which comprised the Secondary Level of education.

It was rightly realized that the Primary Level had to be taken care of if education was to be truly universal and meaningful for the masses. The first step, therefore, in this direction was taken by setting up a Royal Censor Board ("Real Mesa Censoria") whose prime objective was the direction and supervision of education at the lower Level.

This was a part of the larger comprehensive "Plano de Estudos" (Education Plan) unveiled and Decreed in 1772 by the reformer Prime Minister of Portugal, Marquis de Pombal, in which among other things he ordained that:

I. Official Primary schools should be opened everywhere.
II. The Primary teachers should be selected through a public examination by administering a proficiency test for the teachers of the Parish schools.
III. Textbooks should be prescribed and approved by the Royal Censor Board.
IV. The number of vacancies of teachers should be properly identified.
V. The teaching qualifications should be prescribed, etc.

These Orders had the force of law.

Under these same regulations provision was made for the appointment of a Director of Studies who would be the over-all in charge of education both in the country and in the colonies. He would be appointed by the King. At the end of every year he had to submit a comprehensive report to the King regarding the progress of education in the country. He had the powers to take action against any of the teachers if found wanting. He was also empowered to settle disputes, controversies, service matters, etc.

The first Director to be appointed under this "Plano de Estudos" was D. Thomas, Principal of Almeida, of the Santa Igreja de Lisboa.

Going from the academic to the administrative the "Plano de Estudos" formulated the supervisory structure. If at the head of the educational set-up was the Director of Studies, in the colonies there would be a Commissioner of Studies. At the Provincial Level there would be the Schools' Inspector and at the Parish Level would be the quasi-judicial official called the "Regedor".

Earlier the interference of the State in matters educational was not only minimal but also negligible. But with the promulgation of the "Plano de Estudos" the whole gamut of areas and activities under education like the syllabus, the textbooks, the methods, the monitoring, the reporting, the code of conduct for teachers, the pecuniary benefits, etc., were now clearly delineated and directed.

The New Method

Under the "New Method" of Verney certain stipulations pertaining to Primary education which was initially called Lower education ("Escolas Menores, = minor schools) were introduced as follows:

- The teachers' interview should be conducted by a Jury headed in the Dominions (read colonies) by the Commissioner of Studies and comprising of two more members appointed by the President of the Royal Censor Board.
- At the end of the academic year the teachers had to send to the Board the consolidated and individual results of the students along with their remarks regarding progress and attendance so that the Board could issue the appropriate Certificate.
- The syllabus would consist of General rules of Portuguese Orthography, the required Syntax so that the students know to write correctly, the four simple operations in Arithmetic, and Catechism and Civility as these could help the students in character formation.
- The Commissioners (in the Dominions) had to visit the schools without notice at least once a month and get the irregularities corrected on the spot.
- Private tuitions/home schooling was allowed provided the students submit themselves to be examined officially before being admitted to a higher Class.
- No officially appointed teacher, however, could give private tuitions. If found he would be fined 100 "cruzados" the first time and double of that the second time and could even get a punishment transfer to Angola.

The new reforms unleashed by the Marquis of Pombal in 1759 began in Goa with a letter from the Director (General) of Studies, D. Thomas de Almeida to the Chancellor of the Court in Goa, Joao de Souza de Menezes Lobo appointing him as the Commissioner of Studies in Goa. Soon afterwards along with another letter dated 25th of March, 1760 he was sent the copies of the textbooks to be adopted for teaching in the Latin, Greek and Rhetoric Classes impressing upon him the need for quick action. By another letter dated 27th March, 1760 the Governor of Goa, Conde de Ega was also requested to give whatever help was required to implement the orders of the King.

Under this Plan Marquis de Pombal took the landmark decision in 1772 of making Primary education official, free and equally accessible to all for which reason he had to lay down the proper rules and regulations. The idea was to make Primary education mass-based and do away with the exclusive preserve of a few. To support this gargantuan task financially he introduced the "subsidio litterario" tax.

The Pombaline reforms were instrumental in creating two Government posts of teachers in Goa to teach Reading, Writing and Singing, two posts of "Professors" to teach Latin Grammar, one post of Greek language (never filled up), one post of a teacher for Rhetoric and one post of Philosophy. It is another matter that only two Primary teachers, one each in Salcette and Bardez were appointed and one teacher of Latin. The Government was in a way forced to take up the promotion of instruction to fill up the void caused by the expulsion of the Jesuits. But it was also soon realized that funds were needed to carry forward the ambitious education plan.

For this purpose as stated earlier the Government levied a tax called the "subsidio litterario", an educational cess. By an Order dated 17th of October 1773 the King called for the closing of the books of account of the salaries of teachers and other expenses and then opened a new book which would show receipts from the taxes levied on spirited drinks and on the sale of meat on the one hand and expenditure on education on the other hand.

The Royal Censor Board with respect to "the City of Goa" submitted a proposal on the 22nd of March, 1773 which was not only accepted but also incorporated by the King into the other legal stipulations. These various clauses in the proposal were as follows:

- Creation of a Committee as a representative in Goa of the Royal Censor Board comprising of the Archbishop, the Governor and the Military Captain as ex-officio members along with some other competent persons as nominated members which could either be priests or juridical Officers. Their brief would be to get the Laws, Orders, Editals, etc., of the Board implemented in Goa.

- They had to promptly bring to India the Statutes of the University of Coimbra, the laws, the various notifications of the Censor Board in short everything that concerned education in Goa.
- They could seize and forward to the Board books, papers, etc., whose use had been prohibited by the Board.
- They could summon to the office heads of all the institutions and intimate to them the scrapping of any of the prohibited books and fix responsibility for any violation.
- The printing of material in the native languages was to be revived.

Teachers and their Service

Accordingly a notice was issued on the 7th of April, 1774 to the Chief Justice (Ouvidor) to start the process of selecting teachers through an examination and to approve those who wanted to open private schools. To set the process in motion for the selection of teachers the required norms had to be prepared. Officials had to be appointed and certain provisions had to be put in place. For this very reason a set of detailed instructions were issued in connection with the above mentioned examination:

- A competent person was to be appointed to draw up the criteria for assessment, to fix the date, month, and year in which these examinations would be held regularly, to obtain the information of the candidates like their name, age, residence, actual occupation and personal information.
- This examination in charge and the Jury members to be appointed for the examination had to take an oath of secrecy.
- The Jury members had to give their comment at the end of each test.
- Those candidates who had taken Philosophy had also to answer Logic, Ontology, Pneumatology and Metaphysics and had to know thoroughly the system of union of the soul and body.
- The examination would be answered in Latin.

- Those selected would be paid 480 thousand "reis" annually, paid every quarter but always in advance.
- The candidates of Rhetoric would analyze parts of two of the passages of Cicero, would have to respond to the precepts/ principles enunciated by Quintiliano and the Poetics of Horatio, pointing out the beauty in the works of any of the well-known Portuguese writers and the defects in any one of the failed writers. Besides there would be translation of a passage of any of the Portuguese writers from Latin to Portuguese.
- The candidates for Latin Grammar had to select two from any six authors—Cicero, Suetonio, commentaries of Ceasar, Cornelio Nepote, Virgilio and Horatio—for prose passages and one for verse translating orally a short passage from Portuguese into Latin and answering questions on Latin Grammar.
- Instructions as to the examination centres and the mode of answering the examination would be clearly given to the candidates.
- Those appointed for Rhetoric would be paid 440 thousand "reis" annually; and the teachers of Latin Grammar would earn annually 400 thousand "reis".
- Those aspiring to be teachers of Reading, Writing and Counting would be told to write some sentences in Portuguese and prepare a bill which then had to be submitted along with the personal documents for checking of the Orthography and the characterization of letters. Besides this they would also be examined in Catechism.
- Those appointed would get annually 90 thousand "reis".
- Those who had been appointed and placed would figure in the "Mappa da Lei" (Code of Law) of the 6th of November, 1772.

The results of the first examination that was conducted for the appointment of teachers in Goa were then dispatched to the Royal Board (by now the word Censor had been dropped as probably it was found to be a bit obnoxious) on the 2nd of May, 1777. The Jury for these first examinations had comprised of Fr. Antonio Assumpcao for Philosophy, Advocate Vitorino Pereira for Rhetoric, for Latin Grammar Domiciano Francisco da Costa and Luis Antonio Gonsalves and for selecting the teachers of Reading, Writing and Counting, Caetano Ventura de Saldanha and Jose Antonio Martins. A little later by the Decree dated 9th April, 1778, substitute teachers for Latin Grammar and Reading-Writing were appointed in the provinces of Salcette and Bardez. These teachers who were appointed under the Marquis de Pombal's Education plan were called "Mestres Regios" or Royal Masters. Under this same New Method separate instructions were laid down for the "Professors" in different subjects. There were 23 instructions for "Professors" of Latin, 10 instructions for "Professors" of Greek and Hebrew and 13 instructions for "Professors" of Rhetoric.

The Plan took care of all aspects of education. Even books that would be prescribed had first to be approved and notified. For example approval was granted on the 28th of June, 1759 to Antonio Felix Mendes and Pe. Antonio Pereira for the use of their Latin Grammar books for which reason they could be printed only with Government permission.

The Educational Scenario in Goa

What was the educational scene in Goa during this time? Around 1760, Classes (*aulas*) were being conducted in the following places:

Table 2.1: Places where the Early Schools were Run

Sr. No.	*Place*	*Location of school*	*Name of teacher*	*No of students*	*Remarks*
01	Old Goa	S. Pedro Parish	Fr. Augustinho Martins	04	Closed down*
02		Ribandar Parish	Fr. Caetano S. Thiago Lobo	36	
03		Panjim Parish	Fr. Sylvestre de Souza	20	
04		Neura Parish	Fr. Augustinho de Albuquerque	20	Closed down
05		Carambolim (Guadulupe) Parish	Fr. Pedro do Rosario	15	Closed down
06	Chorao	Graca	Fr. Luis Ribeiro	25	Closed down
07		Graca	Fr. Estanislao Correia	10	
08		S. Bartholomeu	Fr. Bartholomeu Xavier	30	Closed down
09		S. Bartholomeu	Fr. Diogo de Abreu	15	
10		S. Bartholomeu	Fr. Jose Manuel	05	
11	Divar	Piedade	Fr. Mathias Rangel	26	Closed down
12		Piedade	Fr. Jose Vaz	06	

(*Contd.*)

TABLE 2.1 (*Contd.*)

Sr. No.	*Place*	*Location of school*	*Name of teacher*	*No of students*	*Remarks*
13		Piedade	Fr. Pedro Gonsalves	01	
14		Piedade	Fr. Phillipe de Braganza	04	
15		S. Mathias	Fr. Antonio Rodrigues	34	
16		S. Mathias	Deacon Francisco Fernandes	03	
17		S. Mathias	Fr. Manuel de Jesus	01	
18		S. Mathias	Menorista Antonio Salvador	04	
19		Naroa (Narveam)	Fr. Antonio Phelippe de Goveia	02	Closed down
20	Jua (S. Estevao)	S. Estevam	Fr. Vicente Ferrao	02	Closed down
21	Bardez	Serula	Fr. Salvador Martins	40	Closed down
22		Serula	Fr. Andre Soares	08	
23		Pomburpa	Fr. Antonio Soares	20	Closed down
24		Aldona	Fr. Roque Fernandes	16	Closed down
25		Sangolda	Fr. Caetano Xavier	20	Closed down
26		Saligao	Fr. Bartholomeu Moniz	26	Closed down
27		Parra	Joao Fragoso	25	Closed down
28		Pilerne	Jose Xavier Martins de Carvalho	14	Closed down
29		Pilerne	Fr. Xavier Pinto	08	
30		Reis Magos (Verem)	Fr. Domingos Antonio Monteiro Xavier	20	Closed down
31		Virlosa (Penha de France)	Manuel de Penha	30	Closed down
32		Candolim	Fr. Caetano Ribeiro	18	Closed down
33	Salcette	Orlim	Fr. Manuel Luis	04	Closed down
34		Orlim	Fr. Antonio Vas dos Martires	06	
35		Varca	Francisco Dias	07	Closed down
36		Varca	Fr. Antonio Rebello	02	

(*Contd.*)

TABLE 2.1 (*Contd.*)

Sr. No.	*Place*	*Location of school*	*Name of teacher*	*No of students*	*Remarks*
37		Colva	Fr. Caetano Rodrigues	04	Closed down
38		Colva	Fr. Francisco Xavier de Conceicao	03	
39		Sancoale	Fr. Caetano Carvalho	12	Closed down
40		Majorda	Fr. Benedito Jacques	20	Closed down
41		Chicalim	Fr. Reginald Burgell	04	Closed down
42		Chicalim	Fr. Antonio de Sequeira	06	
43		Nagoa	Fr. Custodio Baptista	06	Closed down
44		Verna	Fr. Joao Nepomeceno de Rego	02	Closed down
45		Verna	Fr. Manuel Joao de Faria	06	
46		Verna	Fr. Augustinho de Figueiredo	03	
47		Loutulim	Fr. Francisco Xavier da Costa	03	Closed down
48			Fr. Antonio Salvador Monteiro	08	
49		Loutulim	Fr. Jose Mascarenhas	09	

* Since there were no vacancies at times in the Parish churches because of a surfeit of priests, the priests had to stay at home till such time as a vacancy arose. For this reason some of the Classes stopped in September as soon as the new appointments were made by the ecclesiastical authorities.

It is to be noted that there were around 50 Classes opened in the three provinces of Ilhas, Bardez and Salcette. Barring three lay persons and two Seminarians the rest of the teachers were all priests. These priests took to teaching because they did not have any other work to do, they were suitably qualified and they had to engage themselves in some worthwhile activity. They were the only ones who knew Latin and hence could teach a thing or two to the others.

In these three provinces it can be seen that in the year 1760, there were 622 students attending these Classes in around fifty centres. Some teachers attracted more students, some very few. What were the factors that attracted more children to a particular teacher are difficult to know. All these Classes were conducted privately. The Plan of Studies tried to regulate all these Classes. Around this same time in Portugal there were around 526 centres where instruction was being imparted. This meant that only around 12-14 per cent of the school-going population was attending any sort of education. This increased to 22.7 per cent at the time of the establishment of the Republic in 1910.

Officially the Government had appointed the "Mestres Regios". However, the services of these "Mestres Regios" were terminated in 1798 by the Governor, Veiga Cabral citing financial constraints. With the abolishing of those posts of the Royal Masters Primary education was promoted only through the Parish schools and the two Seminaries. Though the next Governor, Conde de Sarzedas did take an interest in education by opening schools in 1808 of "primeiras letras" and setting up of Chairs of Latin, one in Ilhas and two each in Salcette and Bardez the initial impetus had died down and there was only some stunted growth of Western education which consequently meant that Portuguese language and culture failed to take off. Sarzedas opened these five Classes of Latin in 1808 in Cidade de Goa (Pangim), Majorda, Chinchinim, Mapuča and Candolim. The Conde de Sarzedas was, therefore, instrumental in starting the first Secondary schools in 1808. These Classes were reduced to just three, one in each of the provinces when in 1836 by the Decree of 15th and 17th November the new plan for Primary and Secondary schools was unveiled in Portugal. Later on they came to be called the Municipal Lyceums.

Every successive Governor was seized of the problem and though some of them like Dom Manuel de Camara and Dom Manuel Portugal e Castro even wrote back to the King painting a very sorry picture of the state of affairs on the educational front in Goa.

On hindsight Marquis de Pombal should be hailed as a great European visionary and an educational Reformer. He should be commended for showing guts and gumption for taking on the might of the all powerful Jesuits whose writ ran large throughout Europe. Necessity is the mother of invention and circumstances forced Marquis de Pombal to innovate and this like a whiff of fresh air brought in a range of far-sighted reforms in education. More importantly he was thoroughly convinced that it was the responsibility of the State to provide intellectual succour to all its citizens without discrimination or distinction. He was also a liberal-minded person and strongly favoured that Goans should be treated as full-fledged citizens on par with the other Portuguese and not like some second-class citizens.

III
Inclination towards Instruction (1829-1853)

The New Found Zeal

Though the Marquis had given a great fillip to education in Portugal and its Dominions by his pragmatic policy of introducing the "subsidio litterario" the situation in Goa was yet to take off and official instruction was in a pitiable condition described vividly by the Governor, D. Manuel da Camara in 1822, "in a population of 2,60,000, there is not a single house of education" (read school). He complained against the Seminaries where he said that in spite of the State funding them there were only thirty students on the rolls who were haphazardly tutored by the local clergy as they were not really qualified to teach such subjects as Latin Grammar, Philosophy, Theology, Dogmas and Morals. He accused them of using an antiquated and out-dated teaching method. In short apparently he wanted instruction to come under official control.

It also appears that the Governor's plaint was more in support of the Portuguese and their progeny than in sympathy with the locals as a new Constitution had been adopted in Portugal. He apprised the King that because of lack of instruction there was a shortage of people to man the administration. Hence, he proposed that educational institutions should be established sooner rather than later as these would be highly beneficial to the running of the Government. However, he did not stay long to see any tangible results forthcoming. He was succeeded fortunately by another equally zealous Governor, Dom Manuel Portugal e Castro who too wrote to the King about the pitiable situation of education in Goa.

In 1829, only three Primary schools were found to be in existence. After a longish period of inactivity from 1808 to 1830 the Governor, Dom Manuel de Portugal e Castro took the initiative and founded six "public Primary schools" by his "Portaria" dated 5th September, 1831 and located them—with the exception of the one at Ribandar—in the military barracks so that they would be under the direct control of the military commandant of the battalion. On the 9th of September, 1831 he issued a notice making his intentions clear when he stated "I wish to inform that wanting to promote Public Instruction in the islands of Goa and the provinces of Salcette and Bardez and not willing to restrict this important work ....I wish to promote the same Instruction in the New Conquests also ....". He, therefore, advertised the posts and informed about the content for the examination of the would-be teachers. Prior to that on the 5th of September, 1831 he had already laid down and advertised the Instructions to the Teachers of Primary Instruction (Primeiras Letras). But before doing that he first announced through a circular issued on the 13th of June, 1831—the same day he had issued a "Portaria" making it mandatory to have a teaching licence—that he would like to know from all concerned—"Communidades", teachers, officials—the number of teachers, the places where they were appointed, how many had the licence to teach, in which place, what was the teaching method followed, the books adopted and their authors, who had appointed them and who paid their salaries, how much salary was paid to them, etc., to be submitted in a table form so that the information could be viewed at one glance. That probably was the first educational survey in India. There were three types of schools in Goa (in the three provinces) at that point of time; Classes of "Primeiras Letras", Classes of Latin Grammar and Rhetoric and Classes of Philosophy.

After taking stock of the situation the Governor, Portugal e Castro based on the evidence collected arrived at the conclusion that the state of education in Goa was very deplorable with hardly anybody able to understand Portuguese and very few able to either speak or write the language. For this reason he issued the following directions in order to establish the new schools:

1. Because of the military barracks and the families of Europeans and because these places are centrally located the Primary schools will be established in these military areas; in the Artillery centre in Panjim (for Ilhas); in the Battalion of the Gunners at Margao; in the quarters of the Battalion at Bicholim; in the Battalion at Colvale and in the area occupied by the Infantry at Ponda. These schools were meant not only for the children of the soldiers but also for others without any distinction willing to send their children to school.

2. A school would also be established in Ribandar conveniently located where children from the neighbourhood and even from Panjim could attend.
3. These six schools besides having the regular teachers would also get for each school an Assistant, so that the work would get divided and substitution—whenever the teacher was absent—would be possible.
4. These schools would be under the supervision of the Commanding Officers of each place respectively. The school in Ribandar, however, would be under the control of the Military Officer from Pangim.

On the 5th of September, 1831 this same Governor, Dom Manuel de Portugal e Castro issued various other instructions dealing with content in the syllabus, the method to be adopted in teaching the rudiments of the Portuguese language, the textbooks to be followed in the schools, the testing and evaluation of the students, the records to be maintained, the reporting to be done, the academic calendar to be followed and the supervision to be conducted:

- The Primary teachers ("Mestres de Primeiras Letras") would be obliged to teach not only Reading, Writing, Catechism, the main rules of Civility but also the general rules of Portuguese Orthography, whatever Syntax was necessary, that would help the students to write correctly and ordinarily as was stated in the Law of 6th November, 1772.
- The "Mestres" were supposed to know and pronounce clearly and distinctly all the letters of the Portuguese alphabet. After that they had to take up the spelling of the letters of the syllables initially those having one consonant and one vowel and then gradually two, three and even four consonants using the words found in the prescribed textbook, "Escola Nova Christa Politica" written by Dom Leanor Thomas de Souza e Silva for the use of his sons reprinted in Lisbon in the Royal Press. Still some more lessons could be taken up for this exercise by taking up words from other passages so that the students could become fluent.
- After they had learnt to read well and spell the words having one, two or more syllables passing gradually from the first to the second and thus in front. And when the habit had been formed of spelling continuously, they had to read correctly with the proper pauses which demanded different orthographic signs like

the comma, semi colon, colon, full stop, question mark and exclamation mark which were found in the passage, reserving the major explanations to be taken up at an advanced stage.

- The "Mestres" had to take particular care to see that the students kept on repeating always the syllables spelling successively one after the other till the word had ended which was the best method, for in this way when they reached the last syllable they would still be remembering those at the start.
- The "Mestres" were prohibited from using the earlier method which had been prescribed by the law of 30th September, 1770 whereby the students were taught to read through the process of disputations and sentences, etc.
- As soon as the students were clear in reading the letters they had to be taught the shape or the form of the letter through the Catechism booklet by Carlos Joaquim Colbert as per the above cited Law through which they were supposed to learn the Catechism and the principles of the Religion in which the "Mestres" had to instruct them with special care and with preference to any other study. In case this booklet was not available the one by the well-known Fr. Manuel Correia Valente had to be used. Later on they had to use alternatively the "History of D. Joao de Castro" by Jacinto Freire de Athaide and the booklet "Book of children in which the general ideas and definitions of things which children must know are given" whose first edition was printed in Lisbon in 1778.
- After the children had followed thoroughly reading the prose in these books which had been mentioned or in their absence, certain passages from the Sacred History or universal profane History or the History of Portugal or of India, they had to be made to read some book on poetry especially the "Lusiadas" of Camoes taking great care to raise the voice at the stressed syllable, so as to habituate them in the rhythm and the metric cadences and not to allow them to miss any word which they had not pronounced with distinction and clarity.
- As soon as the child had cultivated the habit of holding the indicator to show and pronounce the letters of the alphabet and to spell the syllables the "Mestre" would then teach him Writing, taking great care of the posture of the body, the placing of the arm, the holding of the pen, the formation of the letters and the sharpening of the pointers when he had to apply with sufficient

force, advising him that he had to begin with the more easy and then pass on to the more difficult and at first to form the roots of all the major and minor letters as the *l*, *l*, the capitals C, C and upside down and the j, j. They should observe all the principles which the different authors had given in the "Art of Portuguese Calligraphy" with the result that the students within a short period of time would be able to write the letters of the Writer and the Secretary and lastly the English letters. Towards this end the "Mestres" had to have the "New Art of Writing" compiled by Manuel Jose Satirio Salazar, "Professor" of Writing in Lisbon and printed in the same place in 1807 which they could explain to their students and make them read it frequently as also make them discuss it with one another.

- In the absence of the abovementioned "Arte" any other book could be used as long as the same rules as indicated earlier were followed.
- After the children had learnt to recognize the different letters of the alphabet simultaneously or even later on the different numerals could be taken up for Reading and then they could be made to learn by heart the tables: after that they had to be made to understand the value points which resulted in the successive placing of two or more numerals up to a million.
- They had to be taught the four basic operations in proper order.
- Consequently they could be taught the same four fundamental operations of Addition, Subtraction, Multiplication and Division, of fractions and especially of decimals.
- The Teacher had to explain to the students as early as possible the rules of Portuguese Orthography and all that was necessary using for this purpose the text which was found in the book "Escola Nova Christa e Politica" (New Christian and Political School) which by its clarity and brevity the way it was written was proper for the schools of this country as also it was much more difficult to obtain in sufficient quantity other better books which have similar content.
- The main rules of general Grammar could be explained to the advanced students by applying them to the Portuguese language and whatever syntax was required for it, explaining to them what it consisted of, thereafter making them understand the parts of a Portuguese passage and showing that it did not have any major differences from the Latin passage which had been reserved for the Latin Grammar lessons.

- Similarly they should be made to read some short passages on Chronology, Geography and History appropriate for their tender age. Perhaps the previously mentioned book, "Escola Nova" would suffice especially for Geography in view of the fact that here it was difficult to obtain books following the question-answer method practiced by the students themselves and by repeating it a number of times the students would be able to acquire the general notions of the important concepts without having to learn them by heart, not burdening their memory with such work.
- As the instructions regarding the rules of Civility was expressly stated in the Law of 6th November, 1772, the "Mestres" would have to read and explain in advance and in the absence of other texts the book "Tratadinho Pratico da Civilidade Portugueza" by D. Joao de Nossa Senhora da Porta Sequeira, reprinted in Lisbon in 1818, or the other booklet titled "Tutor Portuguez" reprinted in Bombay in 1828, widely used in Goa, or again the same book mentioned in the above namely "Escola Nova".
- The "Mestres" were prohibited from using the "palmatoria" (a thick wooden palette used for hitting on the palm as a form of punishment) and other barbaric methods of discipline because it is with gentleness, patience and with nice ways that the students should be taught, considering their innocent years and their tender age with complete compassion and showing sensitivity to the children entrusted to him under the important ministry of his teaching: Only in the case of disobedience, of lack of modesty and inattentiveness to the "Mestres" or his peers or even playing pranks on others the students could be punished with the use of the "palmatorio" but only up to a maximum of six counts.
- In the Primary schools the timings were from 8 to 11in the morning and from 3 to 5 in the evening.
- Saturdays were reserved not only for checking what the students had learnt during the whole week especially with regard to Catechism, Arithmetic, rules of Calligraphy and whatever had been recommended but also for discussion among the students as per the topics allotted by the "Mestre".
- There would be no holidays except during the Holy Week, on Sundays, on feast days of Patron saints and on three days during the Carnival.

- The Commandants of the Military battalions in whose quarters or in whose proximity the schools had been established would be the special Inspectors of the schools which would be under their vigilance and care and they would be held responsible for the implementation of these instructions.
- The "Mestres" were supposed to have a notebook with the pages numbered and attested by the Commandant Inspector, in which in serial order they had to write at the time of admission the names of the students, their parents' names, their birthplace, age and residence. They had to leave enough space on the respective pages to write their observations regarding the application, the talent, the attendance and the achievement level of each child, what the child had actually learnt and finally grade his progress.
- Every six months the "Mestres" had to prepare from those notebooks a list of those who had attended regularly mentioning their birthplace, parents' names, his age, time of teaching and the progress of the child. One copy of this list was supposed to be handed over to the Commandant Inspector and the other had to be sent to the Governor with the observations/remarks of the Inspector not only regarding the attendance, application and progress of the children but also regarding the discharging of the duties by the "Mestres" especially those mentioned in these instructions.This list had to be prepared every six months.
- Every six months there would also be a general inspection which would be conducted by persons appointed by the Governor who would examine not only the state of the respective schools, the number of students and their reports but also check if the "Mestres" were observing the duties assigned to them as indicated in the Instructions.
- The "Mestres" were supposed to present in between two monsoons to the person or persons appointed by the Governor every year or at the time of inspection or check the books which had been used to instruct the students, which were different from those officially prescribed and the Dictionary of the Portuguese language by Antonio de Moraes e Silva printed in 1823 or a later edition if possible.
- Whenever a vacancy of a Primary teacher arose it had to be advertised in the official paper so that the prospective candidates could within a period of fifteen days apply to the Governor along with all the necessary documents and Certificates; afterwards

through another announcement the candidates would be informed of the place, day and the time the candidates had to appear for the interview.

- The documents and the qualifications required of the candidates for the posts of Primary teachers in the established six schools were the written application, birth Certificate, a recommendation from the "Mestre" under whom he had studied and a Certificate from the Parish priest; he should expressly mention in the application, handwritten and signed by the candidate addressed to the Governor why he should be given the post.
- The candidates would be examined in the presence of the Governor or anyone so nominated by him by two persons appointed by the Governor, who would examine the candidates in Speaking, Reading, and Writing of the Portuguese language and ask them to do the four basic operations in Arithmetic, as well as in fractions, at the same time testing them in Catechism, Portuguese Grammar and especially in Orthography in conformity with the provisions of the President of the Royal Censor Board of 7th April, 1774.
- According to these same provisions a person had to record the details of the examinations including the information relating to the examinees like their names, their ages, their birthplaces and their occupations. The clerk and the examiners had to swear an oath of secrecy and of fairness assigning to the candidates at the end of the examination certain grades showing clearly the marks awarded for each answer to each of the candidates as per the rules laid down in the above mentioned Order.
- The Certificates, qualifications and the examinations were essential for the appointment of all the "Mestres", whether they would be teaching in schools run by the "Communidades" or in private schools.
- The Government would procure all the books needed for the transaction of the syllabus, for the teaching of Catechism, Civility, Orthography, Chronology, Geography and Grammar as mentioned earlier.

These instructions dealt with all the aspects of the school system. However, it is seen that lot of stress was laid on the appointment of teachers. They were meticulously selected and strict discipline and duty-consciousness was expected of them because the success or failure of the education system at that time depended on the capacity and charisma of the teacher. The teacher had a very big role to play not only in the school but in the whole village or Parish. He was not only a teacher but also an advisor, an educated person, a Government functionary and representative, a power centre and an important person in the whole village. Hence, they were expected to shoulder a huge responsibility.

Instructions to Teachers

Separate instructions were also issued by Dom Manuel do Portugal e Castro on the 5th of September, 1831 for the teachers teaching the Latin Grammar.

After issuing the instructions the same Governor then set out implementing the provisions by announcing publicly the policy of promoting Primary education in the State. He released the following "Edital" (Notice) No. 537 on the 9th of September, 1831in the official bulletin:

Dom Manuel de Portugal e Castro of the Council of the State of his most trusted Majesty, Promoter of the Orders of Christ and Our Lady of Conception of the City of Vicoza, Viceroy and Captain General of the Sea and Earth of the State of India:

> "I make it known that I wish to promote Public Instruction in these islands (Tiswadi or Ilhas) and in the provinces of Salcette and Bardez, and not being able to achieve such an important aim, without first appointing "Mestres" of the "Primeiras Letras" in the main posts in the said islands and the provinces as stated in the Notice, which I had issued expeditiously on the 16th of July, 1828, I have decided keeping in conformity with the Royal Orders in addition to the said Notice to promote equally the same Instruction in the provinces of the New Conquest, appointing for this useful purpose six Primary teachers; one to teach in Panjim, another in Ribandar and the remaining four in the different places in the above mentioned provinces, designated through the "Portaria" which I have directed them to issue on the 5th of this month (September); likewise six substitutes for the six teachers on the payment of six hundred "xerafins" to each of them and to the substitutes three hundred "xerafins" per annum. Those desirous of taking up the posts should apply to me within a period of fifteen days from the date of this publication on plain paper with the Certificate of the teacher under whom

he had been studying and his birth Certificate and the attestation of the Parish priest certified by the Notary Public; those applicants who were residing outside the State and could not produce any of the said documents had to give a declaration in writing citing the reasons for not being able to produce the documents who would then be allowed to attend. At the end of the said period of fifteen days another Notice would be issued announcing the date and time and the Jury members who would test the candidates in Reading, Writing, the four fundamental operations of Arithmetic, fractions, Catechism, rules of Civility, Portuguese Grammar, and especially a portion of Orthography".

The First Officially Appointed Teachers

In keeping with the above stipulations the first teachers were then selected and appointed. The honour of being selected as the first Primary Teachers under the official education system in Goa goes to the following:

(1) Adriano Augusto da Silva Pereira,
(2) Antonio Feleciano Piao,
(3) Vicente D'Araujo,
(4) Henrique Teles da Silva Amorim,
(5) Joao Jose da Fonseca Dias, and
(6) Jose Rafael de Fernandes Noronha.

The appointment of the teachers was followed by the selection of school Inspectors as the Governor knowing full well that an iron hand approach was needed to set the ball of education rolling in Goa as he had found that the situation was not very conducive to learning made haste to appoint the school Inspectors who would keep a strict vigil on the students as well as the teachers. However, the appointment of the these school Inspectors was mired in controversy as the Governor openly showed his bias towards his own countrymen who had been deported to Goa due to some political reasons. But by citing some vague reasons the Governor justified the appointment of the following as school Inspectors:

(1) Frederic Leao Cabreira,
(2) Luis Manuel Correia de Melo,
(3) Francisco Vicente da Cunha,
(4) Joaquim Jose Xavier Henriques, and
(5) Agostinho Jose Lopes Pereira.

After having appointed the teachers and the school Inspectors the Governor issued a Notice on the 27th of October, 1831 that the said teachers should start enrolling students for the classes. Admission would be done from the 1st of November to the 7th only. Knowing full well that one of the major reasons for the limited success of Primary education in Goa was the irregular attendance of the teachers on some pretext or the other the Governor issued another "Portaria" on the 22nd of November, 1831 in which he made it very clear that every time any of the teachers remained absent for more than eight days on whatever grounds, one fifth of their salary would be deducted and this amount would be paid to the substitute teacher. He further enjoined upon the teachers that they should reside at the place where they had been posted.

A Red Letter Day

So after taking care of all the aspects that he could envisage everything was set to start for the first time official Primary education in Goa. In the annals of the history of Education in Goa, the year 1831 should be written in letters of gold because with this event Goa must have been one of the first if not the first in the whole of Asia to experience Western style official Primary education.

Unofficially Primary education was imparted both by the Church and others in many places. However, these were all self-regulated learning centres which depended upon the likes and dislikes of the teacher. It goes to the credit of the Governor that instead of ordering these schools to be closed down and earning their wrath he went about streamlining their efforts. In order to bring in uniformity and exercise control over these private schools that had mushroomed all over the Old Conquests the Governor, Dom Manuel de Portugal e Castro issued the following Notice on the 5th of October 1831:

> "I wish to inform that by the "Portaria" dated 5th of September 1831 and the instructions issued on the same date through which I set up six Public Primary schools and being necessary that the same instructions are also observed by all those paid by the "Communidades" or by those who might have established private schools who wish to teach publicly or even do private tutoring the said instructions are also made applicable to them: Hence the following stipulations have to be complied with:
>
> Those who had been permitted to open Primary schools where the "Mestres" are being paid actually by the "Communidades"

> had to within a period of fifteen days apply for a licence or get themselves examined as per the provisions in the instructions in the presence of the Governor or by persons appointed on his behalf by the Governor in the subject of Reading, Writing, the four fundamental operations in Arithmetic, the integers like fractions, Catechism, Portuguese Grammar, and especially Orthography, applying for this purpose to the Governor on a plain sheet of paper, accompanied by the birth Certificate, Certificate of the teacher under whom he had studied, and the attestation of the Parish priest.
> No person should instruct publicly or even in private without complying with the provisions in the instructions".

The role of inspecting and monitoring these schools had to be done by the local judicial authorities who would check whether the schools had been established after obtaining the necessary permissions.

With that the task that the Governor had set for himself was completed as the school system was well and truly on its way in Goa having addressed both the public and private concerns and taken care of both the administrative and academic aspects of Primary edcuation.

By the end of the eighteenth century the winds of liberal thinking were sweeping across Europe and fresh ideas in education were coming to the fore. These same ideas were then faithfully and quickly transported and implemented in Goa. The French Revolution had demonstrated that people's power was supreme and, therefore, people now craved for more enlightenment.

The year 1831 was the official beginning of Primary education in Goa a date to be endearingly remembered because this gave a head start to some Goans providing them a golden opportunity to come up in life. From this moment onwards there was no looking back and Primary education in Goa first in the "Velhas Conquistas" (Old Conquests) and then in the "Novas Conquistas" (New Conquests) went from strength to strength as can be seen from the growth as well as the developments by way of reforms in this particular field.

A Proper System Being Established

In the meantime in Portugal the laws of Aguiar were enforced and soon in 1835 they were also adopted in Goa making education free and universal. In 1836, consequently by the Decrees of 15th and 17th of

November, 1836 new policies/plans for Primary and Secondary education were approved in Portugal.

Portugal itself was taking education more seriously after it was incorporated in the Constitution as a State responsibility. Hence, as stated above on the 17th of November, 1836 the Queen approved the Plan of Education which had been announced on the 15th of November, 1836 by the External Affairs Secretary, Manoel da Silva Passos in 70 Articles. The salient features of this plan were dealt under the main topics of syllabus, the training, appointment and salaries and the retirement of "Professors", the Method of instruction to be followed in these schools, the schedule to be observed, the examinations and the administration of the schools as can be gauged from the following:

- Primary instruction would consist of:
  - The skills of Reading, Writing and Counting.
  - Civility, Morals and Christian doctrine.
  - Principles of Portuguese Grammar.
  - Brief notions of History, Geography and of the Constitution.
  - Line drawing.
  - Gymnastics/Exercises, age-wise.
- Founding of schools:
  - Any person or a corporation/body was free to establish a school by applying to the local Municipal Administrator.
- All the schools legally established would depend on:
  - The competent authority to transfer the schools from one place to another depending upon the need.
  - To convert a Simultaneous school into a Mutual school.
- Besides the established schools there would be others in all the places wherever possible to accommodate approximately 60 students.
  - For this the Governor had to divide the territory into Circles (Zones) of Primary Education.
- In the Administrative District capitals there would be at least one School of Mutual teaching which would be the "Escola Normal" (Normal School).
  - The disposition of this article will apply to the Cities of Madeira, Funchal and in the archipelago of Azores to the cities of Ponta Delgada, Angra and of Horta.
  - The Normal School and the School of Mutual teaching in the place where it would be located would substitute the old schools of Simultaneous teaching.

  - The Normal school and the Mutual school would have a "Professor" and an Assistant.
  - The Assistant besides his duties under his charge would have obligations to give three lessons at night in a week to the adults who were not able to attend during the day.
- To establish one school for the girls in all the administrative district capitals which did not have a school till that time.
- The appointment of "Professors" depended on the public examination preceding the internship period of sixty days.
  - The appointment would be either permanent or temporary for two years depending upon the merit obtained by the candidate in the examination.
- The authority which would be supervising the schools was empowered to make the temporary appointment.
  - The permanent appointment would be confirmed by the award of the Diploma of the Ministry of the Kingdom in conformity with the merit list drawn up by the authorities.
- At the end of the temporary service the "Professor" had to answer another interview to be placed in a new post; and this would be announced much in advance so that there would not be any discontinuation of service.
  - Ordinarily the temporary "Professor" would be preferred to the fresh candidates.
- The qualifications required of the candidates were as follows:
  - Certificate of Baptism showing 21 years or more.
  - Character Certificate showing good standing in Morals, Politics and Religion from where the candidate had been residing for the last three years, attested by the Provincial head or by the Justice of Peace or the Administrator of the Municipality.
  - Residence Certificate.
  - Certificate showing the candidate free from contagious diseases.
- After two years the two district headquarters would be established.
- In the running of the Normal schools the candidates would be examined in the practical methods of Mutual teaching. In all cases even before this period, the candidates who showed competence and skill in the job and other necessary qualities would be offered the post.

- As long as the Lyceums of Secondary education had not been established in the different district capitals the candidates would be examined through the General Administrators who would act as the Presidents or persons who have been designated as such and would have the power to nominate any Official to serve as Secretary.
    - Two "Professors" from the Primary section from the vicinity had to be appointed in the absence of the "Professor" of the Secondary Level.
    - The Examiners would be invited confidentially by the President.
- The examination would be both oral and written, would be held in public and would last for two hours.
    - In the oral examination each of the examiners would question the candidate one after the other on all the topics of Primary Instruction.
    - The written examination would also be on the same topics and for this each of the Examiners would give one after the other one set of questions to the candidate to reply in the given format.
    - The first set of questions would be different for different topics.
- At the end of the examination the Examiners without consulting each other would mark the candidate in each of the subjects which he had attempted, writing then the remarks in the various columns as prescribed by the various stipulations of Primary Instruction which would be written in clear handwriting along with the name of the candidate and with the signature of the Secretary of the Directorate of Education.
    - The remarks/grades could be Best, Good, Average, Mediocre and Zero.
    - The President of the Jury then had to compile the results to which he would add his particular comments and would submit everything to the competent authority to declare the results.
- The "Professors" of Primary Schools of Simultaneous teaching of any sex would continue to be paid by the Treasurer the same pay as fixed by Law and a further 20 thousand "reis" by the respective provincial authorities.
    - Those "Professors" who had sufficient number of students could introduce the method of Mutual teaching with the

intention of using it in their schools correctly and effectively but by getting it verified by competent authority in keeping with the Decree of the Governor. In such an event the "Professors" would have an increase of thirty thousand "reis" in their salary.

- The "Professors" of the Normal schools and of the schools of Mutual teaching were to be paid three hundred thousand "reis" in Lisbon; in Porto and the provinces on the islands two hundred and forty thousand "reis" and in the other administrative districts two hundred thousand "reis".
  - Any of the "Professsors" who adopted the new teaching method and enrolled a considerable amount of students could obtain from the Governor an annual incentive of up to fifty thousand "reis": provided there was a favourable recommendation from the authority which looked after the schools.
  - The Assistants in the Normal schools would be paid one-third of the salary of the "Professors".
  - For the clerk of the Normal schools a reasonable sum of money would be fixed annually.
  - Whatever is stated here cannot go against the established practice which is actually enjoyed by the "Professors".
- The owners or proprietors of the schools had to treat with dignity the "Professors" in the schools of Simultaneous teaching of either sex, duly disbursing their pension for which they were eligible after ten years of continuous service compensated by a fourth part of their salary; for fifteen years with third part; for twenty five years with half; and for thirty five with the entire salary. Those in the schools of Mutual learning would be given one-third of their salary after ten years of service; for fifteen half the pay; for twenty years two-thirds and for twenty five with the whole salary.
- The pension would be confirmed by the Home Ministry after its approval by the competent authority which would be qualified to check the service as per the documents made available.
- The "Professors" who after their retirement with full pension could and wanted to still continue in teaching their subjects would be paid each year as much as a third of their salary.
- No "Professor" would be suspended without giving him a hearing against any complaint of an individual or without the knowledge of the authority.

- No "Professor" could be dismissed without giving him a chance to appear before the Judicial authority.
  - If the offence had been committed in the discharge of his duties he would be examined by a special Jury.
- The method adopted for Primary instruction was the Mutual teaching method.
- When this was not possible due to lack of students or any other circumstances they would use the Simultaneous method.
- The competent authority would order the school to make an inventory of whatever the school had maintained along with a record of all the school events:
  - The designs and the specimens, the models, the instructions, the special rules, which are necessary for the practicals in the Primary school in each of the branches and the methods.
  - The admission, the examinations, the prizes, and the penalties; the statistics, and the policy of the schools would be the objects of the above mentioned Instructions and regulations.
- The selection and use of the textbooks/compilations would be as per the laid down regulations.
- The Primary schools would be established in public buildings situated in healthy places.
- No "Professors" would take Classes in the house where he was residing with his family unless it was impossible for him to arrange another convenient public place.
- The academic year would start from the first day of October and end on the first day of August. The holidays were as follows:
  - All the Sundays in between;
  - All feast days of the patron saints;
  - All Thursdays of the week when it was not a patron feast day;
  - Eve of Christmas and the following days till the first of January; and
  - The whole of Holy week.
- At the end of the year students would be examined in the content that they had learnt.
- The examination would be held in public in the school hall.
- The Jury members for the examinations would comprise of the "Professor" of the school and a "Professor" from the neighbouring school nominated by the competent authority.

  - The weekly examinations or monthly examinations as per the practice had to be attempted by all which would be decided under the special rules.
- No student would be admitted in the Primary school (1) without a Certificate certifying that he was free of contagious disease and (2) without vaccination or if one had natural "vexigas".
  - The last condition would come into effect only after two years from the date of the promulgation of this Decree.
- All the parents had the bounden duty to send their children to learn in the Primary schools. The Provincial authorities, the Parish priests and the "Professors" in service had to use all means possible to persuade the parents to send their wards to school.
- In the islands the direction would rest with a Council formed for this purpose called the Provincial Council for Primary Education. This would comprise of the "Professors" of Secondary or Superior (Higher) Education residing in the capitals of the provinces presided over by the seniormost among them with the juniormost serving as the Secretary.
  - The role of the President would be to see to the implementation of the decisions of the Council, the Laws, the regulations and the Orders of the Governor
- The responsibilities of the Council would be:
  - To propose to the Government everything that was needed to regulate education depending on their needs.
  - To issue Orders on their own regarding issues not covered under law or the Decree of the Governor.
  - To choose the methods of teaching, the textbooks and the syllabus.
  - To interview temporarily the "Professors" and to propose the appointments.
- In the Overseas Provinces besides these special stipulations which had to be observed there could also be other Decrees issued by the local Government which would be suitably applied taking the local situation into consideration.

Establishing Jurisdiction and Control over Matters Educational

Thus on the Continent as well as Overseas there was to be in each Council an Inspecting Committee comprising of the Administrator of the Council—who would preside—a member nominated by the Provincial Council and the Commissioner who would serve as the Secretary. There had to be also a "Professor", a resident of the area on the Committee who would be nominated by the Directorate and in the Overseas Provinces by the Provincial Council. The term of the Committee would be co-terminus with that of the Provincial Council and when it was formed again the same members could be renominated since the services of the members would be honorary. The following were the various statutes included in the Decree:

- The Inspecting Committee having jurisdiction over the schools of the area would have a delegate from the Directorate of General Administration from whom it would receive Orders and instructions either directly or through the mediation of the Rector of the Lyceum of the District.
- The Inspecting Committee had to pay regular visits to the schools of the area and at least once a month had to check all the books, from the instructional material to the expenditure in the school; from the fulfilling of the laws and the Orders to the existing regulations of the Primary schools; from the shortcomings and the abuses to the improvements which shall be introduced. The Committee had to provide, recommend and amend whatever they thought was necessary as per the law and as per the existing regulations and send a brief report to the General Administration regarding the state of the schools proposing certain changes which were required in the current regulations. The recommendations of the Committee had to be bound together into a compendium and kept in the school. The school provisions had the force of regulations except that they could either be modified or superseded by those of the General Administration. The compendium had to also include all the laws and the regulations of Primary education.
- The local administrative authorities generally had to act as per the directives of the Primary Education Council regarding the furnishing of information and conduct of examinations and at times as per the instructions of the respective delegates of the General Administration Department from whom they would receive the necessary communications.
- The Provincial Council would take on the title and the functions of the Directorate of Primary Education and had to propose whatever new regulations that were needed to be inserted which

having been approved by the Government would be part of the Decree.

Realizing that monitoring and supervision was very important as the school system was sought to be firmly established since normally it was found that both access and retention were difficult to manage in the early stages in the life of a school. One more factor that contributed generally to the collapse of the school system was teacher absenteeism. Hence, indisputably there was need to establish a monitoring body for which reason the Primary Education Council was put in place and the Inspecting Committee was formed so that all decisions for the progress of education could be quickly taken and effectively implemented. The then Governor, General Simao Infante de Lacerda, Baron of Sabroso who had just taken over the reins of the Government in Goa immediately appointed a Committee headed by the Vicar General, Fr. Paulo Antonio Dias to go into the various provisions of the Decree and accordingly to make it adaptable to Goa. The plan submitted by this Committee was accepted by the Governor and was accordingly Decreed by the "Portaria" of 4th July, 1837. The Governor was convinced that without instruction the country (India Portuguesa) could not progress and was of the firm opinion that reforms in this sector were urgently needed. However, this Governor did not live to see the fruition of the work that he had begun earnestly and sincerely as he was called by his heavenly master within a year of his taking over.

Upon his death a Junta comprising of the Archbishop, D. Antonio St. Rita Carvalho, Jose Cancio de Lima, Domingo Luis and Antonio Vieira da Fonseca tried to rule Goa. The last named, however, was replaced within a year by Manuel Jose Mendes, Baron of Candal.

The latter was keenly interested in the development of Goa especially in the field of education. Within a couple of months he issued a circular dated 8th January, 1840 in which he stipulated the following:

- That no student should be admitted for the Latin course if he had not learnt the Portuguese Grammar and other subjects in the Primary school under a legally appointed and authorized teacher.
- That the Parochial/Church/Parish schools should teach only Music.
- That nobody could open a school without the permission of the provincial authorities.

This discriminatory circular raised a storm especially in the province of Salcette because the Music teachers were automatically barred as per the circular from teaching the Portuguese language. The "Camara" (Council) of Salcette made a representation to the Governor that it was incidental for the music teachers to also teach the Portuguese language and they were not really qualified Portuguese language teachers. The Governor being convinced immediately modified his earlier Order and allowed them to continue as before provided they were approved by the provincial authorities through a public examinations.

Pioneering Efforts in Primary Education

The Baron too did not live long to carry forward his work but died prematurely in 1840 paving the way for a new Junta to take over. But this time the Government in Portugal acted quite swiftly and appointed Jose Joaquim Lopes de Lima as an interim Governor which was a good thing to happen for Goa because this Governor was a man in a hurry who gave a great heave-ho to education in Goa. After preparing a favourable climate by holding a meeting with the three Administrators, an Officer of each of the Municipality and the Chief Accountant of the State the interim Governor issued a "Portaria" on the 17th of August, 1841 after holding consultations with various local bodies like the Provincial Councils, Corporations and the "Communidades" and after obtaining the go-ahead from the majority of the members ordering provisionally the following:

- There had to be in each province two types of schools: Municipal and village schools. The expenses to run these schools would be met in the case of the former from the "subsidio litterario" (educational cess) and in the case of the latter from the funds of the "Communidades".
- In every province there had to be three schools, one school of Latin Grammar and Latin language, Logic and Rhetoric and two schools of Portuguese Grammar and Portuguese language, Writing, Arithmetic, Linear Drawing, a Short History of Portugal and of the World, Geography and Chronology. The location of the schools was to be decided by the Provincial Councils and the Administrators.
- There had to be schools in every village having the capacity to admit 40 or more students. Those schools which failed to meet this condition had to be joined together forming a school complex with the main school in the centre where students from different

places could attend. However, the number in each school could not exceed 60.

- In these schools the syllabus would comprise of the skills of Reading, Writing, Counting, Civility, Moral Education and Catechism, some rules of Portuguese Grammar and basic operations in Arithmetic.
- Each of the schools had to have an Assistant who would substitute the full-time "Professor" in his absence.
- In each province a Girls' school too, as and when possible, had to be established.
- In the Girls' school subjects like Stitching, Embroidery and Cutting along with Reading, Writing and the four basic Arithmetic operations would be taught besides Catechism, Civility and Morals so as to instil a love for domestic virtues which were of utmost importance (family life was encouraged).
- In each province there would be a team of school Inspectors consisting of the Administrator of the province as President, the Procurator of the Municipal Council as member and two representatives of the "Communidades" elected for the purpose by the general body of the Provincial Councils and one senior "Professor".

It can be seen from the above that the interim Governor tried to work out the applicability of the regulations announced by Silva Passos in Portugal taking the local conditions into consideration. Besides he showed his acumen by taking only a few of the regulations for implementation so as not to disturb the existing set-up. In fact he tried to take advantage of the existing set-up and only made certain favourable modifications so as to improve rather than impede the growth of education in Goa. With this view in mind he tried to improve the administration and supervision of the schools for which reason he grouped the different schools into school complexes called Circles in the three provinces of Salcette, Ilhas and Bardez. He published the names of the schools as per the Circles along with the names of teachers in the Official Gazette No. 15, of the year 1842. The list is as follows:

Salcette Province

First Circle

Loutulim: Custodio Francisco das Chagas e Silva from Benaulim.

Raia: Pascoal Valeriano from Raia.
Curtorim: Francisco Antonio J. da Rodrigues from Curtorim.
Assistant: Miguel do Rosario Piedade Menezes from Curtorim.

Second Circle

Chandor: Joaquim Santan Coelho de Curtorim.
Chinchinim: Joaquim de Santana e Menezes from Curtorim.
Carmona: Jeronimo Afonso from Betalbatim.
Assistant: Jose Francisco da Conciecao Antao from Cavorim.

Third Circle

Navelim: Jose Salvador Cristovao Diniz from Navelim.
Cuncolim: Antonio de Santana e Costa from Cuncolim.
Margao: Joaquim Manuel Moraes from Margao.
Verna: Joao Salvador Flores from Verna.
Assistant: Joao Inacio Bernicio de Assuncao e Pacheco from Margao.

Fourth Circle

Colva: Francisco Caetano de Souza from Seraulim.
Varca: Benedito Jose Barreto from Benaulim.
Benaulim: Simao de Rosario e Silva from Benaulim.
Assistant: Lucas Floriao de Andrade from Margao.

Fifth Circle

Assolna, Velim, Ambelim: Indalicio Froilano de Melo from Benaulim.
Assistant : Pedro Balthazar de Rosario from Cavorim.

Sixth Circle

S. Tome (Cansaulim): Crispin Dias from Majorda.
Majorda: Jose Philip Pereira from Utorda.
Cortalim: Balthazar das Neves Barboza from Raia.

Bardez

First Circle

Badem : Miguel Constantino do Rosario Martins from Serula.
Socorro : Sebastiao Xavier Pinto from Socorro.
Pilerne : Avelino Francisco from Candolim.
Calangute : Lino Antonio Manuel de Souza from Calangute.
Nerul : Vicente Jacob do Rosario from Candolim.

Candolim : Jose Manuel Braz de Sa from Calangute.
Assistant : Venceslau Antonio Estrocio from Calangute.

Second Circle

Aldona : Manuel Pinto dos Remedios from Serula.
Pomburpa : Vitorino Caetano de Boa Esperanca Menezes from Serula.
Nachinola and Moira : Caetano Felipe Antonio Cordeiro from Assagao.
Assistant : Miguel Francisco de Souza.

Third Circle

Mapuca : Antonio Pedro Floriano Rodrigues from Aldona.
Ucassaim : Gabriel Piedade de Lima from Serula.
Guirim : Caetano Xavier Felix de Sa from Sangolda.
Assistant : Manuel Antonio Damasceno Pinto from Mapuca.

Fourth Circle

Assonora : Antonio Baptista de Trinidade from Assonora.
Revora : Joaquim Francisco de Souza from Calangute.
Tivim : Vicente Xavier de Souza from Tivim.
Assistant : Mateus de Melo from Revora.

Fifth Circle

Siolim : Luis Gabriel de Souza from Calangute.
Assistant : Pascoal Manuel de Mendonca from Colvale.
Assagao : Cosme Caetano Jose de Souza from Assagao.
Assistant : Jose Antonio Martins Raposo from Siolim.

Sixth Circle

Nagoa : Jose Vicente de Gama from Saligao.
Parra : Fr. Aleixo Xavier Pinto de Silva from Canca.
Anjuna : Mariano de Nazareth from Assagao.
Assistant : Pedro Antonio Vicente Paulo de Silva.

Ilhas

First Circle

Pangim : Francisco Xavier de Nazareth from Pangim.
Ribandar : Fructuoso Filipe Neri de Melo from Benaulim.
Sao Pedro : Eugenio Pereira from Sao Pedro.
Assistant : Henrique Alcantara de Souza from Murida.

Second Circle

Taleigao: Rafael Mariano Luis from Taleigao.
Santa Cruz : Pedro de Souza from Pangim.
Merces : Evencio Francisco Monteiro de Santo Estevam.
Assistant : Jose Francisco Salvador de Noronha from Loutulim.

Third Circle

Santo Estevam : Jose Libano de Fonseca from Santo Estevam.
Graca : Jorge Urbano Fernandes from Ribandar.
Piedade : Caetano Xavier Felix de Sa from Piedade.
Assistant : Diogo Joao de Sa.

Fourth Circle

Goa Velha : Lourenco Cristovao Pires from Santo Estevam.
Corlim : Antonio Caetano de Menezes from Sao Lourenco.

This type of arrangement was done to meet certain emergent needs. There was one Assistant teacher for each Circle who had to substitute the full-time teacher during his absence in any of the schools of that Circle. This type of arrangement would also help during the time of teacher transfers and in case the strength of any of the schools got reduced.

It must be remembered that "Professors" were appointed as and when vacancies arose. Besides some teachers would resign either to migrate or for better prospects. For example Fructuoso Felipe Neri de Melo resigned his post as he was selected as a Latin teacher in Mozambique and was, therefore, replaced by Agostinho Xavier Dalgado from Pilerne.

Sorting Out Problems

The interim Governor, J.J. Lopes de Lima left no stone unturned and no aspect untouched in the field of education. He reorganized education which included the Church schools too. He saw that there was a problem regarding the education of children of well-to-do persons who had settled in the Provinces of Salcette, Bardez and Ilhas. Because they were not "Gauncares" (members under the Ganvkari system) they used to take no interest in the affairs of the "Communidades" and reciprocally the "Communidades" too used to ignore them. They were, however, interested in educating their children.

The Governor, therefore, decreed on the 23rd of September 1841 that in addition to the stipulations of 17th of August, 1841, the following should be observed by the Church schools:

- In the Church schools children should be admitted without any fee except those belonging to non "Gauncares" or of those not connected with the "Communidades" affairs, however, if they were very poor then they could be admitted provided they produced a Certificate from the Parish priest to that effect.
- All the other students who were well-to-do and were not connected to the "Communidades" had to pay one "xerafim" every month and rupee one at the time of admission.
- The money would be used for the expenses of the school by the "Communidades".
- The Inspecting team of each Provincial area would decide the best way of charging and collecting the fees and its proper defraying by the authorities concerned.

The Governor then saw that there was a need to open a Primary school—acceding to the demand of the locals—to cater to the needs of the villages of Assolna, Velim and Ambelim and so issued a "Portaria" on the 16th of October, 1841 authorizing the setting up of a Primary school at a central place in Assolna after appointing one "Professor" and an Assistant to be paid by the Treasury as per the established pay scales.

Further he appointed teachers in all the schools of the Municipal areas and also in the Church/Parish schools which had increased manifold. In fact by 1900 the total number of these Church/Parish schools had risen to 94.

Education which was sought to be given a shot in the arm by this interim Governor suffered a crippling setback when this Governor was overthrown by a military uprising on the 26th of April, 1842.

The next Governor, Conde de Antas instead of at least continuing with the good work initiated by Lopes de Lima reduced on the contrary the number of schools from 49 to 26 citing financial constraints which consequently resulted in the decrease in the number of posts of teachers and reduced the financial burden. Later on as if to make amends for the retrograde step he opened schools in the New Conquests, to be precise in the provincial capitals of Pernem, Bicholim, Sattari, Ponda, Zambaulim and Canacona by issuing a "Portaria" dated 14th November, 1842. He was also instrumental in starting the first Marathi Primary school in Pangim through his "Portaria" dated 8th August, 1843. He had started a Primary school in Angediva by making an announcement on the 16th of February, 1843 which school was later on transferred to Vaddem, Socorro in Bardez province in 1872.

After the closure of some of these schools the villages and the Circles from where the Primary schools would continue to function were as follows along with the number of Assistants:

Ilhas

1. Pangim
2. Sao Pedro
3. Santa Cruz
4. Santo Estevam
5. Piedade
6. Goa Velha

For this Circle there would be only two Assistants.

Salcette

1. Margao
2. Verna
3. Loutulim
4. Raia
5. Rachol
6. Curtorim
7. Carmona
8. Benaulim
9. Majorda
10. Assolna

In this circle there would be three Assistants.

Bardez

1. Mapuca
2. Aldona
3. Serula
4. Candolim
5. Nagoa
6. Anjuna
7. Assonora
8. Revora
9. Colvale

For this Circle there would be three Assistants.

By an Order dated 29th of January, 1843, he reorganized the Inspecting Council or the Administrative Council. He ordered that in each province the Council would be headed by the Provincial Administrator as the President, the Accountant of the province/or a member nominated by the Provincial Council and a senior "Professor" who would serve as the Secretary. The above Committees had to report to the Governor and submit to him the full account by the end of February.

Path-Breaking Reforms

Wanting to do away with the religious discrimination which seemed to have spilled onto the educational field he tried to bring the "Novas Conquistas" into the fold of education and thus by "Portarias" issued on 22nd and 23rd of April, 1843 he ordered Primary schools to be opened in the Provincial capitals of Pernem, Bicholim, Satari, Ponda, Zambaulim and Canacona. More specifically the schools were established at Cassabe, Mulgao, Amona and Velguem in Bicholim province, one in Sattari and four in Ponda, Mardol, Marcela and Shiroda in Ponda province. He further discontinued the teaching of Catechism and ordered that only the Portuguese language and Grammar and the four basic operations in Arithmetic had to be taught. Those knowing the Portuguese language, however, would be preferred in the recruitment for Government jobs. He made provision for the payment of teachers through the agricultural societies as the tax "Subsidio litterario" had not been imposed on them fixing their salaries at 240 "xerafim" per annum.

Not much later thinking of regulating instruction in Parish or Church schools also he issued the following "Portaria" on the 29th of January 1843:

> "Having ordered by the "Portaria" of the 14th of November 1842 that the teachers in the Church schools could not be paid like the Municipal ones from the literary tax seems to be unjust as it falls on the "Communidades" of the villages to shoulder the burden which actually they had approved; and the motive for which the Inspectorate or the Directorate had introduced this as per article 14 of the "Portaria" of the 17th of August, 1841 to be represented by two of the members of the "Communidades" without any other qualifications which such a Committee might require: Hence, I now wish to alter the said article 14 and order that the Committee will comprise in each of the Municipal

> Council area only of the Administrator as the President, the Finance Officer or his representative from the same Municipality and a senior "Professor" of the Municipal area who will act as the Secretary. I hope the Committees thus reorganized will function under my authority till the end of next February invariably submit the account of which they had been entrusted as per article 16 as per the need to uphold the regulations of education in general and of the schools in particular".

This he did after heeding to the reasoning that the teachers' salaries in the existing schools had to be reduced so as to enable more schools to be opened and more teachers to be appointed without incurring further expenditure as that would provide more opportunities to students to take advantage of education. He also made alternate arrangements for paying the teachers as these Provinces were both economically backward and did not have any village organization to shoulder the financial burden of meeting the expenses of the school.

By now instruction seemed to have caught the imagination of the people. Hence when the four schools which had been established in Bicholim and Ponda failed to meet the demands of the local population they approached the higher authorities and requested that more teachers be appointed in the school at Cassabe as the lone teacher working there was unable to cater to the increasing number of students: hence, they suggested that four more schools be set up by appointing four more teachers on a reduced salary of 120 "xerafins" who would be paid by the people if need be. The Finance Secretary saw that the demand was genuine and as the people were poor the "Camara Geral" (General Provincial Council) decided to pay the teachers from its own funds. The Governor too was convinced about the need of having the schools and as stated above he issued a "Portaria" on the 22nd of April, 1843 setting up schools at Cassabe, Mulgao, Amona and Velguem in Bicholim Province and Ponda, Mardol, Marcela and Shiroda in Ponda province.

Later on in 1852, eight substitute teachers would be appointed in these schools by the Governor, Barao de Vila Nova de Ourem. By now that is after having ruled Goa for well-nigh three hundred years the Portuguese had started counting Goa as part and parcel of Portugal and started calling it one of their Overseas Provinces in spite of the separation of the Goa territory from that of Portugal by the great expanse of water. To give it further credence Marques de Pombal Decreed that Goans were full-fledged citizens and not Second Class denizens and as such were entitled for representation in the Cortes (Portuguese Assembly) and equally eligible for other State posts and benefits guranteed under the Constitution.

This necessitated that as Portuguese citizens Goans had to be imbued with the Portuguese culture which could best be promoted from the school system as that would be the right place to indoctrinate the young minds by initially making them learn the Portuguese language. Certain Governors like Dom Manuel de Portugal e Castro were extremely disappointed that even after three centuries of Portuguese presence in Goa hardly two or three persons among a hundred knew to speak the Portuguese language.

Laying Down the Code

Now it was the turn of the next Governor, Joaquim Mourao Garcez Palha who was in office for only about a year (1843) to make permanently suitable provisions in keeping with the Code passed in Portugal for the smooth running of the schools and to frame the provisional regulations for the Primary and Secondary schools. These provisional regulations pertained to the discipline among the teachers, the academic calendar, the duties and responsibilities of the "Professors", the duties of students, the salaries of the "Professors", the enrolment and retention of students, the method of teaching and the examination process, etc., were all covered under the following stipulations regarding the "Professors", the school calendar, the duties of students, their enrolment, examinations, school fund etc:

- The "Professors" of the Primary schools in the "Velhas Conquistas" would be paid from the Public Treasury and in the "Novas Conquistas" by the "Camaras Geraes" (Provincial Councils) following the established norms.
- No "Professor" or his Assistant would be suspended without giving him a hearing on any complaint either by an individual or by the Government authority except in the case of absenteeism or any other fault of this nature.
- No "Professor" would be dismissed without being heard before a judicial authority even when through misbehaviour or negligence he did not deserve the trust of the Government.
- The "Professors" had to enter the Class in time and then teach for one hour more or less.
- Application for leave had to be presented in advance to the President of the Committee so as to enable the Committee to

make suitable provisions for the smooth running of the school. Exception: One day's absence due to sudden exigency was excused as the respective Assistant could be expected to take up the Classes.

- Absence due to sickness had to be justified to the President of the Committee by producing a Certificate from the medical authorities concerned within eight days starting from the day he was taken ill which the "Professor" was bound to present as early as possible and then had to produce fresh Certificates for each of the remaining days till his recovery.
- When for certain legally justifiable reasons both the "Professor" and the Assistant happened to be absent at the same time with the approval of the President of the Committee a Senior student had to be asked to mind the Class when no Assistant was available even in the nearby Circle; and if this too failed then a competent person could be appointed by the President.
- In case all the students remained absent in one school and a teacher was absent in another the teacher in the former school could be transferred to the latter by the President of the Committee.
- The individuals who were appointed provisionally to conduct classes in case of emergency would be paid a moderate remuneration decided upon by the Committee and paid for from the School fund.
- The "Professor" and the Assistant of Mutual Learning had to be provided with a substitute. Such arrangement could not be made by the "Professor" or Assistant in the Simultaneous school.
- The transfer of the Assistants from one school to another would be done by taking into consideration the service conditions.
- The "Professors" especially in case of sickness or any other sudden lawful obstacle would have to request the Assistants of their respective Circles to substitute them duly informing the President of the Committee about the arrangement.
- In the absence of the "Professor" and the Assistant it was necessary that the President of the Committee authorized the substitutes officially as per the laid down terms.
- The "Professors" were obliged to show to the person or persons in charge of inspection of the schools the textbooks that were being used in the school which should include besides the Portuguese Dictionary of Moraes, the latest edition of the

Portuguese Grammar of Solano or of Lobato, the Orthography of Pinheiro or of Madureira as well as the following materials:

- The Compendium—Easy Method—by Monte Verde (for Reading).
- One topic from Mr. Besout for Arithmetic.
- Lithographic models for Writing.
- A passage from the constitution of the Archbishopric of Goa and the Catechism of Pe. Manuel Correia Valente or of Carlos Joaquim Colbert or finally the Christian Doctrine (Catechism) of Montpellier.
- The Alphabet Encyclopedia by Monte-Verde for Civility and Morals.
- The Encyclopedic Manual by the same Monte-Verde.
- A compendium with extracts from the best authors from the Ancient History and *New Testament*, also from the *Elements of Sacred History* by Abade de Vallemont translated from French and added with some notifications from Portugal printed in Lisbon in 1767.

- Besides the above mentioned books a Register signed by the President of the Committee for the enrolment of students had to be maintained and another for the registering of the measures taken after being suggested by the Inspecting Committee and other regulations of the school or of teaching.
- The "Professors" had to issue, independent of the dispatches and especially at the request of the interested parties, Certificates of attendance, progress made and other observations as noted down on the Register of enrolment—the page number of the Register had to be mentioned on the Certificate to the interested parties after they had paid the necessary fees of 90 "reis". For the Passing Certificates at the end of their studies they had to pay 150 "reis".
- The Church choir masters or Music teachers who were not actually qualified to teach were prohibited from teaching anything more than what was necessary to follow the Music lessons and the Administrators of the Provincial Council and the Heads ("Regedor") of the Parishes would be held responsible for the implementation of this stipulation.
- The "Professors" and their Assistants had to motivate the students and create the love for learning by means of gentleness and

politeness, admonish them and reprimand them when it was necessary by insinuating certain actions which were more effective than the fear which did not go very well with their innocence and the frailty of childhood.

The School Calendar and School Discipline

- The academic year would start from the 1st of June every year and end on the 15th of next April.
- The normal holidays for all schools, would consist of, apart from the month of May, Sundays and feast days, Thursdays in case no other holiday occurred on that day, the eve of Christmas and the following days till the 1st of January: two days for Carnival and the whole of the Holy Week. In the New Conquests, however, besides these days there would be holidays for Dussehra, Makar Sankranti, Shivratri, Holi, Ramnavmi, Narali Pournima, Jamamastami, Ganesh Chathurthi, Diwali, Bakri Id, Mohorram, and Ramzan.
- Classes in the morning would last for three hours from 8 to 11 and in the evening from 3 to 5. The said time had to be effectively utilized.
- Saturdays were exclusively meant for the revision of whatever had been learnt during the whole of the preceding week with the "Professor" questioning the students or making the students discuss by pitting two students against another two.
    - They had to keep each object in its place.
    - They had to maintain strict silence and sustained attention during the lesson; treat everybody equally; maintain a natural and respectful attitude towards the "Professor".
    - They could not leave the school without permission.
    - They could not speak any other language except the Portuguese language neither using the affected tone or any corruption of words.
    - In the absence of the "Professors" the Class had to be put under the charge of two Head boys appointed as per the circumstances from among the students much in advance taking into consideration the conditions of the locality; they also had to give an account of the absents and carry out the punishments given by the "Professors".

- Whenever the "Professor" or his Assistant entered the classroom the students had to stand up respectfully in their own places and on their knees should recite the prayers in one clear voice. The students had to stand up also when an important person entered the classroom. They had to remain standing till they were told to sit. Before starting the lesson the "Professor" or the Assistant had to call out the names of the students and mark the absentees.
- No student known for anti-social behaviour would be admitted nor given permission to enter as such persons could corrupt the rest of the students; and it was the duty of the "Professor" to keep watch over the students and protect their innocence.
- The "Professor" had to bring to the notice of the weak students their failings and encourage them to improve so as to prevent low results in his Class and if his good advice and other subtle means had not had the desired effect then punishments fitting the fault had to be given by the "Professor".
- No unknown person could be allowed to enter the classroom so as not to disturb the Classes.
- Whenever any disturbance had to take place in the school beyond the control of the "Professor" the day's work had to be suspended and an on-the-spot enqüiry conducted which would then be reported to the Committee through the office of the President.
- The students or their parents had to give in writing to the "Professor" the reasons for their absence. The student who has had thirty absents without reason or sixty with justification would lose the whole year.
- The regimen of the school, the enrolment, the observations regarding the conduct and the abilities of the students had to be taken note of by the "Professor" and in his absence by the Assistant.
- The first 15 days of June were reserved for enrolment of students. After the opening of the school the enrolment of only those students authorized through a dispatch/letter by the Inspecting Committee in which they had justified the delay which might have been either due to illness or other valid justifications which prohibited them from enrolling themselves in time.
- The "Professors" had to have a Notebook with the pages initialled by the President of the Inspecting Committee having seven vertical columns with the following headings: Serial No., Name, Relationship, Residence/Address, Age, Day of Enrolment,

Remarks. In this Notebook under consecutive numbers the students would be enrolled and in the columns under the heading of Remarks whatever was relevant to each of them would be entered, may be their talents, their attendance, their absence both voluntary and forced, their progress, their conduct, the results of Saturday contests, the monthly exercises and the semesters and whatever else could help the authorities to evaluate the child and give a complete idea regarding the moral and intellectual status of the individual.

- No student would be admitted for enrolment without first proving that he did not suffer from any contagious disease; second, without being vaccinated or having natural bladder (this after a year of the publication of this), taking the vaccine by the authority of the Governor; third, should be at least six years of age except in rare cases of abnormal intelligence.
- Those who were enrolled had to pay in this case 150 "reis" for meeting the expenses of the school.
- Those candidates who continued in the same school but fell prey to some contagious sickness would be excused from attending till they had sufficiently recovered.
- A student who had left his teacher in between would not be admitted unless he had produced an attested Certificate from his previous "Professor" stating that he had no objection for his fresh admission.
- Those who had been expelled from a school would be reinstated only by a dispatch/letter from the Committee.
- All the parents had the bounden duty to allow their children to get instruction in the Primary schools: The Provincial Councils, the Parishes and the full-time "Professors" had to use all the means at their disposal to persuade them to enroll their wards in the schools.
- Every six months the "Professors" had to prepare a report referring to all the entries made in the Notebook and had to submit to the President of the Inspecting Committee for onward submission to the Government with his observations or noting.

The Syllabus and its Transaction

- The Art of Reading was the first objective of Primary education; to obtain this aim it was necessary to know the alphabet, the syllables and the vocabulary. It was imperative to phase out the reading skills in a gradual manner so that the students would attain the desired mastery as follows:

- In Class I reading of the Alphabet had to be done.
- In Class II words of one syllable would be spelt and read.
- In Class III words having more than one syllable would be spelt out and read.
- In Class IV they will apply themselves to learning the vocabulary.
- In this same manner they would be taught also Cursive Writing.

- The students had to be shown letters which would also be read out in order to make them familiar with them or syllables had to be spelt which they had to write in pencil and later on when they had already become adept at it they had to write with pen the syllables.
- The students of one Class could not be promoted to the next without being perfectly instructed in the topics of the Class in which they were reading.
- Those who claimed that they were sufficiently trained in Reading would be tested. They would be called upon to read passages from the "Tratados de Moral", Civility and "Doutrina Christa" or any of the other books.
- Similarly the script writing would be divided as follows:
  - In Class I—to trace the elementary lines of the letters, may be vertically as U or may be curves as cc.
  - In Class II—to form after the "promptos" of the previous lesson simple letters with pencil.
  - In Class III—Consequent to the habit of forming the "inculcadas" in the previous they had to write the alphabet dividing it into four types of letters: those that had a closed shape like a, o, c, e; those that lengthened like b, d, t; those that prolonged briefly like p, q, g; and those that were prolonged by one or other part like f, s, o; this would also be followed while writing the capital letters.
- After the students had been trained in the above referred exercises they would go on to write successively the syllables, the vocabulary and the cursive letters.
- In order to follow the above mentioned method there would be a collection of uniform Calligraphy letters.

- The "treslados" had to be changed with relation to the progress of the students; as required they had to be placed on the table in such a manner that everybody was able to see them.
- The Writing had to be checked for errors in the same manner as the act of Writing and depending on the number of mistakes the place of the student in the Class would be determined so as to give an example for emulation; and the same had to be observed also in Reading and Counting; this same occasion would also be used to make corrections regarding the posture, the placing of the arm and the holding of the pen, not allowing the head to incline over the paper more than was necessary.
- The rest of the time the "Professors" had to make the students do the work as per the Class-wise divisions of the alphabet, the syllables, etc.
- The "Professors" had to take the maximum care with their students in correcting the intonation and the pronunciation of the words, to explain to them the sounds of the vowels, of the simple consonants expressed by two letters; of the long consonants, of simple diphthongs, compounds, and nasal; because the defects acquired in the beginning were difficult to correct later on.
- The "Professors" had to make, under the direction of the Inspecting Committee—which will for sake of uniformity prepare an internal regulatory code—the necessary changes in the manner of instruction and the rules included in it, which makes things easy for them to explain the sounds to the students in keeping with the easy method of Monte Verde, Grammar of Solano and others so as to avoid any confusion which may occur especially when the Assistant takes over or an outsider is appointed who may try to use an unknown method or introduce some unfamiliar ideas.
- The "Professors" after having instructed their students to write by hand had to take up Writing of round letters one after the other proportionately. Writing had compulsorily to be taken up every Saturday as per the portion completed during the week and necessary corrections had to be done by the "Professors" at that time.
- The Arithmetic lessons would be divided Class-wise as follows:
    - Class I—to distinguish and write the digits.
    - Class II—to recognize the value in relation to its place.

  - Class III—To learn by heart the tables.
  - Class IV—To learn the four fundamental operations namely addition, subtraction, multiplication and division of integers and complex numbers.
- The Arithmetic lessons had to be conducted in the evening in "subrogacao" of the written text which had to be done in the mornings.
- The lessons of Writing and Arithmetic had to be conducted first. Therefore, it was up to the "Professors" as per the Classes to give them "debuxados" themselves or ask the Assistants to draw the vertical lines and the transversals correcting at the same time the errors. The beginners, however, had to take up lessons which were proper to them and progress accordingly as per the following rules:
  - The Reading lessons and in general all the other lessons would be held by arranging the students of each Class in a semicircle around the teacher's table and by making them read one after the other with the next one correcting the mistakes of the former.
  - At the end of the lesson the "Professor" would praise or "extranhara" the student as he deserved and if necessary impose the prescribed punishments.
- Besides the weekly exercises there had to be monthly and semester ones to which the "Regedor" of the village would be invited by the "Professors" in order to make the occasion a solemn one and the students who had distinguished themselves in these examinations would get prizes as mentioned in the code.
- The remarks obtained in the monthly exercises would be entered by the "Professor" under their names in the Notebook which he had to present during the time of the final examination to the President of the Committee and to the "Professor" who would be assisting him: Besides this as per the regulations the students stood to gain either prizes or punishments which would also be an indication of the dedication of the "Professor.
- At the end of the year the students had to be examined during the last 15 days of April in the content which they had learnt. The following were the features of the examinations:
  - The examinations would be held publicly in the school hall.

- The Examiners' panel would comprise of the "Professor" of the school and a "Professor" from a neighbouring school appointed by the Committee.
- The person deputed by the Governor would become the President of the Committee who had to assist in these examinations and see that no aspersion was cast either on the persons or on the process itself.
- The President of the Committee had to allot the work of asking questions to the students as and when necessary.

System of Reward and Punishment

- The students who had distinguished themselves in these examinations would be awarded prizes as per rules.
- At the end of the examinations the "Professors" had to issue to the students who had qualified the Merit Certificates upon payment of 150 "reis" and 100 "reis" in New Conquests mentioning therein the grade obtained. This had to be done for the following reasons:
  - Without the above mentioned Certificates the students of Primary Level could not be admitted to the Secondary Level.
  - Those who had not been attending any formal school would be admitted only on their appearing for an entrance examination conducted by the "Professor" of the Secondary section in all the subjects as mentioned in the regulations.
- In all the Primary and Secondary schools two types of prizes were to be awarded, honorary and educational objects: the first would consist of small medals with remarks such as good or best and in the second type booklets, "treslados", paper, pens, penknife, etc., were awarded, however, they needed to have some relevance to the textual content.
- Those students who had maintained an impeccable record in all the weekly exercises, monthly and semester examinations and in their conduct and behaviour would be entitled for the first type of prizes. The awarding would be done as follows:
  - The first type of prizes would be conferred on the day of the closing of the academic year by the President of the Committee or any person who fulfilled the laid down criteria.
  - The second type of prizes had to be distributed by the "Regedor" after having fulfilled all the conditions.

- The prize winners were selected by the "Regedor" after going through the records, taking into consideration their achievements and mistakes and then deciding the winners with transparent impartiality.
- After having carried out the distribution of the prizes of the first and the second type the list of the prize winners had to be displayed on the door of the school which entitled the winners of the first type (medals) to wear them on the pockets of their dresses both in their Class and even outside.

- It is a well accepted fact that corporal punishments obstruct the development of natural faculties and, therefore, is never advisable. However the imperfections present in human beings need also to be corrected. Hence, to do that a better option is to make use of moral punishments. These will consist of:
  - Posters or "caroches" with the designation of "fallador" "Travesso" "Bulico' "Desatinado" "Perguicozo" "Mentirozo", etc., written in big letters which would be placed on the head of the student or hung around the neck of the wrongdoer for 15 minutes in the first instance; and if repeated over a period of time the "Professor" had to make him to stand at the door or make him sit alone or keep him on his knees in the middle of the Class, or not allow him to speak with others or separate him from the other students with orders to him not to speak with anybody inside the school for a certain number of days according to the gravity of the offence.
  - The faults which deserve similar punishments besides those that define the said "Cartazes" are as follows: inattention, "motejos" "ameacos" and other similar ones, being insulting to the other students and outsiders who come to the school or those who pass by on the road.
  - If these are repeated and if the defaulters do not mend their ways or their stubborn nature induces them to offend the "Professor" through disobedience and lack of respect or they take recourse to distortion of facts against their classmates or other disorderly means returning back then more stringent punishment would be meted out to them who would then be given corporal punishment making them an example to others. He would be usually given six hits of the dreaded "palmatorio" or some other suitable punishment.

  - When even this had not worked then as a last resort the "Professors" had to refer the matter to the President of the Committee with a list of the foul incidents, of the repetitions and the means which he had used to correct them making out a case for the expulsion of the violaters so as to shield others from being corrupted.
  - Students so expelled could admit themselves again in another school after obtaining the sanction of the Provincial Committee and continue his studies as per the details furnished in the leaving Certificate.
- The "Professor" had to report and recommend to the President if he wanted any student to be dismissed either for rude behaviour or for frequently remaining absent only after he had explored all options open to him like reprimands, punishments, etc.

Teachers' Absenteeism and Fund Management

- The "Professors" and their Assistants who due to sickness could not attend work for more than 40 days would lose one-fifth of their respective salary from day one. Following were the exceptions:
  - In case of voluntary absence for the first time they would lose one-fourth of their salary, for the second time one-half and for the third time if reported to the Government action deemed fit could be initiated against them for dereliction of duty.
  - All these deductions of the salaries of the "Professors" and the Assistants would revert back to the school treasury as well as the remuneration in case of suspension of the teacher.
  - The school fund would consist of the fees from admissions, cost of the Certificates and the deductions if any due to the absence of the "Professors" and the Assistants.
    - — The School Fund had to be used for the following expenses:
    - — The remuneration to be paid for the substitutes of "Professors" and the Assistants.
    - — For the purchase of certain items as mentioned.
    - — For other eventualities with the permission or orders of the Inspection Committee.

- The Safe had to be under the security of a Guard and the "Professor" in charge had to maintain the account which he had to submit to the Inspection Committee or their representative at the time of the ordinary/regular inspection as per the laid down rules.

Sincere Efforts in Vain?

This was a more comprehensive piece of legislation which sought to take care of practically all the aspects of school education. These were prepared by taking the 1836 Code of Regulations promulgated in Portugal by Silva Passos into consideration as the basis for the formulation of all the section-wise rules and made applicable to Goa after adapting them to the local conditions. However it is to be noted that besides the usual conditions of service and discipline the school now was sought to be made a more vibrant and self-sustaining institution. Besides attempts were being made to involve other stakeholders, to give publicity and to garner support for the noble cause of education.

It must have been realized that in spite of the best efforts of the Government the enrolment was not picking up. Getting the people to enrol their wards in the school was an uphill task not only in the 1840s but even much later in 1871 which fact was highlighted by the Governor, Visconde de Sam Januario when he wrote in one of his "Portarias" as follows: "the attendance of the local children in these schools except those that are situated in the Provincial capitals is very thin either through ignorance or through stubbornness of the parents who do not realize the value of this tool of enlightenment and their good fortune that the Government is providing this facility without any ulterior motive....". He was specifically speaking about the newly established schools in the New Conquests. That was, however, the general trend everywhere as the locals still looked with suspicion and misgivings at the Portuguese. But note should be taken of the phrase "without any ulterior motive".

As stated earlier the Governor, Joaquim Mourao Garcez Palha created a Marathi school in Pangim by issuing a "Portaria Provincial" No. 1328 dated 8 August, 1843 in which he laid down the following:

1. There shall be in the capital city a Marathi school located in the house meant for it.
2. The Marathi teacher shall be paid 30 "xerafins" monthly and shall teach the students who attend the Classes to read, to translate, to write and to count.

3. He shall also have to give lessons in Konkani (Canarese) to those who wish so.
4. All those who pass out from this school will be eligible to apply for Government jobs.
5. They would be preferred in judicial posts of the Government and as interpreters in the Provinces or as "Professors" in the "Novas Conquistas".
6. The "Professor" of the school during his absence shall be substituted by a person suggested by him and subject to the approval of the Government would be paid as per entitlement.

This was a tactical move on the part of the local Government as it was noticed that Marathi language could be used not only as a goodwill gesture towards the Hindus—called "gentios"—but also as an effective tool in the management of diplomacy as well as trade and commerce with the neighbouring States. The change in the attitude of the Portuguese rulers towards the Hindus should also be noted though the declaration of the Republic was still a long way off. The same type of attitudinal change was not witnessed towards the Konkani language. It is really intriguing.

Onus on Teachers

Continuing with the reforms path, in 1845 on the 9th of May the next Governor, Jose Ferreira Pestana ("Boletim" 20) published the following notice with regard to the attendance Certificate produced by the "Professors":

> "Being illogical that the "Professors" of Public Instruction attest their own attendance; for which they have I suppose some scruples and it would be unnecessary to attest it or they could keep on doing it as it would not be difficult for them to condone their absence: I hereby declare that the "Regedor" of the respective Parish should inform the Administrator of the Provincial Council at the end of every trimester the absence of any teacher. He had to put up a notice on the door of the Church asking the parents to bring to his notice if any of the teachers had remained absent. The Administrator in his turn had to convey the matter to the Government taking care to verify the correctness of the information".

This showed two things, one the evolution of monitoring and the importance of teachers. Since the whole educational edifice was built on the indispensable presence of the teacher the absence of teachers would have a detrimental effect on the development of the school system and hence teachers were always kept on a tight leash because earlier it was discovered that one of the main reasons for poor attendance was the absenteeism of teachers. In fact everything depended on the teachers. They were really considered as 'masters' of all they surveyed.

This was followed in the month of September 1845 ("Boletim" 36) by another notice by the same Governor whose contents were as follows:

> "Having confirmed to me what the Presidents of the Inspecting Committees of Schools of the Provinces of Ilhas and Salcette had explained that as per rule the admission of students takes place for three months in any term of course with proper justification; that in the Lencastrian schools the students who want to attend in any term as per the system of division which is followed in these schools should be admitted; and finally the Inspecting Committees of Schools, having recognized the justified motive that the students of the Primary Schools who had lost one year due to the discrepancies in the rules which limited the number of justified absents could now be admitted for the examinations of the respective Class".

It must be remembered that there were three types of teaching methods followed till then: The Individual method, the Simultaneous method and the Lancastrian method, (also known by such other names as Mutual or Monitorial) in that order of development and usage. These methods were subsequently to be replaced by the Class system.

It is evident that all efforts were singularly directed at facilitating the enrolment and retention of students with the least empediment. This shows the sincerity of the Government in encouraging the growth of education.

IV
Structuring and Restructuring the System

In the September of 1845 came a major reform in the system of education announced by the Central Government in Lisbon or more specifically the Ministry of Overseas Affairs and Sea Trade, in keeping with the Charter of Laws which had been promulgated in May 1843. If earlier the subjects called "Chairs' were taught randomly now the "Chairs" had to be taught one after the other sequentially. Hence, because of this peculiar arrangement of "Chairs" the Government now had to appoint two full-time "Professors" wherever needed unlike before when one would be full-time and the other as an Assistant.

Similarly to tighten things in the area of supervision too the Government decided to form instead of one school Inspector as per the new regulations an Inspecting Committee of not less than three members. This became the most powerful body governing education as it would be headed by none other than the Governor of the Province and would include the "Professors" of Superior and Secondary education. The Committee enjoyed extensive powers.

Fundamental Alterations in the System

Some of the regulations introduced under these new reforms were as follows:

- In each of the Overseas Provinces there had to be a number of "Chairs" of Primary Instruction meant for the instruction of the inhabitants.
  - The Government upon the recommendation of the Governors in consultation with the Inspecting Council had to fix the number and the locations of the Schools in each of the Provinces.

    - The Government whenever it was convenient had to create new schools or transfer the existing ones by taking always advance information from the respective Governor and his Council.
- In each of the schools students had to be taught Reading, Writing and Counting; the general principles of Morals, Christian Doctrine; Grammar Exercises; Principles of Geography and especially the portion regarding the various Provinces of the Portuguese Monarchy; Sacred History of the *Old* and the *New Testament*; and Portuguese History.
- The Government however was free to order the teaching of any other subject/subjects instead or in addition to as per its needs.
- At the end there would be testing and evaluation in which the student could show his ability in different topics which had been taught to him as far as was physically and morally possible for the teacher, circumstances permitting.
    - The final examination could be administered only to those individuals who had showed competence in all the topics which the "Professor" had covered.
    - When there did not seem to be any purpose in administering the final examination the individual could be motivated to continue for three more years and obtain higher qualifications.
- The salary of the "Professors" would be fixed as per the special circumstances of each Province and the location of the school.
- Those "Professors" who had completed 25 years of continuous service in the teaching profession could retire with pension if they so desired. If a person was unable to teach after ten years of service he would be retired with 2/5 of his salary as pension and those having more than ten years would earn four per cent more for each year for every additional year.
- For calculating their pension the service rendered on temporary basis would also be taken into consideration.
- Besides the schools established in the "Estado da India" and in each of the provinces of Mozambique, Angola, Cabo Verde and S.Thome e Principe, there had to be one main school which would be called the Principal School of Primary Instruction in which besides the designated subjects also had to teach Portuguese Grammar, Linear Drawings, Notions of Practical Geometry, Book Keeping, the natural produce of the province

and the various objects made by the local Industry and Commerce or products worthy of knowing because of their utility in the domestic economy and notions of Physics applied to Industry and domestic Economy.These schools had to be located in places where they would be more useful.

- In each of these schools there had to be two "Professors" among whom the different subjects would be divided in keeping with the special regulations of the schools.
- The "Cadeiras" of the principal schools would be without any individual testing of the "Professors" who through their competence and moral stature might be deserving of the post of teaching. The individuals thus equipped had the right to salary from the day they left for their respective Provinces.
- The Government could grant in keeping with the qualifications of the first ten "Professors" who would be appointed for the five principal schools a total sum of three thousand "escudos".
- Each of these "Professors" of the Principal Schools would earn annually in the Estado da India 300,000 reis; in Mozambique, Angola and S.Thome and Principe 500,000 "reis" and in Cabo Verde 400,000 "reis" all in the currency of the Kingdom.
- In case of absence or prolonged sickness of any of the "Professors" of the Principal schools it was allowed to appoint any individual as a temporary "Professor" of the school who had been or might have been a student of the school as long as he had the age, the knowledge and other qualities necessary for carrying out with dignity the work of teaching which would be entrusted to him.
- These additional "Professors" would serve during the absence, disappearance or sickness of the permanent "Professors" and would be paid one-third of the salary drawn by the full time "Professors".
- The "Professors" of the Principal schools who had completed 20 years in service and were residing effectively in the Estado da India or 15 years in the provinces of Africa would be retired with their last drawn salary as pension if they so desired.
    - The same "Professors" if they were unable to continue in service after completing 8 years and residing in the Estado da India would be retired with one-third of their salary as pension and those completing six years and residing in the provinces of Africa would be retired with half the salary as pension.

- If those that had served in Asia as well as those that served in Africa were retiring due to some sickness would earn beside the one-third or half of their salary another one-twentieth of the salary for each of those years they had served, ten in Asia and eight in Africa.

The Council of Inspection and its Functions

- In each province there had to be a Council of Inspection of Primary Instruction. This Council would comprise of not less than three members; and the Government could nominate to this Council any individual resident of the respective provinces who by their knowledge and other qualities/qualifications would be fit for this job. The Governor of the province would be a member and ex-officio President of the Council. The "Professors" of Superior and Secondary education, of whatever rank and the "Professors" of the Principal schools whenever convenient would also be made members of the Council.
- When beside the President the two members nominated by the King could not join the Council the Governor of the province could nominate in the absence of the appointees of the King persons who appeared to be fit for the posts so that the Council would always be made up of not less than three members.
- One of them had to serve as the Secretary of the Council for which he would be suitably compensated.
- Duties of the Council would include:
  - Presiding over the interviews to recruit "Professors" and to decide on their aptitude. Whenever it was found convenient to the Council it would delegate the responsibility of the interview to two or more of its members.
  - Overseeing their following or ordering them to follow all the laws and regulations related to Primary Education.
  - Implementing all the rules needed for Primary Education in the Province and to taking all measures as per the resolutions taken by the Government.
- The Government had to take all the measures necessary for the implementation of this present Decree and as much as possible attention had to be paid as much as possible to the general legislation on Primary Instruction which had to be followed

especially the Decree of the 20th of September, 1844, more specifically the part related to Primary Instruction.

- The Government had to give periodically an account of the adopted measures to the "Cortes" and the results thereof.

Three major areas had been addressed in the above stipulations laid down by the Ministry of Overseas Affairs and Trade: (1) the establishment of principal schools which were probably meant to be model schools as these were to be set up in all the districts or rather at least one in each district; (2) the appointing of teachers and their service conditions as well as the appointing criteria; and (3) the formation of an Inspecting Council for the purpose of monitoring and supervision.The matter of establishing model schools probably arose because of the various methods of teaching and the Government was now endeavouring to bring in some uniformity as the "Chairs" were being gradually replaced by Classes. On the other hand the interest in the welfare of teachers was probably driven by the fact that more able persons could be attracted to the teaching profession. Education was attracting more and more attention.

Certain Other Relevant Notifications

Earlier in 1844, the then Governor, Jose Ferreira Pestana (Boletim No. 27) had issued the following Order:

> "It has been brought to my notice that in many instances children who could not being economically backward afford to pay 150 "reis" were not admitted in the Primary schools in spite of the Provisional Regulations insisting on enrolment of all children; the first duty of the Governors was to promote education of the people and the Constitution guaranteed free Primary education: for the sake of convenience with due regard to Her Majesty as long as she did not object to it to whom this would be referred those who proved that they were unable to pay the fees by producing a Certificate from the Parish priest and the local judicial authority to that effect should be exempted from making that payment".

This Decree of the Governor soon came to be followed by one issued in Portugal by the Junta comprising of the Queen, the Duke of Terceira, Antonio Bernardo da Costa Cabral, the Baron of Tojal, Jose Joaquim Gomes de Castro and Joaquim Jose Falcao on the 1st of August, 1844 which read as follows (Boletim 44):

- The "Professors" of Primary and Secondary schools could be relieved of their duties by the Government if recommended by the Directorate of Primary and Secondary Education in public interest.
- The Government would be making the rules and regulations and issuing the necessary instructions for the implementation of the present Decree.
- This was in supersession of all previous legislations contrary to this.

A Decree was issued on the 20th of September, 1844 by the Central Government in the name of the Queen whose statutes as far as Primary Instruction (it also included statutes for Secondary and Normal education) was concerned covered the whole spectrum of educational activities and addressed Primary, Secondary and Teacher education. The Decree comprised of six Chapters on Primary education which included around 45 statutes. The areas dealt with were the aims of Primary education, the opening and locating of schools, the qualifying and appointing of teachers, the remuneration and service conditions of teachers, discipline and attendance in schools and schools for girls. Some of the stipulations in this regard have been given below:

- Primary Instruction should be divided into two Levels:
  - The First Level would consist of (a) Reading, Writing and Counting; (b) Général principles of Morals; (c) Christian doctrine and Civility; (d) Grammar exercises; (e) Principles of Chorography; and (f) Portuguese History.
  - The Second Level would comprise besides the subjects of the First Level (a) Portuguese Grammar; (b) Drawing; (c) Geography and History; (d) Sacred History of the *Old and New Testament*; (e) Arithmetic and Geometry with application to Industry; and (f) Book Keeping.
- As the First so too the Second Level could also include additional subjects in place of and in proportion thereof to be decided by the Government.
  - The extent of the content and the method of teaching, as well as the number of lessons of each subject in a week had to be regulated by the Government as far as it was convenient and good for teaching depending upon the different circumstances.
  - The Government would offer prizes of up to the value of 200$00 "reis", to individuals who could prepare and present

compilations/compediums suitable to be used in the Classroom for teaching the different subjects which came under Primary Instruction. (a) For this purpose the Government had to publicize the various programmes/ syllabi; and the Government could establish more than one prize for each of the different subject-wise compilations compendiums if it so desired; and (b) The compilations/ compendiums even though paid for by the Government would still remain the property of the authors if they did not cede their rights spontaneously; but for being ordered to be used in the schools the authors would be subject to the price and conditions of printing them which the Government would impose on them.

- All the schools of Primary Instruction which had been legally created would remain as schools of the First Level. The Government, however, had the right to transfer a school from one place to another after showing the reason for the change.
- The Government would be able to create new schools whenever necessary either of the First Level or of the Second Level.
- As regards the location of the schools they had to be housed as far as possible in a public building or in a place which had been especially designated for the purpose.
- For the setting up and the provision of the Classes of the Second Level other circumstances being equal they had to be established in those Councils which were ready to provide the furniture and the building for the school.
- Whenever a proper building was available for the school no "Professor" could be allowed to conduct Classes in his own house.
- The Municipal Councils could be authorized by the District Councils to fix the salary or remuneration of any resident or individual who having sufficient moral and educational qualifications wanted to undertake Primary instruction in the Parishes in which there was still no publicly appointed "Professor" or no public school. The associations like the "Irmandades" and "Confrarias", could, however, fix the salary of the teacher appointed by them as per their income.

Reforms Promulgated in Portugal

The rest of the stipulations related to the other aspects of Primary education especially the training, appointment and remuneration of teachers.

Regarding the administration of schools the following set-up was proposed in the regulations:

- A Superior Council of Public Instruction would be created with headquarters at Coimbra with the aim of directing, regulating and monitoring all public education.
- This Council would comprise of a President usually the ex-officio State Minister and Secretary of Trade, a Vice President, the Rector of the University of Coimbra or any other as desired, eight ordinary members and any number of extraordinary members, one Secretary and clerical staff to run the office.
- The ordinary members would be nominated by the Government from among the teaching faculty or even retired ones from the University or from any other institution, literary or scientific and from among the other prominent personalities of the country.
- The extraordinary members would consist of the substitutes as well as the heads and the Doctors of the various faculties of the University who were ordinarily residents in Coimbra.
- The clerical staff would be as per the needs.
- This Council would be divided into three sections: Primary Instruction, Secondary Instruction and Superior Instruction. Each section would be under a Director who would be overall in charge, and having a Reporter and a Secretary.
- Under this Council there would be Rectors, Directors, Administrators or heads of various institutions.
- In the Colonies the head would be the Governor and under him the Administrators of the Council.
- Under the Administrators there would be the Commissioner of Studies for each district under whom there would be the delegates and sub-delegates.
- All these officials would be paid for by the Government.

Along with these there were other general regulations aimed at streamlining the complete education system in the country as well as in the colonies.

Minor Periodical Orders

The next Governor, Jose Ferreira Pestana effected three significant changes in the system of Primary education. Firstly, due to demands from the locals he ordered the transfer of the Primary school existing in Pangim to Taleigao. Secondly; he shifted the Marathi school from Pangim to Margao provisionally for two years; and thirdly he established a Girls' school in Pangim. He sought to give further impetus to Girls' education by constituting a special Committee to draw up provisionally the rules and regulations for such schools.

By the "Portaria" of 17th August, 1841 two schools for girls had already been established in Mapuca. Wanting to establish a Girls' school in the capital city he issued a "Portaria" on the 12th of February, 1846 appointing D. Anna Joaquina de Souza Correia as the teacher after consulting the various advisory bodies. She had been selected earlier in 1844. She was appointed on a salary of 60 "xerafins" per month but on the condition that within three months if she had not been able to enrol a minimum of twelve students, her salary would be reduced to 18 "xerafins". This provisional appointment was later approved by the Queen through an official letter dated 18th September, 1846.

Wanting to fill up the vacancies the Governor, Viscount of Villa Nova announced the interview through a "Portaria" dated 12th January, 1854. He then selected D. Ludovina Elvaim de Locio for the post at Mapuca and D. Anna Antonia Isabel d'Unhao as the teacher at Margao.

So by 1847-48 there are found in Goa three types of schools as far as administration and payment of salaries is concerned namely those paid by the State, those paid by the "Communidades" or the Confraternities which were mostly music Classes and those maintained by the Regiments and run by the Chaplains. The total number of students and teachers in each of these categories were 1,419 and 52 plus 68 and 5 in the regional languages, 2,300 and 51 and 220 and 10 respectively. Besides there were Marathi schools which had 68 students and 5 teachers. The following is the list of Primary schools found in 1848 along with the number of pupils and teachers as given in Table 4.1:

Thus it can be seen from table 4.1 that altogether the State employed 57 Primary teachers who were in charge of 1,342 students. The highest number of students in one school is found in Mapuca and surprisingly only one teacher was found managing the whole school unlike Pangim where though only 71 students were reading in the Primary Classes two teachers were found managing the Classes because some managed to get plum postings through influence. The least number of students was found in the school at Santo Estevam with Sanguem coming a close second with only 4 and 6 students respectively.

Table 4.1: Primary Schools in 1848

Sr. No.	*Province*	*Village*	*No. of "Professors"*	*No. of Students*
01	Ilhas	Goa Velha	01	30
02		Pangim	02	71
03		Pangim	01	56
04		Piedade	01	41
05		Ribandar	01	43
06		Santo Estevam	01	04
07		Santa Cruz	01	35
08		Taleigao	01	34
09	Bardez	Anjuna	01	43
10		Aldona	01	33
11		Calangute	01	31
12		Covale	01	48
13		Candolim	01	72
14		Mapuca	01	91
15		Saligao	01	65
16		Siolim	01	48
17		Sirula	01	29
18	Salcette	Assolna	01	18
19		Colva	01	29
20		Chinchinim	01	33
21		Curtorim	01	30
22		Loutulim	01	24
23		Margao	02	63
24		Raia	01	18
25		Cansaulim	01	46
26		Varca	01	49
27		Verna	01	39
28	Paroda (NC)	Mardol	01	14
29		Marcela	01	13
30		Ponda	01	26
31		Shiroda	01	16
32	Zambaulim(NC)	Sanguem	01	06
33		Quepem	01	06
34		Quepem	01	18
35	Canacona (NC)	Canacona	01	09
36		Loliem	01	09
37	Bicholim(NC)	Amona	01	09
38		Bicholim	01	09
39		Mulgao	01	09
40		Velguem	01	09
41	Sattari(NC)	Sanquelim	01	22
42	Pernem(NC)	Arabo	01	22
43		Orgao	01	22
44		Pernem	01	23
45		Parsem	01	23

A Bird's Eye-View of Parish Primary Schools

As far as the numbers are concerned the Church schools did much better comparatively—the total number of schools was 51 and the total number of students was 2,300—though basically they were music classes with a minimum of curricular instruction thrown in as most of the "Mestres" were not competent enough to teach the curriculum and the Parish priest too was not very keen that the local lads learn much more than was needed for Church purposes. Hence only the rudimentary "Primeira Class" (First Class) was established. The whole school was maintained from the funds of the "Communidades" or the Confraternities. Table 4.2 tells us the true tale of these Parish schools:

Table 4.2: Parish Schools in Different Villages across Goa

Sr. No.	*Province*	*Village*	*No.of teachers*	*No. of students*
01	Ilhas	Corlim	01	16
02		Chorao	01	28
03		Merces	01	11
04		Pangim	01	54
05		Santa Cruz	01	36
06		Taleigao	01	20
07	Bardez	Aldona	01	113
08		Assagao	01	70
09		Anjuna	01	16
10		Calangute	01	102
11		Candolim	01	17
12		Colvale	01	13
13		Guirim	01	88
14		Mapuca	01	19
15		Moira	01	70
16		Nachinola	01	42
17		Nerul	01	66
18		Nagoa	01	50
19		Parra	01	94
20		Pilerne	01	21
21		Revora	01	60
22		Socorro	01	101
23		Salvador do Mundo	01	43
24		Siolim	01	89
25		Tivim	01	60
26		Ucassaim	01	87
27	Salcette	Assolna	01	59
28		Benaulim	01	14
29		Betalbatim	01	69

(Contd.)

TABLE 4.2 (*Contd.*)

Sr. No.	*Province*	*Village*	*No.of teachers*	*No. of students*
30		Chandor	01	17
31		Carmona	01	69
32		Colva	01	43
33		Cuncolim	01	37
34		Chinchinim	01	39
35		Curtorim	01	29
36		Cortalim	01	18
37		Loutulim	01	64
38		Majorda	01	37
39		Macasana	01	02
40		Margao	01	39
41		Mormugao	01	22
42		Navelim	01	26
43		Orlim	01	32
44		Raia	01	58
45		Rachol	01	10
46		Seraulim	01	24
47		Cansaulim	01	27
48		Varca	01	28
49		Verna	01	15
50		Velcao	01	44
51		Velim	01	92

It can be seen from Table 4.2 that irrespective of the number of students there was only one teacher as the "Communidades" or the Confraternities were not in a position to pay for two or more teachers. Besides the teaching method that was used was normally the Lancastrian or monitorial. As this set-up in the Parish schools was found to be quite effective the Government mandated that the other schools which were established in due course of time had to do likewise.It is also obvious that most of these schools were well frequented as only the Macasana School shows single digit attendance.

Enrolment in Other Schools

The Regimental schools too did very well as far as enrolment was concerned barring the Mormugao School as Table 4.3 shows.

From Table 4.3 one can infer that it was not only the children of the military personnel who were being instructed and were attending the classes but also some from the neighbouring areas.

Table 4.3: Enrolment in Regimental Schools

Sr. No.	*Province*	*Fort/Barracks*	*No. of "Professors"*	*No. of students*
01	Ilhas	Pangim	01	58
02	Bardez	Mapuca	01	20
03	Salcette	Margao	01	39
04	Ponda	Ponda	01	40
05	Bicholim	Bicholim	01	07
06	Bardez	Aguada	01	19
07	Pernem	Tiracol	01	16
08	Bicholi	Alorna	01	10
09	Canacona	Cabo de Rama	01	11
10	Mormugao	Mormugao	01	0

In 1847-48, it is found that there were five schools in the Marathi language and that too attended by not less than 60 odd students. The following is the break-up as given in Table 4.4:

Table 4.4: Marathi Schools All Located in the New Conquests

Sr. No.	*Location*	*No. of teachers*	*No. of students*
01	Pernem	01	18
02	Bicholim	01	19
03	Ponda	01	19
04	Quepem	01	07
05	Canacona	01	05

In sum one finds that there were a total of 118 teachers in all types of schools and 4,007 students which given the circumstances was a goodly number.

Awakening Consciousness

In the meantime in the Primary schools two problems cropped up. Both related to the New Conquests where the "Professors" less in number were not being paid adequately. Hence, an Order was issued on the 9th of April 1850 that the list of "Professors" who were actively engaged in conducting Classes should be submitted to the Directorate of Accounts who would then make the necessary arrangements. The second problem was regarding the non-teaching of certain subjects like the four operations in some of the schools.

In the meantime having realized the importance of knowing to read and write people from the province of Salcette represented to the Governor that the existing schools were either overpopulated or were located too far from one another so that it was becoming difficult for most of the children to attend classes. Hence, after consulting the Administrator of the Council of Salcette and the Council of Primary and Secondary Instruction it was agreed that there was a need to increase the number of schools not only in Salcette but also in the whole of the Old Conquests. Therefore, in keeping with the Decree of 14th August, 1845 and after approval from the Finance Department and the Government Council a Decree was promulgated on the 13th of May, 1952 by Boletim No. 20 by the Baron of Villa Nova d'Ourem, Jose Joaquim Januario Lapa. The provisions in the Decree were as follows:

- The actual eight substitutes of the classes of Primary Teaching (excluding the Lancastrian classes) would be made full timers and new classes would be established to accommodate them so that they would earn like the full timers from the day they start exercising their new duties.
- The temporary or interim appointments which had been made after promoting the substitutes to regular service in conformity with the rules would continue with the temporary or interim appointment but as "Professors".
- The Municipal Councils of the three Provincial Councils of Old Conquests would furnish to the Government within a period of thirty days the required information basically the locations/sites for the new schools namely: two in the province of Ilhas, three in the province of Salcette and three in Bardez. This proposal had to be forwarded through the Administrator of the Council who would direct it to the Government within a period of ten days in addition to the above period accompanied by his remarks with the plans of the houses which had been identified for the schools and also mentioning the proposed rent (under the Municipality or under the Parish).
- The expenditure for these houses for the schools of Primary education and the other expenses for the purchase of furniture and other articles necessary for the running of the school had to be borne by the Municipal Council. The expenditure would be met from the taxes collected by the District Council and included in the account of the said Corporations. As per circumstances donations of houses as well as furniture from people was preferable to enable the authorities to set up the schools however the school could not be set up in the house of any "Professor".

- The Municipal Councils and their respective Administrators had to in case they had been informed about the location of the new schools propose the change in the location so that there was more or less equal distance from two schools so that they would be accessible to a greater number of students.
- In case of some impediment or sickness or any other difficulty, the "Professor" with whom the house had been entrusted had to make alternate arrangement for the smooth running of the school with the prior approval of the Inspecting Committee of Primary Education of the respective Council or of the Council of Instruction in Ilhas leaving the students free to attend the neighbouring school during this period of absence. If the school was closed continuously for three days a person had to be sent immediately to the school by the Administrator of the Council to take charge of the school temporarily who would then be paid half the salary of the "Professor" for that period of time that he served in the school. If the absence of the "Professor" was prolonged the Government in view of the minutes received from the delegates had to provide a substitute as per the Decree of September 1844.
- In the school under the Council of Primary and Secondary Instruction in Ilhas and in the schools under the Committee of Inspection of Primary education in other provinces there would not be more than two posts in every contiguous circle.
- In the Classes in Panjim, Mapuca and Margao the schools could not be left without a "Professor" for more than eight days. One of the "Professors" from the neighbouring schools nominated by the Council of Instruction or by the Inspecting Committee had to be sent to that school as early as possible.

Overhauling the System Again

The same Governor, Visconde de Vila Nova de Ourem, issued a "Portaria" on the 9th of November, 1854, (Boletim No. 49) detailing instructions regarding the Primary schools of Second Level and Secondary education after getting the approval from all the sanctioning bodies. The following were the stipulations regarding Second Level (Segundo grau) of Primary Education:

- There would be in the provinces of the Old Conquests five schools of Primary education of the Second Level; one in the province of Ilhas located in Pangim, two in Bardez and two in Salcette. This was in keeping with the Decree of 20th September, 1844.
- The Lancastrian schools in Pangim, Margao and the Primary school of the First Level of Mapuca would be converted to the Second Level.
  - The Municipalities of Bardez and Salcette would have to intimate to the Government the locations for the remaining two schools of the Second Level which had been allotted to them and indicate the buildings which would house them. The proposal had to be sent through the Administrator of the respective Municipality who would then forward it with his comments.
  - If there was already a Primary school of the First Level in the said Parish then the Primary school of the Second Level had to be set up in that place by transferring the existing school to another Parish.
- The payment/salary of the "Professors" of the Primary schools of the Second Level was fixed at 50 'xerafins" per month for each teacher.
- In consideration of the greater number of residents in Bardez and Salcette another school of Latin was to be created in each of these two provinces as per the Decree of 14th of August, 1845. The Municipal Councils of Bardez and Salcette would also designate the locales and the buildings for these schools as was done for the other schools. (Consequently these schools were opened in Chinchinim in the "Communidade" house along with all other requirements and the Primary school of the Second degree was opened in Verna with the Council providing the other necessary items. In Bardez the Latin school was opened in Saligao in the "Communidade" house and the Primary school of Second Level was established in Calangute by transferring the Primary school of the First Level to Anjuna).

These were the new steps taken to upgrade Primary education as a visible measure of progress in the State.

V
Full Steam Ahead (1854-1901)

New Reforms

From a tentative beginning in 1831 official Primary Education now started to take on a more defined outlook and became a recognized pursuit. Attempts were made by every succeeding ruler to improve education both vertically and horizontally. Reforms after reforms saw Primary education put on a firm pedestal. However, the response from the locals was least encouraging. The reasons were plenty and of different hues. If for some reasons were political for others they were social and still for others they were economic. The masses as commonly found were simple and ignorant. The school was viewed always with suspicion and with the usual fear of the unknown. Being economically backward they preferred children to help them at home rather than 'waste' time attending school. Knowledge and literacy for the simple folks was at that point in time an unheard of and unwanted thing. Moreover, who wished to learn a foreign language like Latin and Portuguese? Hence, getting the common people interested in the noble cause of education was a herculean task. On the other hand even those few who might have dared to explore the unknown world of knowledge were not only discouraged and despised but also threatened by the landed upper caste who knew that keeping the masses ignorant was to their advantage. So if the success rate in education was nothing to boast about the Portuguese are not to be blamed. The Konknni saying *gorcho bedik, bailo chor* is a fit metaphor for the then prevailing situation in Goa.

As stated earlier the first schools that were established were the Latin schools as in most parts of the world instruction was invariably linked to religious development.Latin was the classical language used extensively by the Church in the religious activities. These Latin schools would help not only in the preparation of candidates for priesthood in the Christian religion but equip them with the language skills.The State authorities too toed the same line using Latin in their temporal affairs. Hence, Latin classes had been established in Goa around 1808. Now, in order to continue with these schools, some substitute teachers had to be appointed. Accordingly the Governor, Visconde de Torres Novas issued a "Portaria" dated 13th September, 1856 appropriating the function of appointing the teachers to the Government. He stated as follows:

> "Having obtained the necessary sanctions from the Council of the Governor, after the stipulation of the "Portaria" of 9th November, 1854 which had been thoroughly explained it was found necessary that any appointment to the post of substitute teachers in the Latin schools outside Lyceum should be made by the Government only as per established norms".

Earlier this same Governor had shown great zeal in taking education to a higher level when he tried to reorganize and give the necessary impetus to education in Goa by establishing the Lyceum (Secondary institution), restarting the Normal school and opening two schools of the Second Level and two schools of Latin in the Provinces of Bardez and Salcette in 1854. He also created a Class of English language in Mapuca. Subsequently in 1855 a Class of French was started in Mapuca and in 1869 a Class of English language was started in Margao.

Besides, he was instrumental in appointing a teacher in the Girls' school in Mapuca, one of the two Girls' schools which had already been sanctioned in 1841. By a "Portaria" dated 12th January, 1854, he appointed after going through the process of selection and getting the approval of the Government Council D. Ludovina Elvaim de Lucio at Mapuca with a salary of twenty "xerafins" per month and in case of absence had to provide her own substitute.

Thereafter he turned his attention to Diu since the Municipal Council had brought to his notice the miserable condition of Primary education in the district. It was pointed out that till then the school was still teaching only Reading, Writing and Counting in spite of the new syllabus adopted as per the provisional regulations of 1848 in which the teaching of Portuguese Grammar, Orthography and Arithmetic was listed. At that time the school was attended by only four students. Therefore, by a "Portaria"dated 10th August, 1854 he declared as follows:

> "I hereby order with the prior approval of the Government Council that the Primary School established in the town square

of Diu would be henceforth known as Mixed school and would have to observe the same instructions given in 1843 as applicable to the school in Daman where the subject of Language and Grammar of Portuguese and Latin, Orthography, Arithmetic and National History were being taught. It is also ordained that till such time as no teacher is appointed especially meant for this school then it would be managed by the Parish priest of Brancavara serving as Assistant to the actual "Professor" of the Primary school, Joao Manuel de Brito drawing a salary of 30 "xerafims" and to the Assistant 20 "xerafims' besides his ecclesiastical income".

This was not the only measure that he undertook in the field of education. He had the inclination to pay attention to what people had to tell him. For some time now the people of Bardez had been bringing to the notice of the Governor that they needed to learn the English language as it was required for dealings in Bombay and other places as the whole of India had come under the sway of the British, Hence, he issued a "Portaria" on the 28th of September, 1854 ordering provisionally the opening of a Class of English in Mapuca, the capital of the Province of Bardez and fixing the salary of the "Professor" who would be appointed to teach English at 40 "xerafins" per month identical to the post created when a class of French had been started in Margao in1850.

Adopting Comenius' Pedagogical Principle

Around this time in Europe the winds of Nationalism were blowing quite strongly and countries like France and England were striving to establish a National system of education. Bitten by the bug probably the new erudite Secretary of State, Joaquim Heliodoro da Cunha Rivara raked up the issue—the first time by a Portuguese top official—of local Konkani language as the medium of instruction almost going against the professed policy of spreading the Portuguese language and culture. It might also have been a fallout of the establishment of the Marathi school and efforts to promote Marathi.

Singlehandedly he brought Konkani into the official education picture. Consequently on the 25th of October, 1859 he got the Governor, Visconde de Torres Novas to approve the directions for filling up the posts of Konkani teachers in the Primary schools. The directions were as follows:

- The first rule of any method was to go from the known to the unknown; the only way to learn a foreign language was to compare it with the mother tongue.
- But for this comparison to be logical and to find the desired effect it was indispensable that the mother tongue—the first requirement for the comparison—had to be adequately or sufficiently known.
- For those whom Konkani was the mother tongue were invited to apply—rectifying the old error that had been committed with this small attempt—to restore its study and promote its culture.
- The first step for its study and culture would be the introduction of the study of its respective Grammar in the schools.
- The disregard of the study of the Konkani language by its own natives was so old and so complete that for a long time now it was found through investigations that the more learned ones among them did not use the language commonly but in general speech because the language did not have grammar nor would it be able to have one.
- Good sense and most rudimentary philosophy did not accept such an absurdity; nobody could admire that which went against good sense and experience to disappoint those who had remained obsessed to such a pernicious error.
- With some diligence it has been discovered that what would have been impossible was not only a possible but also had already taken effect.
- It was also discovered that from olden times learned men had limited the rules of the Konkani language in its various dialects having arranged its Grammar in the Portuguese language and even published it in Portuguese than in the dialect of Goa.
- It was also discovered that besides this a modern Italian missionary (Fr. Maffei?) had composed in the Portuguese language another new Konkani Grammar.
- A new life was sought to be given to the primitive Grammar already printed but almost extinct whose author was Fr. Thomas Stevens and other collaborators who are members of the Company of Jesus (Jesuits).
- The imminent loss of another Grammar till now not edited in the Dialects of the North compiled perhaps in the olden times by a Portuguese missionary whose name was unknown would be avoided.

- Finally throwing some light and saving equally from the risk of loss the modern Grammar by the Italian missionary will also be accomplished.
- The "Professors" have thus in their schools the old Grammar of Fr. Thomas Stevens and the modern one of the Italian priest.
- By the means of these two well laid out Grammars and even with the help of the other from the Dialects of the North easily the "Professors" would be able to gather the practical knowledge which they have of the language and the theoretical knowledge and the method of its rules and its nature.
- It, therefore, depended upon the "Professors" to make the students who entered into the study of the Portuguese Grammar to make them simultaneously to take up also the study of the Konkani Grammar.
- The "Professors" would be able to derive many illustrations and examples from the Grammars of both the Italian priest, that of Fr. Stevens and even from the Dialects of the North without given preference to any one of them as such.
- It would be of utmost importance that the "Professors" having familiarized themselves with the Marathi characters through the introduction of the Grammar by the Italian priest applied in as many examples as possible before teaching their students the value of the same characters in the Roman script, the sentences, words and syllables in Konkani.
- From this Art they would be able to make the students ready with the greatest ease to advance in the knowledge of the Marathi language so useful and so common in these parts of India and according to the opinion of competent men so related to Konkani.
- In the unknown matter of the received customs as it has been mentioned in these directions certain difficulties, hesitations and by chance the repugnance cannot be left to any of the part of the "Professors".
- But it can be hoped that good sense accompanied by the zeal for the progress of their students and the spirit for work would make them more grateful rather than hardworking.
- It may be desired that the "Professors" as soon as they had taken up the first lessons would initiate before their eyes the pair of syllables and the charts of Portuguese names, the syllables and the charts of Konkani names and would be able to proceed in this manner in all the following exercises of the lesson.

- With this the students would develop simultaneously the Reading and the interpretation of Portuguese and Konkani as they would get habituated, almost without feeling it, the mutual correspondence and the version of the two languages.
- In the absence of a Dictionary and books in Konkani which might not be available in the due course of time would, however, be made up in whatever manner possible by the diligence and application of the "Professors".
- These instructions had to be taken as final and no further explanations would be given to the "Professors" as they were not required.

It can well be imagined the turmoil that this new vision of the Secretary must have caused among the teaching fraternity because they themselves had no formal background of the Konkani language. It might also have been a tactical move on the part of the Government to woo back the majority community which earlier they had alienated by their rigid religious policy. The records showed that overwhelming majority of the teachers belonged to the Catholic community brought up on a diet of Portuguese and Christian culture. Hence, there must have been a lot many representations that the new instructions were difficult to follow which might have been foreseen by Cunha Rivara and hence the last instruction becomes significant.

Appointment of Teachers and Other Related Matters

There was indisputable need to make teachers accountable to the whole school system as right from inducing the students to enrol in the school to the conduct of the Classes and maintenance of everything else dealing with the system rested with the teachers. The next Governor, therefore, Jose Ferreira Pestana issued the following "Portaria" on 20th October, 1866 to bring some sort of uniformity in the appointment and conduct of "Professors" and to place the process fully under Government purview:

- The schools of Primary and Secondary instruction maintained by the public bodies like the Municipal Corporations, Parish associations, Confraternities and other similar bodies would be provided with "Professors" as required because they formed a part of the whole set-up of Public Instruction in the State.
- In case of absence of a "Professor" the public body which maintained the school had to propose three suitable candidates

to the competent schools inspection authority and the one who would be selected would substitute the "Professor" during his absence.

- The whole economic aspect of the schools would be looked after by the public body which maintained them and the members, delegated with the function of supervision would visit the school as many times as possible and would give directions and suggestions so as to bring better order and progress in the school.
- When there had been any fraudulent loss of objects the public body or the delegate had to give an account of the circumstances to the competent authority to enable it to proceed with the action required as per the laid down rules.
- The same public body or the delegate when they had realized that in spite of their best efforts the school had not been run properly either discipline-wise or achievement-wise would have to give an account separately to the respective Inspector of schools so that some other steps could be taken which would help in its progress.
- The schools created and maintained by the public bodies would have to follow all the official rules and regulations regarding both discipline and academic performance which were in force in the official schools of the State. The Government authority would then use all the means available with it to see that the public body managed to bring the school on track discipline-wise or achievement-wise so that the abuses were done away with or the defects were corrected.
- In case of suspension or dismissal of "Professors" of the schools run by the Public bodies the rules and regulations for all schools in the State in this connection had to be followed.
- The stipulations in this "Portaria" however did not apply to the schools of Reading and Singing established in the Parishes.

Significant Systemic Changes *et al.*

After the reforms of 1854, another fifteen years later in 1869 to be precise the Portuguese Government came up with a fresh set of reforms announced through a Decree issued on the 30 November, 1869. The major change under these reforms was the division of the elementary course into two classes. The other reforms referred to attendance, age limit for admission, the radius of the school location, the curriculum and the method of teaching. Overall the Government seemed to have tightened its controls still further which meant that education was being taken more and more seriously. The following reforms—those pertaining only to Primary level are mentioned hereunder—which had been announced by the Central Government came to be promulgated in Goa:

- All public education paid for by the State or managed privately was subject to the superintendence and supervision of the respective authorities.
- The authorities to which the above referred were the Councils of Inspectors of Public Instruction and their delegates. The Councils of the Inspectors would be made up of seven members in the State of India and in the Province of Angola and five in the Provinces of Cabo Verde, S. Thome e Principe, Mozambique, Macao and Timor.
- The ex-officio members would be the Governors, in the capacity of Presidents of the Council of Inspectors, and the Prelates of the dioceses or those priests appointed for the purpose as substitutes. Besides these the Councils in India would comprise of two "Professors" of Superior education, one "Professor" from Secondary Level of education and two citizens of proven capability. In the Province of Angola ...... The two "Professors" of Superior education from India had to be proposed by the Public bodies and confirmed by the Governor General whereas in the other provinces like Angola, etc., they had to be nominated by the provincial Governors and confirmed by the Central Government.
- The office of the Council would be located in the capital city of the provinces.
- The following would comprise the duties of the Council both consultative and supervisory:
  - To interpret the various issues which had been ordered by the Governments of the Provinces or by the Central Government *vis-à-vis* the teaching practice.
  - To represent against the topics which are contrary to the interests and progress of instruction in the provinces.
  - To deliberate on the formulation of the regulations for the local schools.
  - To inform the higher authorities about the conflicts of jurisdiction and the competence of the officials of Public Instruction.

- To deliberate over the shortcomings and absence of the "Professors", to propose their suspension or dismissal who deserved of it and to decide upon the questions of discipline and school practices.
- To exercise the function of inspection over all the elementary schools.
- To compile the annual statistics of the schools and other institutions of the province, public and private showing the number of "Professors", and the number of students according to their age, race, sex and the class, mentioning the instructional material used, the attendance in each Class, noting down the absolute and relative capacity of the "Professors" and showing the progress of the students in different Classes or courses.
- To write the annual report which had to show the complete statistics of all the schools of the province, describing the state of instruction in the province, the perceived reasons for its lagging behind or for its progress, including the adequate measures to be taken for its improvement.

- The Councils had to organize at least once a month a meeting presided over by the Governor.
- In the absence of the Governor the meeting had to be presided over by the Episcopal Prelate and in the latter's absence by a member elected for the purpose.
- Besides the monthly meetings the Governor/President can convene extraordinary sessions when required.
- The general statistics and the report about the state of education in the province had to be submitted by the 30th of September of every year and accompanied by the minutes of fruitful discussion, to the Governor of the Province by the 30th of October without fail.
- The Governors had to nominate upon the recommendation of the Councils of Inspection of Public Instruction, local Committees consisting of not less than two members charged with the duty of inspecting the schools outside the town so as to know how they could be made more effective in their organization, more amenable to the local population and in keeping with the indigenous instruction of the place.
- The local inspecting bodies could nominate different delegates for the schools if due to distances they were not able to carry out the inspection in a befitting manner.

- The following were the tasks assigned to the local inspecting bodies:
  - To supervise the observance of all the laws and regulations and punctuality in the school.
  - To visit the schools or direct the delegates to visit them.
  - To maintain uniformity in the use of textbooks and adherence to the rules of discipline and the policies of the schools.
  - To collect the related information of the student population and compile a report on the capacity and the Class of the "Professors" and the progress of the students, sending it from the 30th of November to the 30th of June of each year to the Inspection Council of Public Instruction of the province.
- The services of the members of the Inspection Council of Primary Education would be honorary and would last for a term of three years but were allowed to continue if need be. The services provided by them and the efforts put in by them in this most important branch of education considered as relevant to the overall effect would be suitably rewarded with Certificates of Merit. In a similar manner the services of the delegates and the local Committees would also be acknowledged.
- The services of a Secretary to the Councils or to the local Committees would be provided by appointing a Government servant by the Governors on a part time basis as no appointment could have been done on a permanent basis.
- In each of the Overseas provinces there could have been any number of schools of Primary instruction as per the needs and circumstances of the people.
- The instruction in Primary elementary schools for the boys was to be divided into two levels:
  - For Level I, Reading, Writing, the four mathematical operations both with integers and fractions, teaching and exercises on the system of weights and measures and teaching of Catechism and Christian doctrine which would be for one day during the week for the students belonging to the Catholic religion only.
  - For Level II, Rudiments of Portuguese Grammar, Rudiments of Portuguese Chorography and History, Arithmetic and elements of Geometry with application to industry, Basic Notions of Agriculture and Rural Economy.

- The Governors after deliberating in the General Provincial Council and the Inspecting Council would be able to create "Cadeiras" of Primary education of Level I as per the demand of the population and the circumstances of the locality as well as the "Cadeiras" of Level II whose setting up was necessary which had to be decided by the General bodies of the provinces which would also suggest the salary of the "Professors" and make arrangements for the procurement of furniture.
- The Governors could provisionally nominate the "Professors" of the elementary Primary schools. The confirmation would then depend on the Central Government. *N.B.*—The appointment Orders provisionally issued by the Governors were exempted from the rights of "merce", stamp duty and from other taxes thus with the prior sanction of the Government.
- The Government when it thought fit had the right to order the teaching of other subjects besides those that constituted the school curriculum taught in the Primary schools at Level I and Level II after consulting the Governors, the Overseas Council and the Inspecting Councils. Similarly the Government had the right to fix the salary or the remuneration of the "Professors" appointed in the new schools.
- All children from 9 to 12 years had to attend Primary school closest to their residences with the distance not exceeding three kilometres except those that were sick or handicapped which had to be justified. The Governors after consulting the respective bodies had to adopt suitable measures by which the parents and the teachers would obey scrupulously the above stipulation.
- In schools having Level II there would be public examinations both oral and written during all the trimesters.
- The delegates of the Inspection Councils of Primary education and of the other local bodies would visit the schools of Primary elementary schools both of Level I and Level II during the period decided by the Councils and by the bodies and would test the students passing the competent ones as approved. *N.B.*—The delegates had to inform the Councils and the local bodies about their visit and the tests which had been conducted by them.
- In all the capitals of the Provinces and in the subaltern areas or the districts where its creation would be compatible and if circumstances demanded there had to be a Primary elementary school for the Girls.

- The syllabus for the Girls would consist of Reading, Writing, the four Arithmetical operations in integers and fractions and Catechism for the students belonging to the Catholic religion, all that proper work/functions relevant to females belonging to the common classes.
- The salary for the teachers of Primary education of Level I would be *60$000* "reis" annually in India, *160$000* in Macau and Timor, *180$000* in S.Thome e Principe, *96$000* in Mozambique and *100$000* "reis" in Angola and Cape Verde. *N.B.*—The salaries of the "Professors" of Primary education of Level II could not be more than *350$000* "reis" in any of the provinces.
- When in any part of the locality it was not possible to establish a school or maintain the existing one because of lack of a qualified person to run it perhaps due to the insufficient remuneration paid to the person by the Public body, the Governor could after consulting them appoint a suitable person provisionally with a higher salary after giving satisfactory explanation to the Government.
- The Governors after consulting the local provincial bodies wherever they were functioning and as usual taking the Inspection Council into confidence would make available to the Government a certain number of "Chairs" of Primary education of Level I and Level II, that needed to be established considering the circumstances of the population and its needs and indicating also suitable places where new schools could be found or old ones transferred.
- The "Professors" and the teachers of Primary education who had completed 25 years of continuous service would get the entire last drawn salary as pension. In case it was not possible for the "Professor" to complete 25 years then he would be entitled, as pension, to only 2/5 of the salary he was drawing if he had completed ten years and for those who had put in more than ten years of service but less than 25 years would be paid another four per cent for every extra year.
- Only those teachers who were fulltime and appointed in permanent posts had the right for pension. However, service rendered in temporary posts would also be counted for pensionary benefits.
- The Central Government would subsidize annually Primary and Secondary education in the overseas colonies with supply of

compendiums/textbooks for all the students in all the schools in all the provinces.

- Four years after the schools of elementary Primary Instruction had been in existence all the "Cadeiras" had to be reorganized again in the provinces which had to be vacated afterwards. This would be done by conducting a test for all the students by a Jury of two "Professors" of the school and one delegate nominated by the Inspection Council. *N.B.*—The test programme for the test would be proposed by the school Council to the Inspection Council anticipating the necessity.
- All the candidates both male and female having qualified would be admitted to the tests of the "Cadeiras".

  The conditions for appearing for the test were as follows:
  - Age of 21 years or if possessing any academic degree, then 18 years.
  - A Certificate of good behaviour from the Administrator of the place or by any authority of the Council where he was residing.
- The schools where the attendance was thin would be transferred by the Governors to other localities which obviously would benefit more.
- After three years of continuous service the provisionally appointed "Professor" would become permanent.
- In all the schools in the Overseas provinces the same syllabus and the same textbooks had to be followed.
- The Government would prepare the textbooks which would be adopted in all the elementary Primary schools as in the principal schools and it would order books to be written more appropriate to the level and the locality, which after they had been approved by the Overseas Committee would become textbooks for the schools. *N.B.*—These textbooks would be revised every six years making additions and deletions improving the book in consultation with the Overseas Committee so as to keep abreast of the scientific changes and as per the needs of education.
- The attendant subsidies in meeting the expenses of the Primary elementary education (and other institutions like Normal of Lisbon, (etc) in the provinces like transport, maintenance and attendance of native students of the Overseas possessions would be stopped.
- The salaries drawn by the teachers prior to this Decree would

continue. However, those appointed henceforth would draw their salaries as per the new guidelines.

- The Government would immediately take steps to adopt these stipulations. (*Diario de do Governo*, No. 281 of 10th of December, 1869, Bol. No. 9 of 1870).
- The above stipulations were issued by the Secretary for Overseas Affairs Luis Agusto Rebello de Silva in the name of the King on the 30th of November, 1869.

Coming to Grips with Reality

In spite of the Government's best efforts at spreading education all over Goa the response was far from satisfactory with the locals always looking at the Portuguese suspiciously as they had conquered their land and were trying to impose their own language and culture through education. Due to such a lackadaisical approach the Government was forced to keep on rethinking its strategy. This would often result in either closing down some schools or shifting them elsewhere depending upon the exigencies. At times there would be a need even to open new ones. This went on for quite some time with stability always becoming an elusive factor.

A case in point was the threat of closure of the school at Canacona due to lack of attendance. Instead of doing that the Government thought it fit to modify its policy so as to improve the enrolment and keep the schools functioning. Since this was endemic of all schools in the New Conquests the Governor, Viscount of Sam Januario issued a "Portaria" on the 10th of July, 1871 converting the Portuguese schools in the "Novas Conquistas" into Portuguese—Marathi schools in order to attract more students.

It was brought to the notice of the Governor that there are many difficulties faced by the schools including the filling up of the posts of teachers as sometimes they were filled up after a long period of time and because of differences in the composition of the content or the Jury few candidates would apply for the said posts. To set matters right the Governor, Visconde de Sam Januario, issued a "Portaria" on the 8th of November, 1870 with the following conditions:

1. There would be every year a certain period earmarked for the conduct of interviews for the posts of Primary teachers in the month of January.
2. This would be done by a Jury of five members appointed every year by the Inspection Council among which there would be a

President and a Secretary. *N.B.*—The Commissioner of Studies or in his place the Rector of the Lyceum would be the ex-officio member of the Jury.

3. Those who had been selected and approved by the Council of Instruction would be appointed in the vacant posts during the current year.
4. The Inspection Council of Primary Education had to draw up the schedule for the entire implementation of these stipulations.

Maintaining Financial Discipline

Taking note of the undue expenses incurred in providing instructional materials to the schools and in their maintenance the same Governor, Sam Januario issued on the 2nd of March, 1871 after consulting the Inspection Council the following Order to help the institutions to manage both these aspects through a Central agency so that responsibility could be easily fixed and accounts could be properly maintained in keeping with the reorganization as per the Decree of 1869. He directed as follows:

- The students who were attending the elementary Primary schools of the First and Second Level would pay at the time of enrolling half a "xerafin" and another half a "xerafin" at the end of the year when they wanted to answer the final examination *N.B.*—This had to be recorded in the book of admissions opened anew every year.
- Those who wished to study Latin or Latinity in the respective classes of the Public schools of the Provinces of Salcette and Bardez had to pay one "xerafin" for admission.
- The fees of admission and other fees of the poor students were dispensed with provided they produced a Certificate to that effect attested by the Parish priest and the "Regedor" of the place.
- Only those students who had presented the passing Certificate in the various subjects of Primary education of the First or Second Level acquired in a Public school would be admitted to any Class of Secondary instruction.
- The "Professors" of the schools of Primary and Secondary instruction outside the Lyceum would be able to spend without the permission of the local Inspection Committee a maximum of ten "xerafins" every year for the miscellaneous expenses and cleanliness of the school.

- At the end of the academic year the "Professors" in the Primary and Secondary schools had to submit the bills and the accounts of the school fund to the Inspection Committee along with the documents for examination and approval.
- Having approved the accounts of receipts and expenses the Inspection Committees had to make them deposit the surplus amount in the fund box which would be kept in the custody of the Committee, making note of the amount in a book which would then be countersigned by the President.
- The surplus fund would be used for the expenses towards the purchase of prizes, the repairs of the school and of the school furnitures, for the maintenance of the Secretariat of the Committee and other things that the Government would decide from time to time (Boletim No. 17).

On that same date the Governor issued another "Portaria" in respect of those students who were attending private schools spelling out the manner in which they should be examined:

- The students who enrolled and completed their study in the private Primary schools either in Class I or Class II and wished to appear for the final examination were needed to apply to the local Committee during the first fortnight of March of every year.
- The local Committee then would meet in the second fortnight of the same month and allocate the centres for the examination preferring to seat him in the Parish school or a school in the vicinity which would be communicated to him through a dispatch.
- The examinations of these students who had been admitted by the "Professor" of the school nominated in the dispatch by paying an amount of one "xerafin" into the school account would take place possibly on the same day or the next day on which the students of the public school would be examined.
- The fees of the poor students would be dispensed with provided they produced a Certificate attested by the Parish priest and the "Regedor" of the place.
- All details pertaining to the said examinations had to be written in the respective books of the school with separate pages allotted to each student making the examinees pay half a "xerafin" for a copy of the results of the examination (Boletim No. 17).

Problems with Parish Schools

It was not a smooth ride this implementation of the educational reforms. Many difficulties were encountered as was to be expected. One such difficulty arose in the school at Pilerne in the province of Bardez. As the matter could be solved amicably the Governor, Joaquim Jose Macedo e Couto had to step in and issue a "Portaria" on the 7th of January, 1873 so as to defuse the situation.

The "Gauncares" (members of the "Communidade") had complained to the Governor that the serving Primary and Music teacher had been unjustly suspended by the "Communidade" authorities who used to pay the salary of the teacher and a new one had been appointed in his place without any rhyme or reason. It appeared that the motive for the suspension was because the local Inspection Committee for Bardez did not consider him qualified to teach on the false assumption that the Music teachers come under the control and supervision of the local Inspection Committee.

Actually the duties of the teachers appointed in any of the Church schools was to sing and play during Church services and teach Music and Singing to the children of the village. However, it was incidental to teach a smattering of the language by teaching Reading and Writing so as to enable the children to be familiar with the words sung during service which might also enable them to make some sense of what was being sung and said.

Hence, these Music teachers were not really Primary Teachers in the true sense of the word and, hence, did not come under the jurisdiction of the Inspection Council. The "Portaria" of 20th October, 1866 had also excluded these schools since they had been created and maintained by the local public bodies. So also the Decree of 30th November, 1869 which was in keeping with the "Portaria" of 20th October, 1866 which dealt with the private schools and the appointment of the Church employees opined that it came under the jurisdiction of the Church authorities. It was, therefore, decided by consulting the Inspection Council that the inspection of the school or the appointment, suspension or dismissal of the Music teacher did not concern the local Inspection Committee.

Hence very adroitly the Governor threw the ball into the court of the ecclesiastical authorities. Earlier too when Garcez Mourao Palha tried to interfere with these Church schools there was a hue and cry and the Music schools were allowed to continue as they were.

On the 3rd of March, 1874 the Secretary of the Inspection Council, Francisco Joao Xavier sent the following circular to all the Inspection Committees:

Wishing that the Inspection Council of the State should be fully informed of the state of instruction in the Primary and Secondary schools coming under the charge of the local inspection Committees as also the outcome of these visits of the Committees to the schools of the First and Second Level they are hereby directed—the local inspection Committees of Ilhas, Bardez and Salcette—to observe the following in both letter and spirit:

- At the end of each semester in order to give an account of the current year they had to send to the Inspection Council a list of all students who had attended school mentioning therein their place of birth, their parents and their attendance record as also the textbooks they were studying; and an assessment of what the "Professor" thought of each student regarding his progress, his conduct, etc., and in another special section the Inspection Council had to also give information regarding the "Professor", his abilities both absolute and relative, his regularity of attendance and any other observations the Committee might think fit to inform the higher ups.
- They had to inform by the end of every term as fixed by the resolution of the Council on the 31st of March, 1870 the reports of the visits and the results of the examinations, which had to be furnished in the prescribed format.
- At the end of each scholastic year eight days after the examinations they had to prepare a chart of the enrolment and distribution of the students showing every post, the names of the "Professors", the number of students enrolled, examined and promoted as per the officially prepared format and the list of those awarded prizes and they had to send all this through proper channel through the President to the Secretary of the Council to be published in the "Boletim Oficial".
- Finally they had to inform immediately and directly about the passing away of any of the present or past "Professors" or about any other event connected with education.

Bringing All Schools under State Control

Perhaps the Pilerne school incident had created a situation whereby the other schools too were gradually trying to assert themselves with the result that the Government was being left stranded as a mere by-stander. Hence, it was time for some fresh legislation to rein in the individualistic tendencies. Hence, in 1874, the Governor, Joaquim Jose Macedo e Couto on the 28th of October ordered that all the schools both public and private, Primary and Secondary should be brought under the jurisdiction of the Inspection Council thus expanding its jurisdiction and further empowering it to bring control over the prevailing situation. His writ ran as follows:

- All public instruction Primary, Secondary and Superior funded by the State or run privately was subject to the superintendence and supervision of the State Inspection Council, its delegates and the local Committees as per the Decree of 30th November, 1869.
- It was also the duty of the Inspection Council according to their consultative functions to exercise the function of inspection over all the elementary schools by itself or through the local Committees or through the delegates as per the provisions of the same Decree.
- (refers to Secondary education)
- (refers to Lyceum)
- The Commissioner of Studies or in his absence the Rector of the Lyceum or anybody delegated by him would be the ex-officio member of the Inspection Council.
- The following would be the duties of the Commissioner or the others:
  - To visit all the schools in the territory of Goa, Daman and Diu in order to know the state of affairs of the schools.
  - To know first hand the breach of discipline, the immediate needs of education for which a meeting at short notice had to be called to take the necessary steps.

Instructions for Conducting Examinations

Earlier on the 12th of March, 1874 the Governor, Joaquim Jose de Macedo e Couto had issued a "Portaria" delineating the various stipulations for the conduct of examinations in the Primary Schools of Portuguese, Marathi and Gujarati. The following norms were laid down:

- There would a certain period in the year meant for the enrolment of students for examinations. This would be preferably in the month of January and would be announced in the official bulletin at least 30 days in advance for the interested parties to submit their applications.

- The examinations had to be conducted by a Jury of five members appointed every year by the Council of Inspections with one member chosen as President and another as Secretary. The Commissioner of Studies or in his absence the Rector of Lyceum would be an ex-officio member of the Jury.
- They would be tested in written and oral papers.
- The following was the programme of testing: (For candidates belonging to girls' schools).

Written Papers

1.	Copying of a prose passage (testing Calligraraphy)	= 25 marks
2.	Copying of a Prose Passage (testing Orthography)	= 30 marks
3.	Solving an arithmetic problem	= 15 marks
	Total	= 70 marks

Orals

1.	Reading of a passage from the Classical book	= 25 marks
2.	Basic principles of Portuguese Grammar	= 25 marks
3.	Basic notions of Sacred History	= 20 marks
4.	Christian doctrine	= 25 marks
5.	Arithmetic (four operations)	= 20 marks
6.	Metric-Decimal system	= 25 marks
	Total	= 140 marks
7.	Needle work	
	A. Darning	= 10 marks
	B. Crotchet	= 10 marks
	C. Sewing	= 20 marks
	D. Borders	= 15 marks
	E. Borders coloured	= 15 marks
	F. Stitching	= 20 marks
	Total	= 90 marks

(For students of Portuguese Primary Schools)

Written Papers

1.	Copying of a prose passage (for testing Calligraphy)	= 10 marks
2.	Copying of a Prose Passage (for testing Orthography)	= 10 marks
3.	Solving a problem in Arithmetic	= 12 marks

4.	Solving another problem in metric/decimal	= 12 marks
5.	Two questions on Sacred History	= 10 marks
6.	Two questions on Christian doctrine	= 06 marks
	Total	= 60 marks

Orals

1.	Reading of one passage (prose)	= 08 marks
2.	Reading of one passage in verse	= 10 marks
3.	Basic principles and practice of Portuguese Grammar	= 24 marks
4.	Arithmetic	= 08 marks
5.	Question on metric/decimals	= 06 marks
6.	Brief notions of Geography	= 06 marks
7.	Geography of Portugal and its possessions	= 08 marks
8.	National History	= 08 marks
9.	Rules of Calligraphy	= 06 marks
10.	Rudiments of Pedagogy	= 06 marks
	Total	= 90 marks

(For students of Marathi students)

1.	Reading of a passage in Balbodh or Nagri script	= 10 marks
2.	Writing in the same script	= 10 marks
3.	Reading of a passage in Mody script	= 09 marks
4.	Writing in the Mody script	= 09 marks
5.	Table of integers and fractions of money	= 10 marks
6.	Explanation and exercises on weights and measures	= 10 marks
7.	Naming the years and months in Hindu, Mohammedan and Roman Calendars	= 12 marks
8.	Reading and recitation of Classical Hindu poems	= 08 marks
9.	Rudiments of *Bal Veakoronn* Grammar	= 08 marks
	Total	= 86 marks

Since no mention was made of the levels it was to be understood that the same pattern would be followed for the First and Second level.

Further Directions to the Inspection Committees

On the 4th of August, 1875, the erudite Secretary General of the

Administration, Thomas Ribeiro issued the following instructions to the local Inspection Committees and the inspecting delegates:

- These Committees or the delegates would visit by themselves the schools of Primary instruction maintained through State funds or by private agencies in keeping with the public instruction issued on the 31st March, 1870 and in keeping with the Decree of 30th November, 1869. *N.B.*—They would also be assisted by the administrative authorities and the Parish authorities.
- The "Professors" (both male and female) of the public and private schools must be ready to receive the inspection team with a report of the circumstances of the school.
- During the visit the delegates should carefully check the state of the school, the furnitures, the condition of the house, the hygienic conditions inside and outside the school, number of students present, attendance figures, punctuality, regimen, the method of teaching and the discipline, which the "Professor" had been adopting, the books used for teaching and the overall progress of all the students.
- The delegate had to give instructions and make the necessary corrections putting them in writing in a book or notebook which would remain in the school a copy of which had to be given to the "Professor".
- The delegate had to bring to the notice of the "Professor" if the need arose the principles of pedagogy, in order to improve the teaching of the "Professor"—one of the main objectives of inspection—by developing his capacities and enhancing the quality of teaching.
- They had to inform the "Professor" about the opinion that people had of him in the locality.
- After all the schools under his jurisdiction had been inspected the Administrator of the province at the request of the delegate would call a meeting of the local inspection Committee. In this meeting the delegate had to give his assessment of the state of education in the schools and suggest ways and means of improving it.
- For the purposes mentioned in these instructions the delegate had to proceed with the enquiries if necessary taking the help of the competent local people in the improvement of the school.
- The local Committees would nominate a suitable person in each school where still nobody had been appointed whose task would

be to improve the attendance and the diligence of the students and consequently by all means possible, moral as well as material improve the condition of the school.

- At the end of the inspection and enquiry the inspection Committee had to send a report of the visit to the inspection Council detailing the needs of the school and suggesting ways and means for meeting them if needed.
- The Committees had to prepare a chart/schedule of the visits mentioning the special instructions which the delegates had to communicate to the school sending at the same time a copy to the Inspection Council.
- The Commissioner at his discretion could organize another inspection if needed in any of the schools which had already been inspected.
- The delegate had to be assisted during the Inspection by the "Regedor", the administrative authorities, the accounts people and the Parish authorities. (Boletim No. 63).

The Portuguese laid a lot of store by supervision. There were many reasons. First and foremost because it was a colonial regime the political authorities had to get all the feedback and at the same time keep the schools under a blanket of fear and intimidation so that they should not step out of line and create problems of political unrest or social disharmony in the State. The second reason was to see that whatever was being taught did not have any slant of sedition or anything against the mother country. On the contrary the inspection visit was also to find out whether the process of enculturation was going on smoothly or not.

Bringing More Order in the System

Feeling the need to regulate the appointment of substitutes in the schools the then Governor, Caetano Alexandre d'Almeida Albuquerque issued on the 2nd of August, 1879 the following "Portaria":

- In the case of the absence of any "Professor" due to sickness it had to be seen that the smooth functioning of the Classes was not at all affected which could be taken care of by appointing a person with the approval of the Inspection Committee capable of managing the Classes. *N.B.*—If any of the schools remained closed for three days at a stretch, the Inspection Committee had to immediately make arrangements to send a capable person to restart it.

- If the leave was extended by the "Professor" and exceeded fifteen days the Inspection Committee had to immediately inform the Governor in order to make arrangements to get a quick substitute with the approval of the Inspection Council.
- (refers to Escola Normal).
- The absence due to sickness had to be justified by producing a medical Certificate which the "Professor" had to send within a period of eight days to the respective local Committee and had to get it attested by the health authorities if the leave period was further extended or else his salary would be deducted for the period of absence.
- This applied to all the schools whether they were maintained by the State, the Municipal bodies, the Parishes organizations, the "Communidades" or any other body.
- The local Inspection Committees had to be vigilant to see that no post of Primary or Secondary education in their jurisdiction was left vacant. (Boletim No. 60).

The Governor, Caetano Alexandre d'Almeida e Albuquerque issued another "Portaria" on the 5th of August, 1879, so as to bring in some homogeneity among the different types of schools, to centralize all the other regulations issued from time to time and to streamline the administration of schools. The various provisions of the "Portaria" were as follows:

- The liberty to teach in the private schools authorized under law was, however, subject to the fulfilment of moral and literary conditions established under the same Decree.
- All those who were working as "Professors" in the private schools in the Primary or Secondary sections in any College or Class had to acquire a suitable qualification.
- The qualification should be proved through the documents and by appearing for a public examinations which will be held by the Government in consultation with the Inspection Council of Public Instruction.
- The one who wanted to qualify for a teaching post in a private school had to apply to the Rector of Lyceum and submit his application accompanied by the character Certificate issued by the Municipal Corporation and the Administrator of the Council or Administrator of Accounts where the applicant had been residing for the past three years; and the documents had to prove

his aptitude and show his literary sufficiency to teach and guide the learning of the youth for which he had also to mention the subjects that he had been teaching along with the name and locality of the school where he had been teaching.

- The Rector of Lyceum would then forward to the Inspection Council these applications with his own comments clarifying the status of the said teachers.
- The Inspection Council of Public Instruction could exempt from answering the public examinations those who possessed Diploma of the Superior course of Instruction of the National Lyceum or at least a sufficient number of approvals in the subjects taught in these establishments—if they presented Certificates of merit in Arts or Science or any other recognized faculty—to take up the post of a teacher after consulting the higher authorities.
- If those qualified fail to show the necessary documentary proof that they did have the proper aptitude to teach the subjects in the respective schools or if they failed to prove their capacity by means of a public examination the Governor could deny them the licence to teach.
- The Directors of the private Colleges (Secondary schools) needed a special Certificate of authorization which they had to apply for by presenting certain documents along with a Plan of Studies and Education of the respective College and with an undertaking that they had the necessary means to fulfil all the economic and literary conditions. *N.B.*—For the Directors to be allowed to open a school or run the existing one they had to ensure that:
    - All the teachers teaching in the school had a teaching Certificate in the particular subject they were teaching.
    - All those entrusted with the education of the children had a good moral and civil character.
- The Colleges and the schools were just like public establishments to be visited and inspected by the authorities to which the Directors and the "Professors" were accountable giving all the necessary information required by them.
- Those teachers who did not fulfil the necessary conditions would be penalized with temporary or permanent suspension by the administration of the respective college or school.
- It was up to the respective local inspecting Committees to enforce the stipulations.

Recruitment Rules for Teachers

The Secretary to the Governor, Joaquim Heliodoro da Cunha Rivara prepared the following regulations for conducting licencing examinations for appointing teachers in the Primary schools for Level I and Level II:

- There would be every year a period reserved for admitting candidates for the examination of the posts of teachers. *N.B.*—This period would be in the month of January and would be announced thirty days before the date for submitting the applications counting from the day of publication of the notice on the "Boletim Oficial".
- The Jury to assess the candidates would comprise of five members appointed annually by the Inspection Council out of which one would act as President and another as Secretary. *N.B.*—The Commissioner of Studies and in his absence the Rector of Lyceum would be the ex-officio members of the Jury.
- The candidates for the posts of teachers had to submit to the office of the Governor within the specified period the following documents:
    - Birth Certificate showing not less than 21 years of age or if having an academic qualification then at least 18 years of age.
    - A Character Certificate issued by the Administrator of the Council or of the Administrator of Accounts.
    - Written application.
    - A vaccination Certificate or a Certificate stating that he did not carry any disability which could interfere in his teaching. *N.B.*—The candidates had to put together all these documents and others if there were which would show his qualifications either in Arts or in Science as well as a Certificate showing his teaching experience which would be equal to graduation and would help him in getting preference for the job.
- At the end of the period the Secretary of the Inspection Council would proceed with the scrutiny of the documents:
    - All those whose documents were perfectly in order would be listed in alphabetical order assigned by the Secretary and published in the official paper.
    - The other candidates too whose documents were incomplete would also be listed and published but under a different list

on the "Boletim Oficial" and announced that these cannot appear for the test.

- At the end of this period one day after the Inspection Council had to meet and decide on the day and the time on which the candidate would answer his examination and this would be published on the "Boletim Oficial".

- The examinations would be both oral and written.
- The written examinations would be held first and would be for all the candidates at the same time, same day and same place.
- These examinations would be assessed through voting by the members of the Jury after adding the marks obtained. The grading would be done by comparing the score with the maximum in each of the tests.
- The candidates who had not after adding the subject-wise totals obtained at least one third of the grand total would be excluded from the orals. *N.B.*—Those who had obtained the required scores as per the above article could appear for the orals. Those marks would also be taken into account for the calculation of the final score for the placement in the merit list by the Jury in their submission to the Inspection Council.
- The test for the teachers of the First Level would consist of:
    - Writing of a prose passage from a Classic dictated by one of the members of the Jury.
    - Solving an elementary problem in Arithmetic.
    - Solving of a problem in the decimal Metric system.
    - Answers to two questions on Sacred History.
    - Answering two questions on Catechism and general principles on Morals. *N.B.*—The questions for all the tests would be selected by lots by the first-five students. In the evening of the first day of the examinations the Jury had to meet to finalize a sufficient number of questions for the written as well as the oral tests. Each test would consist of twelve question sets which would be kept in a safe place whose key would be with the President of the Jury.
- The allotted time for the tests could not exceed four hours at the end of which the candidates had to hand over the answer papers properly dated and signed to the President of the Jury who would then initial them in acknowledgement of having fulfilled all the conditions as per the procedures of the examination.

- After the written tests of all the candidates were over the Jury would evaluate each of the answer scripts and each member then would vote/allot marks after scrutinizing the paper with reference to the maximum marks allotted for each paper. *N.B.*—The sum of all the averages obtained in each written test had to be put together by the Secretary in serial order of the names of candidates in the form of a list. This list would then be signed by all the members of the Jury.
- The orals would be answered by the candidates in serial order as per the list in turns of two to four.
- The members of the Jury had to divide the topics of the syllabus among themselves as directed by the President questioning each of the candidates. A maximum of thirty minutes would be allotted to each candidate to be tested on his knowledge and on his ability.
- The orals would be conducted in the following areas:
  - Reading of two passages from a Classic, one in prose and the other in verse, elementary principles on general Grammar, logical and practical knowledge of the Portuguese language.
  - Arithmetic and the metric decimal system.
  - Brief notions of Geography in general and Geography of Portugal and its possessions in particular.
  - National History in brief.
  - Rules of Calligraphy.
  - Rudiments of Pedagogy. *N.B.*—The examination for the candidates of the Second Level would cover topics of greater difficulty in the same areas and a few others.
- At the end of the orals of all the candidates each day the Jury would sit together and assess their scores in the same way as they did for the written tests:
  - Those who had obtained less than one-third of the total of both written and oral tests would be classified as average.
  - Those who had obtained more than one-third but less than half would be classified as sufficient or average.
  - Those who had obtained half of the maximum marks allotted would be classified as good.
  - Those who had obtained two-thirds of the total in both the types of tests would be awarded distinction.
  - In all these three classes of sufficient or average, good and distinction the ranking would be done as per the scores.

- The results of the examination had to be signed by all the members of the Jury and sent to the Inspection Council by the President along with the minutes of the meetings of the Jury also signed by all the members of the Jury along with whatever other documents were used in the said examinations.
- The Inspection Council, having proceeded with the processing of the examinations of all the periods had to classify the candidates taking into consideration the examination results and then draw up the placement list by taking into consideration the qualifications in Arts or Science, the number of years of service in both public and private, the moral, civil and religious outlook, and thus prepare the merit list to be published on the "Boletim Official". *N.B.* In the classification of qualifications, those having—the Normal course would be placed above those having the Lyceum and Science courses and then Lyceum would be above Science.
- At the end of each trimester the Council had to publish on the "Boletim Oficial" the list of vacant posts in the Primary schools in all the provinces of the State so that the eligible candidates could apply within a period of 20 days from the date of publication of the said posts along with all the documents, stating their number on the merit list.
- The candidates included in some of the three classes namely "suficiente" (average), "bom" (good) and "distinctos"(distinction) as per the list prepared earlier could work as a teacher in the open schools; after informing the local Committee about the place of the school and the subjects which he intended to teach.
- The listed candidates under "bom" and "distinctos" who had not been placed in any post of Primary instruction between the two periods could reappear for the examinations along with the new candidates for the vacant posts. The "suficiente" would be placed only if no "bom" or "distinctos" candidates were available in the immediate following year:
    - The candidates classified as "bom" or "distinctos" would have to submit after one year of their qualifying their application and all the other documents as mentioned earlier.
    - The listed candidates had to make themselves available to work as substitutes in the school complexes at a place closest to his residence preferably in the order as they are placed in

the list with the lowest ones placed further away from their residence.

- The teachers for the posts in Girls' Primary schools would also have to apply in the same manner and would also have to follow the same process of selection.
- The Jury for the examination would consist of one member of the Inspection Council as President, a teacher of the "Escola Normal", and one teacher from the official Primary school or in his absence a female teacher of proven merit especially knowing well the feminine arts.
- Every year the Council had to publish the schedule for the conduct of the examination.

The syllabus for the examinations of Primary teachers was as follows:

Written Tests

I.	Writing/Copying of one passage in prose—Calligraphy	10
II.	Orthography	10
III.	Solving one Arithmetic sum	12
IV.	Solving another problem under the metric decimal system	12
V.	Response to two questions on Sacred History	10
VI.	Answering two questions on Catechism and Morals	06
	Total	60

Orals

I.	Reading one prose passage	8
II.	Reading one passage in verse (Os Lusiadas de Camoens)	10
III.	Elements of Grammar and practice of Portuguese language	24
IV.	Arithmetic	8
V.	Metric system	6
VI.	Brief notions of Geography	6
VII.	Geography of Portugal and its possessions	8
VIII.	History of the country special reference to India	8
IX.	Rules of Calligaphy	6
X.	Rudiments of Pedagogy	6
	Total	90

The syllabus for the other categories of teachers for the Portuguese-Marathi schools was the same as above. However for the teachers of the

Girls' schools the syllabus was a toned down one with fewer subjects. The syllabus for the Marathi schools was naturally a different one for example a passage was to be transcribed either in Balbodh or the Mody script. The papers for the teachers of the Second Level would have some minor changes. For example they were tested also in the subject of Drawing.

Thereafter amalgamating all the periodic changes and taking into account the new changes the Portuguese Government came out with a new education policy which was announced through the Decree of 14 December, 1881. Again the major reforms under this new policy was the creation of new schools called the Chapel-schools where the priest would provide religious services to the people as also the educational ones.

The Governor, Caetano d'Albuquerque gave further boost to education by involving the local bodies like the Confraternities and the "Communidades" in the construction of the houses for the Primary schools. Accordingly the "Communidades" of Siolim-Marna, Nerul, Pilerne, Uccassaim, Reis Magos, Saligao, Aldona, Salvador do Mundo, the Confraternities of Rachol, Colvale, Moira, Tivim, etc., contributed from their own funds to construct proper buildings for the Primary schools.

The Goan Spirit Soars

At this juncture it must be mentioned that having learnt a thing or two Goans after having imbibed both the missionary zeal and the language skills charted their own course of establishing schools in Bombay and other places in India and later on even abraod. Bombay now Mumbai became the first destination for the enterprising spirit of Goans. Arguably the first school to be founded by a Goan in Bombay was the "Escola Portuguesa dos Barretos" started by John Barreto in 1783 near the Church of Cavel much before the Government Primary schools could start in Goa. In 1860, St. Xavier's was founded by a Goan, Mr. B.X. Furtado at Cavel again which later on became one of the mostly widely sought after institutions. The Souza School was founded by Antonio de Souza, a businessman originally from Mapuca in 1796 in Mazagaon. There was another school started in the same place by another Goan by the name of Germiniano de Souza. There were two more schools one at Dabul called Goan Union High School and the other Antonio da Silva High School which was initially called St. John Anglo-Portuguese school (Aloysius Soares, Four Centuries of Education, 212).

By the end of this 70 years period from 1831 to 1901 after a plethora of provisions aimed at improving the enrolment and retention rates the situation of the school system as found before the introduction of the major overhaul of 1907 and the declaration of the Republic in 1910 was as follows:

Table 5.1: Enrolment at the Beginning of the twentieth Century

Sr. No.	*Medium*	*Location/Province*	*No. of students of First Level*	*No. of students of Second Level*
1	Portuguese	Ilhas	598	105
2	"	Salcette	1117	143
3	"	Bardez	1347	64
4	"	Pernem	85	—
5	"	Sanquelim	111	—
6	"	Sattari	16	—
7	"	Ponda	138	23
8	"	Sanguem	28	—
9	"	Quepem	75	—
10	"	Canacona	45	—
11	"	Daman	74	14
12	"	Nagar Haveli	—	—
13	"	Diu	64	6
		Total	3698	349
14	Marathi	Sanquelim	24	—
15	"	Sattari	14	—
16	"	Ponda	36	—
17	"	Sanguem	12	—
18	"	Quepem	27	—
19	"	Canacona	18	—
		Total	131	
20	Gujarati	Daman	32	—
21	"	Nagar Haveli	90	—
22	"	Diu	187	—
		Total	309	
Grand Total			4138	349

It can be seen from Table 5.1 that the Government of many attempts did succeed in establishing Primary schools in all the provinces of the Estado da India Portuguesa.At the First level an encouraging figure of 3,698 students can be found enrolled in the Portuguese Primary schools. Another feature to be noted is that the Marathi and Gujarati schools too were doing very well which means the school going culture had already been established in the whole State. In constrast, however, the Secondary level had neither been promoted vigorously nor been attended in large numbers as the total number of students in all schools at the First level was around 4,138 whereas it was only 349 at the Second level making it a percentage of 8 per cent only.

VI
Girls' Education

The dynamic interim Governor, Lopes de Lima was the first to moot the idea of a Girls' school in each Municipal town of Goa. He tried to set up these schools in the Provincial capitals but it appears that his efforts during his tenure did not bear any fruit.

First School Exclusively for Girls

However, the Governor, Jose Ferreira Pestana managed to open the first Girls' school in the State capital, Pangim when he issued the following "Portaria".

"Finding that there was an urgent need to establish a Class (read school) for the girls and the post for which had already been advertised on the Boletim No. 49 in 1844 and the candidate selected. Now the said candidate, D. Anna Joaquina de Souza Correia has represented to me why she should not be appointed. Hence, after consulting the Council of the Governor and the Department of Public Expenditure I mandate the following:

1. That the said Anna Joaquina de Souza Correia be appointed as the teacher in the said school on a salary of 60 "xerafins" per month provided she manages to enroll at least twelve or more students for the Class, finds a substitute who would be able to teach in her absence paying her a decent salary from her own pocket and runs the school for at least one academic year.
2. The salary would be hiked by another 50 "xerafin" annually in case the number of students increases to twenty; it would be hiked to another hundred "xerafins" if the number of students had to go up to thirty.
3. However if the number of students by the end of May 1846 is nowhere near 12 then the salary of the teacher would be reduced

to 18 "xerafins" and another three and a half "xerafin" for every student every month.

4. The teacher was bound to teach the students the syllabus as outlined in the "Portaria" of 17 August, 1841 and conduct the Class as per the regulations given in the "Portaria" dated 6 September, 1843 and such other regulations pertaining to the Primary education of boys if no specific mention was made in the regulations for girls.
5. The Governor desired that facilities for the education of girls having been provided the teacher had to spare no efforts in educating the girls which would be her reward.
6. A special Committee would provisionally supervise the Class and would assist in opening another with the help of the Inspecting Committee.

This initiative had to be approved by the Ministry of Overseas Affairs in Portugal. Accordingly the Queen by her "Portaria" dated 18th of September, 1846 gave her assent to the appointment of Anna Joaquina de Souza Correia as the teacher for the Girls' school and approved her salary and other service conditions.

It was indeed a momentous occasion to have the first Girls' school in the territory and perhaps set a pioneering precedent for the rest of the country. It has, however, to be noted that the Government was wise enough to set a modest and achievable target when it came to enrolment. Further for the success of the school in terms of enrolment and retention the onus was also laid squarely on the teacher thus making the teacher fully accountable.

Limited Expansion

The girls were given incentives to attend school. Seeing the encouraging response two more Girls' schools were set up. When the Governor, the Baron of Vila Nova de Ourem by a "Portaria Provincial" in 1854 reorganized Primary education he tried to expand Girls' education by setting up two more schools, one in Mapuca and the other in Margao in addition to the one in Pangim. In Mapuca by his "Portaria" dated 12th January, 1854 he appointed on temporary basis D. Ludovina Elvaim de Lucio and in Margao he nominated D. Anna Antonia Isabel D'Unhao as the Primary teachers for the Girls schools with a salary of 20 "xerafins" per mensem laying down the same conditions as those made applicable to the teacher in the school at Pangim.

Provisions were also made in the Plan of Studies for Girls' education. The following articles in the Plan of Studies refer to Girls' education:

- In each of the Provinces there should be a school for girls maintained from the funds of the "Misericordia" of the State.
- Here they should be taught Reading and Writing, exercises in Portuguese Grammar, Arithmetic, Principles of Christian doctrine, Civility, Morals, Home Economy, Music, Dance, Embroidery, Knitting and Stitching, Notions of History, Geography and exercises in French and English languages.
- The teaching load should be distributed among three teachers one of whom would be the Rector (head).
- The Governor's Council after hearing the Committee of the "Misericordia" had to frame the regulations of the College (Secondary school), hire the personnel .... and adopt the following principles:
  - They had to be looked after in the school for not more than four years with each school having not less than ten girls.
  - Those having less than 16 years would be admitted in the school on payment of a fee of 1,600 "reis" per month into the treasury of the "Misericordia".
  - Instruction freely available would be the same for internal as well as the external students.
- This school would be under the Director of Studies of the Province in the matter of inspection and proper monitoring.
- The Government would appoint teachers after a public interview to run the school and teach the various subjects.
- The students who had been admitted would have to follow all the laid down rules and regulations.
- It was the duty of the Governor to promote with total dedication the education of girls.

An Assessment of All Types of Schools

The next Governor, Viscount of S. Januario, during whose tenure the well-known poet Thomas Ribeiro assisted as the Secretary of State, was of the firm opinion that public education was the basis of intellectual and moral advancement of civilization. He appointed a Committee on the 12th of January, 1871 to study the educational set-up in Goa and to come up with a plan for its revitalization. The Committee comprised of Joao Antonio d Oliveira, Pe Floriano Mateus do Rosario Barreto, Francisco do Joao Xavier. This Committee was authorized to go into all the previous reports and evaluations and present a plan for a new reorganization of Primary education in the State. The Committee very quickly completed its task and filed a report on the 8th of February which was thereafter made public through the "Boletim Oficial".

The first step the new Governor took was to convert the Portuguese schools in the "Novas Conquistas" into Portuguese Marathi schools as he noticed that the attendance had dwindled to very low levels and people were reluctant to send their children to learn Portuguese. He issued a "Portaria" dated 10th July, 1871in which he stated that "in consultation with the Council of Inspection it has been decided to substitute the existing Primary Portuguese schools with schools of Marathi and Portuguese as it is found that the people due to their ignorance and stubbornness have failed to take advantage of the educational facilities. It is also seen that more than 100,000 people in the New Conquests use the Marathi language for business and other purposes. It is also used in other parts of British India. Hence, the proposal for the creation of Marathi Classes in the New Conquests is favourably considered and the existing Portuguese Primary schools with the exception of those located in the Provincial capitals would be converted to mixed schools of Marathi and Portuguese".

However, the move remained only on paper as teachers to teach Marathi were very difficult to get as the Hindus who were good at Marathi were not sufficiently qualified to teach Portuguese.

However, earlier by the reforms of 1869, separate schools for boys and girls had been established in Goa. This was continued by the Governor, Caetano d'Albuquerque even in 1880 who asked the "Communidades" and the "Confrarias" to build separate school buildings for boys and girls which was complied with by the Associations of Anjuna, Mapuca, Parra, Chinchinim, Calapor, Colvale and Aldona.

Attempt at Boosting Female Literacy

Fresh reforms were introduced in 1869 by Jose Ferreira de Pestana—during his second stint as Governor—which however continued with the two stages of education with a more logical and practical bias. The elementary Level now had two Classes for the boys only. The Girls' school did not have any Classes but the same two Levels were maintained. In spite of such facilities girls' education did not make much headway as can be seen from the fact that in 1892, almost at the close of the nineteenth century there were only around 8 official Primary schools for girls at the elementary, Level. There were, however, some private schools catering to the education of girls. It must also be mentioned here that the efforts of the Governors normally met with little success as the existence of the Girls' schools was usually short-lived.

Francisco Joaquim Ferreira do Amaral was the Governor in Goa from April to November 1886, a very brief spell. Still he made attempts to improve the educational climate in the State. Accordingly he issued a "Portaria" on the 5th September, 1886 establishing a new set of regulations for Elementary education. Sensing how important the reforms could be he tried to do an encore in Portugal where he had been appointed as the Minister for Overseas Trade and Commerce by issuing a Decree on the 31st of October which was made applicable to Portugal and its colonies. The Levels ("primeiro grau" and "Segundo grau") for the first time were made applicable also to the Girls' schools. It was realized that there were 86 Primary schools of the First Level for boys and 08 for girls in the territory of Goa.

The Decline and the Solution

Most of the efforts of the Governors came to naught as the Girls' schools invariably kept on closing down, a similar fate having fallen on these schools earlier in 1871 and in 1882. It was only in 1887 when the Franciscan nuns took the initiative to start a Girls' school in Panjim which survived the vicissitudes of time though in 1911 it was fully taken over by the Government when Dr. Couceiro da Costa was the Governor. When Portugal became a Republic changes took place in Goa fast and furious. The "Colegio Nossa Senhora de Piedade" an institution run by the nuns was closed down and in its place the Government issued an Order on the 4th of January, 1911 establishing a non-denominational institution for girls named as "Escola Nacional do Sexo Feminino" (National School for the Girls). This school had both the levels, "Primeiro grau" and "Segundo grau".

By the reforms of 1907, all Primary schools had been converted to co-education schools as sufficient number of female students was hard to find to attend the Girls' only schools.

In 1920, the Governor, Dr. Jaime Morais chalked out a plan to give a further fillip to education in the State. He touched upon all the levels and the stages of education including Girls' education. He envisaged the setting up of a Women's Institute of education in which there would be a Primary school, a Secondary school and a Special school. The Primary studies would be of five years normally found in the rest of the State, the Secondary again in keeping with the rest would be of four years and the Special course would last for three years.

The "Escola do Sexo Feminino" however did not last for too long as in the year 1952 it was forced to close down and the building along with the surrounding land as well as the furniture was handed over to the ecclesiastical authorities on the condition that an institution for the opposite sex should be run for which the Government would be making a grant of Rs.32,000 available to them.

VII
Reforms Refined (1901-1928)

On the 29th of November, 1904 a notification was issued by Manoel Antonio Moreira Junior at Lisbon in order to put to rest the frequent controversy that used to arise due to the adoption of different textbooks at the Primary Level.

Use of Approved Textbooks in the Schools

The following provisions were incorporated in the said notification:

- In the Primary schools in the overseas provinces those compendiums which had been approved by the official authorities only should be adopted so as to have a uniform syllabus.
- Regarding the texts followed in the colonies the Governors had to invite the authors to submit copies of their books for a contest/bid submitting thereafter the whole process to the Directorate General of Overseas Affairs with its own comments including those of the Inspecting Council of Public Instruction or wherever there was no Council the Governor could approve as per the Decrees in force.
- The contests or bids had to be opened immediately which should not exceed three months. In the meantime the same books followed earlier could be continued with.
- The Governors could also authorize the public Departments in the provinces to supply directly the compendiums to be sold to the students.
- After the list of compendiums for each colony had been drawn up the use of any other book or manuscript by any "Professor" was strictly prohibited.

- If no officially approved book was available and if any other book had been adopted the Governor had to immediately communicate the same to the Directorate General of Overseas Affairs after consulting the Inspecting Council of Primary Instruction.
- This was made applicable to all the Overseas Provinces and the autonomous district of Timor.

The year 1907 was a turning point with far reaching consequences in the history of education in Goa. In fact the reforms—a very comprehensive piece of legislation and a vast improvement on all the previous sets of reforms—were set rolling in the mother country itself when the Ministry of Sea Trade and Overseas came out with a worthy document issued in the name of the King by Ayres Ornellas de Vasconcelhos on the 23rd of May, 1907 for the overhauling of Primary education in Portugal and all its colonies. The following is the text of the reforms published by the State Government mooting some very significant changes as compared to the existing one:

Primary Instruction

- The teaching of the Portuguese language at the Primary Level in the State of India would be divided into two Levels (degrees) called Elementary and Complementary Levels.
- The First Level had to include:
  - Reading.
  - Writing.
  - Basic operations in Arithmetic, simple notions of the metric system especially those referring to measurement and weights, measures, currencies and Indian coins.
  - Elements of linear design.
  - Moral precepts; Christian doctrine for the students who professed the State religion.
  - Elementary Gymnastic exercises and outdoor games.
  - Rudiments of Agriculture of the country.
  - Related notions of Domestic Economy
  - Rudiments of Singing and Music.
- Except: The students of the feminine sex had to take up also Needle Work indispensable to the lower Classes.

The syllabus for the Second Level would be as follows:

- All the portion of the First Level and
  - Elementary knowledge and practice of Portuguese Grammar
  - Rudimentary notions of Natural Science applicable to Agriculture, Hygiene and local industry.
  - Exercises on the Metric system and practice on the Arithmetic operations in integers, decimals, fractions and complex numbers solving common problems of everyday use.
  - Elements of Chorography of Portugal and its colonies, Elementary notions of Chronology, Cosmography and Geography.
  - Colonial History of the country.
  - Notions of Civic Education
  - Elements of Geometric Drawing and copying of simple objects by observing.
- All Portuguese Primary schools had to follow the pattern of two Levels.
- *Exceptions*: For this purpose there had to be separate schools for boys and for girls.
- Admission and Attendance would be as follows:
  - The school-going age for the First Level would be from six years onwards to twelve years and for the Second Level it would be till 16 years.
  - In the Marathi and Gujarathi schools age of the child at the time of admission had to be up to 16 years.
  - Those students who though having completed 12 years had still not appeared for the examination of the First Level would be able to continue attending school unless they had not been making any progress or some disciplinary action had been taken against them.

Everything about Schools

- The establishing, conversion, and the transfer of Primary schools had to be done by the Administrative bodies, by "Communidades" or by any official following the laid down procedures by the Order of the Provincial Government through the Inspector of Primary schools fulfilling the necessary conditions. Except: (a) The Municipal "Camaras" had to inform about the necessity for the creation of the schools and had to take the responsibility if these had been founded at their request, of furnishing the school with the required furniture and other school utilities as well as providing the residential quarters for the teacher when there was no other body or any particular individual who could shoulder this responsibility, of sending for approval the plan of the building as per the terms of Art. 7(b) responsibility assumed by these bodies to which reference is made in the previous article must be accepted with the titular conditions and acceptance given in writing or a public document had to be produced when particulars were asked for.

- Primary schools would not be allowed in unhealthy places.
- The following conditions had to be followed:
  - A school had to function from a centrally located house, having easy access by road and passageways which were in good condition, not having any dangerous neighbourhoods, or bad customs or inconveniences, away from a cemetery and facing in such a way that the gusts of wind do not affect it; it will place the necessary furnitures, a dressing room with hangers outside the classrooms, a covered shed for the recreation of the students, a garden for the horticultural activities and the practice of cultivating fruit trees of the country, which would be under the charge of a horticulturist and an independent house for the residence of the "Professor" wherever possible.
  - The classrooms needed to have proper ventilation to promote school hygiene and had to measure an area of not less than one square metre per child and the height of the roof had to be not less than 3 metres from the surface of the floor.
  - Whenever a house with the above specifications was not available then the height of the roof could have been less but not less than 2.80 metres if the other conditions of hygiene were favourable.
  - No classroom could have besides the door less than two windows and these should be sufficiently big and well placed in order to assure good lighting and circulation of air, for which they had to have ventilators, having enough light on account of better placing of the windows and which permitted the entry of direct light from the left side or on both sides at the same time rejecting the classroom whose

light came from the front or from the rear of the students.

- The floor of the classroom had to be elevated at least by one metre above the ground by stones or by tiles or mud raising it above the ground which would facilitate proper cleanliness and maintenance.
- The roofs when they are not covered with false wooden ceiling or provided with protection against dust had to have tiles so that they could be frequently cleaned. The walls should always be plastered and white-washed.
- Since dust was the main culprit for the occurrence of contagious diseases the floor had to be mopped with some soft cloth in water or antiseptic liquid before being washed and the dust on the table, benches and other material which came in contact with the students had to be wiped with damp cloths which would be washed immediately so that they could be used again the next time
- The students had to be educated formally not to spit on the floor or throw on it the nasal dirt collection by having proper spittoons in the school.
- The school furniture would consist of benches, tables or desks in sufficient numbers for the students. These benches would be movable and as per the different models proportionate to the diverse heights of the students. The desks must be fixed and duly inclined from top so that it may be possible for the students to keep their elbows on them without having to raise the shoulder blade. The benches had to have a back rest of an angled height less than the shoulder blade with the seat sufficiently large to provide enough space for the thighs and of equal height in relation to the desks minus the distance which was required for the elbows of the students. It had to have besides this, three chairs, one for the use of the "Professor", one table with drawers kept on the platform to be closed with a key, one cupboard with glass doors, one cupboard with doors of wood to hold the archival material and the volumes in the library in the classroom and a wall clock.

- The instructional material would comprise of a blackboard of one metre height and one and half metre breadth, a spare board of the same dimensions, an abacus, a collection of weights and measures, a balance and some chorographical charts of the

European continent, adjacent islands and overseas Provinces, a map of the world, a globe, a bunch of small Portuguese dictionaries, a ruler and a wooden compass, one inkpot, two set squares one of 45 degrees and the other of 90, one spirit Level, a collection of geometrical shapes and a cube, a sphere and different charts containing alphabets and syllables. In the schools for girls there had to be also necessary materials for stitching and embroidery.

- The "Professor" would be responsible for maintaining the instructional material and the furniture of the school and it was the responsibility of the teacher to see that it was kept always neat and tidy.
- It has to be recognized and indisputably convinced that the services of teaching should be provided in proper houses which were permanently safe and secure, functioning under favourable conditions and towards this end all efforts and sacrifices must be directed; when, however, it was proved that the Municipal Council could not arrange suitable premises for teaching and it was not possible to acquire land immediately to construct or to appropriate, suitable premises could have been leased temporarily which satisfied most of the provisions under the regulations. The expenses would be paid for by the Municipality.
- If the house offered for the setting up of the school belonged to the Municipality, the "Communidade", the Confraternity or a private party the Inspector of Primary schools had to indicate in his report whether the premises fulfilled all the requisites listing the conditions that could not be met, then taking necessary steps for preparing the building for the purpose for which it was meant. When the house had to be leased, it had to be justified that it was more convenient than all the others given the resources of the Municipality and of the locality and having dealt with the houses ceded by the private parties he had to give his opinion regarding the guarantee of the duration which he could offer along with the house, together with the report mentioning the description of the building/house, the comparison, the hygienic and pedagogic conditions, submitting the whole process to the office of the Secretary General of the Government, accompanied by if possible a plan of the house obtained from the Directorate of Public Works.
- All the informations regarding the setting up of a school had to

be submitted to the Inspecting Council of Public Instruction which would deliberate on the acceptance of the house. Except: After the offer of the place was accepted for setting up the school it would not be possible to function from elsewhere except by initiating again the whole process.

- Whenever it was realized that the location of any school was actually not good for what it was meant the Primary schools Inspector had to propose another spot which had better features which he thought were necessary, where the school services, the health of the students and the materials of the State would be put to better use.
- The neighbouring villages or the Parishes could join together with the aim of creating a common school complex. In such a case they needed to follow the process mentioned in the previous articles. Except: If the villages or the Parishes belonged to different provinces they would then have to get the sanction of the Municipality and the Administrators of the respective provinces.
- Having legally appointed "Professors" to impart education free of cost in the Parishes or in places where official schools were being established the Provincial Government could give grants to these "Professors" when their schools possessed the necessary conditions and they were willing to take care of the poor students by teaching them in Class I and II free. Except: These subsidized schools for all purposes would come under the audit/monitoring of the competent authority and their students were obliged to present at the time of the first enrolment an attested copy of a vaccination Certificate.
- The expenditure made on the purchase of furniture, instructional material and the distribution of the equipment to the schools which had come to be created by the initiative of the Provincial Government or of the existing schools which were not under the control of the "Communidades", "Confrarias", "Mazanias" or private parties would be paid from the School Fund and the repairs to the buildings and the residence of the "Professor" would be carried out at the cost of the Municipality at the request of the Primary schools Inspector when the "Professors" asked for it. Except: If the Municipalities refused to attend to these requests the Primary schools Inspector had to inform the Provincial Government the reasons for their refusal and the need

for the repairs reminding the Municipality of its obligations and insisting on doing the needful through suitable means. For this reason the Provincial Government had to get it in writing from the Municipality that suitable provisions would be made to meet such an eventuality in its budget and in case there was an absolute need and any delay would result in prejudice, it would give permission to proceed with the repairs by drawing money from the School Fund which would then have to be refunded by the Municipality by including the expenditure incurred on repairs in the following year's budget.

Regarding Students

- The academic year had to begin on the 1st of June (working day) and end on the 31st of March. Except; The academic year would begin with the enrolment of the students which had to be done by the 14th or the 16th of June when the actual classes would start. The enrolment would be done on a special book by the "Professors". In the schools where there were Assistants the admission process would rest with the Directors. Students who were enrolling themselves for the first time in Class I had to present a copy of the vaccination certificate. Every time a student enrolled himself in Class II including Marathi and Gujarati schools the candidates had to pay 4 "tangas" which had to be deposited in the current account of the School Fund.
- Besides the normal period of enrolment of the students there would also be extraordinary registrations in the beginning of each month for those students of the First Level who were starting their Primary education.
- By giving a notice to the Inspector of Primary schools a student could at any time of the year change from one school to another.
- At the time of admission the "Professor" after a thorough examination would admit the student in the class or group according to the learning Level of the student.
- All the students had to present themselves in school in time at the beginning of the classes/lessons.
- The time table of each school showing the distribution of periods for each day or week had to be displayed in the classroom.
- The students had to present themselves in the school clean, neat and tidy. The "Professor" upon entering the classroom had to

check the cleanliness of the students and whenever he noticed that a particular student had been coming to school untidy he had to send for his guardian so as to bring to their notice the lapse on the part of the student.

- The students who had been taken ill by a contagious disease would not be readmitted unless and until they produced an attested certificate from the Health Officer of the respective province or from a qualified Medical practitioner certifying his recovery.
- In the Attendance Register the "Professor" had to put everyday once only the absent sign for those students who were absent by putting the letter *F*. Except; In schools where Classes were run both in the morning and in the evening it had to be put in each of the sessions.
- All the days were considered as working days with the exception of Sundays, holidays and Thursdays whenever there was no other holiday during that week. Besides these, the following were also declared as holidays: feast of the Patron Saint of the Parish, the last days of the year from 24h of December to 6th of January, the feast day of Corpus Christi, the Saturday before the Sunday of "quinquagesima" the second and third day of Carnival, Ash Wednesday, the 25th of November, Palm Sunday to the Monday of Pasch, the days of National and international importance, the day of the funeral of any "Professor", the 28th of September to the 10th of October and all the days in the months of April and May. Except: The students of other communities were permitted to absent themselves on the days of their religious celebrations and observance of traditions.
- No holiday would be given or asked for on any other day in the school for whatever reason.
- Those students who attended school regularly and punctually and distinguished themselves by their good behaviour and application or by their scholastic progress would be awarded prizes.
- These prizes would consist of:
    - Public praise in the school given by the "Professor".
    - Public praise and note to the family of the student.
    - Inscription on the Roll of Honour.
    - Stamps, books, honour mentions and dress items given through school funds or through donations.

- The Honour Rolls had to have three columns/categories to inscribe the names of the winners:
  - For attendance.
  - For behaviour and application.
  - For academic progress.

The inscription on the Roll of Honour had to be done every month and these prizes had to be duly written on the attendance register.

To have one's name written on the Roll of Honour for attendance the student should not have had a single absent throughout the month and had to be punctual everyday; For the inscription for behaviour and application students must not have received even one punishment during the whole month and must have been recognized and noted for their application; the inscription for progress would be done of those students who had excelled in the lessons and the practicals.

- The student who gets his name inscribed on the Roll of Honour every month would be given a special prize; a book, a citation of honour, a picture or a dress item which would be conferred on him in a solemn session by the Primary schools Inspector or by the Provincial Administrator after the closing of the schools.
- On the books, on the pictures and even on the dress items meant for the prize winner the name of the winning student would be inscribed along with the worth of the prize, the signature of the authority which conferred the prize and the signature of the respective "Professor".
- The student who in some month did not have his name inscribed on the Roll of Honour for being absent due to sickness duly justified or for any other justified reason would not lose his right to the prize which he could obtain if it had not yet been given away.
- The distribution of these prizes will take place on a particular day so fixed by the Inspector of Schools and after sending a notice in advance to the schools and invitation to the Provincial Government indicating the schools on which the Administrators would have to confer the prizes on the students.
- For the above to take place the "Professors" had to send to the Inspector at the end of each year a list of the students who were entitled for the prizes.
- In order to punish the students for any act of indiscipline inside or outside the school or for having shown disinclination for

studies the following punishments could have been administered depending upon the discretion of the "Professor" and the gravity of the offence:

- The warning/admonishment.
- The reprimand.
- The deprivation of recreation/recess, detention in the school after the end of classes or any other punishments applied in a fatherly manner and which did not affect the health of the students or caused them in jury.
- Temporary suspension from attending school with notice to the guardians/parents.
- Expulsion:
  - The suspension from attending classes had to be done by the Inspector after studying the reasons submitted by the "Professor".
  - Expulsion was the prerogative of the Government after it was proposed by the "Professor" and endorsed by the Inspector through whose office it had to be forwarded to the Government.
  - Expulsion and suspension had to be resorted to only in cases of serious or grave consequences or when the students after being reprimanded with all the above punishments and in spite of notices having been sent to the parents and others had not shown any reformation and would, therefore, be a bad example for the other students.
  - When a case had been made for the expulsion of a student the case papers had to be submitted in duplicate by the respective "Professor" to the Inspector for further needful after keeping one copy in the schools for record.

- While punishing the students the "Professor" should not use expressions which would hurt his dignity or which would be demeaning to him or to this family taking great care in abstaining from taking any action out of anger, passion or sentiment of vengeance, for such manifestations would be a bad example for the education of the students.
- The "Professor" had to have over his students a certain true moral ascendancy in order to be able to continue with advantage in the paternal education of the child. With a rational and good system of punishments and rewards it would be relatively easy

to get the students to learn, to maintain cleanliness, be neat and tidy and be submissive. The punishments must be rarely used so that they are not counterproductive; with persuasion and suave means the objectives of education can be achieved much more quickly and effectively than through severe or violent repression.

Regarding Teachers

- In the Portuguese Primary schools the staff would comprise of one or more "Professors". Except when the schools had more than one "Professor", one of them would be designated by the Government as Director and the remaining as Assistant "Professors".
- There would be a need for an Assistant only if the strength of the students was more than 60.
- The students in Boys' schools would be taught by male teachers and in the Girls' schools by the female teachers.
- The schools of both Complementary and Elementary Levels would be taught by "Professors" who had undergone a complete course of Teacher Training (Escola Normal) under the regency of the same "Professor".
    - The "Professors" of Elementary schools needed to have completed at least the First year of the Normal school to be eligible to be appointed as Assistants in the schools and could teach in Class I of the Primary schools.
    - The "Professors" with the complete qualification of "Escola Normal" course could be appointed in the Elementary schools and would serve as Assistants in the schools of Panaji, Margao and Mapuca in preference to those who had only the First year of Normal course.
- The Directors (Heads) of the schools had to manage the schools and had to shoulder the responsibility of the intellectual, moral and material condition of the school, endeavouring to promote by all means possible within their power the perfection of their establishments. Their educative mission had to extend whenever possible to their relations with the families of the students, having been concerned over the maintenance of the rules and the observance of the Orders issued from time to time by the authorities.
    - In the same schools the Director had to observe the lessons

of the Assistant "Professors" without any prejudice to his own duties in order to take note of any irregularity that might be taking place.

  - The "Professor" Director would be substituted by the Assistant "Professor" in the event of his absence in the school.

- The "Professors" were responsible for teaching in their respective classes with devotion and dedication and in maintaining a close rapport with the students by showing them paternal affection.
- The Assistant "Professors" were to be responsible for the discipline, order and moral education inside the classroom.
- The Director and the Assistants were jointly responsible for the maintenance of the Books of Account of the school or of the Class.
- The "Professors" had to present themselves in the school at the appointed time and would be able to go home only after their work was over.
- In all the schools where there was more than one employee there had to be a muster roll under the charge of the Director where the name of the employee had to be written against which the person concerned would write the time of coming and going.
- During their lectures the "Professors" should not allow any stranger to visit him in his class either to teach or anybody who had not been authorized by the school superiors nor should he be occupied with other work besides that of the school.
- In the schools having an Assistant no class should be left without a teacher. The Director had to put the Assistant in charge or he had to take it up himself or as a last resort had to put in charge at least a student of the class to mind the class while setting them some work to do if nobody else could be found. Except: In the single teacher schools arrangement had to be made to find a suitably qualified substitute or in the absence of the substitute, a capable student could be put in charge.

School Hours and Allocation of Work

- Primary education in Portuguese was to be divided into the following five classes in ascending order:
  - The First Level (Elementary) would be divided into four

classes and the Second Level (Complementary) would include the fifth Class.

- The first Class would be for those newly enrolled students who did not have any idea of the Portuguese language and would be called "Classe Inicial".

- No student would be able to go to the second Class without knowing sufficient amount of Portuguese in order to be able to understand the teaching in that Class.
- All the students would be expressly prohibited who had passed Class I to speak any other language except Portuguese, may be in the Class or during Gymnastics exercises or while playing in the open. This Order had to be prominently displayed and implemented by the "Professors".
- The classroom teaching had to be shown in the respective programmes.
- Teaching of Marathi and Gujarati would be divided into four classes. *N.B.*—In Class I of Marathi the students had to learn the Balbodh alphabets and the syllables, numbers from one to two hundred and exercises in pronunciation and written words in Balbodh (same for Gujarati).
- In Class III and IV there would be translation of passages into Portuguese and the teaching of Grammar.
- The distribution of the remaining instructional topics had to be done in all the three Classes in the respective programme.
- The Class-wise work allocation for the "Professors" would be the responsibility and the discretion of the Director in the schools which had more than one teacher and had to be done at the beginning of each academic year. *N.B.*—The "Professors" and especially the Assistant had to accompany their students all the time as far as possible till the last period.
- Whenever it was not possible to increase further because there was no Assistant the students had to be divided into two sessions, morning and evening. In that case the biggest room in the school would have to be used and the classes of First, Second and Third year students had to be conducted in the morning.
- Instructions had to be given in keeping with the timetable/ syllabus of the respective Class.
- The total number of hours allotted each day to each of the subjects of Primary education would be five including the recess divided properly between the sessions in the morning and in the

evening. *N.B.*—(a) The school had to start at 8.30 a.m. in the months of June, July, August and September and at 9.00 a.m. during the other months. (b) There had to be an interval between one period to the next of not less than ten minutes and in the evening session the interval from one to the other would be after one and half hour. (c) When the "Professor" had to conduct classes in both the sessions the time had to be divided in such a way that he got at least three hours per session.

- The Inspector of schools had to prepare the model time table for the schools which after being approved by the Inspecting Council had to be sent to all the "Professors".
- Upon receipt of the time table the "Professors" had to affix it in the school and the number of periods could neither be increased nor decreased thereafter.
- Instruction in the official schools was absolutely free; the "Professors" could not under any pretext receive any remuneration for any type of instruction from the students.
- The "Professors" could not under any circumstances conduct individual/private classes for the students of that school or any other.
- The following records had to be scrupulously maintained by all schools without fail:
    - Enrolment Register.
    - Register of monthly attendance.
    - Register for recording the visits of the Sanitation/Health Inspector.
    - Inward Outward Register.
    - Stock Register.
    - Register of requisitions.
    - Muster Roll.
    - Tables showing the monthly attendance and progress.
    - Tables showing the leave taken by the "Professors".
    - Tables showing the annual statistics.
- The monthly Attendance Registers and the monthly tables and the Annual Statistics had to be written by the respective "Professors" or the Assistants outside the time meant for instruction; the remaining books had to be written by the Directors in schools where there were Assistants and by the respective "Professors" in the schools where there were no Assistants.

- The annual tables and the monthly tables and the requisitions for the materials had to be sent within the stipulated time given by the Primary schools Inspector.
- The books for correspondence and the printed books would be requisitioned by the "Professors" from the Primary schools Inspector for which payment would be made from the School Fund.
- In the schools where there was an Assistant the promotion of the students from one Class to another rested with the Director of the school who after receiving a written statement of the examinations conducted by the Assistant in his classes would decide on each promotion.
- In the single teacher schools the promotion of the students would be the sole responsibility of the "Professor" which would be based on the performance/competence of each student.
- Each student had to have a notebook named as "Booklet for correspondence" where the "Professor" of the Class had to write every Saturday a summary of the remarks obtained by the student during the days of the week making mention of the particular issues which had to be taken note of. The guardians/ parents/tutors of the students had to record in this booklet the observations which they wished to bring to the notice of the "Professor". The booklet had to be brought to school every Monday morning. The "Professor" would go through the booklet and then keep it in his possession till the following Saturday. *N.B.*—The "Professor" in the summary of his observations had to be prudent and tactful. This was necessary as the susceptibilities of the parents or individuals entrusted with the education of the children should not be hurt; it was imperative to speak the truth without hurting their feelings or without hurting their love for the children and at the same time understanding the weaknesses of the students. The booklet for correspondence had to last for the whole year and was given free of cost to the students.
- The models and methods for the Primary instruction will be the same as those used in the mother country with the necessary modifications/adaptations for easy understanding as per the situation.

Teachers and their Service Matters

The following provisions were inserted for the appointment and other service conditions of the teachers:

- The vacancies in the Portuguese Primary schools had to be filled up by conducting a written interview to which candidates belonging to the State religion only and those possessing the Diploma of the "Escola Normal" or of the new "Escola Mixta" would be admitted for the interview.
- The documentary evidence to be submitted by the candidates had to be given to the Primary Inspector within the specified period as mentioned in the "Boletim Oficial" and had to be accompanied by the following documents:
  - Diploma or Certificate of qualification required.
  - A Certificate of good character from the Administrative authorities of the place where the candidate resides.
  - Certificate of clearance from criminal activities obtained from the Provincial authorities where the candidate resides.
  - Certificate stating that he had undergone compulsory military service when it was applied to the State of India.
  - Certificate from the Health authorities that the candidate did not suffer from contagious diseases nor had any defect or physical deformity which would hamper his work as teacher and that he had been vaccinated.
- Within eight days after the period was over the Primary Schools Inspector had to submit the documents after scrutiny to the Provincial Government which in turn would send them to the Provincial Council for drawing up the merit list.
- The names of the selected teachers would be published in the "Boletim Oficial" indicating the category to which the candidate was found fit and would then be placed in a suitable school when such a vacancy arose or a transfer took place.
- The filling up of the vacancies in the Gujarati and Marathi schools would be done by holding a public interview through a Jury nominated by the local Government with the candidate compulsorily having passed the Elementary and Complementary Levels of the "Escola Normal" or the first and the second year of the present regime.
- The Primary Schools Inspector had to announce the vacancy

indicating at the same time the category and the form of payment of the emoluments:

- The Primary Schools Inspector had to issue the appointment Orders which would be recorded in the teachers' register in the designated schools and then these Orders would be returned with due acknowledgements.
- At the time of payment the "Professor" had to present the appointment Order to the Inspector to enable him to calculate his salary.

- The school charge had to be given to the "Professor" within fifteen days of his appointment—if it was in the Provinces and within 20 days if it was in Daman or Diu—from the date of publication of the appointment in the "Boletim Oficial" by the Inspector or the local delegate in the presence of two witnesses administering to the "Professor" the oath of office and taking an assurance from him that he would do all the work assigned to him by the respective Administrator of the province. *N.B.*—The Authority which would be giving him the charge had to immediately send it through the Inspector of the Primary instruction to the Secretary General of the province to be published on the "Boletim Oficial".
- The appointed "Professor" who without authorization of the Government or without any justification for the delay had not taken charge within the legal time limit and even the one who having taken charge did not enter immediately into service without any authorization or justification would be considered as having rejected the offer. *N.B.*—The authorization of the Government would be given only in exceptional cases if there had been for example a major proven calamity.
- If any post remained without being filled up the Primary Inspector had to immediately communicate this to the Provincial Government and propose the name of any qualified individual in terms of these regulations for appointment as an interim arrangement for the running of the school.
  - In order not to hinder instruction by the delay in filling up of posts the Inspector should be able as soon as possible to put a person in charge to run the school who he considered as fit enough while he would make regular or interim appointment in terms of these regulations.
  - If the "Professor" happened to be absent for more than ten

days he had to be dealt with as per the rules.

- The role of the interim "Professor" would cease the moment a regular teacher had been appointed through interview without waiting for any official announcement from the Superiors.

- After a period of three years of regular service the temporary "Professor" could seek permanent posting in the following manner:
  - For this he would have to apply to the State Government through the offices of the Inspector and the local Government accompanied by a Certificate of regular service during the period referred to which had to be attested by the Secretary of Inspections.
  - The Primary schools Inspector having verified directly or through the local delegate or from the Administrator of the Province the quality of the service provided by the "Professor" would then comment on the application and submit it to the State Government within a maximum period of eight days for further needful.
  - In case it was discovered that the service of the "Professor" was not satisfactory then he would be considered only at the end of the term for that vacant post for which he would be appointed after hearing the "Professor" and after a positive vote from the Inspecting Council.
  - The service rendered by the "Professor" as a legally qualified Assistant would be counted for the post mentioned above.
- To be promoted, the Assistant "Professors" had to apply in the same manner to the permanent posts to the local Government but the process would be on the same lines as follows:
  - For this promotion it was indispensable to have undergone a course of teacher training under the new reforms or a complete course of "Escola Normal" as per the old system.
  - The Governor General could permit mutual transfers between "Professors" of the same category always taking into consideration good and effective service rendered by the "Professor" in a particular school.
- The period of suspension would not be counted for calculating the effective service either for the purposes of promotion or for purposes of permanent appointment.

- The "Professors" had to be given the salary and the work as specified in the budget document and his promotion would be as per the process set out by the Secretary of Inspection of Primary education irrespective of the intervention of the "Professors".
  - Those "Professors" who had not been given accommodation near the school were entitled to get an annual amount given by the Provincial administration, "Communidade", "Mazania" or "Confraria" which would be fixed by the Government as house rent.
  - The interim "Professors" would get two-thirds of the salary of the respective post and the gratuity of the post.
- The "Professor" could not absent himself during the school/ working days from the school without previous sanction from the local Government which he had to request by making an application through the offices of the Inspector.
- When for reason of nausea or any other legitimate cause he had to remain absent from service the "Professor" had to communicate to the Inspector or the local delegate on the same day or as soon as possible by sending some documentary evidence of the sickness suggesting at the same time the name of the person who would be able to substitute him.
  - In case of sickness the "Professor" had to without losing time present to the local delegate or to the Administrator of the Province whoever is nearer a medical certificate proving that he was unable to attend to his duties.
  - The local delegate or the Administrator of the province as soon as he had received the note had to bring it to the notice of the Inspector at the same time arranging a suitably qualified substitute as fast as possible.
  - Every time if it was felt necessary the sickness of the "Professor" could be ascertained and then leave endorsed by the Health official.
  - If the sickness had to go on for more than 8 days leave would have to be endorsed by the public Health Department.
  - In case of death of the spouse or of some elder, child, brother or any other relative leave of absence could be granted for eight days and up to three days in the case of anybody else who had been living with the "Professor".
  - If any person residing along with the "Professor" was

afflicted with a contagious disease the "Professor" would be prevented from attending school till the contagious disease had been diagnosed and he would not be allowed to remain in the house except when he had been authorized by the health official, till the quarantine of the sick and by whatever other means prophylaxis had to be rigorously assured. The "Professor" had to bring the fact to the notice of of the local delegate who would inform the Government through the Inspector going ahead with the arrangements for substituting him.

- The above regulations if not observed could result in loss of salary for the number of days the "Professor" had been absent and could even lose his job if the "Professor" remained absent for more than eight days without justification.
- The "Professor" could be granted up to nine days of paid sick leave by the Health Department in any academic year. *N.B.*—If the sickness continued, then at the end of nine days the Governor after the preliminary inspection by the Department could allow him to remain absent with two-thirds of his salary for up to six months.
- The "Professors" had to be excused from taking Classes on the days when they had to accompany the students of their schools for examinations of the Second Level or when they had been appointed as members of the Jury for the examinations of the First Level.
- The "Professors" who distinguished themselves in the exercise of their duties or had taken part in charitable works or any other good deed in school would be awarded prizes as follows:
    - These prizes would consist of gold, silver or copper medals given away by the local Government.
    - The above prizes would be given to those "Professors" who fulfilled the conditions by the Government on the recommendation of the Inspector.
    - The Primary Schools Inspector had to describe minutely the basis on which he had recommended the names so as to qualify the deserving candidates knowing full well their merits and stating the circumstances which made him recommend them.
    - These recommendations had to be submitted with the required information to the Provincial Government which with the advice of the Inspector of the province would decide over it.

  - The prizes would be given only to the "Professors" who applied for them.
  - The application accompanied by the required evidence and necessary documents had to be sent to the Schools Inspector.
  - The gold medal would be given to only those "Professors" who had put in more than twenty-five years of distinguished service and the silver and the copper medals to those who had put in twenty and fifteen years of distinguished service respectively.
  - No medal would be awarded to a "Professor" who had been penalized in his career.

Disciplinary Action against "Professors"

- The penalties imposed on the "Professors" could have been admonishment, reprimand and suspension with loss of salary, transfer and even dismissal. *N.B.*—The disciplinary actions would be taken by the Governor depending upon the gravity of the case following the proper procedures and giving an opportunity for the "Professors" to defend themselves.
- If any "Professor" had gone against any of the laid down norms as announced by the schools Inspector, the disciplinary process would be started as per law based on the accusations which had to be framed by the Inspector after enquiry and putting on paper his findings as a consequence of the complaint received by him or by any other authority in the following manner:
  - Before initiating any process the school Inspector had to check the genuineness of the complaint and other facts so as to decide on the worthiness of the complaint or whether it was filed with malafide intentions due to local politics or it was a simple case of character assassination.
  - Once the process of accusation starts the accused had to be given a copy of the complaint.
  - The "Professor" within a period of ten days counting from the day the copy of the complaint was given, had to send to the Schools Inspector his defence in writing along with the documents in support if any and the list of witnesses if he intended to produce them as a means of proving his innocence.
  - The witnesses would be intimated through the Administrator

of the province in whose jurisdiction the case fell after receiving a request from the Schools Inspector informing them about the date, the time and the place where they had to depose in the matter. In the event of the witnesses who had been intimated not appearing then the Administrator had to proceed as per the general law.

- The inquiry had to be carried out by the Schools Inspector at the designated place and the evidence had to be written down by a "Professor" so nominated for the purpose acceptable to all. The recording had to be then signed in acknowledgement.
- If it was necessary to enquire with the students of the school to obtain some necessary information these students had to be accompanied by adult persons who were staying with them as family members or guardians to whom they were attached as minors.
- After the process had been duly concluded it had to be immediately sent to the Provincial Government which after examining would decide whether the party was guilty or not guilty of the offence.
- The disciplinary process in which it was proposed to impose the penalty of suspension of more than thirty days or the penalty of transfer or of demotion had to be placed before the Inspecting Council which had to decide on these penalties only through a majority vote.

- Whenever a "Professor" taught doctrines contrary to the devotion which all had to show towards the motherland or to the religion of the State or the morals and good customs and the laws of the kingdom or had committed any crime or caused a public scandal had to be immediately suspended by the Government pending inquiry.
- The "Professors" were not allowed to sell to the students directly or indirectly any lessons or their explanations or any textual material either printed or as manuscript.
- The "Professors" of the Primary schools had to speak in Portuguese and in Konkani to the students of Class I who did not know anything of Portuguese because by using simultaneously both the languages they would be able to learn more easily the rudiments of the Portuguese language. It was, however, obligatory to use only Portuguese in the higher Classes.

N.B.—The "Professors" who did not follow this direction would be duly penalized.

- The "Professors" of the official schools were expressly prohibited from forcing the students to buy other books which had not been adopted by the Government and thus could not teach nor set any questions for examinations on topics which were not included in the prescribed books. *N.B.*—This had to be also made applicable to the "Professors" teaching in private schools.
- Through a special Order the Central Government had to lay down the system for the selection of books to be adopted in schools for Primary Classes in the provinces.
- The retirement of the "Professors" of Primary schools would continue to be governed by the legal provisions which had been promulgated for the "Professors" of the Overseas Provinces by the Government.
- The posts of the Assistant "Professors" had to be filled up by the Provincial Government through a written interview as per the following:
  - The same process that is being followed to appoint "Professors" will also apply to the Assistants.
  - The proof of a good and effective service in any official school will be shown by issuing Certificates by the Secretariat of inspections of primary education as per the informations available with them.
- Whatever was applicable to the Assistants had to be implemented by the Directors of the schools. *N.B.*—For any concessions in the licences to these functionaries the "Professor" always had to be heard in the school where he was rendering his services.

The Conduct of Examinations

Similarly provisions were laid down for the conduct and recording of the examinations for both the Levels. Every aspect of examinations was covered under these provisions. The special feature was the Jury system employed by the Portuguese in the conduct of the examinations. The other striking feature was the oral examinations. The following were the stipulations regarding the examinations:

- The examinations of Portuguese Primary instruction could have been of the First or the Second Level. *N.B.*—In the languages of

Marathi and Gujarati there would be only one examination and it had to be conducted according to the regulations of the respective programmes.

- The examination of the First Level would be for the students who had completed the lessons of that Level and those individuals, who after attending the private schools or schooled at home had to or wanted to obtain the Certificates of that qualification/course. *N.B.* The examination of the First Level was compulsory for admission to the Second Level and would comprise mainly of Reading, Writing and Counting.
- This examination would be held in the month of March in the premises of the official schools as per the following:
  - The examinations of the students of the official schools would be conducted by the "Professor" and the Inspector who could also be substituted by the Administrator of the province.
  - For the examinations of the First Level when it was not possible for the Inspector or the Administrator to assist the "Professor" they could have been represented by the local delegate.
- The "Professors" of the private and official schools had to send in the last days of the month of February to the Primary Schools Inspector, a list of the students desirous of answering the examinations giving their names, parents' names, age, birth place, and the duration in the school of each one of them. The heads of the family would proceed analogously with respect to those students who were under their charge if they had been home schooled.
- The Inspector had to chalk out the schedule of the examinations in which he would be assisting as well as in those in which the delegate or the Administrator of the province would be assisting, conveying the anticipated dates and the schedule to the Provincial Government so that through this it would be brought to the notice of the Administrator of the province.
- The examinations of the First Level in the official schools had to be conducted by the duly appointed "Professor" and in the schools in which there were Assistants by the Directors and whenever they were testing external students then the Inspector had to send expressly an official "Professor" to conduct the examinations of these students. *N.B.* The written answer papers

after they had been initiated/approved/checked by the Inspector, the Administrator of the province or the local delegate would be stored for two years in the archives of the school.

- These examinations would be free and those examined and approved would be promoted by the examining "Professor" who would issue also the Certificate which the school authority had to then attest. The Certificate had to be printed and supplied by the respective school.
- At the end of the examination the Inspector, his delegate and the Administrator of the province had to prepare a list in duplicate of the candidates of the First Level whose examinations had been conducted showing in the list the name of the school, the "Professor" appointed, the name, age, names of parents, place of birth, grade obtained and the date of passing. One copy of the list had to be kept in the school based on which the "Professor" would prepare and give the Certificates free of cost to those who had applied for them; the other list would be sent to the Inspector so that it could be recorded in a special book. The passing Certificates of this examination prepared by the "Professor" had to be sent to the local delegate so that they could be attested with the official seal. *N.B.*—The Certificates of this examination of the First Level could also be requested orally by the Inspector who would then authenticate them.
- The examination of the Second Level was the final examinations of the Primary instruction and was needed for admission to the Lyceum (Secondary education). The syllabi of the respective subjects of the Second Level of Primary education had to have the necessary link with the content of the First Class of the lyceum. *N.B.*—The examinations in the Marathi subject would be held in the "Lyceum Nacional" and the Jury would be constituted as per the Decree; the examinations in Gujarati would be held at the Administrative centres in Daman and Diu.
- The examinations of the Second Level had to commence on the First working day of April and would be conducted in the "Lyceum Nacional" at Pangim, for those who were residing in the New and the Old Conquests and in their respective schools for the residents of Daman and Diu.
- The applications to be allowed to answer this examinations had to be made by the candidates on plain paper, directed and handed over from the 15th of February till the last working day of the

same month to the schools Inspector and should have the name of the examinee, age, place of birth, parents' names, and residence and they had to produce the receipt of having paid an amount of 400 "reis" into the Treasury of the village or the province under the School Fund head. The request had to also state the name of the person who was teaching the examinee along with his designation as a "Professor", or father, relative, or guardian accompanied by a Birth Certificate showing his age to prove that he had completed ten years or he would complete 10 years by the 31st of May along with the Certificate of the First Level of Primary education as per the following:

- The conditions regarding age mentioned above would not be waived under any circumstances.
- Those who produced a Certificate from the Administrator of the province or the Parish priest stating that they were poor would be exempted from paying the fees.

- The schools Inspector at the end of the time period of receiving the applications had to prepare the programme for the examination of the candidates and had to get them affixed on the door of the school which would be venue for the examinations by the 20th of March as well as get them published in the "Boletim Oficial" stating the place, the days and the timings of the examinations and other information that he considered necessary keeping in mind the following:
  - The venues/examination centres had to be shown in an alphabetical order along with the names of the candidates who were appearing in that centre also shown in alphabetical order.
  - Each list had to display the names of the examinees, the names of their parents if there were students with the same name and the tentative day on which a certain candidate would be called to be examined.
- The examinations of the Second Level would be presided over by a "Professor" of the official Secondary school or from the Teachers' Training School having besides the President two more members who had to be "Professors" of the official Primary schools. This Jury had to be nominated by the Provincial Government on the recommendation of the schools Inspector. The following had to be noted:
  - For the composition of the Jury for female candidates the

members had to be generally lady "Professors" and the President had to be a "Professor" of the Secondary school or from the Teachers' Training School.

- When the number of students was large and it was realized that it would not be possible to complete the examinations by the last working day of April then more Juries as required had to be constituted or the same Jury had to take up double the number of students everyday.

- No "Professor" could refuse to be on any Jury whether he was permanent or temporary and had to give his service free of cost when the "Professors" were appointed close to where they had been residing.
- Those who had been appointed on the Jury outside the locality where they were residing would be paid a remuneration of 400 "reis" for each working day besides to and fro transport would be provided by the Administrator of the Provincial Council.
- The "Professors" who did double the work in the Jury would earn a remuneration of 800 "reis" if appointed as Presidents and 400 "reis" as plain members.
- The Schools Inspector if required could appoint one or more "Professors" to help him in the examination work who would not be appointed then on any of the Juries. *N.B.*—This, however, had to be authorized by the Provincial Government.
- Every Jury had to examine at least 20 students per day in the written examinations and four in orals; they would be summoned as per the serial order found on the previously displayed lists. *N.B.* Besides calling those whose examinations were fixed on particular dates everyday a supplementary list with ten students for written and four for orals had also to be prepared as per the serial order so that these could be examined in case any of the designated students were absent.
- Those examinees who remained absent without any justifiable reason on the designated day of examination would be able to appear again for the examination only on the payment of a fee of 400 "reis" and depositing it in the Treasury of the Province of Ilhas or in the Treasury of the districts of Daman and Diu under the School Fund Account head. He had to observe the following:
  - For this the examinee had to apply to the Schools Inspector or the local delegate within a period of three days for proper guidance.

  - If the substitutes who had been called for the examination did not appear then they too had to follow the above regulations.
- The defaulting examinees would be called anew for the examination only after all the originally listed candidates had been examined and would be examined always by the same Jury to which they had been initially allotted provided as follows:
  - If the candidate happened to be absent for the orals then the examinee did not have to appear again for the written examination too.
  - If any examinee had not appeared on the marked day for the second time then it would be considered that he had taken a break from examinations.
- The examinations of the Second Level would comprise of written and oral tests; the female examinees, however, would also be tested in needle work. *N.B.*—The written examinations would come first and the needle work examination would be held in between the written and the oral examination.

Process of Testing and Evaluation

The written tests would consist of:

- Writing of a dictated passage of about ten to fifteen lines.
- Solving a problem of everyday use which had to be solved by one arithmetical operation only and one example of division of fractions or decimals with their respective answers.
- Copying on a rectangular sheet of paper or on plain paper one of the figures used for the teaching of design/drawing.
- Cursive writing:
  - During the written test besides the examiners and the examinees, any authority which was in charge of Primary instruction could be allowed inside the hall.
  - The passage for dictation had to be selected by the Jury from the portion included for the examinations and the questions on Arithmetic and Drawing had to be chosen by lots from about fifty topics given by the Schools Inspector and had to be submitted in a closed envelope to the Presidents of the Jury.
  - The dictation passages, the drawing and calligraphy

questions would be common to all the examinees of the day; Arithmetic sums, however, would be different for each candidate and would be distributed by lots.

- ■ The time allotted for the written test was three hours.

- During the conduct of the test the members of the Jury had to invigilate over the examinees and if anyone was caught using fraudulent means during any of the tests he had to be ordered by the President of the Jury to leave the hall and would be barred from appearing for the remaining examinations.
- Each day at the end of the written examinations the papers would be checked by each of the members of the Jury who then would vote in secrecy. The student who obtained majority of votes of 'sufficient' in each of the tests under '*a*' and '*b*' and majority of votes of 'mediocre' in each of the tests '*c*' and '*d*' would be admitted to the orals. *N.B.*—The results of this voting had to be entered in the records of the written tests which had to be then attested by all the members of the Jury and a list had to be prepared and displayed publicly indicating whether the candidate had been admitted or excluded from the oral examinations.
- The test of needlework meant for the female candidates would last more or less one hour and had to be conducted on the same day of the oral test just before its commencement. It had to consist of different topics on stitching and marking as included in the syllabus like making of stockings, doing crochet and embroidering of white borders. *N.B.*—The female student who had not obtained a majority of votes of 'sufficient' in the test of needlework could not be admitted for the oral test.
- The male students who had been admitted for the orals would be called for these tests in groups of four and in the order of their names on the list.
- The oral tests had to be held publicly and would consist of:
  - ■ Loud reading of a passage of about twenty to thirty lines from the prescribed book presently being followed in the fifth Class of Primary instruction.
  - ■ Understanding of words and phrases of some parts of the passage and Grammar exercises connected with them both practical and elementary.
  - ■ Practical exercises on the black slate and questions on Arithmetic, Geometry and the Metric system.
  - ■ Questions on the principles of Christian moral doctrine

examining the students whose parents were Catholics and Notions of Civic education.

- Questions on the Chorography and national History accompanied by the marking on the map of the Kingdom and the continents, islands adjacent to the Overseas Provinces and questions connected to the teaching of these topics.
- Questions on the rudiments of Natural Sciences and application of some of these rudiments to Agriculture, Hygiene and industry of the country.
- Questions on the domestic economy and on Gymnastics would be as follows:
  - The questions on each subject could not exceed more than fifteen minutes and the total time for the orals for each student would be sixty minutes. The President of the Jury had to distribute the time for each set of questions as far as possible without any bias.
  - These questions had to be asked as per the syllabus of the Second Level and could not deal with any topics which were not there in the syllabus or in the adopted books.

- Everyday at the end of the orals the voting would take place immediately; the student who had obtained the maximum number of "sufficient" in each of the tests under "*a*", "*b*", and "*c*" and at least majority of votes of "average" in each of the tests under "*d*", "*e*" and "*f*" would be promoted.
- The student who had obtained a majority of votes of "good" in each of the written and oral tests "*a*", "*b*" and "*c*" and at least majority of votes of "sufficient" in each of the other tests would pass with distinction.
- The final result of the voting would be recorded on the examination result book of Primary instruction and duly signed by the President and the members of the Jury a copy of which would then be affixed on the door of the building where the tests had taken place. The written tests of these students as well as the respective guidelines had to be sent at the end of the examinations to the Primary Schools Inspector in whose archives they would be preserved for a period of two years.
- The examination record books would be archived in the Secretariat of the Inspection offices but during the conduct of

the examinations they would be the responsibility of the Jury and would be under its charge.

- The examination record books in Daman and Diu had to be kept in the custody of the respective Provincial Administration a copy of which had to be sent to the Secretariat of the Schools Inspector.
- All the record books had to be attested and the pages initialled from the beginning to the end by the Inspector and from these records the Certificates which had been requested would be issued after the necessary fees had been paid.
- The Certificates of the *examinations* of the Second Level of Portuguese, Marathi and Gujarati had to be issued on a stamped paper by the Schools Inspector after charging four "tangas" for each Certificate, keeping for himself one "tanga" and depositing the rest in the Public Treasury.
- The fees charged for the Certificates and deposited in the School Fund had to be paid for by way of stamps, stuck to the Certificates and crossed as per law by the Schools Inspector.

- Those individuals who five years after the publication of this regulation on the "Boletim Oficial" could not or had not appeared for the examination of the First Level would have the following penalties:
  - They would not be appointed to any public post.
  - However, if they joined the State military then they could be granted equivalence with the individuals who had produced the Certificate of the First Level.
- The individuals who had passed the Second Level examination would be preferred in the appointment to any public office to those individuals who still had not appeared for the First Level. *N.B.* In any public post those individuals who had passed the Second Level had to be paid not less than rupees 144.

Monitoring and Supervision

The Portuguese should be credited by going about doing things the right way. They had realized very early that without supervision the progress of education would be slow and haphazard. Hence, they put in place right from the beginning a well-intentioned and multi-layered system of supervision and monitoring. The following were some of the provisions laid down in this regard:

- The highest salary would be paid to the members of the Inspecting Council.
- The post of the Commissioner of Studies had been abolished.
- To monitor the activities of the Primary instruction in the State of India there would be an Inspector of Primary education appointed with the qualification of the Superior education course of the Kingdom, nominated by the Central Government with an annual salary of Rs 720,000 "reis" and 280,000 "reis" as allowances to travel for inspections to different schools across the State.
    - In case the post was either vacant or the incumbent was unable to perform his duties due to sickness then the Director of the Teachers' Training School ("Escola Normal") would be put in charge of the Primary teachers of Nova Goa drawing the same remuneration as applicable to the post of the Schools Inspector.
    - The Schools Inspector would have his office in the building of the Secretariat General of the Government being assisted by a peon who would be appointed by the Secretary General.
    - The posts of the local delegates would continue to be maintained as per the aforementioned regulations and placed under the supervision of the Inspecting Council of Public instruction of the province being subordinate to it. The Inspecting Council had the authority to dismiss those who were found incompetent or negligent in their duties.
- The Administrative, Judicial and Military authorities had to furnish to the Inspector all the information and give whatever help was required which might be asked of them through proper channel for the legitimate discharge of the functions of supervision which had to be properly carried out.

Duties of the School Inspector

- The schools Inspector of Primary education had to also carry out the following duties. He had to:
    - Supervise the functioning of the official schools checking upon the methods used in teaching, the school discipline,

the books, the time tables and the strict coverage of the syllabus.

- See to the observation of the laws and the rules and regulations meant for Primary education keeping the Provincial Government informed regularly of all the means adopted and the measures taken in the implementation of the regulations issued from time to time.
- Inspect the instructional material and the teaching aids as well as the school building and the residence of the "Professor" getting the compliance of the Municipalities, the "Communidades", the "Confrarternities" and the Temple Committees towards their school obligations through the Secretariat General of the Government.
- Exercise direct supervision at times and conduct the examinations.
- Guide and counsel the "Professors" both public as well as private in everything that was connected with education.
- Promote through the Provincial Government the award of prizes and merit Certificates to those who deserved them having demonstrated extraordinary zeal through singular acts concerning education.
- Propose application of disciplinary actions against the "Professors" who were found wanting in their duties allotted to them as per the law and the regulations thus encouraging them to follow always the regulations.
- Fulfil all his duties energetically using his utmost prudence, circumspection and total justice.
- Solicit through the offices of the Secretariat General of the Government information from the officials and the Corporations which were needed for certain educational purposes.
- Tackle if thought just within his capacities all the cases omitted in these regulations which, however, had to be brought to the notice of the superiors immediately.
- Inform the "Professors" and the Committees about the charitable acts in all the matters under his charge.
- Present all the information that might be required to the Secretariat General of the Government.
- Collect the statistics of Primary instruction and send the report annually to the Provincial Government which in turn

would send it regularly to the Director General of Overseas Provinces together with the annual report in which all the changes that had been effected in these regulations for better functioning had to be mentioned.

- Visit frequently and pay surprise visits to all the official Primary schools and the other schools submitting every month a report of the work done and the school visited to the local Government.
- Correspond with the respective Provincial Government through the offices of the Secretariat General of the Government and directly with other authorities and Corporations.
- Take note of all the complaints and the claims addressed to him by the officials and the Corporations which look after education as well as by the private parties dealing with school matters giving an account of all this periodically to the State Government.
- Inform the Governor about the correctness, zeal and the devotion shown by the Municipalities and other Corporations regarding education.
- Preside over the pedagogical Conferences which take place every year and during holidays.
- Inform the Provincial Government about the building plans and the repairs to the school buildings.
- Report the aptitude of the "Professors" teaching in private schools for the award of the "Competence Certificate".
- Observe the following principles:
  - Take note of any negligence, incompetence, lack of aptitude for teaching or rebellious attitude towards the advices and the notices and bring it to the notice of the defaulters again and again by visiting the respective schools till they fall in line.
  - Meet the need to frequently supervise the abovementioned schools and if unable to visit the schools many times both the private and official schools due to lack of time he could make a single visit annually to the official schools which were looked after by dedicated and highly regarded "Professors" whose service merited absolute confidence.
  - Examine scrupulously everything in the official schools

regarding the performance of the "Professors" and the attendance and progress of the students.

- Find the reasons for such lapses as the building having poor hygienic and pedagogical conditions, improper teaching aids or insufficient materials or the residence of the "Professor" lacking certain amenities and seek to know the resources of the locality or place, study the means of removing the inconveniences which he had observed and inform immediately and duly the State Government so that the competent authorities are seized of the matter and start the process of providing the necessary facilities.

- Propose the awards and the prizes to be awarded to the "Professors" who had shown exemplary behaviour, extraordinary zeal and great aptitude in the discharge of their duties.
- Guide and instruct regarding the precepts and the pedagogical rules which the "Professors" must follow who though having the necessary zeal as teachers did not get satisfactory results either due to less proficiency or lack of knowledge of the recent practices of teaching or because of improper arrangements in the school or due to improper methods of teaching, division of Classes or lack of discipline of students.
- Reprimand lightly and politely and always in private those "Professors" who demonstrated little zeal and application in the discharge of their duties which results in disorder in the school and makes the students backward.
- Promote the application of disciplinary action corresponding to the gravity of the offence against the "Professor" after issuing warnings and the notices or else they would bring disrepute and cause the downfall of the school by their improper behaviour and its incurability.
- Examine in each school the number of students as per his convenience checking their attendance and the progress of all.
- State his remarks, his observations and his notings in the school register of every school, public or private that he had visited so that the misuses which he had noticed in the school could be removed. This note had to be signed by the schools Inspector and the "Professor".
- Inspect private schools by making a careful inquiry into the condition of the materials, the methods and the processes of

teaching, the syllabi, the time tables, the books being followed, checking the progress of the students and the education which they had received and also the accounts of the school.

- Keep an eye on the conduct of the "Professors" and the physical conditions of the school which should not pose any danger to the students and give thorough information to the Provincial Government for further action if found in default.
- If he had come across any school where the teaching was carried out by a non-qualified person and if it was found that he had not been duly authorized he had to report immediately to the higher authorities so that through the Provincial Government the school would be ordered to close down. In each Parish or village the Schools Inspector had to collect the correct information regarding the services and the auxiliary services offered by the benefactor organizations to the schools and the students.
- The regulations and attributions which had been promulgated on the 5th of August, 1893 also applied to the Provincial Administrators and the local delegates.

Associations for the School Beneficence

One of the notable features of the Government's efforts to popularize education was the involvement of charitable organizations in the promotion and sustaining of education. The concept was a very laudable one as it sought to make everybody a stakeholder in the process of education of the children. Besides having realized that reward was better than punishment encouragement by way of prizes and awards would attract more and more children and motivate more and more parents to send their children to school. This could be done by forming a village or Parish level organization which would undertake activities for the betterment of the school and the students. Accordingly to fulfil this objective the Government laid down some clear-cut instructions for the forming of these associations as follows:

- In each Parish or village having an official school there had to be an organization promoting beneficence and education consisting of the Parish priest, the "Professor", the local judicial authority and the "Regedor" (head of village).
  - In the Provincial headquarters the organization had to be presided over by the Administrator of the Province and would not have the "Regedor" as part of the school circles.

- If the cluster of schools embraced more than one Parish the respective Parish priest and the "Regedor" would be made part of the organization presided over by the Parish priest of the village where the school was located.
- The "Professor" of the school would be the ex-officio Secretary of the organization. In schools where there was more than one "Professor" the Director of the boys' school would be the Secretary.
- The Provincial Government would be able to include in this organization ladies and gentlemen known for their charity residing in the Parish or outside it who wanted to contribute to the school's benefit as auxiliary members.
- If it was not possible to put in place such an organization by the above method the Provincial Government could appoint three heads of families in each village on the recommendation of the Schools Inspector to arrange the donations.

- These organizations were required for the progress of education in the village to promote instruction and expand it, helping the children to access the school. The contribution and support of the "Confrarias", "Fabricas", "Mazanias" and other bodies and individuals towards education either officially or privately was to be appreciated.
- The income towards these organizations would come from:
  - The amount placed aside in their budgets by the local bodies annually.
  - The income from the various types of donations given to the organization.
  - The income from the fairs, bazaars or fetes which the organization had to hold as many times as possible.
- The Committee had to carry out the following activities in keeping with their beneficence:
  - Distribute uniforms to the students who might need them since their parents were poor and could not afford them.
  - Give books, paper and school utilities to those who needed them and could not afford them.
  - Organize school canteens in order to provide lunch to the poor children under the supervision of the "Professors".
  - Promote rest places and school walks for the sick and the weak.

- Encourage those students who attended regularly and did well in studies by giving those prizes in the form of books, dresses, or even money.
- Promote the recognition by the State of the services rendered by the benefactors of the school through their donations for the improvement in the attendance and learning.
- Give publicity to the school in the Parish by all means possible.
- Cooperate with the Administrative authorities and the local delegate in running the school smoothly in the event of the absence of the "Professors" either due to sickness or any other valid reason.

- The Governor through the subordinates would offer to the Committees all the cooperation which they needed for the discharge of their functions.
- The Committees would organize their budgets and present their accounts to the administrative authorities as per the rules pertaining to these Committees. *N.B.*—The terms and the books of accounts and of receipts and expenditure would be attested by the Administrator of the province.
- The Committees would formulate their own rules and for the proper functioning of the Committee and allotment of duties and submit it to the Provincial Government for approval through the Inspector.
- The Provincial Government would promote a big charitable institution in the city, Nova Goa to promote benefaction and education, meant to help the other charitable organizations in the villages of the country wherever help was required and to give publicity to such institutions and their work as follows:
  - This Committee had to be formed by ladies and the gentlemen (knights) in such number as determined by the Governor those that demonstrate an interest in benefaction and popular education and who by these fortunate means can render good service to the cause of education.
  - The Governor, the Secretary General and the Inspector would be ex-officio members.
  - The Committee would be sub-divided into the Executive, a Festival Committee, Accounts and any other issue which was necessary; each would be made up five members.
  - The service of this Committee would be placed under the control of the Secretariat General where the office also would be located.

The Place of Library in the School

The library is called the soul of any institution. Having realized the importance of such a set-up the Administrative authorities made attempts to promote this facility in every school. It should not be viewed in the present context as the school attached libraries would comprise more of textbooks rather than reference and other reading material. The following provisions were made for the functioning of these school lending libraries:

- Attached to the schools there had to be a small Class library holding all the books adopted in the Primary schools. This library would be the property of the school with the main purpose of helping the students coming from poor families who could not afford to buy books.
- The books of this library were meant for the poor students to whom the "Professor" had to lend during the Classes or even to take home under the express condition that they were to be returned to the library in proper time and in good condition.
- The Assistant "Professors" in the schools in which they had these books, were to be made responsible for the management of this library. In schools having only one teacher needless to say it would be under his/her charge.
- The acquisition of the books was the duty of the Schools Inspector who would purchase them under recommendation from the "Professor" and add to the resources of the library.
- The books had to be catalogued and placed in serial order in the library cupboard which would be made a part of the school furnitures in which should be placed:
  - A catalogue of the existing books.
  - A register to record the issuing and receipt of books to the poor students showing not only their names but also the day of issue/return.
  - A register to show the income and expenditure. The following had to be observed:
    - This register had to be checked by the Administrator of the province and the Inspector every time they visited the school.
    - Every year by the 31st of March the "Professor" in charge of the library had to submit to the Schools Inspector a copy of the inventory of the books along with the report of the activities during the year and the

functioning of the book bank of the library making it a point to record his observations that he thought were necessary.

- The library for its maintenance and replenishment would depend on the following sources of income:
  - A certain percentage of the fees paid by the students for examinations and for registration.
  - Donations from charitable persons and from Societies and from collections from certain wealthy families who had their children in the school.
  - From the fines levied on the parents of the students who had lost or mutilated a book which had been issued to him.
  - From a small subsidy from the School Fund set aside annually by the Provincial Government with the sanction of the Schools Inspector of the province.

Central Libraries for Teachers and Others

But more importantly the establishment of the Central libraries which were meant for the enhancement of knowledge of the teachers and for the reading pleasure of others was a great venture undertaken by the authorities and a step in the right direction. This played a crucial role in promoting the advancement of learning and of the society in many fields of life in Goa. The following stipulations pertained to their set-up:

- In the provinces of Ilhas, Salcette and Bardez they had to set up a library in the Municipal building for the use of the "Professors" precisely called the Central library for Primary schools.
- The library would be managed by one of the employees of the Municipality and would be under his total control.
- The Central school libraries besides possessing books which would be of interest to the "Professors" of Primary education in their educative mission would also be kept open for business for others on Sundays and on feast days and on all those days marked as holidays.
- The books found in the library would be issued to the "Professors" through a request made to the Schools Inspector who would then directly and officially requisition them from the person in charge. *N.B.*—For this reason there would be three school zones (circles): Ilhas, Salcette and Bardez. The first zone would comprise of Ilhas, Ponda and Sanquelim including the

military outpost of Sattari; the second zone would have Salcette, Canacona, Quepem and Sanguem; and the third would consist of Bardez, Pernem and the districts of Daman and Diu.

- The "Professors" could take books from the library meant for that zone only and could not be permitted to have in their possession more than one book at a time and for more than 15 days. *N.B.*—The "Professors" had to compensate the Central school library if the book got damaged when in their possession.
- The record of the books issued would be maintained on a register showing the title of the book, its registered number, the name, the residence and the category of the "Professor" to whom the book had been issued, the date and the entry number of the application and the remark of the Schools Inspector. *N.B.*—For reasons of supervision the Primary Schools Inspector would send with a mention of the service, a note regarding the request duly signed by him and which had to be returned by the in-charge of the library when the book had been restored.
- All the books requested for by the "Professors" from the Schools Inspector or returned for keeping in the library could also be sent by post as bookposts by the officials concerned.
- The acquisition of the books had to be made by the Presidents of the Municipal Councils or Municipal Commissions of Ilhas, Salcette and Bardez after the Schools Inspector had given the green signal. *N.B.*—To meet the expenditure of the libraries all the Municipal bodies had to make a provision in their budgets forcing the Government to oblige them in this duty as far as possible.
- The following were the duties of the library-in-charge:
  - To index the books and store them in order in the cupboards.
  - To make annually a statistical report of the books used and those issued.
  - To record the books every time they were issued.
  - To draw up an inventory of all the material found in the library.
- All the books would be marked with the seal "Central library......." followed by the name of the locality where it existed.

Private Classes and Home-Schooling

Private effort contributed a lot to supplement the efforts of the State in promoting Primary education in Goa. Due to many constraints some of those interested in education had to teach their children at home either personally or by keeping a tutor. Some institutions also conducted Classes for students at their own expense. Nevertheless the Government tried to bring them under its ambit of rules and regulations to exercise control and monitor the imparting of instruction. The following regulations pertained to these private educational agencies:

- Wherever the State did not exercise any Administrative control as per the present regulations those schools would be considered as private.
- The individual who desired to establish an institute in order to impart Primary instruction had to approach the Primary Inspector at least one month in advance and submit an application with the following documents:
  - Diploma of teacher training.
  - Certificate from the police showing no criminal record.
  - Certificate of good behaviour.
  - Name of the institution if there was.
  - Names of the "Professor/s" in charge of teaching along with their qualifications/titles; Certificate from the Directorate of Public Health showing that he did not suffer from any contagious disease and had been vaccinated, a sworn affidavit that the place from where the institute would function was in good hygienic condition.
- The Primary Schools Inspector, having verified the documents had to then submit them with his remarks to the Provincial Government which would then direct the Inspector to authorize the opening of the institute or give reason why it could not be allowed. *N.B.*—The legal title for teaching in the Primary school is a Diploma of Superior Education, or Secondary or the Theology course or the Old course of the Normal School or the new course of the Mixed School meant for the Training of Primary teachers.
- Whenever the institute changed its location or its name or if there was any change in the non-teaching and teaching staff the Schools Inspector and the Administrator of the province had to be duly informed about the changes.
- Analogous information together with the Certificate of teaching had to be acquired by the individual who had started teaching in the school.
- In the Secretariat of the Primary inspection there had to be a Register for the recording of the details of the "Professors" of

private Primary schools. This recording had to be done on a separate page for each "Professor" so that the detailed information pertaining to that particular "Professor" presented at times successively would be easily available.

- Based on this record any Certificate needed for any purpose could be issued as well as additions to the qualifications of the "Professors" could be done.
- The official "Professors" against whom disciplinary action had been taken would not be allowed to open any institution without the consent of the Provincial Government, which would always take into account the severity of the reason for the dismissal.
- The establishment of a school, course or a private institution which had been opened or had been functioning without legal authorization had to be immediately closed down by the administrative authority. *N.B.*—Individuals who had been working in these institutes either on the administrative side or teaching side would be penalized with a one-year suspension of their licence to work or the work permit.
- The "Professors" in the private schools and asylums and any other houses of education with or without boarding facility where Primary instruction was imparted would be obliged to adopt the books, methods and the syllabi approved by the higher authorities for the official schools and would be subject to the official supervision/inspection regarding teaching, hygienic conditions and the instruction imparted in the school.
    - The "Professors" of these private schools would be obliged to keep open the schools all the time and had to allow without any notice the Administrator of the province or the Inspector or his delegate to inspect their schools and show them when required the rules, the syllabi, the timetable and everything necessary for the inspection of teaching.
    - Similarly the same should also be done towards the Health officials when they come on official visit or in obedience to the Orders of the Superiors.
- The "Professors" of the establishments were obliged to submit to the Schools Inspector at the end of the academic year till the 15th of May for the purpose of statistical data the chart as found mentioned in the Decree No. 1 of the 19th of September, 1902.
- The Directors and the "Professors" who refused to submit to

inspection as mentioned above or kept giving explanations to the demands of the authorities or furnished incorrect information would be dismissed from the institution or their official records in the respective book would be cancelled.

- If it was found that the "Professor" had been teaching a doctrine contrary to the veneration which one must have to the Portuguese country, religion and the laws of the State or against the practice of good behaviour by word or by example, would be dismissed from the institute by the Provincial Government. If the "Professor" also happened to be the Director he would be suspended and another person would be authorized to look after the establishment.
    - Same penalty would be imposed by the Government when it was found that the pedagogical and hygienic conditions where the school was functioning from were bad or the teaching did not measure up to the standard or meet the basic requirements.
    - These penalties would be imposed only after giving an opportunity to the accused to defend him in whose defence documentary and testimonial proof would be admitted in the process duly started based on the information furnished by the Primary Inspector and after obtaining the signal from the Inspection Council.
- The individuals and the establishments having legal sanction to operate would be obliged to follow these statutes. Even those who did not have these statutes in their possession would also be obliged to follow them including the teachers so that they would be in a position to obtain the legal qualification within the stipulated time period and prove in the Secretariat of Inspection of Primary education that they possessed the necessary qualifications. *N.B.*—The establishments would be ordered to be closed down whose "Professors" did not comply with the regulations.

Financial Aspects of School Education

It is generally agreed that finances make up a very important part of the management of schools. At times there were financial difficulties and the schools were left to fend for themselves. To meet such emergency situations schools had to be equipped with a workable mechanism that would allow them to tide over the impending problem in order to help the school not only to continue but also to grow. Hence, the Government stipulated that there should be a School Fund to meet the emergency expenses to maintain the schools.

- The following were the resources from where the school funds would be collected:
  - The fees of admission of the students who were attending the National Lyceum as mentioned in the "Portaria" of the Royal Commissioner on the 9th of January, 1897 and from those enrolled in the Teacher Training school.
  - Two-thirds of the amount collected either as term fees, charge for the Certificates and the charge for the marks cards of the students of Lyceum.
  - The income from the admission for examinations and the charge for the Certificates in the Primary schools as per the "Portaria" of 5th August, 1896 (Art. 24 to 136).
  - The funds lying in the school coffers and in the Provinces in the custody of the defunct local Committees as per the regulations of Primary education on the "Portaria" dated 15th January, 1881.
  - The funds allotted for the above purpose by the Municipalities, "Communidades", Parish Committees and the temple Committees in their budgets to help in the construction, repairs and the maintenance of the school buildings placed thus within its limits as per the statutes mentioned in the Decree of 31st October, 1892 article 46.
  - Half of the share of the surplus revenue of the "Confrarias" as per the Decree of 31st October, 1892, the "Portaria" of the Royal Commisssioner of 16th June, 1896 and the Provincial "Portaria" of 15th April, 1899.
  - The education tax/cess of 10th November, 1772 and the Royal Decree of 17th October, 1773.
  - Donations from private individuals or private bodies.
- The School Fund had to be used for the following purposes:
  - Construction or/and maintenance of the school buildings.
  - Purchase of the pedagogic furnitures/articles. *N.B.*—Money from this fund would be used only in case the Municipality or the Municipal Committee lacked the necessary means.
  - Awarding annually prizes to "Professors" who showed extraordinary zeal in their teaching and who were very

diligent and helpful and maintained cleanliness and order in their schools and took care of their furnitures as well as the students who performed reasonably well as a result of the "Professor's" application and hard work.

- Setting up of the Class library.
- Grants to the deserving "Professors" from private schools because of very good results.
- Setting up of new schools as motivation and support to a particular initiative.
- Any other need of the private schools.
- Improvement of things in teachers' training school.
- Cost of the furnitures and the teaching material in the teacher training school.

- The names of donors who contributed substantially towards the School Fund could be given to school buildings.
- The money for the School Fund had to be collected by the Department of Accounts of the province under a special head allotted by the Governor. *N.B.*—Whenever money was to be spent for the construction or the repairs of the school building or grants had to be given to "Professors" in private schools the withdrawal of the money had to be authorized by the Inspecting Council of Public Instruction.
- In every official school there had to be a safe under the charge of one of the "Professors" to keep the fees collected from the students at the time of enrolment. *N.B.*—The statement of accounts had to be shown on a proper register.
- Every year the "Professor" had to send to the Schools Inspector till the 15th of April and also when it was demanded a statement regarding the receipt and expenditure of the respective year and had to deposit at the end of the year in the Treasury of the province where the school was located all the money which had been kept in the school safe under his charge.

Strategies for Teaching

It has already been stated that Primary instruction was divided into two Levels and designated as Elementary and Complementary. The former called "primeiro grau" (First level) comprised of four Classes namely "Classe inicial" (beginners' Class), "primeira Classe" (Class I) "segunda Classe" (Class II) and "terceira Classe" (Class III) and the latter called

"Segundo grau" (Second level) which consisted of only one Class. "Classe inicial" was like kindergarten where school readiness was imparted. The detailed syllabus from Class I onwards was as follows:

In Class I students who did not know anything of Portuguese were admitted. Teaching was done with the main aim of imparting to them gradually the listening and pronunciation skills involving both vowels and consonants and easy understanding and correct pronunciation of words of everyday use and those which they came across in the lessons of Class II.

This Class was supposed to substitute the mother tongue of the students in whose houses Portuguese language was not spoken at all.

Vocabulary: Words had be taught with reference to objects—making use of the Konkani language as little as possible—starting with the words found around the student in the Class and those which the "Professor" thought had to be presented as they would be able to put them to good use, the various objects found in the pictures, etc.

The "Professor" could not leave it to chance the teaching of the vocabulary and teaching had to be done in such a way that the student would acquire gradually the knowledge of the vocabulary used in Class II.

Once the words had been learnt they would be grouped in such a way that they could help in constructing the same phrases as found in the lessons of Class II or form phrases of common use.

Pronunciation: All efforts from the beginning had to be directed towards teaching an exact pronunciation and accent to the students. For this purpose the words had to be pronounced slowly and clearly keeping in mind the represented object and repeating once to each student, many times to others and then to the whole Class till they had obtained the exact reproduction of the sounds which the words represented. Then he had to show an object and then order them to pronounce the word which it represented. The "Professor" had to teach the intonation of the expression and the phrases. In this way the student would get well habituated to reply thereafter in a complete sentence to questions with the words he had learnt.

Syllabus and Classroom Transaction

In Class II the syllabus was both more advanced and more detailed. Note is to be taken of the fact that the methodology too was incorporated in the syllabus itself so that there was very little room left for confusion or neglect.The following directions were given for the teaching of Reading:

- Vowels, their denomination, values and the different combinations which can be made.
- Simple and compound consonants, alone or in combination with the vowels, forming of syllables.
- These letters must be represented to the Class, little by little, by the "Professor" as conveniently as possible, using a graphic likeness or a phonetic analogy.
- Knowledge and use of accents/stresses.
- Composition and decomposition of syllables.
- Reading exercises by syllables, with composed elements of disyllabic words, tri-syllabic and polysyllabic without following the system of spelling.
- Composing and decomposing the words into syllables and then into elements, with an introduction to the teaching of Orthography.
- Reading word by word till the Class could read rapidly and without any hesitation.
- Learning by heart the alphabet in order, needed to help in referring to the dictionary.
- Knowledge of the alphabet in capital letters and the manuscript of the characters.
- Continuation of the reading word by word in different writing styles, printed, lithographic and manuscript.

All the exercises had to be accompanied by the correction of defects in their pronunciation when the students were presenting their lessons, corrections which had been started in the previous Class, and which had to be continued in the following Classes had to be made till the mispronunciation had disappeared.

In all his teaching the "Professor" had to use the maxim 'from easy to difficult' taking special care not to present any new material without the whole Class having learnt perfectly well the previous one and had to try not to burden the children with too many lessons and exercises for their own benefit.

In the early stages of Reading which pertained to a certain Class the "Professor" could make use of the slate where he could then inscribe the number of lessons and exercises as many as his talent and his pedagogical knowledge made it possible or use the printed tables or the lithographs or manuscripts in clear and visible types and even by using moving letters with which he could compose syllables and words.

Whenever he was making use of books or prepared charts he had to take the maximum care in avoiding those exercises that could be learnt by heart easily but badly.

Whenever it appeared to the "Professor" that it would be more advantageous he would present to the Class the manuscript characters before presenting the typographical ones.

For better progress of time and work they had to avoid teaching individually.

Lots of attention was paid to the cultivation of the skill of Writing as most of the records were maintained by hand. Hence there was a need to train the students not only to write but to write in a legible and attractive manner. The old record books bear this out. Manuscript writing in the absence of typewriting machines was commonplace with some persons even acting as official scribers. Accordingly the following directions were laid down for the teaching of the skill of Writing:

As a preliminary step in Writing the "Professor" had to explain to the students the general principles related to the position of the body while writing, the placing of the paper or the slate and the inkpot, the way the pen or the pencil was to be held, the side on which the light, natural or artificial had to be allowed and it was indispensable that a watch had to be kept by constant observation that these principles were followed by the students faithfully while doing any written exercise. Not only the correct execution of the writing but also proper hygiene demands all the vigilance by the "Professor", as also the improper positioning of the body during writing can result in disaster, so also grave deformation in the thoracic box and the organs which contain the bends of the vertebral column and myopia.

At the preparatory stage the students would prefer the slate. Under the guidance of the "Professor" the necessary exercises leading to the education of the fingers for the handling of the pen and the pencil would be undertaken. Then they would be initiated in the penmanship of writing, to put it correctly as per the following:

- Copying on the slates, natural or artificial letters of the small alphabet.
- I, u, n, m, c, e, o, a, v, x, s, r, z, t, d, b, l, h, k, p, q, j, y, g, f.
- Written by the "Professor" on the blackboard or on paper as perfectly as possible.
- The alphabet could not be presented to the Class as a lesson but little by little till the students had acquired a relative graphic perfection which would help in clearly recognizing the letters.

The "Professor" had to show on the blackboard that some letters were derived from others and had to recommend and make the necessary corrections regarding the obliqueness or parallelism both in the body of the letter as well as the stem. With an example of the letters "t", "b", "l" he could teach that the stem needed to have one, two or three heights of the body of the letter and had to insist on the necessity of maintaining the uniform distance between the letters. The "Professor" could not allow the students to use pieces of pencils which were too short as they would obstruct the fingers from holding the pencil in a proper manner.

- The point of the pencil had to be kept sharpened so that the shape of the letters could be copied nicely.
- The superior or the inferior (higher or lower) connection of the known letters forming syllables and words had to be kept at a uniform distance. These exercises could have been done either in pencil or ink on ruled paper in the beginning having the lines for the inclination of the letters copied from the blackboard.
- Copying of the capital letters of the alphabet starting with the elementary lines of its formation, followed by the tracing of the letters, teaching little by little and exemplifying by copying the proper names of persons, cities, rivers, mountains, etc., in order to practice the use of capital letters already studied, revised and perfected by the related exercises. It is imperative that the "Professor" did not discontinue from giving the necessary explanations regarding the denomination of each of the parts that make up the letter, from the starting point, the relative thickness, comparison of the new letter with the analogous ones already known, and application of the new letters so far not learnt, showing the distance of the letters in the same word and the words among themselves in order to arouse and provoke in the students the taste for good handwriting which showed proportion and symmetry. These exercises had to be demonstrated by the "Professor" on the blackboard or on paper and copied by the students on their notebooks within the lines which should not exceed four millimetres.
- *Copying of the numerals*: The inclination of the numerals had to be just like the letters, i.e., 45 degrees.

Subject-wise Syllabi in Class I and II

The following topics made up the syllabus of Arithmetic:

- *Units*: Knowledge of the numbers from 1 to 10 and their representation by means of the digits. Related exercises.
- *Tens*: Formation of the exact numbers in tens, from one to ten. How to utter them and how to write them. Related exercises.
- Formation of comprehensive numbers from ten to twenty. How to call them out and how to write. Related exercises.
- *Addition*: Fractions, sums and sign of addition. Table of Addition. Addition of two or more numbers in such a manner that the total did not exceed twenty. Exercises on mental, concrete and abstract calculations.
- *Subtraction*: Reduction, reducer, remainder or difference and sign of subtraction. Subtraction of two numbers in which the smaller number does not exceed twenty. Exercises on mental, concrete and abstract calculations.
- *Multiplication*: Multiplication, multiplicand, multiplier, product, factors and the sign used in the operation. Multiplication of two numbers such that their product did not exceed 20. Interpretation of the phrases "to duplicate, to triplicate, to quadruplicate and to quintuplicate a number. Exercises on mental, concrete and abstract calculations.
- *Division*: Dividend, divisor, quotient, and the sign of Division. Exact and inexact Division. Remainder in Division. Division of two numbers whose dividend did not exceed 20. Interpretation of the phrases/terms half, one-third, one-quarter/one-fourth, one-fifth, one-sixth, one-seventh, one-eighth, and one-ninth. Exercises on mental, concrete and abstract calculations.
- Formation of numbers between 20 and 30, 30 and 40, etc., up to 100. Four operations performed with numbers up to 100. A table of multiplication. Exercises on mental, concrete and abstract calculations.

As Catholicism was practiced as a State religion the tacit understanding between the administrative and religious authorities had resulted in the official schools also introducing the subject of Catechism as one of the major subjects in the school curriculum. The following syllabus was introduced in the Primary:

- To make the Sign of the Cross, to give blessings, to say the 'Our Father' and the 'Hail Mary'.
- While teaching Catechism, great care had to be taken to see that the students recited the prayers carefully (with breaks) in such a manner that the phrases would bring out the true feelings in them.

The following was proposed under the syllabus of Drawing:

- Copying on the slates the quadrilaterals or on paper the pointed shapes or with the pencil, together as formed examples, by straight lines in different positions, horizontal, vertical, oblique, cross, diagonal, etc.
- Calligraphy exercises.

For the girls under the special subjects the following topics were included in the syllabus:

- Embroidery and stitching.
- Hemming, Use of finger protector and the needle, hem stitch, glove stitch, forward stitch, backward stitch.
- Mark made with flax.
- Use of needles of darning and crotchet. Joining and crèche.

Syllabus in Class III

In Class III continuity was maintained with the topics covered in the earlier Classes. However, the quantum of the content was increased so that there was gradual development of the students. That meant that the pedagogical principles were well applied as can be seen from the following provisions in the syllabus of Class III starting with Reading:

- Reading of short affirmative, interrogative and exclamatory sentences; punctuation marks and their uses, basics of current and accented Reading made very lengthy in the published books and manuscripts whose difficulty was increased gradually paying more attention to the punctuation marks as the sentences had to be understood well by the students.
- The passage that had been read had to be explained carefully giving out the meanings of the words. Lots of efforts had to be made by the "Professor" in these exercises to correct the defective diction which he came across in the language of his students.
- The reading in this Class would be done from a book which contained material having variety, was interesting and useful as the knowledge it offered was easy to understand.
- *Writing*: Copying of good examples of cursive and small bastard letters.
- The "Professors" had to make the necessary corrections in the

copywriting done by the students so that the former would get the students to acquire a handwriting style relatively perfect, clearly legible and proportionate.

- The "Professors" could use prepared notebooks where the difficulty would be increased gradually. In the absence of examples the "Professor" had to use the blackboard to write the exercises which the students had to copy.
- The examples as well as the exercises always had to relate to moral precepts or advice or to hygiene.
- Copywriting exercises for the learning of Orthography.
- *Arithmetic*: Hundreds. Formation of exact numbers of hundreds from one to ten. How to say them aloud and how to write.
- *Thousand*. Formation of exact numbers from one to thousand. How to call them out loudly and how to write. Exercises based on them.
- Formation of numbers between two units of consecutive thousand. How to say aloud and how to write them.
- *Tens and hundreds of thousands*. Formation of numbers placed between tens and hundreds of consecutive thousands. How to say aloud and how to write them.
- Reading of numbers represented by numerals and written while dictating. The four operations done with numbers till 900,000 and tests on these operations.
- Portuguese and Luso-Indian currency; continental money, rupees, "tangas", and Provincial "reis".
- Knowledge of gold, silver, copper and nickel coins as well as paper money. Manner of representing by means of numerals any quantity continental or Luso-Indian as far as possible to know. Luso-Indian weights and measures.
- *Roman numerals*. Various mathematical problems on numerals.
- *Metric system*: Knowledge of metre, litre, gram and their applications. Multiples and sub-multiples of these units, their necessity and their relation to the fundamental unit. Changing the unit. Knowledge of weights used in the practice and in the derivatives of the fundamental means. Exercises based on these.
- *Catechism*: Hail Holy Queen, I Believe, Confession, Act of Faith, Hope, Charity, Attrition and Contrition; Sacraments and short explanation.
- *Drawing*: The same exercises as done in Class II with regard to Drawing done in combination with straight lines and curves or only with curved lines.

- Copying of logos representing articles of common use.
- Calligraphy exercises.
- *Embroidery and stitching*: Consolidation of the work done in Class II and more: The back-stitch and the cross stitch.
- *Markings*: Execution by flax, the alphabet, numerals, date, name, etc.
- *Darning and crotchet.*
- *Music*: Vocal music/singing.

Syllabus in Class IV

In Class IV, the same subjects were repeated. Only in this case the content had increased to double or more than double of what was being taught in Classs III. The following comprised the topics under the syllabus for Class IV:

- *Reading*: Loud reading from the prescribed text and its explanation, substitution of the words, phrases and simple exercises based on the various principles of language in prose or in verse found in the adopted book and generally taught in the Primary schools or some other book of educative value.
  - The manuscripts which could also serve as passages for the exercises of copywriting for the calligraphy to be good had to contain familiar pictures on various topics, memories, applications, acts/minutes, receipts, facts, titles of particular contracts, etc., in letters of various types and whose difficulty had to gradually increase.
- *Writing*: Copying of good examples of bastard, small bastard, cursive, small cursive, capital and small alphabet, abbreviations frequently used, and numerals. These exercises had to be constantly verified and corrected by the "Professor" and which had to continue till the students had succeeded in obtaining a firm, correct and elegant handwriting.
  - Writing the exercises in Orthography on the slate or on paper after being dictated to.
- *Arithmetic*: Million. Formation of numbers with million. How to distinguish million from other units of different order. How to say aloud and how to write. Tens and hundreds of millions. *Billion.* Tens and hundreds of billions.
  - How to read a number represented by a numeral/digit.

  - How to write a number which had been called out. How to read and write a number representing Portuguese currency in "reis" having more than six digits or a number expressed in rupees having more than seven digits. Abstract and concrete numbers. Related exercises.

- *Addition*: Nature of a sum. To prove that the order of the parts is arbitrary. End of addition. Oral and written exercises.
- *Subtraction*: Nature of the remainder. End of subtraction. Oral and written exercises. Multiplication. Nature of the product. To prove that the order of the two factors is arbitrary. End of multiplication. Oral and written exercises.
- *Division*: Practical way to determine the number of the digits of the quotient. The quotient of division of two numbers does not change the value when multiplied or divided if possible, as much as the dividend as the divisor by itself. Ends of division. Oral and written exercises.
  - Conditions necessary for a number to be divisible by another. Equal and inequal numbers. Conditions of divisibility of a number by 9 and its application for the proof of four operations.
  - Decimal numbers. Exercises on the integers and decimals; practicing the four operations.
- *Metric system*: Measures of surface and their applications to the measurement of land. Multiples and sub-multiples of fundamental units. Change of unit.
  - Measures of volume and their application. "Esterre" and its use. Multiples and sub-multiples of fundamental unit. Change of unit. Relation between the measures of volume, capacity and weight. Correspondence between the measures and the weights of the metric system and the measures and weights under the Luso-Indian. Exercises for common use.
  - In the teaching of the metric system the actual weights and the measures had to be used in preference to the models.
- *Catechism*: The commandments, the teachings of the Church, the Articles of faith, the Mysteries of the Holy Trinity, the capital sins and the virtues opposed to them, the theological virtues, the cardinal virtues, works of mercy, brief narration of the life of Lord Jesus Christ, Holy Sacrifice of Mass.
- *Morals*: The teaching of Morals had to be practical, with the "Professor" keeping in mind the task of guiding the students for

their own good, forming their heart and their conscience, directing them accordingly with regard to the following:

- There would always be moral topics and counsels in the lessons, not only the duties in themselves but also in a way they could be carried out. Duties towards the community, towards the members of the family towards our equals and towards God.
- The lessons in Morals had to be given preferably through the means of stories and historical narratives, found in the Old and the New Testament, in the profane history and especially in practical life.
- The moral topics through which it was not possible to understand the old trends had to be encouraged by the "Professor" throughout the school life of the students, whenever he had an opportunity to advise them or to give some beneficial warning.

- *National Agriculture*: Brief notions of the lands in the country from the point of view of Agriculture and some practical knowledge. Elementary knowledge of the main processes of fertilizer and harm: Preparation and arrangement of the land, correctives, stimulants and manure and the furrows. Rudimentary knowledge of widely known trees and useful Indian plants and ways of improving and perfecting culture.Other topics included:
  - Common diseases of plants and the means of combating them.
  - Period of seeding and collecting them and the main agricultural products.
  - Rudimentary notions of Natural Sciences applicable to Agriculture of Goa and indication of the prime material which Agriculture provides for the country's industry.
  - Export and Import of the main agricultural products.
  - This teaching must have a practical side to it as much as possible and had to be taught during the lessons.
- *Drawing*: Very simple drawings of constructions, with the help of the ruler, square, compass and set-squares like:
  - Tracing of straight lines, broken lines and curves and mixed ones in various positions.
  - Right angle, acute and obtuse, rectilinear and curvilinear.
  - Regular and irregular polygons.
  - Equilateral triangle, isosceles triangle and scalene triangle.

    - Parallelogram, cube and trapezium.
    - Pentagon, hexagon, heptagon, octagon, etc.
    - Circumference, circle, centre, diameter, ray, sector, arc, cord, segment, secant, tangent, concentric circles, circular crown, eccentric circumference, tangents and secants.
    - Copying of pictures representing objects of everyday use.
    - Copying of border designs.
- *Domestic Economy*: Acquisition, cleanliness and preservation of the furnitures in the house and the kitchen utensils—Ventilation and cleanliness in the house. Dressing room. White clothes. Manner of whitening and the substances used for that. Foodstuffs. Rice. Fundamental conditions necessary for running a home properly.
- *Singing and music*: Vocal music. Learning of short passages at one time. Knowledge of the notes and their very simple combination. Musical notes.
- *Needle Work and Embroidery*: Consolidation of what had been taught in the previous Class (Class III) and more, like broken stitch, etc.
    - Different ways of marking. Making of simple pieces of white clothes and diverse designs.
    - Stockings and crotchet either plain or in relief.

Syllabus in Class V (Segundo Grau)

The "Primeiro grau" or the First Level consisted of four Classes and the "Segundo grau" or the Second Level consisted of just one Class. It is really interesting to know the reason or reasons for such a division. Normally the certification after answering the examinations of the Second Level was of prime importance. Whoever had done "Segundo grau" commanded a lot of respect and enjoyed opportunities galore to land a Government job. Accordingly the syllabus for this Level was not an easy one and those who were really competent and confident would go in for the Second Level. The following topics were included in the syllabus of the Second Level:

- Reading and exercises on Portuguese language: Continuation of the oral Reading taught at the First Level and recitation of the passages in prose and verse which have been included in the book of Reading for the Particular Class.

- These passages consisted of simple and single narratives including historical facts, descriptions of places, moral narrations, etc.
- The principles of Portuguese Grammar had to be taught through the same lessons which earlier had been done orally and in this way the "Professor" would be adding to the knowledge that the students already had. The topic of the lesson had to be written on the blackboard by the students and Grammar exercises based on the said topic would then be set by the "Professor".
- Every lesson had to have the correct language and complete phrases of the description of the object which it dealt with, that is the name, the place where it was found, the material that had been used in its construction, the artists who were responsible for its quality, colours and Geometric forms and qualities that could be compared with the other objects of the same nature.
- These exercises had to be then copied by the students in their notebooks.
- The teaching of Grammar had to be functional as it was extremely necessary that the students should become proficient in understanding, exposing and writing correctly. The words had to be classified grammatically according to their significance. By means of the intuitive processes separating the concrete from the abstract the studen‘s would be expected to gather knowledge of the nouns, pronouns, articles, adjectives (both qualifiers as well as determinatives), gender as well as number, grammatical agreement, degrees of comparison, verbs (regular and irregular conjugations), adverbs, prepositions, conjunctions and interjections commonly used. Analysis of the sentence relating to the subject, predicate, direct complement and the circumstances of its frequent use, omitting everything which may be "subtilejas grammaticaes" dispensable in Primary instruction.
- The Orthography including the use of the punctuation, could be improved in this class by means of pictures on the various topics as per the choice of the "Professor" with short descriptions of the known objects which the students had to write in their notebooks and had to submit to the "Professor" for his checking who then would make the necessary corrections.
- *Writing*: Continuation of the exercises for improvement of Reading and the recapitulation of the Calligraphic rules taught at the First Level.

- Exercises in running hand on ruled and plain paper.

- *Drawing*: Lines and Angles. To draw a perpendicular line by means of a given straight line. Drawing a perpendicular line from any given point on a straight line. Drawing a perpendicular line from the end of a straight line which could be prolonged. Dividing a straight line into two or four or eight equal parts.
  - Copying seen objects existing in the school; tables, benches, boards, balances, weights, measures, etc., in smaller dimensions, conforming to a scale indicated by the "Professor" with the help of the rules and the set squares.
  - The same exercise for the copying of the Chorographic map or part of it; provinces, districts, regions, course of the main rivers, etc., so as to help in the teaching of Chorography.
- Rudiments of Natural Science especially applicable to Hygiene and Agriculture in the country as follows:
  - Division of the bodies into solids, liquids and gases.
  - Clothes which had to be sewed as per the age, position and climate.
  - The human body, its division into head, trunk and members. The teeth; care to be taken for maintaining them in good condition. Choosing potable water; harm that could be caused by using impure water; practical means of knowing and purifying water; fatal consequences of abuse of alcoholic drinks; importance of the atmospheric air, air pollution, gathering of individuals, healthy or sick, in a small space; gases and the cleaning of the sewers or the septic tanks for the removal of the dirt; gases released by the putrefaction of organic matter; gases released by the exhalations of the swamps, emissions or dust which the individuals are subjected to in their professions.
  - Importance of the cleanliness of the body and dress. Problems likely to arise due to lack of cleanliness. General baths.
  - The Rudiments of Natural Science, included in this programme did not actually constitute a course but were only a series of general facts which could be conveniently given to the children.
  - The material had to be integrated into the lessons and the teaching had to be done by means of an intuitive process with the help of pictures in the absence of or impossibility of presentation through proper objects (realia).

- *Agriculture*: Repetition of the content of the First Level but more in detail
- *Artihmetic*: Unity. Whole numbers. Concrete and abstract numbers. Reciting and writing of numbers. Roman numerals. Exercises.
  - *Addition*. Fractions and Totals. Sign of addition. Nature of addition. Points to be considered in the addition of whole numbers. Table of additions. Tests to show that the order of fractions is arbitrary. Test of addition. Applying it to problems.
  - *Subtraction*. Diminuendo. Remainder, excess or difference. Sign of subtraction. Nature of remainder. Points to be considered in Subtraction. Proving that in the tabulation of addition the remainder did not change its value when it was joined to an additive or subtractive number or in other words the same number was obtained. Test of subtraction. Purpose of subtraction. Problems on addition or subtraction.
  - *Multiplication*. Multiplicand. Multiplier. Product and factors. Sign of multiplication. Multiplication is nothing more than a shorter form of addition. Nature of product. Points to be considered when multiplying whole numbers. Tabulation of multiplication and tests to show that the order of two factors is arbitrary. Test of multiplication, its purpose and application to problems.
  - *Division*. Dividendo, Divisor, quotient and remainder. Sign of division. Points to be considered when dividing two whole numbers. Manner of determining the number of digits of a quotient. The quotient of two numbers did not change its value when either multiplied or divided being possible when the dividend was the same as divisor but the remainder was going to be multiplied or divided by this number, its application.
  - Useful phrases. Nature of quotient. Test of division.
  - Purpose of division. Problems regarding division. Exercises for mental calculation.
  - Number divisible by another or multiple of another. Sub-multiple or factor. Even and odd numbers. Principle on which was founded the divisibility of a number by 9 and its application to the tests of other operations.

- *Fractions*. Their origin in the measuring of continual greatness and the difference between them and the breaking up of numbers. How they are represented and how they are read. The different types of fractions. Decimal fractions or fractional numbers. Extension of the principle of numeration of whole numbers to decimals. How to read and write the decimal numbers. Properties of decimal numbers and their usefulness. Operations on the decimal numbers. Reducing a fraction to a decimal number.
- Complex numbers with application to time, the divisions of the circumference and the currency of the country. Reducing a complex number to a figure. Changing a non-complex number to a complex number. Reducing a complex number to a fraction and from this to a decimal number. Various problems. Idea of the current currency in "India Portuguesa" and the Indian system of weights and measures. Addition and Subtraction of complex numbers in the form of rupees and their sub-divisions and conversion from rupees to "tangas" and "reis" of the times. Exercises and problems on fractions and monetary units. Practical relation of the greater to the smaller and *vice versa* between the Indian measures and the weights and the units of mensuration and the weights of the metric decimal system.
- Exercises and simple problems on the counting of money in rupees and their subdivisions in Indian weights and measures and their conversion into the Indo-Portuguese measures while buying and selling.
- *The metric system*: Its origin and advantages. General principles of its available set. The set that includes the general extension. Large metric numbers and fundamental units of each one of them. Multiples and sub-multiples of the fundamental unit and how they are formed.
- *Measures of length*. Metre and its intrinsic knowledge. Metric measurements. Multiples and sub-multiples. Writing and reading the numbers signifying the measures of length. Effective and nominal measures. The surveyor's rule and its application. Choice and change of a unit. Itinerary measures. Problems.
- *Surface measures*. Square metre. Representing a square metre, drawing multiples and sub-multiples of the square

metre. Writing and reading of the numbers which express surface measures. Choosing and changing the units. Agricultural measures. Problems.

- *Measures of volume*. Cubic metre and how it is formed. Its intrinsic knowledge. Multiples and sub-multiples of the cubic metre. Writing and reading of the numbers which express measures of volume. Choosing and changing the units. "Stere", its multiples and sub-multiples. Problems.
- *Measures of capacity*. Its derivation from volume. Effective measures and their intrinsic knowledge. Litre. Multiples and sub-multiples. Writing and reading of numbers which expresses measures of capacity. Choosing and changing units. Problems.
- *Measures of weights*. Gram and its intrinsic knowledge. Multiples and sub-multiples of gram. Effective measures and their intrinsic knowledge. Choosing and changing the unit. Roman and Roberval balances or weighing scales.
- Relation between the measures of volume, of weight and of capacity. Practice on these relations. Various problems.
- *Elementary Practical Geometry*: Intrinsic notions of figure, volume, surface line and point. Curved and plane surface.
- *Straight line, broken line or curved line*. To trace with a thread and a piece of chalk a straight line in any board which is claimed as "serar" How to draw a straight line of great dimensions for measuring of lands with a metric scale. Vertical, horizontal line. How to determine whether a line is horizontal in a construction by means of a thread of "prumo". How to determine the horizontal with the mason's Spirit Level.
- Spirit Level of a bubble of air. Idea of the Spirit Level with water; how it works. Parallel lines, perpendiculars and obliques. Angles, Polygons. Regular and irregular polygons; their names, as per the number of sides.
- Triangles and quadrilaterals.
- The "Professors" had also to show the students by means of polygons cut out from cardboards of different colours the triangles, hexagons and squares and these combined with regular octagons without keeping intervals as these geometrical forms are many times used for floors and for pavements, etc.

- The lady "Professors" would be able to similarly show the girl students so that it would help them when they had to make bed sheets, bags, etc., from the remnants of the cloth which could not be used for anything else. With the indicated Geometric forms they could have been taught to prepare an article that could be used in the house, useful and nice.
- *Circumference, circle and centre.* Practical way of tracing a circumference. Ray, diameter, chord, tangent and secant. Arc and the circular sector. Division of circumference into squares and degrees. Protractor and its applications.

- *Chorography*: Demonstration of the shape of the earth. The rising and setting of the sun. Day and night. Relation between the year, month, week, day, hour, minute and second. Leap year and normal year. A solar day and a civil day. Elementary knowledge of the word Geography, administered through models, stamps, maps or designs on slates that the students have already acquired through their knowledge of their locality where they were living or those which they had visited.The following then should be taken up:
  - Division of the world into five parts. Oceans. Situation of the Hispanic peninsula, of the continent of Portugal, the adjacent islands and the overseas possessions, especially of "India Portuguesa". Division into Provinces; their limits shown on the maps. Administrative divisions of continental Portugal, islands and overseas possessions. Capitals and important cities. Mountains, rivers, ports and important capes.
  - The geographic meaning of "India Portuguesa". The main rivers, ports, mountains, streets, rail lines, capes, islands and frontiers.
  - Administrative, ecclesiastic, military and judicial divisions of India. Cities, towns and important possessions. Production and population.
- *History*: Foundation of Monarchy—Ruling dynasties in Portugal and names of Portuguese Kings. Notable events during the reign of D. Afonso Henriques, D. Diniz, D. Joao I—Discovery of Brazil—D. Joao IV and D.Pedro IV—Campaign for liberty. History of India Portuguesa.
- *Grammar*: Simple exercises in grammatical analysis of passages in prose. Verbs, nouns, adjectives, prepositions, adverbs,

conjuctions and interjections. Practical exercises on Orthography.

Syllabi in Mixed (Vernacular and Portuguese) Schools

Besides the Portuguese schools there were also Marathi-Portuguese and Gujarati-Portuguese schools. The former were mostly located in the New Conquests and the latter ones in Daman and Diu. Being mixed schools obviously the programmes in these schools were tailored as per the specific needs of the students attending these schools. Probably this might have been one of the first attempts in the world to introduce the bilingual method of teaching. Consequently the Programme/syllabus enforced in the schools was different as can be seen from the following. In Class I the topics were as follows:

- *Reading*: Study of alphabet, rules of syllable formation, habituating the students to a correct pronunciation and explaining to them the sounds of the vowels and the consonants. Oral Reading, done slowly in the first and the second book of Gujarati; oral exercises of spelling some words of a seen passage.
- *Writing*: Characters, syllables, words and numerals in block letters on the slate.
- *Arithmetic*: Counting of numbers. Tables of multiplication up to 20.

The same topics were continued also in Class II. However, the amount of content had increased and more work was allotted to the students as can be gauged from the following:

- *Reading*: Oral Reading from the third and the fourth books. Recitation of passages from these books. Understanding the meaning.
- *Writing*: This was done on a notebook or copybook in Gujarati handwriting, in big letters. Dictation exercises in Gujarati of the seen passage.
- *Arithmetic*: Oral counting and writing of whole numbers. Four fundamental operations on the whole numbers: addition, subtraction, multiplication and division.
- *Geography*: Definition of Geography. Idea of the shape of the earth. Division of the world into five parts. Ocean and its division. Chorography of "India Portuguesa".

In Class III the same topics more or less were persisted with but as usual with an increased emphasis on the subject matter as can be seen from the following:

- *Reading*: Oral Reading from book 5 to 6 in Gujarati characters and Balbodh for Marathi schools. Recitation of passages from the same books. Understanding the meaning.
- *Writing*: Writing on the copybook some cursive lines in small letters and medium letters. Dictation in Gujarati from the books read.
- *Arithmetic*: Operations on complex numbers. Addition, subtraction and multiplication of fractions in Gujarati called "Ampane". Measures, weights and Luso-Indian currency.
- *Geography*: Situation, limits, administrative divisions, judicial, military and ecclesiastic divisions of Portugal and its colonies, seeing their respective maps. Geographic nomenclature of India Portuguesa; main rivers, ports, mountains, streets, railways, capes and frontiers. Mountains, rivers, ports, capes and important cities of Portugal and its colonies.
- *Grammar*: Definition of Grammar. Orthography. Lexicology. Grammatical classification of words; idea of nouns, of gender, and number of nouns, formation of plural of nouns in general; irregular formation of feminine; knowledge and use of the seven cases in declensions.
- *Drawing*: Elementary notions of linear drawing.

The "Professor" will make known to the students in Portuguese the Grammar terms and the terms in other subjects used in the Gujarati language.

There was a different set of subjects in Class IV. As per the school structure Class IV was the end of "Primeiro grau". Hence, an attempt was made to sort of round off the whole course keeping in view the subjects covered under the "Primeiro grau" syllabus of Portuguese schools. The following subjects comprised the syllabus of Class IV in Gujarati and Marathi schools:

- *Reading and Writing*: Reading from the prescribed text, nouns, articles, adjectives, as qualificatives, the Gujarati characters and Balbodh letters from Book VII. Feelings expressed in the Gujarati and Balbodh characters.
- *Calligraphy*: Perfection of letters.

- *Arithmetic*: Division into "ampane". Highest common factor (HCF). Least Common Multiple (LCM). Operations on decimal fractions. Correspondence between the measures, weights, currency Luso-Indian and of the metric system.
- *Decimal metric system*: Measures of length, of surface, of capacity and of volume. Stere.
- *Chorography*: The Constitutional Charter of Portuguese Monarchy. The Organic Charter of the Overseas Provinces. Form of Government and dominant religion in Portugal. Population and production of Portugal and its colonies.
- *History*: Founding of the Portuguese Monarchy. Ruling dynasties in Portugal and names of the Portuguese kings. Major events during the reign of D. Afonso Henriques, D. Diniz, D. Joao I—Discovery of Brazil—D. Joao IV and D.Pedro IV—Campaign for liberty. History of "India Portuguesa" especially of Daman and Diu.
- *Grammar*: Simple exercises on grammatical analysis of the seen passages in Class. Verb, noun, adjective, preposition, adverb, conjunction, and interjection. Practical exercises on Orthography.
- *Drawing*: Drawing with pencil such common objects as furnitures, utensils in school, of kitchen, etc., by looking at them.

In Class III and IV the students had to translate from their respective Gujarati or Marathi books of Reading, passages into Portuguese as per the terms of the regulations which the "Professor" had to enforce during the Class hours by adopting the conversational approach which would make the students listen to Portuguese sentences, try to understand them and then try to speak in Portuguese though evaluation would be done in Gujarati.

Pre-scribing of Textbooks

In June 1907, the Minister, Ayres de Ornelhas de Vasconcelhos issued a notification prescribing the different textbooks to be followed in the schools. The various stipulations were as follows:

- In all Primary schools whether in the Overseas Provinces or in the autonomous district of Timor the officially approved books should be adopted for a common system of education whose term would be six years.

- During the first period of their prescription the Government would call for bids from writers of textbooks for those regions having differences of race, economic conditions, special features, etc. However these had to be approved as textbooks for particular Classes by the Consultative Committee of the Overseas Affairs.
- The Government would lay down the form and the conditions for the bids which would be executed by the Governor and inform the Directorate General of the Overseas Affairs.
- The selection of the books had to be done by the Inspectorate of Schools wherever these had been established or else by a Committee appointed for this purpose by the Governor. The list then had to be published on the "Boletim Oficial".
- In case the books were exhausted or in case of any other calamity the Governor had to make additional copies available to the public.

Conversion of Schools Into Co-education

By 1912, after Portugal had declared itself a Republic there were three types of schools as far as the composition of students was concerned: the boys', the girls' and the co-education. And within no time because the enrolment figures were always coming down in the girls' schools all the schools were converted into co-education schools by the "Portaria Provincial" No. 965 dated 16 November, 1921. Under the reforms of 1912, more such schools were started. But as stated earlier by 1921, all schools had been converted into co-education.

We know that earlier there were schools which would teach only up to the First Level and there were others which would teach up to the Second Level. The Republican Government which had taken over the reins of power in Portugal had decided to make education both secular and universal. Accordingly by a Decree No. 504 in 1913, it converted all schools teaching up to the Second Level to co-education. The first such co-education school was opened in the village of Merces not far from the capital city of Pangim in June 1913. In the latter half of 1913 the Portuguese Government by a Decree issued on the 8th of April, 1913 created twenty new schools, 19 of which were located in Goa their number taluka-wise was as follows:

1. Canacona 03
2. Ponda 03
3. Pernem 03

4. Quepem 03
5. Saguem 03
6. Bicholim 02
7. Sattari 02

The Government enjoined upon the school authorities to open these schools as fast as possible within a period of two months. With the declaration of the Republic the Government seemed to be in an unholy haste presumably trying to make up for lost time because the education levels in Portugal were one of the lowest in Europe which on hindsight was one of the major reasons for the backwardness of the country.

In May 1913, the Governor, Francisco Manuel Couceiro da Costa issued a "Portaria" stating that henceforth a teaching licence would be required for "Professors" of private Primary schools besides having a Diploma of a course of Superior education or Secondary or Theology studies or a Certificate of the course of "Escola Normal". Those who were in service without the licence had to obtain one within a period of five years from the date of the above publication or else they would be sacked from their jobs. However, those who had the Certificate of competency which had been conferred on them as per the earlier legislations could continue teaching.

The Council of Public Instruction and its Functions

In order to manage the growing number of schools and school personnel the Government started taking more interest in its administration. In October 1918, the Secretary General Francisco M.Peixoto Vieira issued regulations regarding the constitution of the Council of Public Instruction after it was decreed by the Governor General, Jose de Freitas Ribeiro (1917-19) in 1917. It underwent some changes understandably with a view to giving it a wider representation. The composition, functions, duties, etc., were as follows:

The Council would comprise of three experts representing Arts and Sciences nominated by the Governor and six elected members, one from Medical School, one from Commercial Institute, one from the "Escola Normal", one representing the Primary Teachers and two from Lyceum for a period of three years. All had to be permanent "Professors" from Nova Goa (Panaji) except the Primary Teacher who could be from any part of Goa and hence was paid a travelling allowance of Rs. 3. All others were treated as honorary members. However, they were entitled for leave on the day of the sessions. Those from Nova Goa, capital city were entitled for one day and from outside the city were entitled for two days leave.

The procedure to elect the members of the Council too was laid down. They were to be conducted by the respective Directors in the institutions. In the case of Primary Teachers they were to be held at the Municipal centres. All Primary Teachers, ordinary, extraordinary, regular, substitutes, part time and assistants could vote by secret ballot. The votes were sealed, stamped and sent to the Council's office which would open them, count them and communicate the results to the respective heads. If there was a need for re-election, that too would be communicated. In case of a tie the seniormost candidate would be declared elected.

The Council once constituted had intrinsic magisterial powers. There were two types of sessions, ordinary and extraordinary. Ordinary sessions were held before the 5th of every month. Extraordinary sessions would be called for only if some special circumstances warranted them. No session could take place without the President or Vice President and without a majority of the members being present. The officials of the Inspecting Council or of the Directorate had to attend the meetings if thought necessary for the sake of providing information whenever required.

The Council's members would be divided into three Committees, one for Primary and Teacher education, one for Secondary and Special education and the third for Superior or Higher education.

The members of the first Committee would comprise of the teachers of Primary schools, the teacher from "Escola Normal" and one of the "Professors" from "Lyceum" who would also be the President of this Committee. The second Committee would look after the affairs of the Secondary and Special instruction. This would comprise of the remaining elected "Professor" from Lyceum, the "Professor" from Medical school, and the elected "Professor" from the Commercial Institute and one of the nominated members who would preside over the Committee. Lastly the Committee to look after the Superior instruction would comprise of the "Professor" from Medical school, and the remaining two nominated members one of them acting as the President.

Thereafter the rules for the conduct of business during the meetings were laid down. Any decision to hold good had to be carried by a majority vote. If any presentation had to be made then the President would fix the date, time and venue for its discussion. The documents would be sent to all the members before the day of the discussion. No member could keep the resolution for more than 48 hours. No member could speak during the meeting without the permission of the Chair and no member could be allowed to speak for more than three times on the same topic unless it was the reporter or the proposer. The issues submitted to the Council had to be accompanied by all the relevant information from the departments and the required documents for proper deliberation. The minutes of the meetings had to be recorded and then signed by the President and all the members present for the meeting.

All sessions would commence with the reading of the minutes of the previous meeting which would then be approved and signed. This would be followed by the reading and distribution of the correspondence and other urgent matters. Then the discussion would start on the items listed on the agenda of the day. In case of extraordinary sessions the issue would be immediately and seriously dealt with.

The following duties were assigned to the President:

- To assist in conducting the sessions.
- To propose the items for discussion and control the proceedings, conduct the voting and announce the results.
- To maintain order during discussion.
- To implement or order to be implemented the rules and regulations related to public instruction.
- To give charge to the new members and announce the induction of new members and the Secretary into the Council.
- To convene the extraordinary sessions.
- To distribute the documents and the agenda to the members concerned.

In the absence of the President, the Vice President nominated by the Governor from among the members would take the place of the President. The duties of the members were listed as follows:

- To attend and participate in the sessions both ordinary and extraordinary.
- To propose, indicate, and contribute to the progress of education and carry out the functions of the Council.
- To ask in the meetings for clarifications and informations needed in the discharge of his duties.
- To write projects and reports and replies to issues assigned to him.

One of the members was appointed as the rapporteur. This reporter had the following duties entrusted to him:

- To prepare the agenda items and to carry out the duties assigned to him.

- To provide to the Secretary of the Council all the necessary documents, informations and documents or any other work and clarifications required for the understanding or explaining the issues.
- To propose to the Council any action required to be taken pertaining to this section.
- To request for an extraordinary meeting when certain urgent issue was to be discussed.
- To give his opinion in writing on any issue after thorough examination referred to him.
- To participate in the discussions.

The Secretary of the Council held the pivotal position in the organization with the following functions and duties coming under his purview:

- The Secretary was nominated by the Governor from among the officials of the General Secretariat on an annual remuneration of 60 "reis".
- He had to assist in all the sessions, read the correspondence, attend to the other paper work and present information and clarifications which he should obtain from the Government or from any of the members of the Council.
- He had to write the minutes of the meetings and also do any other work assigned by the Council.
- To present in the correct format the issues to be debated in the meetings.
- To sign in the name of the Council or the President any correspondence of urgent nature.
- Get any information or clarification from any public office required by the reporters.
- To take down point-wise the deliberations and decisions of the members of the Council and of the instructions of the President.
- To maintain the books of Minutes, inward/outward register and record the distribution of the items.

The Council was obviously constituted for certain specific purposes namely as an apex advisory and supervisory authority. Definitely it had a very important role to perform in the overall educational set-up. Hence some very important functions were assigned to it some of which were as follows:

- To recommend titles of books of literary, artistic and scientific value.
- To propose steps needed to be taken for the progress of education.
- To carry out extraordinary inspections of institutions under their purview.
- To decide upon the proposals of the Governor presented to the Governor's Council either on the general organization or any of the branches of education, to examine the projects for the framing of rules, general or special, to examine the proposals for setting up of institutions, to decide upon the admission, examination, Diploma and Certificate fees, to recommend the list of textbooks to be followed or prohibited in the institutions, to direct the institutions to adopt the teaching methodology as well as the teaching programmes, and the subjects to be taught, to draw up the conditions for the appointment of Primary Teachers and setting up of private schools, to frame rules for the appointment, promotion, transfer and interviews of Primary Teachers, conditions and penalties for the suspension, transfer or dismissal of "Professors", to review the decisions of the School Councils regarding penalties and expulsion, to settle conflicts regarding jurisdiction, to give permission to strangers to teach or open schools and to decide on all matters on which it was consulted or empowered by law.
- To prescribe after proper examination books approved by the Governor for use in the Primary schools and the "Escola Normal" for a period of six years. The books were at first kept open for public scrutiny for a period of not less than six months.
- To allow any of the members to develop any teaching learning material.
- To take up matters only after the School Councils had been consulted.

Every now and then educational Administration was being altered so as to strengthen it. By a "Diploma Legislativo" dated 29th June, 1923, the Directorate of Instruction (Direccao dos Services de Instruccao) was created. Subsequently a couple of years later in 1925, the Governor General, Jaime Alberto de Castro Morais (1919-1925) changed it into the Department of Primary Education (Reparticao de Instruccao Primaria) and integrated it with the General Secretariat.

By now the Prime Minister, Antonio de Oliveira Salazar had assumed the dicatatorial role and taken full control of Portugal and so in 1933 he completely revamped and re-established the whole administrative set-up in the colonies detailing the positions, hierarchy, duties, areas of jurisdiction, disciplinary actions and division of labour between the central administration and the provinces. The massive tome ran into five parts with the first part having eight chapters, the second part three, the third part with six chapters, the fourth part with only three and the fifth with four chapters. The Governor was of course the highest authority in the colony.

A Primary Teacher's Typical Calendar of Activities

The annual calendar of activities of a "Professor" in the Primary school would be as follows:

June

1. First day—Reopening of schools.
2. 10th to the 15th—Admissions of students to various Classes with proper documents and charging the prescribed fees.
3. 15th—Submit in the Department of Instruction the salary bills of the school personnel accompanied by the duty certificate of the previous month by keeping a copy of the documents in the school records.
4. 16th—Hold the final examinations of the first three Classes through a duly appointed jury of "Professors" as per the established rules and also register those who were being admitted for the first time in Classes II, III and IV upon payment of necessary fees.Meeting of the School Council for the distribution of Classes, the school time table and giving assent to the bases of direction to be given to the teaching.
5. After 16th—Submit a copy of the minutes of the meeting to the Department of Primary Instruction along with the record of admissions, promotions, etc. Enlisting of the members both ordinary and full-fledged of the School Benefit Fund and collecting the allotted quantum of funds from this date to the end of the year.

July

1. Day one—Meeting of the School Benefit Fund General

Assembly to decide the admission test of students to be enrolled in the four Classes and to enroll members and fix the quota for the month.

2. Till the 5th—To send to the Department of Primary Instruction the monthly chart of attendance by keeping a copy in the school.
3. Till the 15th—Send the salary bills to the Department along with the duty certificate.

August to October

1. First day—Admission test for students to be enrolled in the first four Classes. Enlisting of members and fixing the quota.
2. Till the 5th—Submitting the monthly attendance report.
3. Till the 15th—Submitting the salary bills.

November

Meeting of the Committee on School Benefit Fund.

1. First day—Admission test, test for promotion, enlisting of members.
2. Till the 5th—Submitting the attendance report.
3. Till the 15th—Submitting the salary bills.

December

1. 2nd day—Admission test and enlisting of members
2. Till the 5th—Submission of the monthly attendance report.
3. Submission of salary bills.

January

1. 7th day—Admission test in only the first-three Classes and enlisting of members of School Benefit fund.
2. Till the 5th—Submission of the monthly attendance report.
3. Till the 15th—Submission of salary bills.
4. Till the 15th to the 20th—Issuing of attendance certificate by the "Professors" appointing as members of the examination Jury.

February

1. First day—Admission test of students in the first three Classes and enlisting of members.
2. Till the 5th—Submission of the monthly attendance report.
3. Till the 15th—Submission of salary bills.
4. From 10th to the 20th—Submission of list in triplicate of candidates for the examination of First level.
5. From 15th to the 28th—Submission of list in duplicate of candidates for the examination of Second level with all necessary documents.

March

1. First day—Admission test of students of the first-three Classes and registering of members.
2. Till the 5th—Submission of the monthly attendance report.
3. Till the 15th—Submission of salary bills.
4. 15th—Closing of Classes.
5. Till the 30th—Submission of all accounts to the Accounts Department.

April

1. Month of final examination of the Second level.
2. Till the 5th—Submission of attendance report in dulicate along with the receipts and the attendance certificates in triplicate.
3. Till the 15th—Submission of salary bills.

May

1. Till the 14th—Submission of salary bills. The record of students (those who joined or left) of the year just ended and the budget for the coming year.

VIII
The Great Push Forward (1929-1950)

Earlier we had seen how education had made slow progress going by the number of schools and the enrolment figures. Though the education saga began with six Primary schools in 1831 by the end of the century they had increased to only 105 which included 88 Portuguese, 10 Gujarati and 7 Marathi with a total of 3,895 students attending Classes in the Portuguese schools and another 131 and 309 attending Marathi and Gujarati respectively. Another 20 years later that is by 1920-21 the scene was looking a little bit healthier after the Government introduced a slew of measures to promote education more aggressively in the "Estado da India Portuguesa" after the declaration of the Republic with around 150 schools of Portuguese and around 74 Marathi schools—this included the privately run schools too — and another 20 schools in Gujarati. The total number of students enrolled in the above schools was around 10,000.

A Few Enrolment Statistics

The slow progress can also be gauged from the following statistics shown in Table 8.1:

Foundations for the Further Promotion of Education

In 1927, the then Governor Pedro Francisco Massano de Amorim issued a "Diploma Legislativa" on the 16th of September spelling out the foundations for the promotion of education in the "Estado da India Portuguesa" keeping in view the peculiarities of the place realizing that the form adopted in Portugal could not be ditto copied in Goa.

He laid down the following foundations:

- *Base I*: In the Estado da India there would be Primary, Secondary, Special and Superior education.

Table 8.1: The Enrolment Scenario in 1920

Sr. No.	*Provinces*	*Portuguese/Marathi/Gujarati*		
		1900	*1920*	*1950*
01	Pernem	85	136	121
02	Bardez	1411	2679	1048
03	Sattari	30	66	87
04	Sanqueli/Bicholim	135	343	239
05	Ponda	197	301	436
06	Ilhas	703	1765	2381
07	Salcette	1160	—	4296
08	Quepem	102	196	216
09	Sanguem	40	82	167
10	Canacona	63	129	261
11	Mormugao	—	496	678
12	Daman	—	—	—
13	Diu	—	—	—
14	Dadra & Nagar Haveli	—	—	—

- *Base* II: Primary education in Portuguese language would have two Levels (degrees—graus): the first one having four Classes and the second one having the fifth Class, in accordance with the regimen already followed in the State, adapting the programmes of Portugal to the regional needs, joining to them the brief notions of History of Portuguese India and giving a convenient extension to the programmes of Class I so that they could learn practically and intuitively the Portuguese language keeping in mind above all that they had to learn to read, write and count and maintaining the remaining subjects of the syllabus in the form of lessons. The general regime to be adopted in the schools was co-education.
- *Base* III: There would be examinations at the end of the First and the Second Level. The examinations of the First Level had to be conducted in the premises of the official Primary schools by a Jury comprising of three members under the chairmanship of the local representative with one citizen nominated by the Government and a "Professor" who may be from the official school or from a private school. The examinations of the Second Level would take place in the premises of the respective provincial headquarters.
    - The Juries for the examinations of the Second Level had to be presided over by evidently capable persons with one permanent for the place and the other to go from place to

place. The permanent member would be a "Professor" from the official school and the mobile one would be from the private school who had either qualified through "Escola Normal" or had a legal title (Certificate) to be working as a private teacher of the Primary Level as per rules in force.

- The "Professors" holding a Diploma from the "Escola Normal" had to for this purpose apply to the Department of Primary Instruction to be included in the list by presenting a copy of the Diploma which would be returned to him.
- The list of the candidates as well as the members of the Jury of both the Levels would be organized without any distinction between the students of the official Primary schools and the private schools in such a manner that the candidates would have in the Jury a respective "Professor".

- *Base* IV: The teaching of the Marathi and Gujarati languages would be checked by the Government and organized in keeping with the "Diploma Legislativo" No. 103 of the 7th of November,1924, obliging the Government to proceed with the organization of the syllabus providing as much choice as possible for the adoption of books in Marathi and Gujarati as may be adopted in these schools.
  - With regard to the appointment of "Professors" to the vacant posts or to the posts in the Marathi and Gujarati Primary schools there had to be public interviews (tests) among Portuguese citizens.
  - The inspection of the schools had to be done by well-qualified persons knowing well the languages in which education was being imparted.
  - Private instruction in Marathi, Gujarati and Urdu organized under the model of official instruction would be subsidized by the Government when the Directors of these schools were Portuguese citizens or these schools were maintained by institutions whose statutes had been approved by the Government. These grants would be given only when they fulfilled the financial conditions of the State.
- *Base* V: In order to facilitate the pedagogical improvement of the "Professors" of Primary schools and help in the establishment of Primary schools and model kindergartens "Professors" would be sent from this colony (read Goa)—not more than three at a time—at the cost of the Government after being selected to the

National pedagogical centres or foreign centres to undergo courses of improvement which could not be for more than two years. In such a case the "Professors" upon their return would have to continue in their previous post and scale. They also had to present a report of their work and they had to serve the State for at least ten more years.

- *Base* VI: It refers to Secondary education.
- *Base* VII: It refers to the courses under Political Economy, Direct Administration, Marathi, Sanskrit, etc.
- *Base* VIII: It refers to Special Education.
- *Base* IX: It refers to Vocational studies.
- Base X: It refers to Superior/Higher Education.
- Base XI: The Special Diplomas awarded with the prior sanction of the Council of Public Instruction would help in regulating the functioning of all the establishments of education in this colony as well as all the free and private teaching. Those regulations which were bound to change the actual form of teaching had to be submitted to the sanction of the Council of the Government who would decide on the part related to the salaries of the "Professors" either permanent or on contract.

Enrolment Figures Five Years Later

Table 8.2 shows giving details of the Primary schools established up to 1925:

Recruiting Teachers Officially

In August 1928, another "Diploma Legislativo" was promulgated by the same Governor, Pedro Francisco Massano de Amorim, in which he laid down the rules of recruitment for the posts of "Professors" of Primary education which were as follows:

- The schools had to be divided into three categories: (a) Schools located in the provinçial (Concelhos) headquarters of Ilhas, Salcette, Bardez and Mormugao; (b) Those located in the headquarters of other provinces; and (c) Those located in all the remaining places.
- The appointment of candidates with professional Diplomas would be done in a school of the third category through a written test to fill up any vacancy resulting from a transfer to the other categories.

Table 8.2: A Complete View of Primary Schools established up to 1925

Sr. No.	Village	Location	Year of establishment/ transfer	Remarks	P.P. No.	Local Representative	No. of Teachers
01.	Aldona	Tercena	14/11/1842 & 21/04/1881(girls)	—	1470 &248	Dr. Honorato Elvino de Souza	02
02.	Anjuna	Tembi	14/11/1842 & 31/05/1855 (girls)	Had two houses	1470 & 15	Adv. Caetano Marian Vas	02
03.	Assagao	Centrai	24/08/1912	Had boys and girls school same year	Decree	Bras Antonio de Souza Ticlo	02
04.	Assolda	Gudem	24/08/1912	—	Decree	Chondru Sadashiv Sinai Cheldencar	01
05.	Assolna	Culmoroda	16/10/1841	—	1951	Francisco Xavier Antonio de R.Monteiro	
06.	Benaulim	Pulvaddo	17/08/1841 24/08/1912	Boys and then girls	No number. Decree	Dr.Felipe Joaquim Velho	03
07.	Betalbatim	Pocvaddo	02/12/1870	—	Despacho	Adv. Rodolfo J.V.Crasto Menezes	02
08.	Bicholim	Bitoliput	14/11/1842 & 24/08/1912	Boys and Girls	1469 & Decree	Xencoro Sinai Colvalcar	02
09.	Borim	Tolopa	16/11/1921	—	965	Jose 10Francisco Rodrigues	02
10.	Calangute	Naikavaddo	17/08/1841 then 31/05/1855 from 09/11/1854 and 09/09/1878	First came the First Level school then the Second Level and then the girls school	No number given. 65. Not given. 357.	Adv. Pedro Antonio de Souza	03

(Contd.)

TABLE 8.2 (*Contd.*)

Sr. No.	*Village*	*Location*	*Year of establishment/ transfer*	*Remarks*	*P.P. No.*	*Local Representative*	*No. of Teachers*
11.	Calvim	Calvim	19/09/1916	—	36	Dr. Honorato Elvino de Souza	01
12.	Camarcazana	Pedem	09/09/1881	—	504	Tome Martinho de Souza	01
13.	Canacona	Chaudi	14/11/1842 & 14/12/1880 & 08/02/1882	Created then again and then allotted the place	1470 Decree 08	Adv. Francisci Antonio Rodrigues	01
14.	Candolim	Pintosvaddo	14/11/1842 & 07/10/1910	Boys then girls	1470 369	Francisco Antonio das Dores e Sa	02
15.	Cansaulim	Near Rly station	05/08/1852	—	72	Lencastre Pereira de Andrade	02
16.	Carmona	Siro-Alemao	14/11/1842 and 05/08/1852 & 24/08/1912	Closed down twice	1470 92 Decree	Andre Socorro de Noronha	02
17.	Cavelossim	Fonsavaddo	22/07/1899 & 14/05/1907	—	272 & 125	Aniceto Assuncao Dias	02
18.	Chandor	Cavorim	13/05/1852 & 05/08/1852	Boys and girls	62 & 92	Adv. Antonio Francisco de Santana Pereira	02
19.	Chinchinim	Igrejavaddo	17/08/1841 & 05/01/1882 & 31/12/1892	Elementary. Girls. Elementary and Complementary	No Number. 14. 787.	Dr. Antonio Simplicio dos Barros Dias	02

(*Contd.*)

TABLE 8.2 (*Contd.*)

Sr. No.	*Village*	*Location*	*Year of establishment/ transfer*	*Remarks*	*P.P. No.*	*Local Representative*	*No. of Teachers*
20.	Chorao	Boktavaddo	11/06/1895	Transferred from Mandur	399	Pe. Jose Libanio Paes	02
21.	Colva	Primeirobairro	17/08/1841	—	No number	Dr. Jose Vicente Hipolito de Santana Mascarenhas	02
22.	Colvale	Mazalvaddo	05/09/1831 14/11/1842 06/09/1875	The First school was closed down in 1841 and then restarted. Then came the girls school.	531 1470 & 136	Adv. Jose Maria Lobo	02
23.	Cortalim	Povoacao	13/05/1852 & 05/08/1852	Was not functional in May	62 & 92	Pe. Pascoal Manuel da Piedade Gomes	01
24.	Cumbharjua	Mologanta	31/12/1892	—	787	Lucio Fermiano de Sa	03
25.	Corlim	Igrejavaddo	7/10/1910	—	369	Feleciano Querobino T.V.Sequeira	01
26.	Cuncolim	Igrejavaddo	25/01/1871	—	Despacho	Jose Cassio Inocencio Fernandes	02
27.	Curchorem	Curchorem	27/05/1899	Transferred from Tilamolla	201	Pe. Francisco Alcuino dos Remedios Costa	01
28.	Curtorim	Povoacao	14/11/1842 & 07/10/1910	Boys and Girls	1470 369	Dr. Lubin Peres da Costa	02
29.	Dhargalim	Arabo	22/05/1879	Transferred from Parsem	276	Dr. Caxinata Laad	01
30.	Dramapur	Not given	15/01/1914	—	34	Dr. Jose Camilo Roque Dias	01

(*Contd.*)

TABLE 8.2 (*Contd.*)

Sr. No.	Village	Location	Year of . establishment/ transfer	Remarks	P.P. No.	Local Representative	No. of Teachers
31.	Durbhatt	Durbhatt	07/10/1884	Transferred from Kundaim	498	Rudraji Bascora Naique Pratap Rau	01
32.	Goa Velha	Salaria	14/11/1842 &24/08/1912	—	1470	Dr. Jose Antonio Octaviano Rodrigues	01
33.	Guirim	Monte de Gurim	21/02/1881	—	135	Pedro Caetano do Rosario de Souza	01
34.	Loutulim	Igrejavaddo	14/11/1842 & 24/08/1912	Boys and Girls	1470 Decree	Dr. Caetano Gracias	02
35.	Macasana	Macdem	24/08/1912	—	Decree	Dr. Fidelis Antonio Fernandes	01
36.	Majorda	Godinhovaddo	14/11/1842	—	1470	Adv. Inacio Xavier Trifonio Godinho	02
37.	Mapuca	Khorlim	17/08/1841 14/11/1842 & 17/08/1841	Announced in 1841 but functioned from 1842. The girls school started functioning only from 1854 with the appointment of the teacher	Not mentioned. 1470. Again not mentioned.	Lucas Antonio Bras de Sa	03
38.	Marcaim	Odal	16/11/1921	—	965	Anant Givotoma Camotim	01
39.	Marcela	Marcela	14/12/1880 16/11/1921 28/06/1922	Created, closed down and re-opened	Decree 965 798	Siurama P.S.Amonkar	01
40.	Mardol	Mardol	25/07/1921	—	583	Joaquim Bernard Misquita	01

(*Contd.*)

TABLE 8.2 (*Contd.*)

Sr. No.	*Village*	*Location*	*Year of establishment/ transfer*	*Remarks*	*P.P. No.*	*Local Representative*	*No. of Teachers*
41.	Margao	Northern road	05/09/1831 & 14/11/1842 & 17/08/1841	Boys in military barracks then Liceu bldg. Girls	531 1470 12	Adv. Lazaro Gonzaga Faleiro	05
42.	Merces	Carmichembhatt	25/04/1913	—	206	Dr. Jose Irineu A. dos R.Furtado	02
43.	Moira	Alto do oiteiro	29/09/1879	—	640	Caetano Fidelis da Gama	02
44.	Morjim	Modlo vaddo	24/08/1912		Decree	Dr. Tedoro de Souza	04
45.	Mulgao	Pardi	22/04/1842 & 16/11/1907 & 1/10/1925	Opened then closed then reopened	No number then 1967 then 840	Xanum Raugi Sinai Mulgaonkar	01
46.	Nachinola	Vangar	11/09/1923	—	Despacho	Olenzorio Jeremias de S. Rita Lobo	01
47.	Nagoa (Bardez)	Arpora	14/11/1842 26/07/1913	First order cancelled and then reestablished in 1913	1470 then 398	Adv. Jose Sergio Xavier do Rego	02
48.	Nagoa (Salcette0	Capelavaddo	11/03/1914 & (03/07/1921) & 26/05/1925	Closed down once	125 313 438	Joaquim Salvador de Noronha	01
49.	Navelim	Navelim (small)	17/08/1841	—	Not given	Roque Santan Piquito Cardoso	03
50.	Nerul	Fottavaddo	24/08/1912	—	Decree	Lourenco J.M. Mendonca	02

(*Contd.*)

TABLE 8.2 (*Contd.*)

Sr. No.	*Village*	*Location*	*Year of establishment/ transfer*	*Remarks*	*P.P. No.*	*Local Representative*	*No. of Teachers*
51.	Neura	Igrejavaddo	07/03/1882	—	154	Adv. Aquino Jose de Noronha	02
52.	Nuvem (Salcette)	Beloy	07/10/1905	Transferred from Rivona	299	Adv. Jose Napoleao de Menezes	01
53.	Orlim	Sambate	26/08/1899	Transferred from Carmona	301	Jose Gaspar Gomes	02
54.	Pangim	Fontainhas & Camara bldg. (2 schools)	05/09/1831 & 17/08/1841 effective on 12/02/1846	One for boys and the other for girls	531 & 105	Adv. Francisco Xavier de Miranda	06
55.	Parra	Balemvaddo	17/08/1841 21/02/1881	For boys and for girls	No Number 135	Dr. Sebastiao Jose da Graca e Costa	02
56.	Pernem	Nanoda	14/11/1842 & 23/12/1913	Boys and Girls	1469 & 625	Sripad Sinai Telinga	01
57.	Piedade	Goltim	14/11/1842 & 31/12/1892 (two Levels) 14/11/1909 (girls)	—	1470, 787 307	Custodio Vicente Gomes Pereira	03
58.	Pilerne	Moicovaddo	17/07/1878	—	303	Dr. Cosme Valerio Inacio Delgado	02
59.	Pomburpa	Golnavaddo	24/08/1912	—	Decree	Dr. Feleciano de Vila Nova Lobo	01
60.	Ponda	Cassabe	14/11/1842 31/12/1892	Single and then both Levels	1470 787	Dr. Felizardo Lourenco do Rosario Hercules de Almeida	02

(*Contd.*)

TABLE 8.2 (*Contd.*)

Sr. No.	*Village*	*Location*	*Year of establishment/ transfer*	*Remarks*	*P.P. No.*	*Local Representative*	*No. of Teachers*
61.	Quepem	Sirvoi	14/11/1842	Created	1470	Adv. Jose Luis de Souza	01
			15/07/1850	Closed down	No number		
			23/03/1863	Transferred from Loliem	44		
			24/08/1912	Girls school	Decree		
62.	Raia	Magilvaddo	14/11/1842	—	1470	Dr. Luis Caetano Elfistone de Melo	02
63.	Reis Magos	Ambecandem	13/05/1852	—	62	Ricardo Micael Teles	02
64.	Revora	Nadora	14/11/1842 21/11/1881 & 26/07/1913	Closed down twice and then finally opened in 1913	1470. 672. 397	Ornelas da Conceicao Pinto	01
65.	Ribandar	Nobres	05/09/1831 07/10/1910 (girls)	—	531 369	Dr. Antonio Sinval da Costa	02
66.	Saligao	Ararim	05/08/1852	—	92	Dr. Teodomiro das Neves Carvalho	02
67.	Sangolda	Mae de Dues	1923-24	—	Despatch of Governor	Napoleao Duarte	01
68.	Sanguem	Municipa Square	14/12/1880	—	Decree	Antonio Piedade Lourenco C. Fernandes	02
69.	Sanquelim	Administrative building area	14/11/1842	—	1649	Dr. Claudio V.B. de Albuquerque	01
70.	Santa Cruz	2nd Bairro	14/11/1842 & 24/09/1881 (girls)	—	52 529	Teofilo Eufemiano Xavier Pinto	03

(*Contd.*)

TABLE 8.2 (*Contd.*)

Sr. No.	*Village*	*Location*	*Year of establishment/ transfer*	*Remarks*	*P.P. No.*	*Local Representative*	*No. of Teachers*
71.	Santo Estevam	Mangueiral	14/11/1842 &24/08/1912 (girls)	—	1470 Decree O	Evencio Francisco Monteiro	03
72.	S. Lourenco (Agasaim)	Baixo de Igreja	24/07/1908	—	269	Lino Francisco Xavier Palha	01
73.	S. Pedro	Palmar Jumbo	14/11/1842	Functioned again from 1/10/1925 P.P. 839	1470	Joaquim Rafael dos Barreto	02
74.	Satari	Keri	16/11/1921	—	965	Jose A Maia de S. Menezes	02
75.	Seraulim	Not given	02/05/1861 12/08/1912	—	By A.C.D of the confraria and then Decree	Dr. Lasaro Agostinho da Costa	01
76.	Serula	Badem	14/11/1842 30/09/1855	Located First in Porvorim then shifted to Serula	1470. 89	Dr. Acurcio Rafael Fernandes Veloso	03
77.	Siolim	Bamonvaddo	05/08/1852 & 07/10/1910	Boys and Girls	92. 369	Antonio Jose Domingos de Sa	02
78.	Shiroda	Bazar	24/08/1912	—	Decree	Gopal C.S.Guddo	01
79.	Taleigao	Santissimo	30/09/1844	—	1174	Dr.Aleixo Honorato Xavier Martins	02
80.	Telaulim	Telaulim	16/11/1921	—	965	Jose Carmo de Azavedo	01

(*Contd.*)

TABLE 8.2 (*Contd.*)

Sr. No.	*Village*	*Location*	*Year of establishment/ transfer*	*Remarks*	*P.P. No.*	*Local Representative*	*No. of Teachers*
81.	Tivim	Igrejavaddo	05/08/1879	—	521	Dr. Angelo Manuel Nepomuceno de Sousa	01
82.	Tropa	Main roadside	23/09/1921 20/10/1925 30/01/1926	Transferred from Sarzora then closed down twice and finally reopened in 1926	780 894 65	Antonio Jose Domingos de Sa	01
83.	Ucassaim	Dumpem	13/05/1852 & 05/08/1852	Was not opened First time	62 92	Dr. Estevao Jeremias Mascarenhas	02
84.	Valpoi	Central place	14/11/1880 & 08/04/1886 & 05/04/1898	Opened and then transferred to Galgibaga and then reopened	Decree then 194 then 230	Antonio Jose dos Martires e Souza	01
85.	Varca	—	22/04/1926	—	291	Pe. Joaquim Francisco de Oliveira	01
86.	Vasco	National street	05/09/1899	Transferred from Vaddem	325	Vicente Alvares	03
87.	Velim	Zuino	15/12/1887 24/08/1912	Transferred from Balli. Then came girls school	807 Decree	Tentente cor Antonio Joao Mascarenhas	02
88.	Velsao	Igrejavaddo	24/08/1912	—	Decree	Marcelino Barreto	01
89.	Verna	Igrejavaddo	09/11/1854	Established in 1855 and approved in 1858	108 Decree 31	Adv. Francisco Joao de Melo	02

    - The first appointment of such a candidate would be considered provisional and would become regular only after a period of two years of effective service.
    - In the written test for the first appointment preference in the merit list would be given to those who had put in temporary service as per their length of service after taking into consideration the marks on the professional Diploma.
    - The temporary appointment would always be made of those candidates approved in the interview and as per the merit list prepared by the Jury.
- The vacancies that would occur at the Second and the First Levels would be filled through a written test among the permanent "Professors" of the schools in the Classes next below who had at least one year's experience in the following manner:
    - The merit list of the candidates after the written test, had to be prepared after adding the marks of the professional Diploma, points obtained for every five years' of experience and points for having obtained at least the remark "good" in the confidential report.
    - Those who had obtained the remarks 'good' and 'sufficient' would qualify for the written test.
    - Those who had not completed the course of "Escola Normal" would get one third of the marks less than those who had completed the first year of the old "Escola Normal" or two years of the present course.
    - The filling up of the vacancy in the higher Classes would be done only after the transfers through a written test in each category had been gone through.
    - While the actual regular "Professors" would continue in service for the vacancies in the schools of the first category they would be able to attend the interview simultaneously for the schools of the second and third category.
- The interview for the transfer of the "Professors" of the schools of the third category had to be as per the stipulations above.
    - As with the regular "Professors" the transfer of the provisional "Professors" would also be under the same rules.
- If during two successive years the provisional "Professor" had to get the remark "deficient" then he would be terminated in his service as a teacher.
    - The appointment of the provisional "Professor" would be

converted into a permanent one if he had obtained the remark "good" in the first two years or three remarks of "good" in a period of four years or else his services as a teacher would be terminated.

- The transfers and the promotions had to be done at the request of the interested except in cases of transfer on disciplinary grounds.
  - Every year in the first-fifteen days of March the general interview would be held for which an official announcement would be made by the Department of Primary Instruction. Those interested had to apply along with the documents which had not been submitted earlier and stored in the Department.
  - By the 15th of April the merit list had to be ready showing the marks of each candidate of the different categories of the schools as per the rules by the Department and had to be recorded in the service books and published in the "Boletim Oficial" for the sake of making any representation within a period of 15 days from the date of the publication.
  - The merit list drawn up by the Department of Primary Instruction would be approved or modified by the Governor and announced through a "Portaria" after consulting the Council of Public Instruction having presented to them all the criteria followed in drawing up the list and after going through the representations of the candidates.
  - In case there was a vacancy in any category the provision by transfer would come first announced within fifteen days in the respective category, to which the "Professors" of that category would appear for the interview after having submitted an application in which they had to mention the schools that they would prefer and the order of preference to which they had the right, producing the documents needed for the purpose after which the interview for the promotions would start proceeding in the same way as per the number of vacancies which had arisen in the category immediately lower than the previous.
  - In the same manner the interview for filling up the provisional and interim vacancies would be held as per rules.
  - In case no candidate appeared for any of the categories then the "Professors" belonging to the lower categories would

be admitted without taking into consideration the length of service and if the interview remains inconclusive the post had to be filled by a provisional "Professor" as per the terms of these regulations.

- With all things being the same preference regarding placement would be given in the following order of merit:
  - The local candidate.
  - The candidate who used to reside not more than five kilometres from the school in which no ascendant or descendant was found.
  - The wife of a Government official who did not reside more than five kilometres from the office where the official was performing his duties.
  - The candidate who was a "Professor" of a higher level of education.
  - The candidate who proved to be more qualified either in Arts or Sciences.
- The spouse, however, had absolute preference to the local school where the other spouse had been working.
- The candidates who had submitted their applications or documents which might have had some deficiency of formalities or some documents missing would be called officially by the Head of the Department of Primary Instruction and told to rectify the deficiency within a maximum period of 10 days from the date of having received the notice.
- The conditions of equalization of a Diploma from the Capital (Lisbon) would be regulated by the respective city legislation.
- In the schools of one post there would be only one "Professor" or one lady "Professor" according to the classification obtained in the interview. In those schools with more than one post if the number was even there would be equal number of men and lady "Professors", if odd then more would be appointed as per the classification in the interview.
  - This rule would apply also to transfers.
  - In places which had more than one school not more than 500 metres away from each other for the purpose of filling up the vacancies they would be considered as one.
- The "Professors" who had been granted unlimited licence would be placed without interview in the school of the same Class in

which the teacher had been exercising his duties from the date of his request for the licence.

- Of the "Professors" who had come to attain the age of superannuation within another two years would be interviewed for posts only in the higher Classes and not lower.
- The "Professors" in the schools of the same category could exchange their places by observing certain conditions after having rendered at least two years of good and effective service in the last school allowing the change to be determined only in exceptional cases and for reasons of personal problems which were worthy of considering.
  - The changes could be authorized at any time of the year but they would become effective only at the beginning of the next academic year and they would be able to join from the 1st of April to the 31st of May.
  - Any change once permitted would be allowed to become effective only with the authorization of the Governor after consultations with the Council of Public Instruction if the "Professors" had applied for it.
  - The Department of Primary Instruction having received the applications asking for the changes had to set in motion the process with certain information regarding the quality and the effectiveness of the service of the "Professors", the moral conditions in which the change was required and was possible within the existing rules.
- The change would be negated if any of the "Professors" were being dealt with on disciplinary grounds as it would be considered as absolutely and permanently impossible for the "Professors" to exercise their duties as it would be contrary to the spirit of the rules in force.
- The Head of the Department of Primary Instruction was bound to send to the "Professors" till the 15th of June of each year officially the chart of the qualifications and the assessment of the service which these had rendered in the previous academic year.
- The Head of the Department of Primary Instruction during the inspections of the schools had to enter in the book meant for this purpose his remarks for the number of times the "Professor" had been absent during his tenure—which could influence his qualification—and issue necessary instructions to correct any

defect deciding to inspect again the same school within an interval of one month in order to verify if his instructions had been complied with or not. This entry against the absence of the "Professor' would serve as a criterion for his classification.

- The "Professors" who had already been classified by means of the marks would be classified again by applying the adopted critieria of this Diploma in the following manner:
  - Good—10 marks and above; and
  - Deficient—Less than ten.
- This equivalence would be done by a Committee comprising of the Director of the Civil Administrative Services, the Director of "Escola Normal" and the Head of the Department of Primary Instruction and then present the report to the Council of Public Instruction which would then decide over the matter.
- In the years in which the marks regarding the qualifying service had not been taken into consideration proportionate marks which they would have obtained during those years in which they had qualified for service had to be allotted to them.
- The "Professor" who could not conform to the qualifying service criteria would be able to within ten days from the date of having to received the intimation complain to the Head of the Department of Primary Instruction and when the latter thought that the complaint was justified the "Professor" would be allowed to reappear for the interview by making a petition and submitting it in the Department of Public Instruction for onward submission to the Governor who would then take a call after consulting the Council of Public Instruction.
- Thirty days after the publication of the Regulations, the Head of the Department of Primary Instruction had to present a proposal before the Government for the placement of the Primary "Professors" within the respective zones (circles) of the schools of the first and the second category having previously obtained the sanction of Council of Public Instruction.
- The officiating "Professors" would be kept in the schools in which they had been already placed when they had obtained less than three good remarks in any number of years as per the equivalence established by this Diploma.
- The "Professor" appointed in the schools located in the main areas in the North had the right to the advantages which had been offered to them by the terms of the existing legislation.

Changes Effected in the Laid Down Rules

On the 2nd of May, 1929, the person in charge of the State, Acursio Mendes da Rocha Diniz was authorized by the Council of Public Instruction after it had been proposed by the Department of Primary Instruction and endorsed by the Government Council in the absence of the Governor to issue the new Rules and Regulations regarding Primary education which had been earlier issued but then subsequently withdrawn as there were some inappropriate entries. The following were the various provisions in the modified rules:

- The Primary education aimed at providing the child with the basis of a general culture, preparing him for a social life which had to start at the pre-Primary education level basically intuitive and administered under the form of lessons of things without systematization of syllabi, timetables or exercises and at the Primary level inclined towards mainly the function of Reading, Writing and Counting and working with hands and having adopted convenient the methods and syllabi same as those in force at the Centre (Portugal).

The following provisions were specifically aimed at the Pre-Primary education level:

- The Pre-Primary education would be started through schools that had to be established as per the earlier Decrees of 10th May, 1919 and 6th November, 1923.
- The First school would be set up in Pangim and would serve as a model for others.
- The regulating of the Pre-Primary schools would be the object of the special Diploma to be published.

Then came the set of regulations for the Primary level. These were as follows:

- The Primary education in Portuguese language would consist of two Levels (*graus*), the First one having 4 Classes as presently being followed in the Colony and the Second Level by Class 5 as in the previous regime, giving it a convenient extension to the syllabi of Class I in order to make them learn the Portuguese language practically and intuitively so that above all it will be convenient to teach Reading, Writing and Counting and being able to teach the remaining subjects in the syllabi taught in the form of lessons of things.

- Besides the Gymnastics, practice of Hygiene and Choral Singing it would include the following other subjects at that level:
  - Drawing, Geometry and Manual Work.
  - Dictation, Reading, Writing, translation and Grammar.
  - Arithmetic and Metric system.
  - Chorography of Portugal, of the State of India and of the colonies, History of Portugal, brief notions of the History of "India Portuguesa" and Civic education.
- The general regime adopted in the Primary schools is of co-education.
- The academic year in all Primary schools would commence on the 10th of June and end on the 31st of March. The instructional year would begin from the first working day which followed the 15th of June and would end on the last working day of February.
- The period ordinarily for admissions in the official Primary schools would be from the 10th to the 14th of June and would end in the last five days of February.
- Outside this period but till the end of August the Head of the Department of Primary Instruction could permit admissions in any Class if requested by the father of the child, the tutor or the guardian of the student/candidate.
- The students of Class V for every term at the start or at the time of closure of admissions had to pay towards the General School Fund, a fee of 6 "tangas" for the benefit of orphans without any means and for the children of poor parents.
- The receipts of the opening and closing of admissions of the students of Class V as well as the documents and the Certificates and the examination guides for the foreign students of the school had to be entered in a special book showing all the receipts till then collected and had to be deposited in the Treasury of the Province till the 31st of March in the account of the General School Fund.
- Besides the normal period of admission there would be a second period of extraordinary admissions which would be from the 1st to the 4th of September for the students of Class I and II who had been undergoing home schooling.
- The Head of the Department of Primary Instruction could authorize the transfer of the enrolment of the students from one official school or private school to another, either official or

private taking steps to inform the Directors of the school that he would be leaving and the one he would be joining.

- The transfers thus referred to as well as for the home schooling or private tutoring could be made till the 31st of December and from there onwards in advance only in exceptional cases duly justified.
- For the initial enrolment in the schools of Primary instruction the student had to present attested certificate of vaccination which had to be kept in the school till the end of the academic year.
- For the purpose of enrolment at the Primary level the Records and Registration section and the Department of Civil Registration had to issue free of cost Birth Certificates as an extract on plain paper declaring therein that it had been issued for that particular reason.
- The Department of Primary Instruction had to provide the Records section and the Department of Civil Registration the forms which would be needed for this purpose as per the model provided by these regulations.
- The Directors of the official and private schools had to send to the Department of Primary Instruction till the 10th of July a nominal report Class-wise of all the students who had sought admission in the school.
- The school would start functioning as far as possible in all the Primary schools from 9.00 a.m. There would be five periods every working day of the school except on Thursdays which would be a rest day.
- Two or more "Professors" taking Class simultaneously in the same room was prohibited.
- If there was a single hall for two "Professors" they had to take up their Classes alternately without any change in the timings till provision was made to expand the school building.
- Each period would be of 40 minutes with a break of 15 minutes of rest and recreation. Between the third and the fourth period there would a break of at least one and half hours.
- If the local circumstances, however, were not suitable then the above stipulation could be altered through an amendment proposed by the Director of the school to the Head of the Department of Public Instruction.
- The time tables and the syllabus of the Primary schools prepared by the Head of the Department of Public Instruction, taking into

consideration the proposals presented by the Directors of the schools till the end of June had to be prominently displayed in the classrooms.

- After having received the time table the "Professor" would not be allowed either to increase or to decrease the number of periods or even to reduce the duration of the periods
- The methods and the processes of teaching would be dictated and supervised by the Head of the Department of Primary Instruction.

- All schools, official and private would have during the academic year, two days of National and provincial holidays, Sundays and Thursdays as holidays, three days after the Sunday of Carnival and Thursday, Friday and Saturday before Easter Sunday as holidays.
  - On the days of National and provincial holidays and on Sundays the National flag had to be flown in all the schools.
  - The evening before the National and Municipal holidays the "Professors" had to deliver a short patriotic speech to the students on the significance of the day.
  - For the Hindus three days holidays would be given on the occasion of Ganesh and one day for Diwali and for the Muslims the day of Ramzan had to be declared a holiday.
- The school breaks would be from the 6th of October to the 25th of October and from the 23rd of December to the 6th of January and the summer holidays would be during March, April and May barring the period of examinations.
- As a rule only those children who had completed at least six years of age during that particular year could be admitted for enrolment.
- The age for attending official Primary school could not be more than 14 years.
- The students had to come to school clean and tidy.
- The children who suffered from some contagious disease or any other sickness which the local health authority thought was contagious would not be allowed to either enroll or attend school. Any other person too having the above conditions would not be allowed inside the school.
  - The students who manifested some skin infections or head scalp had to be sent to the local health official who had the authority to bar the child from attending school due to his sickness.

- If a student had been stopped from attending school and wanted to rejoin he could do so only on the recommendation of the local health official or any other medical practitioner after he was certified as fully cured and his interaction would not pose any danger to his companions.

- If in any school there was an instance of sickness which the doctors diagnosed as contagious then the respective health official had to investigate if the cause/source of the sickness was in the school itself and prepare a report a copy of which he had to then send to the Directorate of Health Services.
  - The persons who resided with the affected student would not be allowed into the school premises.
  - In cases of sickness suspected to be contagious the "Professor" had to communicate the case immediately to the health official in terms of the law disclosing also the fact to the Head of the Department of Primary Instruction.
- If there was in the school a "Professor" having special competence to teach the first three Classes he would be authorized to do so.
- In the Class I intuitive and practical learning of the Portuguese language had to take place, directed preferably by "Professors" who had knowledge of pre-Primary teaching.
- No student could pass Class I without knowing sufficiently the Portuguese language since he had to understand the lessons in Class II.
- All the students had to be expressly prohibited from speaking any other language in Class except Portuguese even during the Gymnastics exercises and outdoor games period.
- The principle of rotation would be followed in the Primary schools. The "Professor" would accompany as a rule the students whom he had been teaching from the Class I to the last Class.
- As a rule each "Professor" would be allotted the charge of a Class or a batch of up to 50 students.
- No "Professor" could be allotted work in more than three Classes cumulatively except if the school had only one post.
- If the average attendance in a particular Class managed by the "Professor" was more than 50 students he could propose to the Department of Primary Instruction its separation into two sections and creating another post of a "Professor".

- In the schools in which there was a School Council this proposal had to be previously approved by the Council.
- Whenever the "Professor" had to teach in two sections the Class timings/periods of each of these would be three hours per day including the short intervals for rest.
- The above "Professor" would be a special Diploma holder appointed with a monthly salary above the normal.

Establishing of New Schools or Classes

The following regulations were then put in place for the opening of new schools:

- The construction of school buildings had to follow strictly the rules of Hygiene and Pedagogy established as per the Decree of 20th January, 1917, which had remained unaltered till date.
  - The school building when leased had to fulfil the following conditions. They had to:
    - Be centrally located for the school population which would attend it.
    - Be located in a healthy and easily accessible place.
    - Be away from unpleasant establishments like "tavernas" (liquor shops) or factories.
    - Be at a minimum distance of 200 metres from any type of burial place.
    - Have toilets, lavatories, dressing rooms, dinner hall, garden and a covered shed for recreation.
  - The classrooms had to have at least 1.25 sq. m. per child, a passage of not less than 4 m, big door and two windows with panes with each one not less than 1/6th of the surface of the wall. When no light entered from the two sides of the Class the benches and desks had to be arranged in such a manner that the students would get light from their left side.
  - The classrooms needed to have ventilation and the floor had to be unobstructed to enable the students to walk freely and tiled so that it could be maintained clean and in good condition.
  - The roofs when not thatched had to have a false ceiling of wood and painted white. The walls had to be coloured, green, yellow or ash coloured of two shades, darker shade from

the ground to a height of two metres with the rest of a lighter shade which would be washable.

- If a proper building was not available the one which satisfied the above mentioned conditions more or less had to be leased in which case the corridor could have been less than 3 m.
- The above conditions would apply for the first-two years from the date of publication of this regulation to schools which function in buildings of the State and even when they have their own buildings the conditions apply for all the Primary schools in existence.
- The leasing of any building for a school should be done after obtaining the sanction of the sanitary official.

- The school furniture had to be as per the technical, hygienic and pedagogical specifications and had to be approved by the Government for which reason copies of the models had to be submitted for maintaining its record in the Department of Primary Instruction.
- Besides the necessary number of desks for the students there had to be at least in each Class a table and a chair for the "Professor", cupboards for notebooks and other instructional materials for the students and a stand for the regional Museum.
- The minimum didactic material for a student would comprise of a black slate, a collection of weights and measures, a Roberval balance, a decimal balance, standard measures, compasses to measure the thoracic dimensions, a collection of geometrical solids, a pack of chorographic cards of the continent, adjacent islands and overseas possessions, a collection of geographical maps, a stand for the cards with alphabets, twenty collections of moving characters, and a collection of necessary utensils for Manual Work and Art Education.
- The dwelling of the "Professor" had to have at least five rooms including a kitchen.
- The expenses for the furniture, instructional material, the school utensils, repairs to the schools, the rent of the leased building, the dwelling of the "Professor" and the subsidies were to be met from the Public Treasury, the other public bodies and the administrative Corporations or from individuals or private institutions which must maintain themes per the terms of the procedures for the creation of schools.
- In the event of non-observance of the stipulations mentioned

under the present regulations by the public bodies, administrative Corporations and individuals or private institutions the school might be forced to close down.

- The public bodies and the administrative Corporations had to make provision annually in their accounts for the recurring items of expenditure/funding needed for the maintenance of the schools which were under its charge in terms of the present regulation and the legislation in force and when they had not followed the instructions, the Government before approving the budgets would make them include those items of expenditure/funding.
- The "Professors" who had not got residential quarters would get their rent of the house reimbursed by the Municipalities under the terms fixed by a special Order.
- In case a school was closed down due to an epidemic or some natural calamity the "Professor" would not lose his right to his usual remuneration which he used to draw during his tenure.
- The public bodies and the administrative Corporations and the private associations had to provide a temporary "Professor" whenever a school had been restarted till the vacancy would become regular.
- The "Professors" of the official Primary schools who had been or were going to be appointed by the Government at the request of the Corporations or of any of the citizens and maintained fully or partly at the expense of these public bodies would belong to the group of official "Professors" and would be paid directly from the public Treasury.
- It was the duty, however, of the public bodies to furnish to the Accounts Office within the stipulated time period the estimated amount required for the entire maintenance of those schools or for the one which they were committed to since its inception for which a certain amount used to be released from the School Fund.
- All had to obey the conditions laid down by these regulations and could make an application to the State for the appointment of the one "Professor" but if stipulated enrolment had been met then a second "Professor" could also be appointed
- Except in unforeseen cases as per law, meetings of any type in the official school premises without authorization of the Government were expressly prohibited.

Shutting Down of Schools or Transferring Them

Clear provisions in the rules were laid down regarding the creation, transfer and closure of schools as can be seen from the following:

- The actual official Portuguese Primary schools were grouped according to the plan done at the time of creating the schools conforming to the regulations in force.
- The creation, changing or the closure of Primary schools or even the lapsing of the posts of "Professors" would be subject as much as possible to a general plan of establishing and spreading Portuguese Primary schools which would be organized by the Department of Primary Instruction and approved by the Governor with the approval of the Council of Public Instruction after getting it passed by the Council of the Government (permanent section).
- The creation of schools or of new posts of "Professors" in the existing schools would always be determined by means of a process chalked out in the Department of Primary Instruction and accompanied by the following documents:
    - List of students according to their school going age, residing in the area where the school was going to be located, organized by the local office in coordination with the village head and in case it was in the capital of the province by the Secretariat of the Municipal Council assisted by the respective "Regedor's" office.
    - A report as per the approved model regarding certain conditions of the place where it was going to be established had to be prepared by the Head of the Department of Primary Instruction with the sanction of the sanitary authority.
    - A list of the furniture and the necessary instructional materials as well as the budget for its acquisition had to be submitted to the "Fazenda" referring to the deposits that had been kept aside for these expenses.
    - The opinion of the local delegate of Primary Instruction or in his absence the opinion of the local office would be considered:
        - — In case the building was being donated a report had to be filed as per rules after the Health authority, the representative of the Public Works Department and the

Head of the Department of Primary Instruction had inspected the site.

— In case of creation of the new posts the procedure indicated above would be dispensed with.

- The procedures for the transfer or the closure of the school or of a post of a "Professor" would be made/done as under:
  - With the documents like the list of students etc.;
  - Statistics chart of the last three academic years;
  - Attendance chart and the progress of the students during the months of the school year which was still going on; and
  - Any other information about the same matter which would be useful to the Government.
- (Transitory) The schools which actually had been wrongly constructed because of lack of proper building or not having proper hygienic and pedagogical conditions had to be closed down if found wanting after a thorough inspection by the Sanitary Inspector, Head of the Department of Primary Instruction and the representative of the Public Works Department. It would, however, be allowed to function again only when a proper building and other conditions were in place.
- The closing down of a school could not be done without an inspection by the Council of Public Instruction and the approval of the Government which would try to consider all the necessary aspects especially the attendance in the school for which reason if need be a new building could be constructed.
- Any school whose enrolment for the past three consecutive years had been less than twenty would be closed down, if the motive for such a situation could not be exactly verified. If it was due to the existence of a small school-going population or if the cause was a consequence of the respective "Professor's" incompetence or negligence of his duties or his obstinacy in persisting with his own ways the school would continue to function and the respective "Professor" would be subject to legal action under the disciplinary process.

Appointment and Other Service Conditions of Teachers

After making some necessary modifications these rules which are not much different from those of 1928 or rather which are an improvement of those same rules were issued. As per these rules the appointment of teachers, the process of selection, their categorization and their service conditions would be regulated as follows:

- The "Professors" of Primary Instruction coming under permanent appointment after having passed the designated interview/test would constitute one group.
- In the appointment of teachers of Primary instruction the following had to be observed:
  - All the schools would be divided into three categories: (i) those situated in the administrative capitals of the provinces of Ilhas, Salcette, Bardez and Mormugao; (ii) those located in the administrative capitals of other provinces; and (iii) those situated in other places.
  - The initial appointment of candidates with a professional Diploma would be made in the school of the third category in the post created by the transfer of the "Professor".
    - — The first appointment would always be considered provisional which would become permanent after two years of unblemished record of service.
    - — In the documental interview for the first appointment only the marks shown in the professional Diploma would be considered. However, preference in the merit list would be given as per the length of service to those who had some experience in teaching.
    - — The interim appointments would be done taking into consideration the place of the candidates in the merit list.
- The posts which would occur in the schools of the second category and the first category would be filled up through an interview among the permanent "Professors" of the schools of the category immediately below who had at least one year of permanent service in the respective Class.
  - After the interview the merit list of the candidates would be prepared by adding the marks obtained in the professional Diploma, a mark/point for every five years of service and a mark/point for every three remarks of "good" in the evaluation of his service.
  - For this purpose the service of the "Professor" had to be evaluated by giving the remarks of "good" or "deficient".
  - Those "Professors" who had been appointed without having completed the course of "Escola Normal" would have their

marks obtained in the First year of the old Escola Normal reduced by one-third if they had completed only the first year of "Escola Normal" or by reducing to half the marks obtained in both the years of the "Escola Normal".

  - The filling up of the posts in the last category would only be done by transfer also through an interview/test in terms of the number of posts available in the said category.
  - As long as the existing "Professors" continued in service for the posts in the schools of the first category the posts in the second and third categories would also remain the same.
- The interview/test for the transfer of the "Professors" of the schools of the third category would follow the norms as mentioned above.
  - Having done the transfer of the permanent "Professors" the transfer of the provisional "Professors" would also be done under the same rules.
- If for two successive years the provisional "Professor" had been getting the remark "deficient" he would be given the termination order for his service as a teacher.
  - The appointment of a provisional teacher would be converted into a permanent one only if he had obtained during the first two years the remark "good" or three remarks of "good" during a period of four years failing which his services as a teacher would be terminated.
- The transfers or the promotions would be done only at the request of the interested party except in the case of disciplinary action.
  - For the above purpose annually in the first fifteen days of March a general interview would be announced to which all the "Professors" could apply through proper channel through the Department of Primary Instruction submitting together the necessary documents if they had not been submitted and recorded in the Department previously.
  - By the 15th of April the merit list had to be prepared showing clearly the marks obtained by each "Professor" of each category as per the rules framed by the Department of Primary Instruction following the criteria as far as the length of service is concerned. The list then had to be published in the "Boletim Oficial" for the purpose of receiving objections if any within a period of fifteen days from the date of the said publication.

- The merit list prepared by the Department of Primary Instruction would be approved or modified by the Governor General before announcing it after hearing the Council of Public Instruction to which they had submitted all the documents which had served as the basis for the merit list and taking into account the objections raised by the interested parties.
- In the case of there being a vacancy in any category it would be first announced within fifteen days of its occurring to which the "Professors" of the category would be able to apply through an application in which they had to declare their preference of the schools they would like to be transferred to indicating also the preferences to which they had the right providing the necessary documents to back up their claim after which the interview for promotion would be held. In the same manner the vacancies in the lower categories too would be filled up immediately.
- Similarly the interview would be conducted for filling up the provisional and interim vacancies proceeding in the same way as above.
- If there were no candidates for any of the categories of schools the interview would be thrown open to "Professors" from the lower categories without taking into consideration their length of service and if the interview could be held then the post would be filled up by appointing a provisional "Professor" as per the rules in force.

- With all things being equal the order of preference followed in the selection of candidates for the posts would be done in the following serial order:
  1. The candidate who was the resident of the place where the school was located.
  2. The candidate who resided not more than five kilometres from the school in which there could be rising or declining "provido".
  3. The spouse of a Government servant who had applied for the post in the school which was not more than five kilometres from the office where the spouse worked.
  4. The candidate who was a "Professor" of a school of the higher category.

5. The candidate who proved that he had better qualifications either academic or scientific.

- The spouse who sought transfer to a local school where he/she would be with the other spouse would , however, have the absolute preference.
- The candidates posted in the schools after the interview whose documents or applications were not in order would be called officially by the Head of the Department of Primary Instruction to correct the defects within a period of 10 days from the date of receiving the notice.
- The applications seeking admission to the interview for the posts of "Professors" provisional or interim had to be addressed to the Governor accompanied by the following attested documents:
    - Diploma or Certificate of having qualified legally as a teacher.
    - Birth Certificate proving that he had completed 19 years of age as shown on the qualification of the candidate of the "Escola Normal" and when he had not served as a teacher should not have been more than 35 years. If he had worked earlier then this limit would be 35 years plus the amount of time he had worked as teacher or as a Government official.
    - Certificate of good moral and civil conduct.
    - Certificate from the police (no criminal cases).
    - Medical certificate to show that he was not suffering from any contagious disease, had good health to work as a teacher, did not have any defect or physical deformity which could hinder his school activity and had been vaccinated against an attack of smallpox within the last seven years.
    - A signed written declaration under oath pledging his respect and his loyalty to the institutions assigned to him.
    - A list of the qualities and the years of service as per the regulations.
    - Certificates or documents to prove that he had literary and scientific qualifications.
        - The above documents would then be filed in the Department of Primary Instruction within a period of 15 days from the date of publication of the notice.
        - Those candidates who had not been appointed as "Professors" would be excused from furnishing the documents since these documents could be found in

the process of other previous tests if the period of validity of any of them had not lapsed. In certain circumstances, however, the "Professors" who had served in the interim posts could be exempted from presenting the duly signed and stamped documents.

— The production of the Certificate from police was compulsory. The validity of this document was 180 days.

- The candidates who had qualified in the capital city (Lisbon) would be subject to the equivalence of the Diploma as per the respective legislation in force in the city.
- The Head of the Department of Primary Instruction had to send the results of the interviews to the Government through the offices of the Directorate of Civil Administrative Services within a maximum period of 30 days counting from the date of the end of the test accompanied by the following:
  - Information of the date, the vacancy and how it had occurred indicating also the date of its publication on the "Boletim Oficial".
  - Information regarding the budget.
  - Copy of the announcement of the interview.
- In the schools where there was more than one "Professor" no post was supposed to be filled up by interview without first verifying whether the school attendance had exceeded the legal number of students or not.
- The "Professors" who had been dismissed could not be admitted again for any interview before they had completed a period of five years.
- "Professors" exempted from the interview at their own request would be interviewed again for any post after one year only.
- In schools where there was only one post it will be filled up with one "Professor" or one lady teacher according to the Classification obtained in the interview. In case there was more than one post if the number of posts was even there would be equal number of male and female teachers and if there was an odd number of posts then more number of teachers would be posted as per the selection in the interview.
  - The same rule would apply in case of transfers too.
  - In places where there were two schools not more than 500 metres away from each other both would be considered as one unit for the purpose of filling up the vacancies.

- The candidates appointed by virtue of a test could continue in the previous post in the school where they were already serving and in case they turned down the appointment they would be considered afresh whenever such a vacancy arose.
- The period for taking charge of the new post was 15 days in the district of Goa and twenty days in the districts in the North.
  - The "Professors" transferred through the conduct of a test would be able to take charge till the last working day of the month of February and start their duties from the 10th of June.
  - The appointment had to be preceded by a medical examination and the charge would be given by the Department of Primary Instruction recording and signing in the respective book with all the legal formalities preceded by the declaration of honour by the candidate by which he would swear his loyalty to the Constitution and the laws of the Republic and by which he would carry out faithfully the functions which they had entrusted to him.
  - If the candidate had been residing in the districts in the North he would be able to take charge in the Secretariat of the Government of the district following the usual formalities. The copy of the charge and the legal papers had to be sent to the Department of Primary Instruction and recorded in the respective book.
- If the candidate was residing in the North Districts he would be examined by the Health Committee of the respective district.
- The "Professor" could have been excused for not having taken charge of his post within the stipulated time limit only in case of natural calamity or any other unforeseen circumstance.
- In this case a candidate classified immediately below would be nominated.
- The "Professors" in the case of unlimited permission who had been told to join back his post could only be placed without interview in a school of the same category as that in which he was working on the date of his applying for a licence.
- The "Professors" who would be attaining their age limit within two academic years would be barred from appearing for the interview for a post in another school from a superior category to a lower one.

- The "Professors" of schools of the same category could change their places which would not come under any of the conditions mentioned earlier if they had put in at least two years of good effective service in the previous school, allowing such a change only in exceptional cases and for personal reasons which they had to take note of.
  - The changes could be authorized in any term of the year but they would come into effect only in the beginning of the next academic year, at the time of taking charge which would be between the 1st of April and the 31st of May.
  - Any change once permitted would come into effect only with the authorization of the Government after the approval by the Council of Public Instruction when the "Professors" had applied for it.
  - The Department of Primary Instruction having received the request for the change had to start the process with sufficient information regarding the quality and the effectiveness of the service of the "Professors", the moral conditions on account of which they had applied and if it was fitting into the rules in force.
- The change would not be granted if any of the "Professors" had any disciplinary proceedings pending against them or if they had already been certified to have been incompetent to exercise their functions or if it would be contrary to the spirit of any of the rules.
- If a "Professor" who had been given an interim posting had refused the offer without proper justification he would be excluded thereafter from the list.
- The appointment and the service of the interim "Professor" would end with the closing of the academic year or at the end of the annual examinations of those Classes which he had been conducting.
- Those interim "Professors" who had been appointed to substitute the permanent ones during their sickness were exceptions and their tenure would end immediately as soon as those "Professors" joined back in their service.
- When a citizen makes a donation of a school building to the State the posts in the respective school to which the donor had the first right would remain unfilled till the work of the building was completed within a period of time as fixed by the donor.

- The Head of the Department of Primary Instruction was obliged to send to the "Professors" till the 15th of June of each year the seniority list showing also the qualifications and the experience of the previous years.
- The Head of the Department of Primary Instruction during the inspections had to record in the book meant for this purpose the deficiencies and shortcomings of the "Professor" which could influence his qualifications and issue necessary instructions for correcting his defects making it a point to inspect again the same school within an interval of less than a month during the same academic year to verify whether his instructions had been carried out and noting down again the defects if any. This record would be used at the time of drawing up the seniority list.
- The "Professors" who had been classified by taking the marks into consideration would be placed as per the following equivalence:
  - "Bom"—10 marks and above.
  - "Deficiente"—less than 10 marks.
- This equivalence had to be made by a Committee comprising of the Director of Civil and Administrative Services, Director of "Escola Normal", and the Head of the Department of Primary Instruction and present it to the Council of Public Instruction which would then take the final decision on it.
  - In the years in which he did not have any remark regarding his qualifying service, remarks proportionate to the number of years would be inserted by the authorities.
- The "Professor" who did not conform to the qualifying of his service had to within a period of 10 days from the date of receiving the official communication claim from the Head of the Department of Primary instruction and in case that too was turned down he could then approach by means of a petition submitted through the Department of Primary Instruction within the same time limit, the Government who would decide on the petition after hearing the Council of Public Instruction.
- The Head of the Department of Primary Instruction had to decide over the complaint which had to be dealt with within ten days from the date it was received in the Department for which the complainant had to be issued a receipt; when the petition or complaint however had to be sent to the Government the Head of the Department within a similar time period had to inform the complainant about it.

- In the capital city as soon as it was possible a model school would be created so that practical courses on methodology for the improvement of the Primary teachers could be administered.
- In the model school it would be possible to appoint three "Professors" who had undergone a course of improvement in Lisbon or any other foreign course and two in service "Professors" from Goa selected through an interview among all the "Professors".
- Thirty days after the publication of these regulations the Head of the Department of Primary Instruction had to put up a proposal to the Government to place the Primary "Professors" from the group of the First and Second category, after obtaining the sanction from the Council for Public Instruction.
- The permanent "Professors" would be retained in the schools in which they were teaching if they had at least three remarks of "good" in four years according to the equivalence established in these rules.
- If no suitable candidate had been found for filling up the vacancies in the Northern Districts by the second half of May under a proposal from the Head of the Department of Primary Instruction permanent "Professors" in sufficient number would be selected by a Committee for one year to begin with from the junior-most in the third category to fill up the vacancies in the following order: Diu, Nagar Haveli and Daman.
    - The term of the Committee referred to above could be extended for successive years at the request of the interested when they had received good information about them.
    - The vacancies arising out of the deputation to the North Districts would be filled up by the interim "Professors".
- The deputed "Professors" who had not been able to complete the full academic year would be the first ones to be appointed for the subsequent year.
    - If, however, the Health office declared that the deputed "Professor" was under risk in the North he would be recalled and appointed as interim "Professor" with his post going to one of those residing in those districts.
    - The interim appointment in such cases would not be according to the merit list of the interim "Professors".
- If the "Professors" who had been deputed to the North Districts refused to take up the post then they would be placed outside

the group without salary they would remain so in this manner till they agreed to be considered for deputation.

- The "Professors" of the North Districts would be entitled to the benefits as per rules in force.

The Duties and Responsibilities of Teachers

Not only the division of labour but also the system of checks and balances by now had been well refined. Being sticklers for discipline everything was put down in black and white so that no dispute should arise as to the duties and responsibilities. The Director and the "Professors" had clear cut duties and responsibilities. This legislation lays down specifically the various roles they had to perform:

- In all the schools of Primary instruction there had to be a Director, named by the Government among the permanent "Professors" of the respective school as proposed by the Head of the Department of Primary Instruction.
- Charged with the post of Director of the school (Head of the school), besides the obligations that he had as a teacher, the following were additional responsibilities:
    - To administer the school;
    - To promote the progress of the school, to coordinate the work of the teachers, to encourage their initiative and professional efforts and to establish between them a good rapport.
    - To communicate to the head of the Department of Primary Education, the irregularities that had, if any taken place.
    - To organize and to write the daily accounts of the school
    - To inform the authorities about the education of the students, about their moral and intellectual progress.
    - To submit for the approval of the Head of the Department of the Primary Education, mainly during the academic year, the budget of the workers and the cleanliness of the school, taking into account the school Committee if there was one;
    - To keep the account of the fees, the guides and the Certificates of attendance and deposit the amount during the month of March in the Public Treasury under the School Fund.
    - The junior-most teacher had to serve as the Secretary of the school.

- The teachers had to fulfil the following:
  - The teaching and the education of the students was their duty, taking interest in their moral and physical development, applying the methods and the processes of the modern pedagogical science which would be very helpful for teaching and for the child whose rights they sought to defend.
  - To accompany the students during recreation, not to spy on them but to guide them in their games, establishing with them an affectionate and educative familiarity.
  - To create in the child, through education, a deep and intense love for his country and love for the public institutions.
  - To participate in the development of the school as his duty, to keep it clean and beautiful, to look after the acquisition of the school material, creation of a museum and a library and organization of the auxiliary and beneficial institutions.
  - To lend to the school all the prestige by its exemplary organization and good discipline, obtaining for it the respect of the local people.
  - To be present in the school at the regular time and leave the school only after completing the respective tasks.
  - To obey all the rules, regulations and the orders originating from the local official superiors.
  - To organize the daily diary of the Class or Classes in which they had to note, briefly, the matter taught during the day and the homework for the following day.
  - To treat equally all the students, inculcating in them the sentiments and the courtesy.
  - To conduct oneself properly in life and in the society, always being aware of the highest mission of the educator and showing, by example, an educative action in the locality, in such a manner that it would invite all the respect and consideration.
  - To maintain the attendance register of the Classes.
  - To direct the students, while doing the written exercises, manual work and drawing.
- The school discipline must not be based on authoritarianism, intimidation or violence but based on the rights and duties of the child:

- The discipline must be maintained in the school with the interest in teaching, making it attractive, pleasing and harmonious with physical and intellectual development of the child, provoking his curiosity and attention and inculcating in him the habit of work, acquiring a respectful esteem that the teacher deserved from his students; developing his affection, creating in him the confidence and the sense of individual responsibility and perfecting in him the character and the education of his desire.
- To correct the mistakes committed by the child, the teacher had to try to know his physical condition, his crises and functional disturbances, his intellectual and affective development, the environment in which his life went on, knowing thus the particular motives and strengthening them for a preventive system.
- The punishment had to be given paternally. The teacher had to inform the parents or the guardians of the child so that they could help him in his education or obtain a medical certificate when it was judged to be convenient.
- The appreciation, the compensations or prizes were to be given to the students taking into consideration not only the individual progress but also without any unhappy comparison with others, lowering of character or making them lose their confidence which if given properly should on the contrary strengthen them.
- The teacher could expel a student in case of flagrant and exceptional violations, or when all the normal pedagogical recourses had been tried and if it could contribute to a conducive atmosphere in the school making it as a prime example for the others.
- The expulsion would come into effect only after the authorization by the Provincial Government and through the process duly initiated by the Head of the Department of the Primary Education and this being justified with documents sent by the teacher.

- The teachers during the teaching hours could not take up any other work besides teaching, or abandon the Class or attend to visitors.
- The teachers could not accept any other duties in the community affairs like "Mazanias", neighbourhood responsibilities or local

administration nor exercise any other official or particular functions which could hinder his exercise of his duty.

- The teachers could correspond with their local superiors only through proper channel of the Department of Primary Education and in schools through the school Director wherever there was one.
- The teachers had to promote among the students the organization of Stoicism (doctrine of voluntarism, pluralism, etc. which institution had the provisions to strengthen the physical and moral education of the children.
- Selling of any school objects and items to students by the teachers was prohibited.
- The school records would comprise of the following to be filled in as per the relevant models provided along with the regulations:
  - School Diary.
  - General Registration book;
  - Monthly attendance Book;
  - Register of school inspection;
  - Register of correspondence dispatched;
  - Register of the inventory of furniture and school utensils;
  - Requisition Register;
  - Daily attendance Register;
  - Register of terms of examinations;
  - Monthly record of attendance and evaluation;
  - Monthly record of leave granted to the employees;
  - Annual statistics record;
  - Income and expenditure book; and
  - Record of the meetings of the School Council.
- The school Directors had to send to the Department of Primary Education till the 10th of every month the Attendance Register duly attested, the attendance account, referring to the previous month; till 15th of April, the annual statistical record; and till 5th of each month, the leave record, of leave granted in the previous month for the personnel of the school and the respective heads of the salary duly filled in.
- The salary heads for teachers had to be verified by the Department of Primary Education, signed on the reverse by the Head of the same Department and sent to the Public Treasury for the purpose of passing and making the payment till the 20th of each month.

- The books and the printed materials for the use of the schools had to be sent to the Department of Primary Education obtained through legal means and for which provision had been made in the budget under the General School Fund.
- In schools where there were more than one teacher there had to be a School Council which had to be constituted by all the effective teachers of the school, presided over by the Director and with the following attributions:
  - To assist the Director in his functions of pedagogical nature;
  - To take note of the necessities of the school and to provide them;
  - To chalk out the plan of the teaching programme;
  - To appreciate and to apply the best practices and processes for teaching;
  - To deal with the organization and the administration of the library, museum, cash boxes and school canteen;
  - To organize the distribution of the lessons/periods of each Class;
  - To organize the excursions, pedagogical walks and the holiday programmes within the scope of the Funds of the school;
  - To propose to the Head of the Department of Primary Education the modifications that the necessities of teaching and school hygiene dictate;
  - To advise about issues which, though the Director being competent to resolve, seem tricky to him; and
  - To organize at the beginning of the year and to submit to the approval of higher authorities the distribution of periods to the teachers.
- The School Council had to meet at the beginning and at the end of the academic year; at the end of the third semester and every time that the Director called for it or when two or more teachers requested for it.
- The junior-most regular teacher had to serve as the Secretary and take down the minutes of the meeting.
- The Chairman of the School Council had the casting vote during voting in case of a tie.
- The meeting of the School Council, at the end of the third semester, had to take place especially, in view of the notebooks, to appreciate and to take note of the remarks which had been given to the students.

- The register of evaluation had to contain and show the averages; and
- The periods had to correspond to the academic trimesters, the first one ending on the 31st of August, the second one on the 30th of November and the last one at the end of the academic year.

Other Matters related to Teachers

What was the role of a teacher? What were the various functions a teacher had to fulfil in the exercise of her profession? These were clearly outlined in the following statutes:

- The residence of the teacher had to be in the school complex; if, however, the school building had no residential quarters, the teacher had to reside as close as possible to the school.
- The teacher on no account could remain absent from school during working days and leave the headquarters without the permission of the Head of the Department of the Primary School. In case of urgency due to which the teacher had to remain absent, the teacher had to inform the Head immediately and justify the absence later on.
- The married teachers, if residing in the same Parish where the schools were located not more than 5 km away were allowed to live together.
- The teacher had to be paid bonus and whatever emoluments were due, in case his services were terminated due to some contagious disease or due to some catastrophe legally justified.
- If any school could not function due to lack of premises or due to the non-availability of residential quarters, the teacher had to be placed as far as possible in any other school of the same Class and of his preference, in the same district.
- The services rendered by teachers of an official nature relating to their profession would be counted in the same manner for all purposes.
- In the schools where there was only one teacher, once the post was vacant or the teacher was legally prevented from performing his functions, the Head of the Department of Primary Education had to immediately propose to the Governor the appointment of an in service teacher for substitution. If, however there was more

than one teacher, the Classes of the teacher suspended, would be under the charge of another teacher of the same school, who would join the Classes into two sessions till a substitute teacher was appointed in place of the suspended teacher.

- In case of sickness of a teacher for more than three days it was compulsory to present the medical Certificate. Each Certificate could justify only the leaves in sequence and not the intervening period.
- The teachers in the Primary schools married and pregnant were granted leave of 60 days, 30 days in the last month of pregnancy and 30 following the child's birth.
  - During this period the teacher enjoyed all the rights and perks as if she was in effective service without considering the leave for any other purpose except this.
  - Fifteen days before, at least, the one who desired to go on leave had to communicate to the Department of Primary Education, attaching the Medical Certificate, in order to make arrangement for her substitution.
  - If on account of sickness, the teacher was not able to present on the last day the application for leave he had to observe the regulations regarding the absences and permissions.

Regulations Governing Home-Schools

Since schools were few and far in between at least in the earlier days many of those who could afford it used to conduct Classes at home for their children.Travelling to and fro if the school was located kilometres away was alos a problem since transport facilities were rarely available. In such a scenario the only option for those who wanted to educate their children was to engage a tutor and be one himself. The long arm of law however did not exempt such schools from the laid down regulations. The following provisions refer to homeschoolers:

- Any school or any private course of Primary education in Portuguese language was free provided it obeyed the prescriptions of the present regulation. The opening of a school or a course of free education had to be applied for in writing to the Governor who would grant permission only on the understanding that the school or individual would follow the regulations as laid down and also maintain the standards of hygiene.

- Private teaching/tutoring could be done only by individuals who had registered themselves in the Department of Primary Education.
  - The registration of teachers for private tutoring could be done on a separate page for each teacher on which all information would be written in serial order in such a way that whenever it was needed it could be extracted in the form of a Certificate having legal sanction and legal basis.
  - Only those teachers who had the legal qualifications could be registered for private tutoring.
  - In areas where there was a lack of teachers or conditions to function as Primary school teacher were not favourable, any individual could be authorized to teach, provided he was qualified at least in the course of the Lyceum.
  - The application requesting the registration with the Department of Primary Education as teachers of private teaching, had to be submitted in the same Department along with the following documents:
    - — The Certificate stating that a course of Normal School had been completed;
    - — Birth Certificate;
    - — Certificate of Police Clearance;
    - — Certificate of vaccination; and
    - — Medical Certificate issued by the Medical Officer, proving that the candidate did not suffer from any contagious disease or any other physical defect that could inhibit him from exercising the functions of a teacher.
- The applications requesting permission to work as a Primary teacher had to be submitted to the Department of Primary Education along with the necessary documents including the Certificate of the general course of Lyceum.
- The private schools of Primary teaching were subject to the inspection by Department of Primary Education and the Medical officer:
  - The teachers of these schools and Principals, Directors of hospitals and any houses of education where they had Primary schools, were obliged under the penalty of expulsion, to furnish all the informations to the Department of Primary Education and to the Medical Officer, the Classes

and the school hours and to provide to them when demanded, all the documents which were judged necessary for the inspection of teaching and the hygienic and pedagogical conditions of the buildings.

  - The Head of the Department of Primary Education, during his visits to the private schools, had to check the notebooks regarding the practical exercises of the students.
  - Annually and at the beginning of the academic year, the Department of Primary Education had to inform the District Councils and the Head of Police whether the private schools had been authorized to function or not.

- The private schools of Primary teaching were subjected to most of the dispositions of the present regulations and were expected to maintain the books of general registration and monthly attendance according to the official models.
- The establishments of private teaching which functioned without legal authorization and which did not follow the dispositions of the present regulation, would be provisionally suspended by the administrative authorities, after a requisition was issued by the Head of the Department of Primary Education after following the due process of law.
- The complete suspension of any school or course of private Primary teaching had to be ordained by the Governor, after consulting the Council of Public Education taking into account the report from the Department of Primary Education, the defence of the interested party, the proofs of witnesses and documents and the comments of the Head of the Department of Primary Education.
- Home schooling under the responsibility of the parents or the tutors of the students was permitted by the Government.
- Teachers were prohibited from giving private tuitions in the school premises whether it was for the children of the same school or any other school, but could do home schooling, without violating their official duties.

Other Initiatives at Spreading Education

The Government obviously put in a lot of efforts to spread education which showed in the various initiatives it tried. Besides opening regular schools and allowing private and individual teaching the Government made use of night schools and mobile schools in order to bring education closer to the people. The following regulations were put in place for the purpose of night Classes:

- In the Primary schools of the localities where circumstances demanded night courses could be started with prior permission of the Governor.
- The night courses were meant to help in the Primary education in Portuguese language of both adults and boys of more than 14 years who probably were not able to avail of this education or to complete it.
- The night courses had to be overseen by the Director of the school where they had been started.
- The teachers conducting the night course and having a special Diploma were entitled for a monthly remuneration.
- The night courses would start on the 10th June and end on the last working day of the month of February. The registration for the night courses was permanent.
- The night course would not be conducted for less than 12 registered students and could be suspended if the daily regular attendance was less than 10 students.
- The books of registration and attendance had to be maintained the same way as it was being done in the other Primary schools. The attendance records had to be sent, every month separately to the Department of Primary Education.
- The duration of the Classes every night would be of 2 hours.
- Whatever was applicable to the day schools was also applicable to the night schools except the dispositions of this regulation if found contrary.
- The timings for the night courses had to be fixed by the Head of the Department of Primary Education.
- None of the students of the night courses could appear for the examination of Primary education without showing regular attendance during one academic year and demonstration satisfactory progress.

Improvement of Educational Qualifications

Provision in the rules was also made to allow those who wished to upgrade themselves and improve their academic performance and record. The following regulations refer to this aspect of the school system:

- The first preparatory course of education, in Portuguese language, would consist of 5 Classes. Of the 5 Classes the first 4 Classes would make up First Level and the 5th.Class would form Second Level.
- The passing/promotion of students from one Class to another, till Class IV, would be done by the respective teachers after judging them to be sufficiently qualified. The Head of the Department of Primary Education, after verifying personally or through a locally appointed delegate could order the demotion of a student who could not continue in the higher Class, where the teacher had placed him, as he failed to fulfil the requirements. For the lapse on the part of the teacher action deemed fit would be taken against the defaulting teacher.
- The students who had been promoted to the next Class had to be issued a Progress Report pertaining to the last attended Class in which the student was reading and an Attendance certificate as per the format charging the student, as the cost of the *impress,* an amount of four "tangas", that would be deposited in the General School Fund. Those students who had been irregular in their attendance could not be promoted to the next Class, that is, if the number of absences exceeded one-third of the number of days of the academic year.
- There would be public examinations of Primary education, both for First Level as well as Second Level.
    - The Jury for the examinations of First Level which had to take place in the respective official Primary school, would consist of the local delegate as Chairman, the official teacher or the private teacher who was teaching the student as a member, and one citizen appointed by the Governor as the third member.
    - The Jury for the examinations of the Second Level, which had to be conducted in the headquarters of Primary schools of the respective districts, would be made up of: (1) a teacher of the Secondary School level or Normal Primary School, or in his absence, by any prominent citizen, preferring someone who had undergone the complete course of the Lyceum or of the Normal School, (2) an official or private teacher who taught the student; and (3) an official Primary teacher.
    - The Jury for the examinations of Second Level had to be

appointed by the Governor after being proposed by the Head of the Department of Primary Education, in consultation with the Council of Public Instruction.

  - Only those teachers of private schools would be appointed on the Jury for the examinations who had been legally registered in the Department of Primary Education and who had undergone a course of Normal or General education in the Lyceum.
  - The list of the Examiners would be drawn up in such a way that no discrimination would be done either to the students of official schools or of private schools since each Jury would have a respective teacher in that group.
  - The examinations of Primary education had to be conducted during the period from 15th February to 31st March. However, the examinations could be extended or postponed through the intervention of the Governor whenever such a need arose.

- No student could appear for the examination of Primary education, unless he had completed 9 years at the First Level and 10 years at the Second Level or would be completing in that current year.
- The number of students called daily for each of the examinations would be 10 from the First Level and 5 for the Second Level respectively with all examinations completed on the same day.
- A Diploma would be awarded on the successful completion of the examinations of each of the Levels.
- For the examinations of Second Level, the Jury constituted at each of the headquarters, had to examine a maximum of 100 students.
- The teachers of the official and private schools had to send in the last 10 days of January to the Department of Primary Education, the lists of students in duplicate of Class 4 and Class 5 who had qualified to answer the examination of the First Level and Second Level giving their names, age, residences, names of parents or guardians, etc., and the number of years in the school. With respect to those students doing home-schooling the heads of the family had to proceed with the formalities. Along with the lists, the birth Certificate of the students whose age did not conform with that on the registration book of the official school also had to be sent.

- Along with the lists those students appearing for the examinations of the Second Level had to pay a stamp fee of Re.1, 2 "tangas" and 6 "reals".
  - These stamps had to be the unused ones of the official school.
  - Those students, who had attached a legal document proving they were poor, would be exempted from paying the fees.
- The students of open schools (private or home), who were applying as candidates for the examination of the First Level or the Second Level had to attach to their application besides the other documents demanded, a vaccination Certificate and the receipts of the prescribed payments issued by the teacher of the official school of the Parish.
- The lists of the students appearing for the examinations in the official schools had to be accompanied by the Progress Report and regular attendance Certificate in Class 4 or Class 5 as per the given format.
- Students registered in official schools could not be admitted for examinations, through home schooling or private teaching, except if they had done the transfer to these agencies before the 31st of December.
- The Head of the Department of Primary Education had to prepare the examination timetable and communicate it much in advance to the respective schools for the knowledge of the interested persons.
- The students who wished to appear for the examinations of the Second Level had to attach their respective reports, Diplomas or the passing Certificates of the First Level.
- The examinations of Primary education of the First Level as well as the Second Level would consist of written examinations, orals and practice of manual work.
  - The written and practical examinations were complementary.
  - The written, practical and oral examinations would always take place on the same day, with the written and practical examinations in the morning and the oral examinations in the evening with a break of not less than 3 hours.
- The examinations of the First Level would take place in each official school in the second half of February on the days and time fixed by the Head of the Department of Primary Education.
  - The written and practical examinations would be based on the matter mentioned below:

- A dictation of a simple text of about 8 to 10 lines from the book of literature officially adopted for 2nd, 3rd and 4th Class for the purpose of evaluating the Orthography and Calligraphy of the examinees.
- The solving of a simple problem by using an easy method and an Arithmetic problem with the respective examinations.

- Drawing in pencil of any visual object on a plain paper without the help of a ruler or any other instrument.
- Free construction of any object of common use in paper, cardboard, mud, plasticine, verga, palm leaves, "esparto" or any other material according to the liking of the student and its use in the region.
- The girls had to, besides this, answer an examination on Needle work included in the syllabus in the four Primary Classes.
- The oral examinations consisted of the following:
  - Reading and then explaining a simple text from the book approved for Classes 2, 3 and 4; and
  - To write whole numbers and decimal numbers on the blackboard and then read them; to do exercises on decimal and complex numbers; to solve simple problems and do mental calculations, everything that was included in the syllabus of the First Level.

- The duration of the written and practical examinations of the First Level could not exceed 3 hours.
- The oral examination of the First Level for each student would last, as per rule, 10 to 15 minutes.
- The examinations of the Second Level would take place in the month of March on the day fixed by the Head of the Department of Primary Education more or less on the same lines as that of the First Level.
  - The written and practical examinations would be based on the following material:
    - Dictation of 12 to 14 lines from the textbook of literature approved for Class 5 through which the Orthography and Calligraphy of the examinees would be evaluated;
    - Solution of simple problems involving one or more operations related to practical life, found in the syllabus of Arithmetic and Sets of numbers;

— An exercise in drawing done in pencil on a plain paper, consisting of a representation of a visual object without the help of a ruler or any other instrument; and
— A free construction of an object of common use in paper, cardboard, plasticine, verga, palm leaves, "esparto" and any other material used as per the liking of the student included in the syllabus and generally used in the locality.

- ■ The girls had to, besides the above, appear for an examination in Needle work taught as part of the syllabus in Primary education.

- The duration for the written and practical examinations of Second Level could not exceed 3 hours.
- The oral examinations of the Second Level would consist of the following:
  - ■ Reading and explaining of a simple text from the book approved for Class 5;
  - ■ Grammatical exercises written on the blackboard; and
  - ■ Questions on the topics included in the syllabus. The oral examinations would be of maximum 30 minutes.
- Each of the written, practical and oral examinations would be scored by each member of the Jury on a scale of 0 to 20 marks.
- The allocation of minimum marks for each aspect would be as follows:

At the First Level

Dictation	2
Arithmetic (problems and sums)	2
Drawings	1
Manual works	1
Literature	2
Explanation	2
Mathematical problems Problems	2

At the Second Level

Dictation	2
Arithmetic (Problems and sums)	2
Drawing	1
Manual work	1

Reading	2
Explanation	2
Grammar	2
Arithmetic	2
Geography, History and Civics	1
Agriculture	1

- The marks shown above were only indicative and arbitrary and were distributed just in order to help the examiner in scoring section-wise and then summing up the total out of 20.
    - At the end of the examinations, there would be a meeting of the members of the Jury in a secret session, each examiner presenting his marks record either of the First Level or of the Second Level, completely filled in and duly signed and then organizing the record as per the given format which would show the final result of each examinee. These records then had to be sent at the end of the examinations to the Department of Primary Education, along with the written and practical examinations papers and the marks for Needle work, all records duly signed by all the examiners.
    - While calculating the final marks a half mark or more in every section would be rounded off to one. For calculation of the final average the exact average of the marks given by each examiner had to be taken into account.
    - The Jury, while evaluating all the written and oral examinations, had to take into account also the manner in which the examinee exposed and expressed himself in Portuguese.
    - The examination of Needle work though not included in the calculation of the final average had to be passed by scoring a minimum of seven marks.
    - The candidate who had obtained less than ten marks would be detained.
    - The Diplomas and Certificates of the successful students would be described as very good, good and sufficient, corresponding respectively to the final averages of 18 to 20 marks, 14 to 17 and 10 to 13.
- The final results of the examinations of the First Level as well as of the Second Level had to be written in special books which would be kept in the Department of Primary Education for the purpose of issuing the Certificates.

  - The person in charge of writing the Certificates had to write them on a stamped paper, authenticate them with the white seal of the Department of Primary Education and charge an amount of rupee one towards the General School Fund as per rules and one "tanga" for issuing the Certificate. These Certificates would be endorsed by the Head of the Department of Primary Education.
  - The same record had to be maintained also in the school by the respective teacher in a special results book for students as also in the statistical records which after the end of the school examinations had to be submitted by the Chairman of the Jury to the Department of Primary Education.
- All the written examination papers had to be signed by the members of the Jury and sent, after the examinations to the Department of Primary Education, where they would be archived for two years and then destroyed.
- The Chairman of the Jury had to select the topics and the sub-topics for the written and practical examinations and had to direct the examining teachers on which topic they had to question the students so as to avoid asking questions on matters outside the syllabus.
- Any disagreement which might have arisen during the examination regarding the interpretation of the regular dispositions among the teachers and the Chairman of the Jury had to be solved by communicating the incident to the Head of the Department of Primary Education.
- The student, who had not completed his examination due to justified reasons, could do so before the same Jury till the last scheduled day of the examinations as allotted by the Department of Primary Education.
- The Head of the Department of Primary Education had to propose to the Governor the names of teachers needed for the conduct of the examinations including the official Primary teachers who could not remain absent at all from service during those days. The teachers appointed for examination work would be granted transport allowance and suitable remuneration on the days of examination only for working as members of the Jury. This had to be done so as to allow the examination process to go on smoothly.
- No student was permitted to appear for the examinations of the

First Level and the Second Level in the same academic year except when they had already completed 10 years of age.

- The examination of Needle work had to be conducted by the teacher concerned.
- The Diplomas or Certificates would be issued free of cost as per the format given by the Department of Primary Education and the record properly maintained at the end of the examinations duly signed by the members of Jury.
- If both the regular and the substitute candidates failed to appear for the examinations it would be conducted with the number of students present who perhaps would voluntarily offer themselves to be examined on that day.
- The Chairman of the Jury for the examinations of the Second Level when they were not residing in the locality where the examinations were going to be held, were entitled for a one time conveyance allowance and monetary assistance which would be fixed by issuing a special order.
- The official teachers appointed as members of the Jury, when they are staying outside the headquarters of the examinations, were entitled for travel allowance and all the perks for each working day which would be granted as a special case.

Tightening the Administrative Controls

The Portuguese also laid a lot of store by supervision and hence they put in place strict rules for overseeing the teaching in the classroom as well as the administration in the schools so as to convey a healthy picture of school education in the State. The following rules pertained to administration and monitoring in the schools:

- The administration and inspection of Primary education in the State would be under the Governor through the intermediary of the Department of Primary Education, with the Director as the Chief Inspector of Primary Education.
  - This Department was to be integrated into the Department of Civil Administrative Services.
  - The staff of the Secretariat of the Department of Primary Education would be suitably established through a special rule, in harmony as per the demands of the service.
- The functions of the Head of the Department of Primary Education were not to be in conflict with any other duty or as an

editor of books or as an author who could not in any case promote any of his books in the colony. The transgression of the disposition would be punished with demotion after following due legal process.

- There had to be in each Parish, where there was an official school, a local delegate appointed by the Governor, proposed by the Head of the Department of Primary Education, directly under this Department.
- Duties of the local delegate:
  - To promote diligently the development of education in the Parish area, using all means at his disposal so that the school was regularly attended;
  - To propose to the higher authorities, after consulting the teacher of the school everything that may be judged necessary to improve the hygienic and pedagogical conditions of the school;
  - To visit regularly the schools and check upon the registration and attendance books;
  - To use the means at his disposal for increasing the amount in the School Fund;
  - To preside over the examinations of Primary education of the First Level; and
  - To communicate to the Department of Primary Education any problems or irregularities which he had come across.
- The appointment of the local delegate of Primary education was made taking into consideration the known moral qualities of an individual, residing permanently in the respective Parish and qualified in a Secondary or a Higher education course. In case there was no such person having any of these qualifications, the best delegate would then be chosen.
- The following were the duties of the Department of Primary Education:
  - To prepare a Register of the teachers of Primary education;
  - To make a General Register of the official schools, private schools, private courses of Primary education, Principals and school employees;
  - To permit and initiate the creation of schools, the transfer of schools and the conversion of schools from one type to another;
  - To hold interviews and give salary raises to the "Professors".

- To archive the books of records of all the examinations of Primary education;
- To communicate to the schools the information that had to be sent to the higher authorities;
- To organize the general and annual statistics of Primary education;
- To file the copies of the correspondence of the Department with other Departments, Schools, authorities and Corporations relating to the services of Primary education; and
- To allot the heads of salaries to the Department of Primary Education and process the salaries of the office employees and of the teachers of Primary education of all official schools.

- The incumbent clerk will exercise the functions of the Secretary in the Department of Primary Education.
- The expenditure for the employees of the Department of Primary Education would come under the budget head of the General School Fund for the employees of all the schools.
- The clerk had to furnish all the informations to the employees and give clarifications to the requests by the Head of the Department of Primary Education, had to carry on as per norms, to issue Certificates when requested, to collect and disburse the salaries, to keep under his charge the seals of the Department and to fulfil any other function which the Head of the Department of Primary Education had to allot to him from time to time.
- In the absence or the temporary non-availability of the clerk, the Governor could appoint, on the proposal of the Head of the Department of Primary Education, a person who could be a permanent substitute to him. This appointment would normally be of a Primary teacher.
- The Department of Primary Education would have annexed to it a pedagogical Library stocked with reference books, the acquisition of books being done with the prior sanction of the Governor and paid from the School Fund which annually figured in the respective budget. From this fund the Head of the Primary Education would be able to acquire in the same way books which he had found useful and relevant for the school libraries.
- The Head of the Department of Primary Education would be appointed by the Governor through the open documental

recruitment simultaneously in the Ministry of Colonies and Department of Services of Civil Administration of India, to which only the official teachers of the Metropolis could be admitted, with those who had published better pedagogical works being preferred over others.

- When there was a vacancy or the Head of the Department of Primary Education could not attend to his duties due to some constraint the Governor could appoint one of the employees to perform the Director's duties.
- In the absence of the Head of the Department of Primary Education for the purpose of inspection, the clerk of the Department had to attend to the routine and urgent work and to sign the correspondence of the Head.

- The Head of the Department of Primary Education had to perform also pedagogic and fiscal functions :
  - The pedagogic function consisted in directing and harmonizing the process of teaching, may be general or may be special, acquainting the teachers with the methodology and the teaching process, without discouraging the individual initiatives which they might have taken since such a step showed the scientific probity of the system.
  - The monitoring function consisted of verifying the functioning of the schools and the performance of the teachers, carried out without breaking the laws, regulations in force and the resolutions taken.
- Besides the above duties the Head of the Department of Primary Education had to perform also the following ones:
  - To orient the teacher in his teaching and educational activities through modern pedagogical processes, holding conferences and conducting model lessons for this purpose.
  - To visit frequently without prior notice all the official and private schools, submitting a monthly report to the Government of the work done by the schools and his school visits.
  - To promote the creation of school museums and libraries for the teachers as well as the students and also organize courses for their improvement for the "Professors", as per the needs of the schools and the locality.
  - To urge the establishment of utilities for children, in front, behind and around the schools, and encourage them to

conduct walks and school excursions and other educational activities.

- To evaluate at the end of the year the service rendered by the "Professors".
- To propose to the Government for reasons of pedagogical order or technical formality or moral health the suspension, transfer, dismissal or retirement of the "Professors", penalties which could only be imposed after holding and concluding disciplinary proceedings in terms of the laid down disciplinary rules.
- To observe and order to be observed the laws and the regulations of Primary instruction.
- To exercise other obligations assigned under the framework of Law.
- To inspect the instructional material and the school utensils as well as the school buildings and the residential quarters of the "Professors", requesting the Municipal Councils, the "Communidades", the "Confrarias" and the "Mazanias" to fulfil their school obligations
- To promote through the Provincial Government prizes and rewards to all the citizens who deserve them because of their contribution to education.
- To organize the holding of examinations and to exercise by himself or through his delegates/representatives utmost vigilance, inspecting carefully this particular activity.
- To prepare the annual report and to direct the preparation of the general statistics of Primary instruction which would be made by the Secretary of the Department showing all the changes which were good for education and to send them to the Government till the end of June.
- To sign the salary bills of all the "Professors" of Primary instruction and other functionaries of the Department.
- To correspond with the Provincial Government through the intervention of the Director of Administrative Services and directly with the local delegates, the "Professors" of Primary instruction and other authorities and Corporations requesting for information and necessary documents for the proper discharge of his duties and for the preparation of the report and other matters.

- To give all informations which would be asked for by the Government.
- To take note of whatever complaints or claims which might have been addressed to him regarding the service of employees and public bodies which are looking after education as also by the private ones asking for an account with the Government.
- To inform about the manner and zeal with which the Municipal Councils and other Corporations had been paying attention to their school obligations.
- To propose higher rewards and corresponding prizes to the "Professors" who having shown exemplary behaviour also demonstrated zeal and great competence in the discharge of their duties.
- To initiate disciplinary proceedings against those "Professors" who stubbornly refused to heed to the warnings and notices, for having misbehaved or for having neglected their duties in the schools.
- To organize the merit lists of the candidates to send to the schools and to prepare the respective procedures.
- To take action in all the cases of default after asking for necessary instructions from the Government.
- To administer the money in the General School Fund which according to the budget was meant for the acquisition of books, paper and other articles of use, for cleanliness of the Primary schools, the school libraries, and the supply of textbooks, pedagogical material and anything else which may be necessary for teaching in the Primary schools making the Director of the school responsible as the material had been acquired through the requisitions made by him.
- To order to close down, through the offices of the respective provincial Administrator, the private schools that had been functioning without legal authorization or without complying with other provisions in the existing regulations.
- To communicate to the higher authorities if the Head of the Department of Primary Instruction had noted in any of the "Professors" the tendency to inculcate in the hearts of the students through words or through actions ideas contrary to the country to the Republic and to its laws.
- To visit repeatedly on inspection and to proceed strictly

against them if the Head of the Department of Primary Instruction had noted down any negligence, lack of competence or less pedagogical aptitude for teaching, or had ignored the advices and the notices.

- To inspect at least once if unable to inspect frequently due to lack of time or to inspect three times in each year all the official schools which was necessary for singling out the dedicated and competent "Professors" whose service merited due recognition.
- To examine in the official schools with great care everything that referred to the study material.
- To investigate the reasons if as a result of his inspection it was seen that the building lacked essential hygienic and pedagogical conditions with insufficient school articles and a "Professor" who was far from satisfied with the more modest means available. To remedy the situation he would get to know the local resources, study the way of removing the inconveniences which had been observed and inform the Government about everything by forwarding his report along with the suggestion to the competent authorities.
- To advise and instruct regarding the precepts and the pedagogic rules which must be observed for the effectiveness of the classroom practice of the "Professors" who in spite of being dedicated did not have the required proficiency or were in the know of things in the latest methods and hence did not obtain satisfactory results either in the internal organization of the school or in the selection of the methods of teaching.

Textbooks and their Proper Use

Care was taken to see that students were provided with proper textbooks and other instructional materials. Accordingly the Government laid down norms for the publication and use of textbooks and other books. The following regulations gave certain directions for their use in the schools:

- Every five years the Government would hold a selection test for a period of six months for choosing suitable school books. In the respective notification before the selection test the conditions in keeping with this regulation would be clearly stated along with the date of the test and the date and hour of the closure.

- The editors or the publishers who desired to present some of their work during this selection test had to produce against a duly issued receipt in the Department of Primary Education two copies each of their books meant either for the students or for the teachers. The candidates would have to prove that they were in keeping with the civic rights.
- The books submitted for the selection test would have to satisfy the following conditions:
  - Had to be in tune with the syllabus mentioned in the regulations.
  - Had to be printed in tipography or dactilography.
  - On the frontispiece the name of the applicant should have been displayed. Along with the application they had to enclose a chart mentioning the name of the writer pertaining to each division/chapter/lesson in the book which would be opened in the meeting of the Council of Public Instruction in which the material would be approved.
  - The material in tipography or dactilography had to be numbered and all the leaves had to be signed by the applicant. Whatever amendments or corrections had to be made had to be duly initialled.
  - In all the works done in dactylography the first page always had to be printed in tipography showing the format and type of letters adopted and the graphics to be found on the printed pages indicating clearly the place where the other remaining pictures had been inserted.
    - — The designs approved on the book had to be numbered and attested by the President of the Council for Public Instruction or by a person to whom this work had been delegated so that they could vouch that the pictures shown on the printed book corresponded to the pictures presented to the authorities earlier having been presented together with an example as per the requirements.
    - — The kind of letters in which the text had been composed in the books had to be indicated previously in the preface as per rule and these must be selected from the types which had been officially listed.
  - Each example of the dactylographic work had to be bound with the printing done on white paper.

- To indicate the minimum price for which each copy could be sold.
  - — The works that did not satisfy these conditions would be rejected by the Council for Public Instruction.
  - — The approved works had to be presented in the Department of Primary Education within a period of six months counting from the immediate day of the publication of its approval in the "Boletim Oficial".

- The hygienic conditions which the books had to satisfy were as follows:
  - The paper had to be white, very lightly yellowed or ash and absolutely devoid of shine; sufficiently spacious so that the printing on one side did not fudge the matter on the other having minimum of decorative or fancy work.
  - The colour of the printed letters had to be clearly black, in the methods of writing permitting the compression of the letters.
  - The type should not be difficult to follow.
  - The length of the lines could not exceed 0m.08 in the books meant for the students.
  - The minimum margin had to be 0m.023
  - The gap between lines could not be less than two points for texts which did not exceed twelve points and to four for higher ones.
  - In the composition any of the types indicated in the preface could be used selected from among the letter types given on the General Catalogue of the National Printing Press of Lisbon and which were found to be reproduced in the "Diario do Governo" no. 98, II Series, of 22nd April, 1920 pages 1.487 and 1.488.
- The authors or the publishers of the approved books had to present a copy of each of them duly authenticated in the Department of Primary Instruction for the purpose of review by a special Committee nominated by the Government which would go into the hygienic conditions of the book and the harmony with the measures mentioned in the preface.
- If after any work had been approved the author or the proprietor declared to the Government that he wished to offer it to the State the donation would be accepted with the work being printed and sold by the Government at the cost price.

- The books meant for the students would be the following:
  - Reading book for Class II, III and IV.
  - Writing book for Class V.
  - Arithmetic and Geometry books for Class III, IV and V.
  - Geography and Chorography of Portugal, of the State of Portuguese India and the colonies for Class IV and V.
  - History of Portugal and brief notions of "India Portuguese" for Class IV and V.
  - Botany and Agriculture for Class III, IV and V.
  - Lessons on practical topics.
  - Notebooks of Calligraphy
  - Choral singing and Music for Class II, III, IV and V.
- A special selection test would be held in the Colonies for books coming under some of the above categories. However, most of the books approved and prescribed by the Council of Public Instruction would be from those adopted in the mother country.
- The choice of the book for initial Writing and Reading would be left to the discretion of the "Professor", since the method to be followed had to obey modern pedagogical principles.
- The Department of Primary Instruction had to recommend to the "Professors" the teachers' books which were supposed to be useful in upskilling them in teaching in the Primary Classses.

Plans for an In-Service Teacher Training Institute

The Government was interested in having a special school so as to improve the standard of teaching. With this in mind it tried to put in place the objectives of this institution and the directions that this school should take for which reason it set down the following:

- The Government would be able to create in the model school upgradation/training courses meant for the "Professors" of Primary instruction.
  - Those who attended regularly these upgradation courses would be awarded a Merit Diploma.
  - Those "Professors" who attended the courses of upgradation/training would get the benefit of added service which would be counted as part of their service. The financial costs to be paid to the teachers would be established by issuing a special notification.

- In order to facilitate the pedagogical upgradation of the Primary "Professors" and the establishment of the Primary schools and the pre-Primary models initially three "Professors" would be selected and deputed as per the stipulations laid down in a special Diploma at the cost of the Government to the National or foreign pedagogical centres for these upgradation courses which however could not exceed two years. These "Professors" had to revert back upon their return to their original posts without any enhancement in their salary and were obliged to present a report of their work and compulsorily serve the State for the next 10 years.

In order to take care of whatever was not still covered in the foregoing rules and regulations it was sought to be taken care of in the following dispositions:

- In the cases omitted in the present regulations the legislation in force at present in the country thought practicable with the vote of the Council of Public Instruction and sanctioned by the Council of the Government (permanent section).
- All the alterations introduced in the legislations of the Primary Instruction of the mother country had to be adopted in this State after duly adapting them through the Council of Public Instruction.
- The promotions of the "Professors" from one category to another for a period of six years would be continued with.

Suitable Changes in the Above Plan

Since the sanction had been given to make alterations in the above legislation as per the local needs the Governor, Joao Carlos Craveiro Lopes found that some of the stipulations could not be implemented and had to be modified to suit the local conditions. Accordingly after studying the reforms he asked the Directorate of Civil Administrative Service whose first Official, Francisco Xavier Lucio Carneiro de O. Nogar had issued the "Portaria" on he 30th of January, 1934 making clause by clause changes in the current legislation on Primary education which were as follows:

- The periods (teaching) which were designated to be of 40 minutes were increased to 50 minutes with an interval of ten minutes in between instead of 15. Between the third and the fourth periods there would also be an interval of two hours instead of one and half hour.

- Instead of March or April the interview for filling up the posts of teachers by transfer would be held annually in the month of January which would be done by the Department of Primary instruction within a period of ten days only instead of five days thus filling up the posts vacant till that date. The interview would be intimated to the "Professors" through an official communication from the Department of Primary Instruction making reference to the documents and books existing in the same Department.
- The evaluation of their service during interview would be limited to those who were either in permanent service or on probation. This service would be counted up to the date of the publication of the notification.
- In schools which had only one post a "Professor" would be appointed as per the classification in the interview taking the circumstances into consideration. In schools which had more than one post and if the number of posts was even there would be an equal number of male and female teachers and if the number of posts was odd then the number would be more of either male or female depending upon the classification obtained in the interview.
- In all the Primary schools there had to be a Director (Headmaster) who besides the duties allotted as a teacher would also have the following additional work:
  - The charge of the Director would be exercised as a rule by the senior-most "Professor" but in case the Head of the Department of Primary Instruction thought that this "Professor" did not have the necessary qualities then it had to propose another name to the Governor from the same school who was considered as more suitable for the exercise of that function.
  - In conformity with this alteration the expression senior-most had to be substituted in most of the remaining articles by "Professor" Director.
- Corporal punishments were to be prohibited absolutely and not used selectively and sparingly.
- The official "Professor" was prohibited from running a boarding school.

- The following expression had to be added to Article 124—dealing with cases of sickness—after the words 'duly cured' that only those cases which the Head of Primary Instruction thought worthy of taking up should be considered for review under the disciplinary regulations.
- The following "that for the examinations of the Second Level Juries would be constituted for groups of fifty each in every circle/area headquarters" was to be inserted in Article 137.
- The Article 146 was to be substituted as follows: The time allotted for the orals of each of the candidates of the Second Level would be less than 40 minutes and more than 20.
- Similarly in Article 149 it was to be added that whenever a candidate remained absent due to sickness or any other duly justified reason he would be called for the Second round on the day fixed by the respective Jury and he would have to answer the examination which he had missed due to absence on the last day of the functioning of the examination Jury. The justification for the absence should be given within 24 hours.
- The female candidates if they had not obtained a majority of remarks of "sufficient" at least in the tests of Needlework would be barred from appearing for the other examinations.
- The following change had to be made in Article 155: The Certificates had to be issued on stamped paper or on pressed paper on which was stuck the respective stamp authenticated with the office seal of the Department for which rupee one would be charged as contribution to the School Fund as per rules plus two "tangas" and three "reis" as processing fee. For a copy of any other Certificate not mentioned here the processing fee would be 12 "tangas" which would be claimed by the Secretary of the Department as emoluments.
- The following refers to Article 159: The marks for academic progress had to be given by the School Council at the end of the academic year for the work done by the student during the whole year. These marks had to be duly recorded in the respective school registers. These marks pertained to students reading in Class 2, 3 and 4 respectively. For them the promotion criteria would be as follows:
    - The students of Class 2 whose average marks were more than nine and had a good conduct would pass immediately to the next Class.

- The students of Class 3 and 4 whose average marks were more than nine at the end of the Second term were to be admitted for the final examination.
- Those students from any Class who had during the year remained absent for one-third of the number of instructional days or more in the whole academic year could not be promoted or admitted for the final examination except when the "Professor" took the responsibility for his promotion or admission for the examination.

- For the sake of the above rule the academic period to be considered was from 16th of June to 15th of September as first term, the second term from 16th of September to 15th of December and the third from the 16th of December to the end of February.
- The final examinations to promote students from Class I to Class II had to be held in the first fortnight of February by taking help of another "Professor" from the same school if there were more than one teacher.
- The student who had been promoted to the immediate next Class would be given a Certificate of attendance as per rules.
- The conduct of the students in each of the academic terms was to be evaluated by the respective "Professor" from the School Council by giving them either of the remarks "Bad", "Bearable" and "Good".
- If any of the students had obtained the remark "Bad" for two terms in any of the Classes in that academic year then they could not be promoted to the next Class nor could they be proposed for the examination.
- In the last five days of the academic year a meeting of the School Council had to be called to approve the attendance and the conduct of the students of Classes 1 and 2 and "Classe Inicial".
- As an exception the promotion of students reading in "Classe Inicial" could be made at the beginning of October itself.
- The third clause of Article 171 had to be replaced with the following: The Governor by a special notification and under the proposal of the Head of the Department of Primary Instruction could order any "Professor" of the Primary schools to work in the Department who would then be substituted putting him in charge of carrying out inspections of schools whenever the Head so desired. This "Professor" would receive besides his normal

salary a special remuneration fixed as per the rules in force.

- In case no substitute was available then a "Professor" would be appointed on temporary basis who would be paid from the money of the General School Fund.
- Again Clause 5 of Article 184 was to be changed into "the service of the "Professors" at the end of the term would be counted".
- Article 195 had to be altered as follows: The selection of books for the instruction of Reading and Writing so also for the Speaking and Written language in the "Class inicial" and in the Class I would be done by the Council of Public Instruction leaving however the method to be followed in teaching the children in the hands of the "Professor" but as per the modern pedagogical principles.

Transfers and Appointments of Teachers

When Paulo Bernardo Guedes took over as the new Governor the first thing he did was to issue a "Portaria" dated 3rd January, 1946 regarding the posting of "Professors" in the Primary schools of Portuguese in the State in supersession of the previous Order which had been issued in 1938 as follows (province-wise) (Table 8.3):

Table 8.3: Number of Posts in Different Provinces

Sr. No.	*Name of Place*	*No. of teachers*
1.	**Ilhas (Tiswadi)**	
	1. Chorao	4
	2. Cumbharjua	1
	3. Corlim	1
	4. Goa Velha	2
	5. Mandur	2
	6. Merces	3
	7. Neura	2
	8. Panjim	5
	9. Piedade	4
	10. Ribandar	3
	11. Santa Cruz	4
	12. S. Estevao	7
	13. S. Lourenco	2
	14. S. Pedro	1
	15. Taleigao	3
2.	**Bardez**	
	1. Aldona	2
	2. Anjuna	2
	3. Assagao	1

(Contd.)

TABLE 8.3 (*Contd.*)

Sr. No.	Name of Place	No. of teachers
	4. Calangute	2
	5. Calvim	2
	6. Camacazana	1
	7. Candolim	2
	8. Colvale	1
	9. Guirim	1
	10. Mapuca	2
	11. Moira	2
	12. Nachinola	1
	13. Nagoa	1
	14. Nerul	1
	15. Parra	1
	16. Pilerne	1
	17. Pomburpa	1
	18. Reis Magos	2
	19. Revora	1
	20. Saligao	2
	21. Sangolda	1
	22. Serula	2
	23. Siolim	2
	24. Socorro	2
	25. Tivim	1
	26. Tropa	1
	27. Ucassaim	1
3.	**Salcette**	
	1. Assolna	2
	2. Benaulim	4
	3. Betalbatim	3
	4. Carmona	3
	5. Cavellossim	2
	6. Chandor	3
	7. Chinchinim	4
	8. Colva	4
	9. Cuncolim	4
	10. Curtorim	4
	11. Dramapur	2
	12. Loutulim	4
	13. Macasana	2
	14. Majorda	5
	15. Margao	6
	16. Nagoa de Sal	2
	17. Navelim	3
	18. Nuvem	2
	19. Orlim	3
	20. Paroda	1
	21. Raia	4
	22. Seraulim	2
	23. Telaulim	2
	24. Varca	2
	25. Velim	4
	26. Verna	2

(*Contd.*)

TABLE 8.3 (*Contd.*)

Sr. No.	*Name of Place*	*No. of teachers*
4.	**Mormugao**	
	1. Cansaulim	3
	2. Cortalim	3
	3. Vasco da Gama	5
	4. Velcao	2
5.	**Pernem**	
	1. Arambol	1
	2. Dhargalim	1
	3. Morgim	1
	4. Pernem	1
6.	**Sanquelim**	
	1. Amona	1
	2. Bicholim	1
	3. Mulgao	2
	4. Sanquelim	1
	5. Usgao	1
7.	**Sattari**	
	1. Birondem	1
	2. Codal	1
	3. Querim	1
	4. Valpoi	1
8.	**Ponda**	
	1. Borim	2
	2. Durrbatt	2
	3. Marcaim	1
	4. Marcela	1
	5. Mardol	1
	6. Ponda	1
	7. Shiroda	1
	8. Verem de Ponda	
9.	**Sanguem**	
	1. Collem	1
	2. Rivona	1
	3. Sanguem	2
10.	**Quepem**	
	1. Assolda	1
	2. Canaguinim	1
	3. Curchorem	1
	4. Quepem	2
11.	**Canacona**	
	1. Canacona	1
	2. Maxem	1
	3. Sadolxem	1

(*Contd.*)

TABLE 8.3 (*Contd.*)

Sr. No.	Name of Place	No. of teachers
12.	**Damao**	
	1. Damao praca	2
	2. Damao pequeno	2
13.	**Nagar Haveli**	
	1. Silvassa	2
14.	**Diu**	
	1. Diu	2
	2. Gogola	1

From table 8.3 it becomes evident that a total of 222 teachers were teaching in the various schools located in 14 Provinces which included Daman, Diu and Nagar Haveli. The highest number of teachers was to be found in the province of Salcette which apparently had the highest number of Primary schools. Again understandably the New Conquests had less number of schools and consequently less number of teachers in the Primary schools.

Initiatives of the Governor, Quintanilha Dias

By a "Portaria" bearing No. 4.971, dated 29th October, 1949, Fernando de Quintanilha e Mendonca Dias modified a few rules for the conduct of the final examinations and the organization of the examinations of the First and Second Level of Primary instruction and of the examinations of Portuguese language in the private English schools. The rules were as follows:

1. The examinations of Class I, II and III would be held in the first week of March admitting students from Class II to the examination of Class III only those who had obtained during the mid-year in Class II marks not less than nine. Except the promotion of students from "Class inicial", First and Second level examinations would be conducted in the first five working days of the month of October.
2. The examination of the Class III including those of mixed (Portuguese-Marathi, Portuguese-Gujarati would be held five days before the month of March and those of Class IV from 12 of the same month.

Subsequent to this the same Governor, having taken note of the diminishing school population of the official Primary mixed school of

Portuguese-Marathi in Quepem and considering that there would be better results if the school was transferred to the Parish of Cacora (Kakoda) of the same province and on the recommendation of the Council of Public Instruction and the Permanent Section of the Council of the Governor, the Governor General of the State of India taking recourse to the powers granted by the Article 31 of the "Acto Colonial" and by 19 of Article 33 of the "Carta Organica" of the Kingdom ordered by a "Portaria" dated 7th September, 1950, the Primary school of Portuguese-Marathi mixed instruction was transferred to Cacora from Quepem (town).

By now in Europe and elsewhere the Swedish teaching method called Slojd had gained a lot of importance. Keeping abreast with the times the Governor, Quintanilha Mendonca e Dias framed a Class-wise syllabus and tried to introduce it in a big way in the schools in Goa. By a "Portaria" bearing No. 5.107 dated 21st September, 1950 he stated that considering the need to systematize and give a big push to the teaching of educative work in order to develop the natural aptitudes of the students under the proposal of the Inspection section of Education and after consulting the Council of Public Instruction and the Permanent Section of the Council of the Government, the Governor General of the State of India by the powers granted by Article 31 of the "Acto Colonial" and by 19 of the article 33 of the "Carta Organica" of the Portuguese Kingdom determined the following:

Class I

Modelling: Free modelling

Paper Works: Double folding, to crease, to plait, and to tear or cut paper; dividing the paper into equal parts, folding the paper into simple articles like hats, boats, etc.

Class II

Modelling: Modelling of fruits, pages and objects of common use; free modelling.

Paper works: Simple and varied doubling; outlining simple, preparatory exercises for weaving and interweaving

Working with banana, coconut and jackfruit leaves: Baking of articles of common use which can be prepared with these leaves.

Class III

Modelling; Copying of models; modelling with clay (relevos de terrenos), free modelling.

Paper Works: Continuation of the doubling of paper; Preparing covers for the books, embossing, superscribing, etc., paper cutting of symmetrical and geometrical figures, dolls, objects of common use and others of simple contours; weaving, collage; frieze; decorative combinations of circumferences, squares, rectangles and triangles; mosaics, centres and corners.

Working with Thread, Fibre and Hay: German knots, galley knots, running knots, etc., crossbars, holders for the vases, meshes, etc.

Working with the Coconut Leaves: Preparation of slippers, shoes, roofs of palm leaves, baskets etc.

Working with the Seeds of Melon and Water Melon: Hand basket, purses, curtains, baskets, etc.

Class IV

Modelling: Paper flowers, animals, solids, and geometric figures and objects of simple contours (contorno).

Paper Work: Freehand sketches on paper; straight lines and stars, curved lines and rose-like, small carpets, curtains and wall-hangings, etc.

Exercises on thick cloth with pins on paper or thin cardboard, straight and curved lines and their combinations; moulding of the tracing paper, flowers and animals; transparent ornamental motifs, letters and words.

Collage and Cartonage: Execution of paste, card-cases, moulds, boxes, calendars, screens, buckets, etc. Execution of the same work with collage of the decorative motifs drawn on coloured paper.

Working with the ribs of the leaves of the coconut tree with or without box: Curtains, brooms, cages, stairs, carts, chairs, baskets for paper, etc.

Working with Wood: Use of the pen knife, small hammer and nails, execution of the handles of the knife, paper forks, boxes, boats, and other simple constructions.

Working with Cotton and Hay, Grass: Making of hand basket, small baskets, diverse animals, spinning, etc.

Besides chalking out a detailed syllabus the Secretary to the Council of Public Instruction, Alvaro Ribeiro notified on the 18th of October 1950 a model for the written and practical tests in the Primary schools which had been prepared and submitted by the Chief of Inspectorate of Education, Elvira de Noronha.

In June 1952, another "Portaria" was released stating that "A Primary school of official Portuguese education was established in Diu meant for those who had crossed the upper age limit for enrolling in normal schools".

Again the Governor, Fernando de Quintanilha e Mendonca Dias published on the 13th June, 1952 the following "Portaria" in the "Boletim Oficial": The post in the above school would be filled by transfer of a permanent teacher with the Inspectorate of Education drawing up a list of the "Professors" teaching in Class II and Class III.

Then came the rules for appointing teachers in the Portuguese-Urdu schools by a "Portaria" 5.534 dated 24th July, 1952, by the same Governor.

Notifications from Time to Time

In the meantime another "Portaria" was issued by Manuel Maria Sarmento Rodrigues from the Ministry of Overseas Affairs on the 4th of December, 1953 stating that in the placement of "Professors" in the private schools of Primary education in the Overseas Provinces, preference had to be given to the "spouses" of the Government functionaries in service who had been placed in the locality where existed a school or a post.

The next Governor, Paulo Bernardo Guedes because pressure was being exerted to take plum postings decided through a "Portaria" 6.077, dated 1st July, 1954, to grade the Urdu schools as follows:

1. Panjim School,
2. Ponda school, and
3. Nanuz school.

The posts in the above schools would be filled in the given order and the new teacher if any would be posted only in the last school.

Again the same Governor to set to rest the confusion regarding issuing of Attendance and Enrolment Certificates at the same time decided *via* the "Portaria" 6.249, dated 9th of December, 1954, as follows:

No Certificate of enrolment or Attendance simultaneously in Class III and Class IV should be issued to any student, private or domestic unless the student produced a Certificate stating that he had cleared Class III or during inspection proved that it was with the papers of Class II.The Certificate of Class III had to be kept in the school. Those Certificates issued in contravention of this rule were to be considered as null and void.The admission given on the basis of these Certificates had to be cancelled by the "Professor" Directors. Those who disobeyed the above would have disciplinary action taken against them.

With regard to the posts of Inspectors so that those appointed should be morally above the Primary teachers he ordered the following by a "Portaria" 6.026, dated 8th April, 1954:

Because of the Primary teachers serving as Inspectors of education it was established that they had to qualify with the remark of "very good". The posts of School Inspectors were being performed by "Professors" of Primary education with both good references and the remark of "average" when the latter one was not at all admissible.

The Governor then shifted his attention to the enrolment of students and by a "Portaria" 6.848, dated 17th January, 1957, legislated the following:

- The minimum age limit for enrolment in the official Primary schools would be 6 years completed or about to be completed in that calendar year.
- Those students who had completed 16 years would not be allowed to attend school except if they were enrolled in Class III or IV in which case they would continue till the end of the academic year.
- The minimum age limit to register for examinations of the First Level or the Second Level was respectively 9 and 10 years completed or due to complete in that calendar year upto December 31st.
- Except those students who might have passed out in the official or private schools when the "Professor" had declared that they had no problem if they were admitted for the examinations.

Another few "Portarias" were issued by the Governor, Bernardo Guedes concerning the time limit for teachers to apply for interview, extension of the period for admissions in Primary from 24th of May to the 4th of June (which was later on extended to 30th of June), conducting the examinations of Class I, II and III during the last five days of the instructional year as well as announcing the minimum standard of passing from Class II to Class III.

An interesting event that took place during his tenure was the establishment of "two cash prizes instituted in the name of Dr. Ubaldo Pais in the Primary school of Assolna for the students of Assolna, Velim, Cuncolim and Ambelim; one for the student standing first in Class I and the other in Class II. Rules for the award were also framed".

Efforts Continue Till the End

The last Portuguese Governor, Manuel Antonio Vassalo e Silva by a "Diploma Legislativo" dated 15th June, 1961 established Portuguese schools of Primary education in the following places thus creating another 30 posts of Portuguese teachers:

Table 8.4: The Newly Created Posts Province-wise

Provinces	*Pernem*	*Bicholim*	*Sattari*	*Sanquem*
	Corgao Querim Tiracol	Latambarcem Mayem	Poriem Cotorem	Bhatti Curdi Dabal
Provinces	*Quepem*	*Canacona*	*Nova Goa*	*Bardez*
	Avedem Cusmane Xeldem Fatorpa Molcornem	Gaondongrim Bhattpal	Dona Paula	Sauntavaddo, Calangute Dando, Candolim Namoxim, Guirim Duler, Mapuca Marna, Siolim Revora
Provinces	*Ponda*	*Salcette*		
	Adpoi-Agapur, Queula Kundai Ponchvaddi	Ambajim, Margao Aquem Baixo Deussua, Chinchinim.		

Significantly it is apparent that barring ten posts the remaining twenty were all in the New Conquests. This indicated that the Government with the change in its policy was concentrating on equitable distribution of educational opportunities for its people. Due to it s neglect and consequent backwardness the government was paying more attention to the New Conquests as is evidenced from the various measures undertaken by the Government.

IX
The Final Act (1950-1961)

All the legislation that had been promulgated and modified, adjusted, improved upon and experimented with from 1831 for more than a century finally snowballed into a comprehensive code of rules and regulations pertaining to the total school education system in the State which set out the functioning and administration of all schools in a systematic orderly and disciplined manner. So in 1958, a complete set of rules and regulations was approved and published for the benefit of all. Prior to that, the rules and regulations that were promulgated in 1931 were being followed. The present document issued by the Secretary General Rui de Azavedo Guimaraes was a comprehensive piece of legislation which had evolved after undergoing numerous additions, modifications and deletions as we have read in the foregoing chapters. It was then printed in the form of a booklet having twelve chapters and included everything from admissions, appointments to duties and responsibilities of teachers and even the various formats for issue of Certificates, maintenance of records or even preparation of lessons. A thorough reading of this important piece of legislation, therefore, becomes necessary. A translated version which was drafted in the form of Articles since it was a legal document is provided hereunder:

CHAPTER I

Section I—On Teaching

Nature and objectives of Primary education:

1. Primary Education consists of two Levels of education: elementary and complementary.
2. Primary education would be imparted at all Levels in the official

schools in the Portuguese language (medium of instruction) and at the elementary Level it could also be in Portuguese-Marathi, Portuguese- Gujarati and Portuguese-Urdu. *Exception*: As per established norms private schools, home schooling and individual tuitions could also impart Primary education.

3. Education was entirely free and schools were exempted from paying taxes and stamp duties, the registration in the official Primary schools was free, including the attendance, the testing and examination of students, the examination forms and the respective Diplomas/Certificates.
4. There was no imposition of stamp duty or charging of any other emoluments. The medical Certificates and the church Certificates or those issued by the "Regedores" for the purpose of complying with the law/rules as laid down for Primary education were free of cost.
5. The education in Portuguese was spread over four years with each Class normally of one year duration with the First three years making up the Elementary Level and the fourth year as the Complementary Level. *Exception*: However, for those who normally do not speak Portuguese there would be an Extra Class in the official Primary schools called the "Classe inicial ou preparatoria" (initial or preparatory Class).
6. Primary education was supposed to help in the physical, intellectual and moral development of the children and provide them with the necessary knowledge in general for their dignified living, for their individual progress and for their integration in the economic and social milieu in which they were living. *N.B.*— In the first-three Classes it was basically taken that the students would learn to read, write and count, understanding the simple facts of life around them, and practice the civic and moral values related to their duties towards God, country and family. The fourth Class besides the foregoing, would take upon itself to provide the notion as far as possible of the position of Portugal, both continental, insular and overseas in the contemporary world, through the study of its History and Geography preparing at the same time their entry into the various social functions and imparting the necessary knowledge for the continuation of their studies at the next Level.
7. The above competencies would then be tested in the examinations, held normally at the end of the academic year for Class III and IV,

with the fulfilment of the attendance requirement.

8. A special Diploma/Certificate would be conferred on completing the course provided the established rules were followed and the syllabus taught was as close as possible to the one followed in Portugal.

Section II—Compulsory Instruction

9. All those who had completed seven years of age till the 31st of December and were less than thirteen had to compulsorily attend Primary school till they had passed any of the examinations, elementary or complementary.
10. The compulsion of Primary instruction included the compulsion of registering and be it as student of official Primary school or of private school, had the compulsion of attending regularly as regulated by the present set of rules.
11. Those entrusted with education were responsible for the compliance of related orders in the implementation of this compulsion having undertaken to promote the enrolment and to guarantee the regularity of school attendance of the minors under their charge. *Exception*: In effect this legislation considers that the father, the mother, the tutor and the guardian through the very undertaking as parents, tutor or any other competent entity or by virtue of the simple authority of the fact were to be held responsible.
12. It is the responsibility of the Directors of the schools and the respective "Professors" to encourage enrolment and regular attendance by the children at their proper school age, acting in this regard together with the families and explaining to them the need of education for inculcation of values and the sanctions which can be imposed they failed to enroll their children.
13. The following were excused from attending regularly Primary education: (a) those who were physically handicapped or mentally incapable, (b) those who resided more than three kilometres away from any Primary school either Government or private, since no transport would be provided for them. However, those who were physically handicapped but otherwise in good health had to be admitted into special schools if these were within three kilometres from their residences. This had to

be implemented by the person in charge of education through the teachers.

CHAPTER II

Section I—School Survey

14. From January to April every year throughout the "Estado da India" the exercise of collecting data a school survey would be organized and would include all the children both males and females separately from the age of seven to 13 completed or about to complete in December of those who did not have any certificate or proof of having attended or appeared for examinations in any of the schools of Primary education.
15. To conduct this survey Committees would be constituted in each Municipal area or Parish.
16. These Committees would function from the libraries or the offices of Civil Registration and would be constituted by the respective "Conservador" or an official who would serve as the President, appointed by the head of the Municipality and by a "Professor" of a school located in the Municipal town observing however the system of rotation in case there was more than one school. *N.B.*—In the capital city in place of a teacher, a functionary of the Department of education could be appointed as a member of the Committee. If necessary the Directorate of Civil Services could add one or more "Professors" of the Municipal town to the Committee. The survey operations and other services of the Secretariat of the Committees would be carried out by the functionaries under the Department of Instruction of which they would form a part.
17. The Committees of the Parishes would function in the local Primary school or there was more than one then in the one designated by the Directorate of Civil Services and would be constituted with the Director of the school as President of the Parish Committee, with the teachers and the Civil Registrar if the place had one as members. *N.B.*—(a) The absence of the President of the Parish Committee at the meetings of the Committee would not be a justification for the postponement of the work; (b) In the Parishes where there was only one teacher he would assume the charge as the President of the Committee and the functionary of the Civil Registry would take charge of

organizing the survey; (c) in the Parishes where there was no school at all the President of the Committee would be the "Regedor" or any teacher of the neighbouring Parishes nominated by the Directorate of Civil Services; and (d) in the Municipal towns which consisted of more than one Parish only one Committee would be formed.

18. On the first working day of January the Committees of the Municipal areas had to start their work in the respective "conservatorias" or offices of the Civil Registry where they would fill out the individual entries with the name, address, relationship, profession of the parents and date of birth of the children who had completed or were going to complete in that calendar year the age of seven. *N.B.*—(a) The Committee had to examine the corresponding registers of the previous years regarding the surveys, in order to include in it the children whose births had been inscribed late; (b) the entries referred above had to be submitted accompanied by particular note till the 20th of the same month, to the President of the Committee of the Parish where the parents of the children resided; (c) regarding those children who had expired after the inclusion of their names in the entries sent to the Committee of the Parish in the preceding five years the Municipal Committee had to prepare a list which would be submitted within the stipulated time to those Committees.
19. At the end of the exercise which they had been entrusted with the Municipal Committees had to enter on the proper register the minutes where the number of entries sent to each of the Parish Committees was written showing clearly the male or female sex of the children. By the 20th of January a copy of the minutes had to be sent to the Directorate of Civil Services.
20. From the 21st of January to the 20th of February the Committees of the Parishes had to prepare centre-wise and sex-wise, the lists in which the names had to be written in the chronological order of their birth, followed by the identification marks matching the entries submitted by the Municipal Committees not only of the children living in the Parish but also of those who though not being born there, had been residing in that place continuously and had completed or were going to complete in the calendar year seven years of age.
21. The Parish Committees within the stipulated time would proceed

with the revision of the lists drawn up five years earlier by eliminating those who had died or had passed some of the examinations of the Primary education or were cut off from the school perimeter and adding to the lists those that had been born elsewhere and were now residing in the Parish.

22. The survey of those children residing in places connected to the school centres of the neighbouring Parishes would come under the Parish survey where the centres were located. The entries relating to the children in these places, therefore, had to be made till the 31st of January by the President of the Committee of the survey to which these places belonged.
23. The Survey Committees of these places had to submit by the 31st of January to the respective Parish Survey Committees the details of the children who had relocated themselves in these Parishes or in the school centres.
24. To implement the above stipulations the Parish survey Committees would proceed with a well-designed inquiry format so that all children residing in the respective areas and subject to the obligation of attending school could be included, for which they had to solicit the cooperation of the Parish priests or any other administrative entity, including authorities and functionaries of the State who could not refuse to co-operate.
25. The President of the Parish survey team would sign alongwith the members of the Committee the lists pertaining to each of the six years covered by the survey and send them by the 10th of March to the school delegate or to the Council of Goa or to the Directorate of Civil Services. *N.B.*—From these lists two more detailed lists would be prepared corresponding to the centres that were functioning in the Parish or in the school circle.
26. In the last meeting of the Committee the report of the work undertaken would be drawn up and signed by all the members a copy of which would be submitted along with the lists to the school delegate or to the Council of Goa or to the Directorate of Civil Services. *N.B.*—The entries of the children inscribed in the original list would remain with the President of the Committee.
27. Having received the respective reports and after the names of those who had answered some examinations or the other had been eliminated they had to be checked by the school delegate or by an official of the Department of Education and returned, with the exception of two copies, to the respective Parish Committees

which would distribute them to the different educational institutions. *N.B.*—(a) The authorities then would compile all the data into a well-formulated table showing in alphabetical order the Parishes, the centres and the wards and then the children as per their sex in the survey/census; (b) If need be the official of the Education Department would appoint one or more "Professors" from the Municipal town to complete the work.

28. The Department of Education had to prepare a report to be presented to the Director of Civil Services who would then evaluate the results of the survey work and then reward those who had worked hard and take to task those who had neglected their work.
29. The subordinate staff had to render all the help asked for through the good offices of the President of the Committee of the Parish.
30. The census work had to be carried out without neglecting their regular school work and was compulsory and without any additional remuneration for the members of the Parish Committee.
31. The lower officials of the Department of Education who refused to help or showed negligence or bad faith in the work which had been entrusted to them or put under their charge would invite disciplinary action against them.
32. The teachers whose services had been hired for the census work could not remain absent enjoying holidays without completing the work entrusted to them or assigned to them.
33. The expenditure for the exercise of the census work would be borne from the funds provided for in the budget.

Section II—Admissions

34. Only those who had completed minimum 7 years till 31st of December of the respective year could be admitted in the first Class of Primary Elementary Level either in a formal school or at home or individually.
35. The registration had to be done by the Director of the school at the request of the guardian of the minor. *N.B.*—(a) for the proper implementation of this the Director of the school could allot the work of registration to any of the other teachers.
36. The normal period for admission was from 25th of May to 4th of June. *N.B.*—Before the start of the admissions the Director

would announce either by pasting a notice in a prominent place as far as possible the duration for the admissions, the penalties to be imposed on the guardians who did not follow the stipulations regarding the compulsion of attending school as well as the names of the minors, attending school for the first time.

37. Without prejudice to the application of sanctions to the whole process, the admission of a child subject to compulsory attendance could be facilitated till the first day of the third period of the academic year.
38. The registration act imposes always on the child the attendance compulsion till the end of the academic year.
39. The first registration done on the books of registration within the stipulated period signed by the Director of the school, would consist of:
    (a) Complete name, birth date, nationality, residence and names of parents or guardians of the enrolled.
    (b) Complete name, State, profession, residence of the guardian.
    (c) In case the child was enrolled on behalf of the family by a benefactor, the name of the institution had to be mentioned.

    Exception: Only in case of some doubt arose or when the enrolled had not figured in the books of registration then he would be exempted from producing the Certificate of age or his personal details. It was, however, always necessary that a certificate of vaccination against contagious diseases had to be produced.
40. The registration of the children who had attended the same school was done by a simple recording in the respective terms showing the Class to which they belonged.
41. The registration of children who had attended other schools would be done upon furnishing of a pass Certificate in the previous Class the one from which he was supposed to have passed out or in which he had been reading.
42. It was prohibited in principle for the student to attend any school outside the official circle in which he resided. *Exception*: (1) The attendance in schools situtuated outside the circle should be authorized every year; (2) The responsibilities if in contravention of these articles would rest solely with the teacher who had registered the child; and (3) In case of false declarations regarding the residence those in charge of education would be penalized as per rules.
43. Those students who for the first time were attending school would

be registered normally in the first Class or the "Class inicial". *Exceptions*: (1) Whenever the students showed disinterest since they were too old for the Class they would be admitted to Class III by giving them a simple test; (2) Those students tutored at home or individually in terms of article 46 and who in the following year enrolled themselves in the next Class would be admitted by the Director of the school through a prior verification of his knowledge/learning as per the terms of the previous paragraph.

44. The private schools authorized to provide Primary education could admit within the stipulated period to the official schools any student subject to the conditions of learning.
45. The private schools had to intimate till the 10th of June the Directorate of Civil Services and the official schools the exact place where the children could enter their names, their parents' names, their nationality, their addresses as well as the name and the residence of the person in-charge of the child's education.
46. The admissions of those who were tutored at home or individually had to be made in the school circle to which the child belonged through the Director of the official school till the 20th of June. (1) For the execution of this article there will be in the official schools a special book as per the model annexed to this regulation.
47. After having received the desired detailed information the Directors of the school had to verify which of the surveyed students in-spite of not having answered any of the examinations of Class 3 or 4 had not registered themselves and advise the respective in charges in writing by the 20th of June to get them registered within a period of five days from the day of receiving the notice, informing them at the same time of the penalties they would be subjected to if they failed to comply with the stipulations of law.
48. The Directors of the school had to communicate to the Directorate of Civil Services the names of the in-charges of education who, after receiving the notice could not carry out the process of enrolment. *Exceptions*: (1) The Directorate of Civil Services till the 30th of every month would direct the defaulters through a registered AD letter within a period of ten days to pay voluntarily the respective fines. If the letter was returned or the notice had not been signed the notification would be sent through an

intermediary of the competent administrative authority. (2) The fines had to be paid in the respective schools and they would become ineligible for any increase since their payment had been made voluntarily; and (3) If at the end of the time limit, the proof of having paid was not produced he would be sent by the Directorate of Civil Services to the tribunal of the Municipal area for a proper decision. This announcement would then be subjected to judicial enquiry to find out if there had been any violation of constitutional facts or of the documents of notification.

49. The in-charges of education who till the 20th of June had not enrolled the minors as per the obligations or had not presented to the Director of the school a convenient record of the enrolment would be subjected to a penalty between Rs. 5 and Rs. 20.
50. Besides the penalty fixed in the previous article the in-charges of education would be punished with a fine between Rs. 20 to Rs. 50 for not effecting the enrolment till the end of the first academic term.
51. The penalties in the previous articles would be imposed on the in-charges of education if after having been intimated in writing by the Official or any school authority to give the information had not done so within a period of ten days.

Section III—Organization of Terms

52. The fixing of the number of terms for each school was the prerogative of the Director of Civil Services taking into account the number of students registered and as per the provisions in the budget (1) The number of terms that the schools would have in each year would always be different from those existing in the previous year, which had to be communicated to the respective Directors till the 31st of May by the Directorate of Civil Services (2) Normally the number of students in each Class could not exceed 40.
53. The Directors of the school in consultation with the school Committee had to work out the organization of the terms within the notified rules meant for the "Professors" and the students and which had to be made known by noon of the 5th of June. *Exception*: In case no order to the contrary had been received, the Directors of the schools could fix the same number of terms as were had in the previous year.

54. Education would be separate for boys and girls. *Exception*: The system of co-education would be allowed in schools in which there was only one teacher or when the school building and the number of teachers and students of each sex prohibited such a separation.
55. A regency of more than one term would not be given to any "Professor" except at different times and in schools in which there may be an excess of student population. *Exceptions*: (a) Normally a group would be constituted of only one Class. However, under exceptional circumstances there would be two (b) The number of students in each Class had to be more or less equal with some difference of less students in the lower Classes; (c) while distributing the Classes among the "Professors" attention should be paid to the span of teaching experience with those who had joined later being given the lower Classes; and (d) the repeater students would be distributed equitably in the same Classes.
56. The Heads of the school had to communicate by the 10th of June to the school official the number of Classes, the number of students in each Class and the number of Classes allotted to each teacher. *Exception*: (a) Whenever there was a situation contrary to the rules as far as the allotting of Classes/periods among the "Professors" was concerned, the Heads had to send together with the plan of distribution of periods a report justifying the action of the Head; and (b) the school officials had to communicate to the Directorate of Civil Services till the 20th of June, in alphabetical order of the Parishes or the cluster of schools the number of Classes, the number of students in each Class, and the Classes/periods distributed to each of the "Professors". They also had to send the reports which they considered worth studying by the Directorate of Civil Services.
57. After having studied the distribution done, having dealt with the reports sent, having made the clarifications which had to be then conveyed to the school officials and to the school Heads and the "Professors" concerned, the Director of Civil Services had to confirm the distribution made or suggest the convenient changes that needed to be effected.
58. The Heads of schools would then consider as ratified the distributions made by them if till the 20th of July nothing had been communicated to them to the contrary.
59. (refers to students of Normal School).

Section IV—Transfers

60. The transfer of students from one school to another and the transfer between private schools would be permitted at any time of the academic year provided an application addressed to the school Head where the student was seeking admission was made. *Exceptions*: (a) The transfer of students from one school to another of the same locality was permitted only till the 31st of December and by the orders of the Director of the Civil Services, by moving an application by a duly qualified person; and (b) The transfer of students of the official schools to private schools or home school would also be permitted till the beginning of the third quarter of the academic year, through an application addressed to the Director of the School in which the child had been enrolled; (c) The transfer of students from a private school to an official school would also be permitted when the parents or the tutor of the minor changed residence to a locality where no private schools of Primary education were to be found through an application addressed to the Director of Civil Services in which the reason for such a request had to be mentioned.
61. The transfers would be made by the officials of education and the applications would be addressed to the Director of the school which the minor was attending. *Exceptions*: (a) The Director of the School would then send to the Directorate of Civil Services the applications which had to be attended to by the superiors and would retain the remaining after mentioning therein the declaration of identity, the enrolment and the attendance of the student; and (b) Through the declaration referred to above the Director of the School would admit the student whose attendance was satisfactory.

CHAPTER III

Section I—Time Table

62. In all the Primary schools the scholastic year would begin on the 25th of May and would end on the 31st of March; the academic year would begin on the 5th of June and end on the last day of February. *Exceptions*: (a) The holidays for the Primary schools during the academic year besides Sundays and days of

National and Municipal importance were three days immediately before the Quinquagesima Sunday and three days before Easter Sunday; (b) For the Hindus these would also be taken as holidays: 2nd and 3rd day of Ganesh Chaturthi and Diwali; for the Muslims one day each for the festival of Ramzan, Id ul Adha (Bakri Id), Id Mila udin and Moharram; for the Parsis, the day of Pateti; and for the Christians the feast of St. Francis Xavier and the souls of the departed; (c) On the days of National and Municipal importance and on Sundays the National flag would be flown in the schools; and (d) In the evenings of the National and Municipal holidays the teachers would give their students a short patriotic lecture on the significance of the day.

63. The mid term breaks would be from the 14th of September to the 04th of October and from the 23rd of December to the 6th of January; the long holidays would be from the end of the scholastic year to the beginning of the new scholastic year without any prejudice to the services of payment and enrolment.
64. Every school day would consist of five sessions/periods of 40 minutes duration each except on Thursdays when there would be only two periods being of religion and morals, gymnastics and games, activities appropriate to the Youth Corps (Mocidade Portuguese) or for the girls with the teaching of stitching and needle work. (a) All schools that function normally would start at 8.30 a.m.; in schools which function with teachers alternating between the two sessions the morning session would begin at 8 a.m. and the evening session at 1.30 p.m., with each of the teachers maintaining the proper timings continuously; and (b) In all the schools there would be an interval of more or less 15 minutes between the third and the fourth periods and others of ten minutes between the remaining.
65. The intervals are for all purposes a part of the functioning of the school for which reason the "Professors" must not during these periods lose interest in their students.
66. The organization of the time table or the plan of weekly distribution of subjects period-wise after consulting the school Council, would be the responsibility of the Directors of the schools who had to prepare the time table as per the instructions given by the Directorate of Civil Services (a) The time table would be implemented provisionally from the first day of the academic year; (b) The Directors of the schools through the local

education official had to send as soon as possible to the Directorate of Civil Services the time tables which they would be implementing after they had been approved or altered; (c) The Inspectors making certain changes which they thought were necessary would submit the time tables of different schools to the Director of Civil Services and only after he had approved them would implement them in full force.

67. In every Classroom a copy of the time table had to be affixed easily visible to all both students as well as the "Professors" so that it could be followed during that term or all the terms (a) The distribution of the subjects to be taught during the different periods would be changed only in exceptional circumstances which had to be recorded in the "Diary of Lessons" (Log Book)
68. The lessons had to be prepared in advance and the main points had to be written in the Log Book (a) The Log Book had to conform to the model annexed to these regulations and had to be completed in keeping with the norms established by authorities earlier; and (b) Failure to comply with this stipulation would invite disciplinary action as a case of negligence and mishandling of professional duties.

Section II—School Attendance

69. Students must be present in the school in time from the beginning of the school session tidily dressed.
70. The attendance referring not only to the physical presence but also to the progress and conduct of the students would be registered in the respective book.
71. Only in case of natural calamity the students were permitted to remain absent from Classes or other activities of the school.
72. Always whenever a student remained absent from school the teacher had to by the following day bring it to the notice of the respective Director along with the reasons which led to his absence. *Exceptions*: (a) In case the authorities had not been informed the Director of the school should communicate through the local administrative authority within 24 hours and in writing to the teacher that he had to justify the absence within two days immediately indicating the relevant provision; (b) The Director could condone only that absence which had been justified by valid reasons; but the Director whenever necessary had to

constitute or order to be constituted an inquiry into the veracity of the reasons.

73. Absence could be condoned for the following reasons:
    (a) Sickness of the student;
    (b) Death in the family;
    (c) Contagious disease of a person with whom the person lived;
    (d) Inaccessible residence and hence difficult to communicate
    (e) Solemn family get-together; and
    (f) Other facts which could evidently be considered as sufficient justification.
74. In the attendance register besides marking the students absent the reasons given for their absence too had to be indicated and the reasons for granting or non-granting of leave had to be written.
75. The tutors in each case had to enquire about the reasons for the absence or the irregularity of attendance and always as much as possible bring it to the notice of the Director of the school.
76. Irrespective of the penal clause in provision No. 49, the teachers who knowingly or through negligence had marked students absent for three days without asking for any explanation or without any justification would be liable for action under provisions in No. 80. (a) Recurrence of such incidents during the same academic year would invite action with twice the amount of penalty as the previous one.
77. The Directors of the schools of official instruction and private schools had to bring to the notice of the Directorate of Civil Services till the 5th of each month the infringements in the teaching practice committed by the teachers in the previous month. *Exceptions*: (a) The Directors of the official schools who did not comply with the principle mentioned in the foregoing provision would also suffer the same action as proposed for the teachers without prejudice to other disciplinary action; (b) The Private Primary schools which did not comply with the provisions mentioned above would be closed down temporarily or indefinitely depending upon the seriousness of the infringements committed; and (c) The action as spelt out above was the sole prerogative of the Governor.
78. The Directorate of Civil Services after having taken note of the infringements mentioned above should initiate action as per rules given in No. 48.

Section III—School Discipline

79. School discipline as a formal element of education had as its objective to create order and the necessary quietude in keeping with the academic environment and to contribute to a worthy development of the mental faculties of children as per their physical growth and spiritual and moral progress. *Exceptions* (a) The "Professors" had to treat all students in equal measure without any distinction, with love and care as they were his own children; (b) School discipline must be maintained by means of persuasion and only in cases of total ineffectiveness of these measures, punishments should be resorted to; and (c) Corporal punishments are prohibited.
80. Whenever some student shows stubbornness to the fatherly affections of the "Professor" this should be brought to the notice of the Class Teacher so that necessary steps deemed fit could be taken. In case the Class Teacher had to find it difficult to put the child on the right path it would be a fit case for the Directorate of Civil Services which would have to provide in the event of its intervention certain corrective measures.
81. Without prejudice to the claims to any other prize the students who distinguished themselves in school by their regular attendance, their conduct, application and progress should have their names written on the roll of honour during the last period of the day.

CHAPTER IV

Section I—Academic Help

82. Financial assistance to poor students in the official Primary schools would be given from the school and canteen funds. *Exceptions* (a) The two organizations mentioned above are meant, generally speaking to encourage the enrolment and regular attendance through material and moral help to the students who were found to be economically backward.
83. In every school it was obligatory to have a school fund.
84. The school fund was set up specifically for the following purposes:
    (a) To provide the students free of cost or at reduced prices, essential articles like books, needed for their learning;

articles for their current consumption like medicines, vests and pants;

(b) Maintain or subsidize the school canteen and vacations;

(c) Support walks and school excursions;

(d) Develop in students an associative spirit and social cooperation.

85. The canteen would function in a proper building adjoining or detached from the school and at the initiative for establishing it could come from the State or any person or entity.

86. The specific objectives of the school canteen were as follows:

(a) To provide free of cost on school days snacks to the needy students who attend Classes regularly;

(b) To help in the formative efforts on the school;

(c) To cultivate in the students a spirit of cooperation and Christian charity promoting within its ranks membership duly authorized by the Class teachers; and

(d) To develop the best collaboration as also other works of social assistance especially in the protection of and support to children.

87. The students who did not fit into the above category could also avail of the snacks in the school canteens by paying the indicated price.

88. Always when any property worth Rs. 50,000 or more was donated towards the canteens the State would take charge of the construction of the respective buildings and would give the donor the right to indicate the "Professors" for filling up of two of the vacancies or open a central place as canteen to benefit schools around.

89. The generosity mentioned in the above clause had to be accepted by the Governor by publishing such an offer on a case to case basis in the Official Gazette.

90. The Government would be able to provide premises for the school canteens in the State Government buildings provided it caused no inconvenience for the services for which these had been specifically attached.

91. The State through the intervention of another section namely the National Organization of Portuguese Youth (Mocidade Portuguesa) would monitor the private initiative in establishing and running of canteens through certain means which they thought were suitable.

92. The deeds of endowment/donation for the canteens were exempted from stamp duty and from other charges as well as from the respective registration and certification process at the Registrar's.
93. All those who wanted to contribute with some donation or service would be admitted as members of the canteen and school fund organization:
    (a) As per their contribution the members would be of two types: ordinary and special. Those who contributed Rs. 5,000 and above or paid a monthly instalment of Rs. 15 would be special members; and
    (b) the students could enrol as ordinary members.
94. The following would constitute the income of the school fund and the school canteen:
    (a) The fees from the members;
    (b) The interest from the funds instituted in its favour;
    (c) The income from receipts of public collections and school feasts;
    (d) The subsidies from the State, from "Communidades", from the administrative bodies, from associations, from public administrative Departments or from any other entities; and
    (e) Any other donations.

    With the exception of one above the income of the school fund would comprise of:
    (a) The profit arising out of the sale of books or any other school materials;
    (b) The subsidies given on account of the income from the sale of limited books of Primary education, edited in this State itself;
    (c) The net income from the cultivable agricultural lands that make part of the school compound as long as no school canteen existed; and
    (d) The interest from the loans and payments as per the terms of this order.
    (1) The following constituted the income of the school canteen:
    (a) The profit from the selling of snacks as per the rules; and
    (b) The net income from the cultivable agricultural lands which made a part of the school compound.
95. The school fund and the canteen fund would have as its organs; a General Assembly and a Directorate. *Except*: (a) The General

Assembly would comprise of all the members and would function under the guidance of a Committee of three members whose President would be designated by the Director of Civil Services; and (b) The Directorate would comprise of three to five members having a President designated by the Director of Civil Services; and two representatives selected from the teachers of the circle.

96. Whenever it was convenient the Governor would be able to nominate an administrative Committee comprising of three to five members to run the administration of the school and canteen funds.
97. The "Professors" would get the students interested in the working of the funds encouraging them to register as members and calling them to cooperate actively in its functioning.
98. The reports and the accounts of its management would always be submitted annually for the consideration of the Director of Civil Services.
99. The name to be given to the canteen and the school society was the prerogative of the Governor.
100. The contribution of the teacher in the functioning of the canteen and the school society would be duly considered at the time of promotion/placement.
101. The functioning of the school society and the school canteens would be regulated by proper statutes approved by the superiors.

Section II—Organization of the Portuguese Youth

102. In all Primary schools, official as well as private frequented/attended by the male students a principal centre of the organization had to be established.
103. The Director of each of these centres would be nominated by the regional delegate of the organization from among the male "Professors" teaching in the school where the centre had been established after consulting the Directorate of Civil Services. Except in the schools where there were no male teachers a female teacher could be appointed to direct the centre.
104. The activities of the Portuguese Youth Organization would be conducted as per the established plans drawn up by the Commissariat and with a schedule that would be prepared in consultation with the Commissariat and the Directorate of Civil Services. Except the activities of the Portuguese Youth

Organization would be integrated into the teaching time table and would figure as one of the components.

105. All the male students enrolled in any of the said schools whether Government or private, home or individual were obliged to register themselves with the Portuguese Youth Organization in the schools in which the centres had been established.
Except: The home schooled or tutored students who did not attend regularly the activities of the Youth Organization would be obliged to enroll in the official or private schools under penalty of making them subject to the established sanctions in the rule book if they failed to do so.

106. The incumbent "Professors" of the male students were obliged to attend and participate in the activities of the Youth Organization. At the time of Classification/promotion of teachers the zeal and the interest shown in the activities by the "Professors" would be taken into account.

107. The private schools which could not implement this rule regarding the activities of the Youth Organization would be fined Rs.100 to 200 or with jail as per the gravity of the offence.
Except: The penalties would be imposed only by the Governor at the instance of the Commissariat of the Youth Organization through the Directorate of Civil Services.

Section III—Educational Cinema

108. In the localities where there were cinema halls exhibition of films could be organized for the students of the Primary schools.

109. The programme would be worked out between the theatre owner and the Director of the Directorate of Civil Services. *Except*: They had to show only those films which had been Classified as meant for children.

110. The time schedule would be organized in such a manner that they would not end later than 20.30 hrs.

Section IV—Feasts, Walks, Excursions and Exhibitions

111. With or without prejudice to the weekly timetable feasts, walks and school excursions would be able to realize exclusively educational objectives. *Except*: (a) Always because of the scheduled time table any of the activities cited in the present article

might interfere with the usual timetable for which reason it was necessary for the Directors of the schools to seek prior authorization from the Directorate of Civil Services. This request had to be accompanied by a practical plan duly approved; (b) The feasts, the walks, the excursions and the exhibitions were always to be integrated into the activities of the Portuguese Youth Organization and the students would be able to participate in such activities which the stipulations of the school thought were suitable; and (c) After having observed the feasts, the walks, the excursions and the exhibitions the respective reports had to be submitted through proper channel to the Directorate of Civil Services and to the Commissariat of the Portuguese Youth Organization.

112. There would always be school feasts/festivals which had to be decided in advance or even suddenly if the Director had to agree to it.

113. The closing of the academic year must be accompanied by an exhibition of the work of the students to which permission of the higher authorities was not needed (a) The school exhibition was not to present to the public the qualities of the "Professor" or of the families of the students but the spirit of observation and the capacity of understanding of the students according to the pedagogical processes, along with the efforts and the methods of the "Professor". For this reason no work could be done only with the objective of being exhibited and the exhibition would be a faithful, truthful and complete documentation of all the activities of the school during the year; and (b) After the closure of the exhibition the exhibits would be returned to the students.

114. The "Professors", who would be exempted only in case of sickness with leave duly approved, had to accompany the students that took part in the walks, excursions and other activities, co-curricular and official acts as they might have been designated by the Director of the school or by any other higher authority. Any unauthorized absence during these activities would be viewed seriously and invite disciplinary action.

CHAPTER V

Section I—Testing and Evaluation in School

115. Testing and evaluation of the students would be done twice a

year both in the academic subjects as well as in their conduct. The scores, however, would not be taken into consideration for the final examinations or for promotion (a) the students would be Classified as per the following remarks: Very Good, Good, Average, Mediocre and Bad. The remarks had to be written in the students' report cards and given to the guardians on the 31st of July, 12th of September, 16th of November, 20th of December, 31st of January and 20th of February.

116. For this purpose each student had to have a marks card as per the annexed model in which the given remarks would be written (a) Two days prior to each of the given dates the marks card would be taken by the students to show their guardians who would take note of the remarks and then would return them as soon as possible; and (b) If the remarks had not been written on the marks card then the teacher would be held responsible for the lapse.

117. The remarks showing the evaluation would be given separately in each subject. The evaluation would be the responsibility of the individual teacher but the ultimate objective was the cognizance by the school Council.

118. Students would not be admitted for the final examination or the passing/qualifying examination if:
  I. The students had scored less than average in the finals of the last two periodic tests.
  II. They had got a "Bad" in the second periodic test except if in the other two tests they had obtained not less than a "Good".
  III. They had scored a "Bad" in the last periodic test.
  IV. For some reason or the other they had not been evaluated in the two periodic tests and had got less than a "Good" in the one in which they had been evaluated.
  V. They had the remark "Bad" in Conduct in the last two tests.
  VI. They had remained absent for more than one-third of the attendance and had scored less than a "Good' in the last two tests and the absence had not been justified. However, whenever a student was transferred from one school to another and the attendance did not permit him to be evaluated the evaluation could be done as per the declaration made in the previous article.

119. The students who had not been included in any of the clauses of

the preceding article would be admitted to the final examination as per the established norms in these regulations.

Section II—Final Passing Examination

120. The final passing examinations had to be conducted normally within eight days following the end of the academic year. *Except*: If at the end of the First term some student showed that he was competent to pass the Class he could submit to the Director of the school a request for holding a passing test in the last week of the term since such an application was required to be given by the guardian of the child stating that the child was advanced in years for that particular Class in which he was presently studying and the "Professor" to whom the student had been allotted would make a part of the Jury and had to take the responsibility of his promotion; and (2) Such students who had been promoted in the above manner had to immediately report to the Class in which they had been promoted. However, they could be admitted to the final examinations of the new Class at the end of the academic year if in the remaining two terms they had scored in the new Class less than "suficiente" (average).
121. The final examinations had to be conducted observing all the rules issued by the Directorate of Civil Services duly published in the "Boletim Official".
122. In the official Primary schools which were functioning in both sessions the final examinations would be held by two "Professors" appointed by the Directorate of Civil Services; when there was only one Class then the respective "Professor" would organize and evaluate the students so that there was not much discrimination in the scores.
123. When two "Professors" had been appointed as mentioned above in case of disagreement over the promotion or detention of any student the matter had to be dealt with by the Director of the school by asking them to give the student under question again the written and practical tests as also the orals which would be conducted in his presence and then a decision deemed fit would be taken. *Except*: If in case the Director of the school was one of the "Professors" who had evaluated the student then the school delegate had to as soon as possible appoint another "Professor" who would immediately conduct the proceedings as per the laid down rules.

124. The Directorate of Civil Services had to nominate a "Professor" from any Government school to preside over the conduct of the final examinations in the private schools. *Except*: The final examinations of the students studying privately or coached at home would be held in the school in which he had been registered together with the students of the official school.
125. The "Professors" who scored the tests and Classified the students were responsible for their promotion.
126. The tests having concluded it was necessary for the Directors of Schools to get the necessary scores written down and then record the results after consulting the other documents based on which the evaluation had been done. *Except*: These results should be kept in the same school for one year and should be packed and sealed.

Section III—Examinations of Primary Classes

127. It was the stipulation of Primary Education that after due approval examinations either of Class III or of Class IV had to be held.
128. The examinations of Class III was not compulsory for the students of the official Primary education who wanted to appear for the examinations of the next Class. *Except*: (1) In the case of those students of an official school who wanted to appear for the examinations of Class III it was necessary for their guardians to apply in writing to the Director of the respective school till the 20th of January; (2) The requests for admission to the examinations of Class III had to be accompanied by a payment of stamp fee but the Directors of the school could demand that the signature of the guardian be attested by a notary always in case there was some doubt regarding its authenticity; and (3) The indication of the above paragraph applies to those students registered as home schooled and individually coached who had to apply to the Director of the school where they had been registered.
129. Till the 30th of January the Directors of the schools both official as well as private had to communicate to the Directorate of Civil Services separately showing the number of students appearing for Class III and for Class IV, also indicating the number of those students whose applications depended on the end of the

academic year since they could not be included in any of the stipulations under 118. *Except*: The Directors of the official schools had to also include in their communication the names of the home schooled students and the individually coached ones registered in their schools and who met the legal requirements of appearing for the examinations.

130. Till the 20th of February the Directors of the official and private schools had to send to the Directorate of Civil Services after having properly filled in, the examination forms of the confirmed candidates for the examinations of Class III and Class IV. *Except*: (1) The forms which had to be as per the model annexed herewith would be filled in and signed by the Directors of the respective schools or in the case of home schooled or individually coached students by those who had been involved in their instruction; (2) These forms then had to be submitted separately for Class III and Class IV accompanied by a list in duplicate showing the names of all the students arranged in alphabetical order without mentioning the sex or the type of education; and (3) The responsibility of giving the correct information would rest with those persons who filling up the forms.

131. The Directorate of Civil Services would accept till the 1st of March the forms of those candidates wanting to appear for the examinations of Class III and Class IV who met with all the legal conditions with a late fee of Rs. 15 paid by way of court fee stamps.

132. Upon receiving the communications referred to above the School Inspectors after going through them would prepare and forward to the Director of Civil Services a complete plan of all the examinations to be held in the year showing clearly the number of Juries to be appointed, their composition, the venues/centres where the examinations were going to be held, the days of the examination sessions and any other factor needed for making things clear to those interested. *Except*: All the above formalities had to be completed before the 5th of March so that everything could be published in the "Boletim Oficial".

133. The Juries of examination for the Primary instruction would comprise of three in-service "Professors", with one of them serving as the President and the other as the Secretary. *Except*: (1) The President of the Jury who had to be a Diploma holder should be competent enough to enforce the legal aspects, to direct

the conduct of the examination, to preside over all the meetings, to endorse the written tests of the candidates, to communicate to the superiors any untoward occurrences and to carry out all the acts which the law demanded of him; and (2) One of the "Professors" could be from the private schools but legally appointed by the authorities.

134. Examinations of Primary education had to be conducted in those centres where enough number of students had been registered and proper accommodation was available. The examinations had to begin normally from the 12th of March.

135. Till the 8th of March the Directorate of Civil Services would send again to the Directors of the school where the examinations were being held the examination forms stating those that have been accepted and those that had been rejected and to the Presidents of the Juries the lists of candidates centre-wise. *Except*: (1) The Directors as well as the Presidents of the Juries would make everything public whatever had to be known by those interested in the examinations; and (2) After the publication of the examination details the Directors of the schools had to send the examination forms to the Presidents of the Juries in keeping with the stipulations in 137.

136. When it is discovered that a candidate was not fulfilling the legal conditions for appearing for the examinations besides the penalties imposed by law which would have to be undergone by the person who had given false information, the candidate would be barred from appearing for the examinations since the final result had still not been prepared.

137. The examinations of Primary instruction comprise of written and oral tests (1) The timetable of the written examinations would be prepared by the Directorate of Civil Services, the timetable of the orals would be determined by the Presidents of the respective Juries in conformity with the established rules; (2) The candidates who failed to appear for the examinations on the appointed days could get a second chance to appear if he applied within three days from the date of examinations by paying a fine of Rs. 15 by way of fiscal stamps which should be affixed to the application and submitted to the President of the Jury or in his absence to the Director of the School where the examinations were being held; and (3) As soon as the examinations ended the Presidents of the Juries had to-

immediately convey to the Directorate of Civil Services the names of those candidates who had remained absent; and (4) The second chance to appear could not be given before the expiry of eight days after the examinations.

138. The topics/questions and regulations for the written examinations would be framed by the Directorate of Civil Services which would get them printed beforehand as was necessary and maintaining the confidentiality. *Except*: (1) The topics/questions would be sent to the Presidents of the Juries much in advance by sealing them in an envelope and they would be in their charge till the end of the examinations.

139. In the examinations of Class III there would be written examinations in the subjects of Drawing, Orthography, Calligraphy, Composition and Arithmetic; in Class IV the written examinations would be held in the subjects of Drawing, Composition, Interpretation and Grammar, Orthography, Arithmetic and Geometry and History and Geography. *Except*: All the written examinations of Class IV would be confidential.

140. The written examinations unless changed by the Directorate of Civil Services would begin at 8.30 and would be in the following order along with the duration:

(a) The examinations of Class III:
   1. Drawing—40 minutes
   2. Orthography—30 minutes
   3. Calligraphy—10 minutes
   4. Composition—30 minutes
   5. Arithmetic—50 minutes

(b) The examinations of Class IV:
   1. Drawing—50 minutes
   2. Composition—40 minutes
   3. Interpretation and Grammar—50 minutes
   4. Orthography—30 minutes
   5. Arithmetic and Geometry—60 minutes
   6. History and Geography—50 minutes

Except: (1) The tests in Class III would all take place on the same day whereas those of Class IV would take place with the first-three subjects on the first day and the remaining three on the second day; and (2) Between each subject there would be an interval of not less than 10 minutes.

141. The students were expected to enter the examination hall a few

minutes before the commencement of the examinations as they had to be allotted their places and because of the announcements which would be made by the President of the Jury which had to be in keeping with the rules of the tests.

142. The time when the examinations would end had to be indicated in advance.

143. Outside persons were prohibited from entering either the examination hall or the corridors or even the centre.

144. The examinees had to take with them the following:
   (a) For all written examinations: Paper for rough work for calculations, pen or pen and ink, pencil and eraser;
   (b) For the Drawing examination: The required material.

145. The attested forms with the topics/questions of the examination had to be opened at the beginning of each examination by the President of the Jury and in the presence of all the Committee members. *Except*: The President of the Jury could hemself explain to the candidates or through any other member the correction or interpretation of any question which seemed vague or which by chance appeared to be having errors and the explanation would always be given in a loud and clear voice and to all the candidates as without the correction it would not be possible for the candidates to answer properly.

146. All the test papers had to be signed by the President of the respective Jury within the first 15 minutes of the test. *Except*: (1) After the expiry of the time given for each of the tests the papers had to be collected and submitted to the President of the Jury; (2) The test would be arranged as per the terms fixed by the Directorate of Civil Services for maintaining secrecy and confidentiality and the anonymity of the tests in Class IV; and (3) The marking of the tests should be done in conformity with the stipulation in 1 of the Article 115 and as per the instructions issued to the examination Jury.

147. The results of the written tests would be decided as soon as possible and with the simple remarks of "Admitted" or "Not Admitted". *Except*: (1) After the results had been decided they should soon be entered in the respective results book/register along with the Classification and these would then be counted, closed and sealed in an envelope to be sent to the Directorate of Civil Services either personally or through post within the shortest time possible. (2) In the proper register these should be

recorded, signed by all the members of the Jury which should include all the examinations and the names of all the candidates both "Admitted" and "Not Admitted".

148. In the examinations of Class III the following candidates would be excluded from appearing for the written tests:
   I. Those who had not obtained at least the remark of "suficiente" in the subjects of Orthography and Arithmetic and "mediocre" in Composition.
   II. Those who had one "mau"(Bad) and not a single "bom"(Good) or "muito bom"(Very Good).

149. In the examinations of Class IV the following could not be admitted:
   I. Those who had not obtained at least the remark "suficiente" in the subjects of Exposition and Grammar, Composition, Arithmetic and Geometry and at least "mediocre" in Orthography.
   II. Those who had one remark of "mau" in any of the remaining subjects and did not have any "bom" or "muito bom" in the subjects mentioned above.
   III. Those who had three remarks below "suficiente".

150. Those candidates who did not come under any of the above stipulations would be admitted for the oral examinations.

151. The orals would begin on the first working day after the announcement of the results of the written examinations.

152. The oral examinations were public but persons who did not have place to sit or those in some way or the other were going to interfere with would not be permitted in the examination hall. *Except*: (1) In the examinations of Class III the testing would last for 15 to 20 minutes while in the examinations of Class IV they would last for 20 to 30 minutes; and (2) Whenever needed the President of the Jury could prolong the examinations by another 5 minutes.

153. The orals of Class III will comprise of:
   (a) Reading, Exposition and Grammatical Analysis of a prose passage selected officially or when that was not possible whatever had been used in the school in which the student was studying could be used.
   (b) Arithmetic and Geometry exercises worked out either on the slate or mentally.
   (c) Questioning on the other remaining topics/subjects.

154. The examinations of Class IV would consist of the following:
    (a) Reading, Exposition and Grammatical Analysis and Logic of a prose seen passage used in the school which the student was attending.
    (b) Exercises in Arithmetic and Geometry.
    (c) Questioning on the other remaining topics/subjects.

155. Every examination would be conducted by two Committee members as per the subject/topic allocation done by the President of the Jury in advance who had to ensure that the examinations were conducted in conformity with the established pedagogical and legal norms, intervening whenever necessary during the oral examinations.

156. As soon as the examinations were over in any of the topics mentioned above the examiners had to hand over the Classification of the students to the President so that he could immediately take note of it. *Except*: (1) The oral examinations normally would be conducted for a group of eight students at a time of Class III and six of Class IV and at the end of the examination of the group the Jury would meet to do the evaluation taking into consideration also the marks obtained in the written examination, and (2) The results would be made public immediately after the evaluation by the Committee in the said meeting.

157. In the examinations of Class III the following candidates could be re-examined:
    I. Those who had secured a remark lower than "suficiente" in some of the subjects mentioned in 153 (a) and (b).
    II. Those who had a remark "mau" in the orals in the subjects mentioned under (c).
    III. Those who had in the final score of both written and oral three remarks of "average".

158. In the examinations of Class IV the following candidates could be re-examined:
    I. Those who had secured a remark lower than "suficiente" in some of the subjects mentioned in 154 (a) and (b).
    II. Those who had a remark "mau" in the orals in the subjects mentioned under (c) and (d) of the same article.
    III. Those who had in the final score of both written and oral three remarks lower than"suficiente".

159. Those candidates who did not come under any of the above conditions could be promoted.

160. In the examinations of Class IV those students who cumulatively did not get any remark lower than "suficiente" and got at least the remark "bom" in the written examinations of Exposition and Grammar and in Arithmetic and Geometry and in the orals under (a) and (b) of article 154 and had in the total at least six remarks of "bom" and "muito bom" would be Classified as passed with distinction. *Except*: (1) The expression "passed with distinction" had to be written in the sheet where the results were written, on the book of results and also on the Certificate.
161. After the examinations were over the Jury had to send the prepared results to the Directorate of Civil Services as per rule.
162. The Directorate of Civil Services would award Certificates only to those students of Primary education who requested for them.

Section IV—Appeals

163. The guardians or the candidates themselves if of major age or free and have been disallowed from appearing for the written examinations of Primary instruction could appeal against the decisions of the Jury. *Provided*: (1) The applicant, at the time of applying deposited an amount of Rs. 10, without which the application would not be accepted; and (2) The amount would be returned in case the appeal was upheld and the candidate would then be admitted for the orals; in case the appeal was not upheld the money would go into the fund of the school where the student had been registered.
164. Having received the application with all conditions duly fulfilled the Director of Civil Services had to order the marks of the candidate to be checked or refer it to the Inspectorate or to two "Professors" of Primary education of his choice so that the assessment could be done again. *Except*: (1) This Classification was final and would be endorsed by the Governor; and (2) In case there was some mischief on the part of the Jury disciplinary proceedings would be initiated against them.
165. In case the appeal was upheld then the candidate would be examined in orals by a different Committee appointed by the Director of Civil Services not by the existing one. *Except*: If necessary he would appoint a special Jury in order to conduct the orals after the results of the written examinations had been declared as pass.

CHAPTER VI

Section I—Establishing Schools

166. Schools would be established in proper buildings conveniently furnished and stocked with didactic material and necessary effects.
167. The State had to provide in all the populated habitations, the existing buildings with sufficient rooms constructed in conformity with the legal stipulations and as per the pedagogical recommendations and school hygiene.
168. In places where no building existed as per the above conditions a house which fulfilled the following conditions would be leased to serve as a school:
    (a) It should be located in a more or less central place.
    (b) It should be situated in healthy surroundings and should be easily accessible.
    (c) It should be at a distance of at least 200 m from any cemetery, tavern, police station, market, factory or industry which could interfere with the smooth functioning of the Classes.
    (d) It had to have toilets, lavatories, dressing rooms, garden and a covered porch for recreation.
    (e) Each room should measure not less than 1.25 sq. m. per each student, the passage could not be less than 4 m, should have a large entrance, two glazed windows which should be enough for light to enter, a hygienic floor, painted walls either with white colour or clear grey and the roof painted white without frames or ornate. *Conditions*: (1) The Health Department had to be informed whenever a house was being taken on lease for a school; and (2) No "tavernas" or manufacturing factory or any other installation could be allowed in the vicinity within 200 m of the school which could interfere with the proper functioning of that school.
169. In each of the Classrooms the following furniture had to be placed:
    (a) Table and chair for the "Professor";
    (b) Two chairs;
    (c) One cupboard for the material;
    (d) One black board of stipulated dimensions;
    (e) A cupboard for teaching aids;

(f) Sufficient number of desks as per the following specifications:
   (i) As per the approved model; and
   (ii) They should be arranged in the Classroom in such a way that the students would receive daylight on their left.

170. Each school should have at least the following material:
   (a) One globe;
   (b) Maps of Portugal, its islands, India and the other Portuguese possessions around the world;
   (c) Collection of maps of all continents;
   (d) Scale (Planisferio);
   (e) A measuring tape of at least 15 m;
   (f) A Geometry set;
   (g) Accessories of the black-board: a one metre rule, square, compass and a protractor; and
   (h) White and coloured chalk sticks.

   Except: In each school placed conveniently there should be a photo of the Head of the State.

Section II—Plan of the School Buildings

171. In the Department of Education there should be a complete plan of all the school buildings clearly drawn up as per the model annexed herewith. *Except*: In each school there should be the duplicate copy of it which should be in the possession of the respective Director.

172. The plan should show the following informations:
   (a) The owner of the school;
   (b) The date and the cost of construction;
   (c) Date of major repairs carried out and the expenditure incurred as far as possible;
   (d) Photos and the plan or a simple sketch of the building, its annexed parts and the plot;
   (e) Date of founding of the school, its name and its location/address;
   (f) Names of "Professors" who taught in each of the years; and
   (g) The annual statistics, the enrolment, the attendance, the promotion, and the conduct of examinations.

Section III—Functioning, Creation, Shifting and Closure of Schools

173. The Primary schools would be clubbed into groups or circles as per the map annexed to the form by the one who is in charge of education and they should be within the radius as per the established norms.
174. The school buildings meant for the running of Classes for the students of Primary instruction and except in cases expressly anticipated under law, it was totally prohibited to have any sort of gathering without the express authorization of the Governor.
175. The establishing of schools or of constructing new Classrooms in the existing schools had to be done always through an elaborate process by the school Inspectors and in keeping with the regulations mentioned in the following documents:
    (a) A list of children of school-going age residing in the particular area which would be covered by the school was to be prepared by the Committee of the said Parish/village in consultation with the head of the village ("Regedor"), or with the Secretary of the Municipality helped by the "Regedor" if it was within Municipal limits.
    (b) A report had to be prepeared regarding the condition of the building, its location which would be checked by the school Inspectors along with the sanitation Inspector.
    (c) The amount of furniture and other school material required along with the expenditure for its acquisition. If the school would be set up privately, the NOC from the Directorate of Public Accounts and Expenditure showing the funds available for the expenses. *Except*: (1) In case of gift of the building the process would be as per the rules under No. 2 after the Director of Civil Services had visited the place along with the Sanitation Inspector of the locality as well as a representative of the Public Works Department; and (2) In case of creation of new Classrooms the above may be dispensed with.
176. The establishing of schools or creation of posts of "Professors" comes under the powers of the Provincial administration, to be proposed however by the Directorate of Health Services and Instruction and ratified by the Council of Instruction. *Except*: (1) Whenever there was a need to set up any school or to increase the number of posts of "Professors" the Directorate of Civil

Services had to direct them in such a way that Classes could be conducted smoothly from the very first day of the new academic year; and (2) When it was found that it was not possible to start the Classes before the 31st of August the new schools or the new Classes had to start functioning only from the beginning of the next scholastic year.

177. The shifting of a school from one place to another would be considered as if one school had been closed down and a new one was being opened and hence would have to observe the rules as in 175 to 178.

178. Those schools where the attendance for consecutive three years had been less than thirty and the school statistics showed that the number would not increase had to be shifted. *Except*: (1) The shutting down of any school was the prerogative of the Governor and after being proposed by the Directorate of Civil Services; and (2) The process for the closing down of any school would be done by taking into consideration the school statistics of the last three years and of the immediate past year.

CHAPTER VII

Section I—Night Classes

179. It will be the Governor who would decide upon the opening of night Classes through a "Portaria" as and when he thought fit.

180. The admission to these night Classes was permanent and would be for the whole academic year which would the same as that fixed in Article 62. *Except*: Those interested could enroll themselves till the 31st of October.

181. The "Professors" who conducted these night Classes would be paid during the time of their services a monthly remuneration of Rs. 60 which would be allocated under the designated budget head.

182. The minimum number of students required to open and run a night Class could not be less than 20. *Except*: (1) Whenever the number of students was less than twenty or the attendance had been less than fifteen in two consecutive months the night Class had to be shut down without following any formality just by informing the Directorate of Civil Services; and (2) The "Professor" and the Director were jointly responsible for the guarantees given as per the above paragraph.

183. The "Professors" of the night Classes had to put in 12 hours of work divided throughout the week for six working days of the week. *Except*: (1) The timetable would be as fixed by the Directorate of Civil Services.

184. The Registers of admission and of attendance, the records of Class examinations and final examinations of the students of the night Classes had to be the same as those of the day Classes. *Except*: (1) The examinations of the students of night Classes would be held along with the students of the day Classes; (2) The students of the night Classes were not subject to the application of these relative regulations of education.

185. The "Professors" of the night Classes would be appointed annually and preference would be given to those already in service in the same school.

CHAPTER VIII

Section I—Books and School Libraries

186. In the Primary schools both official and private they had to use the books and compendiums ordered by the Governor General. *Except*: (1) Every year in March the list had to be published on the "Boletim Oficial"; and (2) The same books could be continued with if they had not been replaced in the new list.

187. The approved books adopted in the capital city (Lisbon) if found to be better had also to be adopted in the Primary schools in India. *Except*: (1) If no such book was used in the capital city for any of the subjects of Primary education in India or when it had been determined that these books were not that much superior then the Directorate could give permission to print the locally prepared text books.

188. For the selection of such textbooks as per the above the Governor had to order a public scrutiny of books from one to five years old. *Except*: (1) The scrutiny would be open for six months and the conditions for the presentation of the books would be published in the "Boletim oficial".

189. The approved books would then be published by the Government Printing Press and only in case it was not possible for the Government then by others. *Except*: (1) In case these books were published by the Government Press then the Accounts section

would have to make the necessary provisions in the budget and the books would become the State possession; and (2) Also by a notification of the Governor the remuneration to be given to the author would be reasonably fixed along with the price of the book. The Government Printing Press would be responsible for the editing of the text books; and (3) The prescribing of the text books would be the responsibility of the Council of Instruction which could take on board two "Professors" of any stage to review them.

190. The Directors of the Primary schools had to create "attached" to the school libraries in order to help the intellectual and moral development of the students. *Except*: In the libraries of the Primary schools books approved by the Censor Board for Children's Literature of the capital city or by a Commission of the State for the local publications had to be stocked.

191. The Director of each school had to frame proper rules for the maintenance of the library and get them approved by the Director of Civil Services.

192. The school fund could be used to procure the necessary books for the school libraries.

CHAPTER IX

Section I—Categories of Teachers

193. The teaching staff of official schools of Primary education consisted of two types of "Professors":
   (a) Permanent "Professors" or from official Primary education cadre; and
   (b) "Professors" recruited during contingency.

   The permanent "Professors", legally eligible to work as official Primary teaching staff were given the designation of cadre "Professors".

194. The cadre of the "Professors" of official Primary education was the one that was approved by law and incorporated in the general budget, the "Professors" belonging to it were those who are included in it and who had been appointed as per the terms of Legislative Diploma No. 1817, of 24 July, 1958.

195. The contractual "Professors" were appointed, for a period not exceeding the scholastic year, to the vacancies that might have

occurred in the schools, for replacing the permanently or provisionally appointed "Professors" during their absence or impediments and for attending to the requirements of teaching due to excess of students:

1. The contractual "Professors" could be selected for examination work, and in such conditions, the appointment would remain valid upto the end of scholastic year.
2. The expenditure column in the general budget had to show proper entry for the payment of salary of the contractual "Professors".
3. The permanent "Professors" who had been posted at Daman and Diu and who had declared their intention to continue there would be entitled to all the perks during holidays.

Section II—Filling of Posts and Appointing "Professors" in the Zone

196. The official schools of Primary education were to be of the same category, for the purpose of provision, with the exception of the one in the Cidade de Goa (Panaji) as that designated to serve as Practice school for the students of the "Escola Normal".

197. The teaching cadre of each circle/zone would be fixed by the Governor, by a Decree in which he would approve the general plan for posting the "Professors" in the schools as per the teaching requirements.
    1. The male "Professors" would be placed in the schools attended by students of masculine sex, and only female "Professors" would be placed in the schools attended by students of feminine sex.
    2. When the interview for the boys' or girls' schools could not be held for two consecutive years, the Governor could appoint after calling for applications from any interested persons, a male or female "Professor", irrespective of stipulation in the above paragraph.
    3. The vacancies in private institutions would be filled up as per the following principles: in schools having only one vacancy, a male or female "Professor" would be provided; but in the schools having more than one vacancy and the number of posts was even, then the number of male and female "Professors" would also be equal, and if it was odd then it did not matter whether the male were more or the female were more.

198. The filling up of vacancies that would occur in the official Primary schools would be done first by means of transfer, after receiving applications, and based on the merit list drawn up of the "Professors" of the official Primary teachers' cadre who had at least one year's service in the place they were working and in case no such candidates were available or had applied for transfer, then anybody from amongst the candidates approved in the interview for inclusion in the cadre would be appointed.

199. For the purpose of transfer referred to in the previous clause, the Directorate of Services will compulsorily publish, in the month of January each year, in the Official Gazette (Boletim Oficial), a merit list of all the "Professors" belonging to the official Primary education cadre with reference to 31st December of the previous year.

1. In the merit list those "Professors" who had less than one year's teaching service at the place they had been working, a note would be inserted showing the duration at the place of their current posting.
2. The list referred to above was subject to claim and appeal within the following time period: for claim, within a period of fifteen days from the date of publishing of the list in the Official Gazette; for appeal, within thirty days from the date the official decision had been given on the claim.
3. The merit list, after deciding on the various claims, would be made again or withheld by the Governor.

200. Without prejudice to the applicants' rights, the Governor could then send, under the advice of the Director, in case of schools till then not provided with any teacher, in-service "Professors" of the same cadre from other schools for a period of not more than one year.

201. For the purpose of preparing the merit list, for each noting in the service records of the "Professors" of '*muito bom*' (very good) one mark would be allotted, a half mark for '*bom*' (good) and one-fourth for each noting of '*suficiente*' (sufficient), taking the first-fifteen years of service into consideration.

1. In case of similar scores the reasons for preference in the gradation would be:
   (a) Longer period of school service rendered to the State, whatever may be the title of appointment;
   (b) Better educational qualifications;
   (c) Seniority in age.

2. To the experience clause, "Professors" of co-education teaching schools, those of extinct '*Escola Nacional do Sexo Feminino*', '*Escola Profissional*' attached to workshops of the State, Elementary Agricultural School of Sanguem, Schools of Arts and Trade of Sattari and Daman and Instituto Luso Indiano, half mark for each year of service rendered in these schools would be added to the limit of fifteen years and as long as the service was not value added by other means.
3. Besides the period of fifteen years referred to in the final part only the values of '*Muito Bom*' would be added.

202. In the first issues of the "Boletim Oficial" of the months of March, July and November the Directorate would publish a notice announcing the vacancies existing on that date in the teaching cadre of the schools and inviting the "Professors" of Primary education cadre, constituting the merit list, to apply for their transfer, within the time limit of fifteen days. The persons or private entities who might have offered or donated sums or properties of a value of not less than Rs. 50,000 for school building or for school canteen could recommend the appointment of one or two teachers for these schools, whenever there were vacancies from amongst the candidates who had passed out from "Escola Normal"

203. In case the vacancies were to be filled by transfer preference would be given to the spouse of the public functionary who had his residence within a five kilometre radius from the school. In case there were two or more candidates competing for the same vacancy, the one having a better place in the merit list would be preferred.

204. Regarding vacancies in the annexed Primary school of teacher training preference would be given to those Primary teachers who had scored not less than 15 marks in the Diploma of Teaching and a Classification of '*bom*' in two teaching years.

205. The rest of the vacancies would be filled with candidates approved in the interview for entrance in the cadre.

206. For filling up the posts the order of Classification/merit in the interview for entrance in the cadre would be strictly observed. The "Professors" residents of Daman and Diu having their roots and families or the families of their spouses in these districts had to be given preferential treatment in the placement of teachers

in the Primary schools in Daman and Diu as was followed in the transfer of teachers.

207. The "Professors" reintegrated into the cadre after extraordinary leave would be admitted to the interview for transfer, independently of the condition of permanence of one year in the school, could however obtain the transfer only in the case none of the competitors satisfying that condition intended to take up the post.

208. The "Professors" who had been transferred or placed as per the terms of these regulations would start functioning in the school where they had been placed or had been transferred only from the beginning of the new academic year and never in the middle of the year, except in case of candidates who had been newly recruited and had not been working as contractual "Professors".

209. The entrance of "Professors" in the cadre of Primary teachers was done by means of a competitive test/interview, to which the candidates qualified after passing out from any of the national teachers' training schools and aged between 18 years and 35 would be admitted.

210. During the month of February of each year and after the verification of the existence of vacancies, the Director would publish a notice announcing the opening of the competitive test/ interview and would fill up the vacancies within the period of sixty days.

211. The applications requesting admission to the competitive test/ interview had to be addressed to the Governor, handed over within the time limit to the Directorate accompanied by the following documents:

(a) Birth Certificate;

(b) Diploma, Degree or Certificate of competence for the practice of Primary teaching;

(c) Certificate of no Criminal offences;

(d) Certificate of good moral and civic behaviour, given by the Administrator of the Province in which the candidate was domiciled;

(e) Documents proving that the candidate had done his military duties;

(f) Certificate from the Health Board stating that the person was physically fit to work in the Primary teachers' cadre;

(g) Certificate of vaccination against small-pox;

(h) Declaration to which the law No. 1901 dated 21 May 1935 refers;

(i) Document proving that he/she had not been dismissed from Public office due to disciplinary reasons; and

(j) Any relevant other document that could help his place in the merit list.

The applicants had to present the identity card mentioning its number at the time of handing over the application.

212. The Directorate would publish in the 'Boletim Oficial' the Government Gazette within the period of ten days the merit list of candidates. Together with the merit list, the names of the excluded candidates would also be published indicating the reason for their exclusion.

213. Within a period of fifteen days, from the date of publication of the merit list, any competitor could address to the Governor a claim against his exclusion from the test or against the merit list.

214. After the claims were decided or when the period for filing the claims was over and after obtaining the approval from Governor the final merit list had to be published in the 'Boletim Oficial'.

215. The appointed candidates had to take office within a period of thirty days, counted from the date of publication of the appointment Decree in the 'Boletim Oficial'. At the time of taking up office the appointees had to present again the identity card and the Diploma of public functioning, and had to hand over the declaration demanded by Article 3 of law No. 1901, of 21 May, 1935.

216. In the first "Boletim Oficial" published after 10th May, a list of schools having vacancies during the following academic year would be published along with the reasons for such vacancies. Till 31st of the same month, all the contractual "Professors" could request their appointment to any of the schools having vacancies, indicating the order of preference.

(1) The appointments would be done taking note of the requests of the interested persons, giving preference to the more qualified; and

(2) Those who had not requested for any school or had been chosen to the ones they had requested would be placed in conformity with the requirements of the service.

217. The contractual "Professors" who did not present themselves

within the period of ten days after the announcement of their appointment in the "Boletim Oficial" would be exonerated and would not be reappointed before the completion of a full period of two years after the publication of the previous appointment:

1. The Diploma-holders who had been appointed to a school as per their request but had not joined the service within the period of ten days would not be appointed to any school in identical conditions before the completion of two years;
2. The teachers who had been transferred from Daman and Diu had to apply within the fixed period of time for their transfer to be taken note of and to be considered if they had not yet been posted in any of the schools as per the list announced in the notification and if they had not posted to ask to be appointed within the fixed time limit.
3. In case of request for resignation during the academic year, the same provisions of this article would apply to the contractual "Professors".

Section III—Classification of Service

218. The service of "Professors" of official Primary education would be Classified as "muito bom" (Very Good), "bom" (good), "suficiente" (Sufficient) and "deficient" (Deficient) at the end of each academic year.

219. The Classification would be done by the Director after getting the information from the school Inspectors.

220. In the Classification of service of "Professors" attention would be paid to:

(1) Any appreciation made by superior authorities and mentioned in the official documents;

(2) The moral behaviour of the "Professor" in and outside the school;

(3) The pedagogic aptitude of the "Professor" would be verified as under:

(a) In the teaching of the students checked during the inspection and by the performance of his students in the examinations;

(b) In the preparation, gradation and execution of lessons;

(c) In the event of the students having taken care of the exercise books and the books; and

(d) In the maintenance school discipline.

(4) The actions of the "Professor":
   (a) In maintaining order, cleanliness and conservation of furniture and teaching material;
   (b) In his interest in the hygiene of the students;
   (c) In his participation in the activities of '*Mocidade Portuguesa*' (Portuguese Youth Organisation);
   (d) In his compliance of laws related to compulsion of education;
   (e) In his relation with the families of the students;
   (f) In his participation in the functioning of the school fund and school canteen;
   (g) In the organisation of school functions, walks and excursions; and
   (h) In his participation in the organisation of census and the execution of school documentation and statistical maps.

221. Each school must be inspected at least once a year.

222. It should be communicated to the "Professor" in a confidential note, any shortcoming observed during the inspection, giving him corrective instructions.
   (1) The "Professor" could give explanation to the Inspector, within a period of fifteen days, justifying his actions considered erroneous and the objection to the suggested instructions.
   (2) In case of his justification not being accepted, the "Professor" could complain to the Director, within a period of five days to be counted from the time the communication was made to him and even request for a new inspection by a different person.

223. The Classification of service of teaching staff had to be done till 31st May of each year, but for contractual "Professors" it would be done till the 30th of April.
   (1) The Classification of teaching staff would be done of only those having more than six months of service; and
   (2) The conferring of Classification 'deficient' during two consecutive years, or during three interpolated years, constituted a basis for disciplinary action.

224. The Classification note and details of the effective service relative to each year of service had to be communicated to the "Professors" of the cadre till the 15th of June and till the 15th of

May to the contractual "Professors".

225. The "Professor" not agreeing with the Classification or with the effective service could appeal within a period of fifteen days to be counted from the day of receipt of official communication to the Director who could then modify or maintain the same. His decision, if found unfavourable, could be appealed against with the Governor General, within an identical period to be counted from the day of reception of official communication.

226. For all legal purposes, for the "Professors" who had been called to render service in the organisations dependent on Education Department, their last note of Classification would be maintained as long as they continued in these institutions, except when they had bad annual reports. The service of "Professors" would be counted as per the terms established in this notification.

227. The service rendered by the "Professors" outside the organisations dependent on the Education Department would not be counted an teaching service for any purpose.
There was anexception however to this. If any person had rendered service in any public job, which under law, could be done only by delegation of duties in '*Estado da India*' or in the Departments of Central Government such service would be counted.

Section IV—Rights and Duties of "Professors"

228. The "Professors" of Primary education, as Portuguese citizens and civil servants, enjoy all rights and all the duties as expressed in the Political Constitution and in the '*Estatuto do Funcionalismo ultramarino*' (Overseas Civil Service Statute).

229. Besides the general duties of citizens and the duties of civil servants of Portuguese Overseas colonies, it was especially up to the "Professors" of Primary education to:
   (a) Teach the students with the double objective of administering them the knowledge contained in the syllabus of Primary education and of forming the character and the spirit;
   (b) Watch the students during recreation and direct them in their games.
   (c) Create in the spirit of students a profound and intense love for God, for Portugal and for the Family, and due respect to the constituted powers of the Nation and to the established social order;

(d) Treat all the students equally with affection and care, instilling in them the work habits, politeness of sentiments and courtesy in the behaviour;

(e) Take care of health of the students and ask for the intervention of health authorities whenever it was felt necessary;

(f) Collaborate in the development of his school, contributing for its good maintenance and beautification, acquisition of school material and organisation of its auxiliary institutions;

(g) To be present in the school at the appointed time, leaving the premises only after respective work was over, and doing all the writing work that was allotted to him;

(h) Organize and have always in order the "*Diario de Licoes*" (daily work schedule book/log book);

(i) Fill in the work books of the students and register in the charts of annexed models their respective marks;

(j) Make efforts for obtaining continuous pedagogic and scientific perfection and best output of education;

(k) Make the school prestigious, by its model organisation and good discipline, making it respected and attractive for the local population;

(l) Attend with affection the parents and guardians of the students, helping them with the knowledge to educate the students better;

(m) Proceed always with maximum seriousness, avoiding conflicts and frictions with the authorities, public functionaries and families of students

(n) Be present for all the solemn civic and school functions to which he had been invited and render one's co-operation as soon as it was indicated or requested;

(o) Conduct one's life in the society in a way deserving of respect and consideration from everybody, setting an educative example in the locality;

(p) Carry out all the laws, regulations and orders emanating from superior official stations.

230. The "Professors" during the working hours should not be busy with any work outside their teaching and education of students; leave the Classes or receive visits of persons not connected with the work.

231. The "Professors" who did not perform the functions of Directors

could correspond with superior authorities only through proper channels.

232. The "Professors" of Primary education were prohibited from working in any other profession, unless they had the permission from the Governor.

233. The "Professors" of official schools of Primary education could not teach in the private Primary schools, give tuitions to any students of official Primary schools and teach students who were not their children or grand-children. It was even prohibited to allow others to give tuitions at their residences. The infringement of this provision in this article would be punished with the punishment No. 3 of article 354 of "Estatuto do Funcionalismo Ultramarino" and with the No. 5 in case of repetition of the incident.

234. The married lady teachers who were expecting would be exempted from service for thirty days at the time of delivery.
   (1) During this period the lady "Professors" would continue getting their salaries.
   (2) The duration of this leave would be counted as effective service, and subtracted for the purpose of concession against sickness.
   (3) The lady "Professors" had to send the necessary communication to the Directorate, informing fifteen days before the day she intended to go on leave, together with a medical Certificate from the competent authority attesting the fact.

CHAPTER X

Section I—Direction and Administration of Schools

235. In the schools where there were two or more divisions, there would be a Director, who would be an permanent "Professor", appointed by the Director of Services and also removed when he thought it was necessary, and in the schools having more than four divisions there would be also a Deputy Director, appointed or removed in the same conditions by the Director:
   (1) In the schools having only one "Professor", he would be considered as Director for all purposes.
   (2) The Directors of schools, in their absence or leave would

be substituted by the Deputy Directors, if appointed or by the in-charge of the school.

(3) Always, if there was no effective working "Professor", the in-charge of the school would be an additional "Professor", and in his absence a contractual "Professor" designated by the Director of Services.

236. The powers of the Director of the school would be as follows:

(a) Observe, execute and implement the laws, regulations and orders of superiors;
(b) Administer the school and represent the same;
(c) Co-ordinate the work of the "Professors" and establish a good harmony amongst everybody, leading them with great affection and rectitude;
(d) Organize the school census in his zone or area;
(e) Supervise the discipline of all services;
(f) Admit the students and distribute them in the divisions after consulting to the school Council;
(g) Arrange and have in order always the books and registers of the school of the part that he is concerned with, and monitor the other work pertaining to the "Professors";
(h) Work out the monthly and annual statistics of attendance and the balance sheet of the school bank and of the school canteen and send these documents to the Directorate of Services within the established deadlines.
(i) Work out the annual report in the given format to be sent to the Directorate of Civil Services by the 30th April;
(j) Promote the creation and growth of the school bank and normal functioning of canteen, in such a way that all the needy students would be able to benefit from them.
(k) Close the accounts of the school bank and the canteen and send them to the Directorate of Services by 31st of March;
(l) Promote co-curricular activities like functions, walks, excursions and school exhibitions;
(m) Communicate immediately to the Directorate of Civil Services any irregularities, whose removal was not being within his powers and give all the clarifications asked for;
(n) See that all the families are informed of the students behaviour and win their co-operation;
(o) Send to the School delegate whatever was required about the service period of the school personnel;

(p) Communicate, without delay, the arrival and departure of the teaching and non-teaching functionaries of the school;
(q) Take steps demanded due to the urgency of service, in such a form that it would not suffer alterations that could damage it;
(r) Communicate to the health authorities all the facts which were within his powers; and
(s) Sign all books and registers of school as required.

237. The Directors of the schools, except when it concerned the subjects that had to be treated by the intervention of the school delegates, could correspond with the Directorate of Civil Services.

CHAPTER XI

Section I—Statistics and School Record Keeping

238. For maintaining the school records there had to be in each school:
(a) Bulletins regarding the registration of admissions of students;
(b) Registration books of the official schools;
(c) Registration books of individual or home schools;
(d) Attendance registers for boys and girls for each course;
(e) Inward correspondence register;
(f) Outward correspondence register;
(g) Muster roll;
(h) Inventory register;
(i) Monthly attendance charts;
(j) Annual statistics charts;
(k) Students' booklets;
(l) Charts of students' progress;
(m) Logbooks;
(n) Students' Health records; and
(o) Account books of school funds and canteen funds.
The records had to be maintained as per the official formats given.

239. Till the 5th of every month the Director of the School had to send to the school delegate the monthly record charts of attendance, the duplicate copy of the progress reports of the students, a comparative statement of the accounts of the school

fund and the canteen fund, and by the 30th of April the annual statistics.

240. At the time of maintaining the school records the following had to be borne in mind:
   (a) Number of students enrolled during the year or at the end of the month.
   (b) Number of students admitted till the end of the year or the month through enrolment or through transfer.
   (c) Number of students who left the school for whatever reason during the year or month.
   (d) Number of students left on the rolls at the end of the year or month.
   (e) Half yearly or fortnightly attendance
   (f) Maximum relative attendance in a month or a year
   (g) Minimum relative attendance in year or month
   (h) Regular attendance annually or monthly
   (i) Number of presents
   (j) Number of absents
   (k) Number of students promoted
   (l) Number of students sent up for examinations
   (m) Number of students passed.

CHAPTER XII

Section I—Orientation and Inspection of Primary Education

241. It was within the powers of the Director of Civil Services to supervise in the orientation and inspection of the Primary education.

242. It comes under the charge of the Chief of the Directorate of Instruction all the functions of education that should be followed as per the instructions of the Director of Civil Administration.

243. The school Inspectors and the school delegates were the agents of orientation and inspection of Primary education, under the supervision of Director of Civil Services.

244. The school Inspectors had to conduct their functions in harmony with the Act No. 41.472 of 23rd December, 1957, concerning especially:
   (a) Giving opinions on all subjects related to Primary education and submit them for the decisions of the Director of Services;

(b) Working on the reports that had to be decided by the Director of Services;

(c) Organizing topics for the examination papers of Primary education, collecting suitable information for same and submitting their work for approval to the Director of Civil Services;

(d) Directing and checking the composition and printing of the question papers when it was necessary;

(e) Organizing the examinations of Primary education, submitting their work for the approval of the Director of Civil Services;

(f) Offering suggestions related to improvement of services of official Primary education;

(g) Visiting frequently all the official schools, inspecting the Classroom teaching and verifying whether the functioning of schools and the discharging of functions by teaching staff was done without breaking the laws, regulations in force and the decisions and precepts determined by the higher authorities;

(h) Directing the "Professor" in his teaching work by showing modern pedagogic processes, giving model lessons if it was found that the ones resorted to by the "Professors" were less convincing;

(i) Promoting the creation of school museums and libraries for "Professors" and students as also organizing the improvement courses for the "Professors";

(j) Proposing at the end of the scholastic year the Classification remarks on the service of the "Professors";

(k) Cooperating with the chief of the Education Office in preparation of biographical register of "Professors" and school records;

(l) Giving clarifications to the "Professors" on different teaching matters;

(m) Proposing the acquisition of school furniture as well as all the teaching material;

(n) Taking cognizance of complaints, representations and reclamations that might be directed at him, regarding the working of Primary education, and transmitting to the Director of Civil Services, the matters which did not come under his powers for solution of subjects;

(o) Arranging visits to the houses or rooms that may have to be used for starting of schools, courses or Classes of Primary education, proposing the approval or rejection, depending on the satisfaction or legal conditions;

(p) Suggesting the creation, transfer, conservation or suppression of schools or the work place of the "Professor";

(q) Look out for correct observation of laws and regulations by the Primary education services teaching staff, and should take measures within his powers, for this purpose, informing always the Director of Services whenever such cases came up.

245. The posts of school delegates had to be filled up by permanent "Professors" of Primary education appointed fulltime by the Governor and designate to them their functions.

246. It was the duty of school delegates to take care of regular functioning of Primary education services in respective districts, promoting full execution of laws, regulations and superior instructions, and principally:

(1) To render all the clarifications to the Directorate of Civil Services, which might be asked;

(2) To work out the school statistics;

(3) To approve the acquisition of furniture and school material explaining its necessity to the Directorate of Civil Service;

(4) To supply to the schools of the district the necessary books, booklets and printed registers and the dispatch material;

(5) To manage the funds put at their disposal for the cleaning and for the dispatch work;

(6) To inform the Directorate of Cvil Services about the need for appointment of contractual "Professors" due to increase in student population;

(7) To keep vigil on the discipline in the school;

(8) To communicate all the incidents in the school that might not be according to the law, regulations and instructions of superiors;

(9) To keep vigil on the proper execution of services of school administration;

(10) To send to the Directorate of Civil Services, a note with exact attendance of all the "Professors" and menial personnel of the schools in the district with respective payment papers, duly filled in;

(11) To cooperate in the work of school census; and

(12) To cooperate with the Director of Civil Services, with the Chief of the Education Department and with the school Inspectors, in all matters concerning Primary education.

247. The Directorate of services would promote at the opportune time the organization of pedagogic conferences.

248. The themes of conferences would be proposed by the school Inspectors and distributed by them and by the "Professors" after having been approved by the Director of Civil Services.

249. Any "Professor" could present an original work that would be included in the programme of conferences if it was approved by Director of Civil Services.

250. No work could de presented in the conference without the knowledge of the Director of Civil Services.

251. It was for the Director of Services to preside over the pedagogic conferences, but the chief of the Education Department could represent him or a school Inspector and if none of these functionaries were present then by the school delegate of the district.

252. In the pedagogic conferences, besides pedagogic and didactic subjects, topics of cultural or medico-school subjects could also be discussed which the Director of Civil Services had considered to be suitable though not belonging to Primary school education.

253. The attendance for conferences and for the courses was compulsory for the "Professors" expressly designated but it was optional to the remaining ones.

This was the last time that any reform would be introduced by the Portuguese Government because on the 19th of December, 1961 they say Goa, Daman and Diu was liberated and became a part of India.

Epilogue

The study of the evolution of Primary education in Goa gives one an insight into not only the attempts and their types made and not made by various Government authorities but also the instructional changes that were being regularly made both in keeping with the reforms in the mother country as well as in tune with the philosophies and methodologies that were being propagated in Europe from time to time. Some of the striking features of Primary education that held sway for almost hundred and eighty years in the "Estado da India Portuguesa" are worth taking note of if not for any other purpose then to satiate one's academic interest at least.

The first example and the best is that of the sweeping reforms of Sebastiao de Melo, the Marquis de Pombal. The eighteenth century was witness to some great educational theorists like Rousseau, Pestalozzi, Marquis de Condorcet, etc., who initiated some path-breaking philosophical and pedagogic movements like Naturalism, National system of education, Realism, etc. This seemed to have had a profound effect on Marquis de Pombal who seemed to have been more influenced by the French (this can be seen from his favour the Verney's New Method which seems to be akin to the Frenchman Basedow's "The Book of Method" and taking a cue from them introduced his significantly trail-blazing reforms.

The Avant-Garde Reforms of Pombal

Bent on giving a great fillip to education as it was gaining more and more importance in Europe he realized that funding was a *sine qua non* and, hence, hit upon the idea of raising funds through the levy of an educational cess on the sale of meat and wines. This smart move put funds at the disposal of education for which reason in Goa two more posts of Government teachers could be created in the provinces of Bardez and Salcette apart from the two existing ones. But in spite of funds being available there were a few Governors like Veiga Cabral who were regressive in their thinking and thus instead opening new schools closed down even the existing ones. However, the next Governor, Count of Sarzedas, making use of the Royal Order of 9th September, 1799 established in 1808 the "Escolas de Primeiras Letras" which were the real precursors of systematic official education in the State.

Free Education

So from a purely pseudo-religious activity carried out by the Missionaries in the Parish schools to serve their own purposes education after the expulsion of the Jesuits in 1759 and later on of the other Orders in 1836 education became a State subject. However, it was still to free itself from the shackles of religion and become truly free and liberal. It goes to the credit of the Marquis de Pombal that education was finally snatched away from the hands of the Religious and given a secular tinge. Later on the revolution in Portugal by the Liberals in 1820 also helped in maintaining the momentum. No doubt it would take almost another hundred years with the birth of the Republic in 1910 to rid education of its religious coloration and make it truly secular.

Appointing of Teachers

It was somewhat like a free for all. There was no set method. There was no set term and there were no precise books. Marquis de Pombal's reforms saw to it that this *laissez-faire* state of affairs was put to an end and order and control was introduced into education. That is why the first thing he proposed was the licencing of teachers. All those who were interested in conducting Classes had to first of all appear for an examination. This automatically meant that they had to be registered. With registration came control and the place of functioning would have to be disclosed along with the other data like the number of students, the fees charged if any, the duration of the course, the books being followed, the method being used, etc.

Prescribing Textbooks

With this procedure it came to light that any book that the teacher fancied was used as a textbook. By getting the teachers to register it was not only to bring them under State control but also to weed out the out-of-favour books being used under the Jesuit method of teaching. Moreover by introducing a common textbook uniformity would be established which could help the students in case they shifted their places of residence.

Authority

But more importantly the Government made it amply clear that the sole authority in all matters educational rested with it and issued necessary instructions from time to time laying down the rules and regulations on how to conduct the Classes. It established itself as the authority to grant permission to open schools, to subject themselves to inspection, to use the prescribed textbooks, etc. In short the State appropriated to itself full authority to regulate and control education in the State without brooking any opposition. In fact Portugal was already late in joining the other European countries in State control of education as Prussia had already made attendance compulsory in elementary schools as early as 1717 and followed it up with the General School Regulations in 1763. In France the hot topic in the mid eighteenth century was National Education and in England the closest anybody to such a system was the Monitorial Method propagated by Joseph Lencaster and later on Andrew Bell. This is the reason why History and Geography were given the pride of place in the school curriculum.

The Number of Schools in 1700 in Goa

During the days of the Religious Orders almost all education was in the hands of the priests and as such all Classes (they were called as such because education was limited to learning the Latin language) were run by them as many of them were without a job for two reasons: (1) There were from 1758 to 1862, a total of 3,733 priests out of which 3,096 were secular priests. Between 1844 and 1849 itself a total of 322 priests were ordained by the Bishop, Dr. Silva Torres when there were only about 20 vicariates. (2) The tussle between the "Padroada" and the "Propaganda Fide" led to the unemployment of many of the priests. Hence, many of them took to teaching or conducting Classes. A look at the chart given on pages 22, 23 and 24 makes it amply clear what I mean as around 47 priests were conducting Classes officially in different Parishes all over Goa.Besides these there must have many others who were giving private tuitions without being registered.

Priestly Class as Teachers

In fact it is very interesting that certain human behaviour invariably remains the same irrespective of the clime and time. Just as in the Hindu system the reins of education lay in the hands of the priestly Class because of which they were the masters of the scriptures so too was the case with the priests in the Catholic religion. From this literary power emerges a volley of holds over others which many abused in nefarious ways. When the trend was to make literacy a preserve of only a few it stands to no reason why the priests of the Catholic religion set up Classes and tried to disseminate the three Rs. There could be one explanation and that is they wanted more and more candidates to join the Seminaries so as to create armies of Missionaries as Goa was considered as the Centre of Evangelization of the Orient.

Incidentally it must be mentioned here that one of Goa's greatest sons, Ven. Blessed Fr. Joseph Vaz was conducting such a Class in the Parish of Nossa Senhora da Piedade (Our Lady of Piety) Church on the island of Divar in the year 1759 and had six students under him. There were three more priests teaching in that Parish though at that time with Pe Mathias Rangel having the highest number of students, 26.

Number of Students and Population

In the year 1760, there were 660 students enrolled in the Classes run by the priests not counting the others who used to conduct Classes either occasionally or individually. Presuming that such a situation existed there might have been another hundred odd students learning the rudiments of the language in the three provinces of Tiswadi, Bardez and Salcette which increases the total to around 800. Since there was no such thing as a Class system it was a one time affair. If one assumes that every year on an average 600 to 800 children were tutored then the literacy rate in those three provinces must have been very high and almost the whole population amounting to probably 60 to 70 thousand was reasonably educated. This makes a very impressive figure which could be comparable to many of the European countries projecting Goa as very progressive in the mid-eighteenth century.

The Primary School Teachers

As far as qualifications were concerned there were three types of teachers:

those who had completed the training course of the "Escola Normal", those on who due to their long experience as teachers were conferred the title of "titulo de capacidade" and then because of the shortage of teachers those who were given a temporary right as "regentes". But those who were appointed on permanent basis had to undergo a rigorous interview which included a written test and orals. Seemingly the whole process was transparent and at the end a merit list was prepared and published. The teachers were also given the lofty title of "Professor", the Heads of the schools were called Directors and secondary schools were known as "Colegios".

It is interesting to note here that the Portuguese had a graded structure for the schools. There were three grades, first, second and third based on certain criteria like urban (location), enrolment of students or even performance in examinations. Those who had put in more years of service would have the privilege of working in the grade one schools. The newly recruited teachers would generally start in the grade three schools with a probation period of two years. There was also a reward system in place for those teachers who showed lot of dedication and application.

But the talking point among the Primary teachers was the regular pedagogical conferences where many of them had an opportunity to present innovations and programmes for the improvement of Primary education in the State.

Students' Enrolment in Schools

The first aspect that strikes one is the period of admissions. Besides a fixed period at the beginning of the academic year students could be admitted at any time of the year normally at the beginning of every month. This arrangement was made because of two reasons: (1) Some children were home schooled or privately tutored and would enroll themselves just before the commencement of examinations or only for examinations; and (2) As the Government was interested in promoting Primary education such a facility was extended in order to make things easy for enrolment of students.

It was the responsibility of the "Professor" to get the village children to enrol in the Primary school. For this he had to first conduct a survey trying to find out how many children were there of school-going age. In this he could have been assisted by the village "regedor". To help him further not only to register the children but also the retain them there was the School Benefit Committee. They would raise the resources to support the needy children by way of books and stationery. Every school had a special fund called the Canteen Fund which would be utilized to supply eatables to the poor and the needy. Besides this the Government would encourage the locals to start charitable societies which could fund the educational activities. The Government was also not averse to taking donations especially in the form of infrastructure (read houses) and in return would grant the donors the privilege of nominating two suitably qualified persons for the posts of "Professors" in the school. To meet the espenses of maintaining the premises the Government had put in place the School Fund.

The variety of efforts that the Government put in to expand Primary education as can be gauged from the reforms are to be appreciated. Any time admission, free textbooks, Government funding, free canteen facilities, involvement of individuals and charitable organizations of well-to-do persons, etc., were all aimed at improving the Primary school situation and finally in 1869 even compulsion. But in spite of their best efforts as one Governor writes "the locals don't want to send their children to school out of ignorance and stubbornness".

The Curriculum and Classroom Teaching

The curriculum though was overhauled periodically there was no fixed time frame. Besides the academic subjects it would be interesting to note that certain subjects like Civility, Morals, Drawing and Craft (Sloyd) were given a lot of importance treating them on par with subjects like History and Geography.

In the Classroom one of the strategies used to encourage and motivate the students was what was called in Portuguese "chamado". Every time a student did better than the others he would be made to sit at the head of the Class in the first place as a reward for diligence. Another strategy that was used both to motivate good performance and extract good behaviour was to write the name of the students every week in both the categories on the blackboard under the roll of honour which would stand the student in good stead at the time of the final examinations.

Curiously the Portuguese used the school as a lesson to others to curb not only the obnoxious practice of *paan* eating among the locals but also the habit of spitting. That is the reason why when the whole country was being painted 'red' Goa was free of that menace till a few years ago. In all the Primary schools in the early stages spittoons were installed and students were trained to spit in these receptacles. Indirectly the students learnt not to spit all over the place.

The Portuguese paid a lot of attention to health. While selecting the spot for locating the school as a pedagogical principle it was essential to see that it was away from undesirable influences like "tavernas", cemeteries, police stations, toilets, etc. Besides at the time of admission of the child a certificate of inoculation was compulsory. The students were checked for cleanliness on a daily basis by the teacher. They had to wear clean clothes. They had to pare their nails regularly and they had to crop their hair short. The inspecting team always made it a point to check upon the cleanliness of the school both inside and outside. Hygiene and cleanliness was given a lot of importance which explains the fact that Goans have assimilated well the concept of cleanliness unlike many others in the rest of the country.

The pièce de resistance, however, of the school system was the examination system. It was made up of both written papers and orals. The oral method of testing has many benefits for the student. It builds up his self-confidence, it teaches him to think on his feet, it improves his verbal expressions, it emboldens him to face an audience, etc. It is also a good occasion for the Jury—another prominent feature—to assess, keeping aside the occasional personal bias, the student from different angles like subject knowledge, the level of understanding of the student, the articulation of words and his language skill, attitude, aptitude and thinking skills. There were also some other aspects of the examination system like selection of topics, accommodating the justified absentees, the eligibility for continuing the examination process, the deciding on the final score by the Jury and even the recording of the scores.

And finally the last aspect of the school education that attracts our attention is the importance that was given to supervision and monitoring. It appears that the Portuguese had realized very early that supervision was an integral part of the process of schooling if schools were going to give the desired results. Hence, the School Inspectors were armed with extensive powers so that the teachers as well as the textual materials and the students were kept on a tight leash. Besides the Inspector, there was also the local authority the "regedor" and even the School Benefit Committee and finally the Director of Education as the highest inspecting authority.

Girls' Education

In June 1968, the Directorate of Education, Goa hosted a conference on "The Development of Women's Education" in the country. One of the papers presented was titled "Development of Girls' Education" in which the paper presenter states that the percentage of girls attending primary school in the country in the year 1965 was around 35 per cent whereas in Goa it was around 45 per cent. Further on she makes another telling remark saying "we also find that in Goa there is not much resistance to the enrolment of girls in mixed schools". She goes on to cite the actual figures saying that out of 196 middle and high schools in Goa only 24 schools were exclusively for girls. This good trend continued so that today we find that more than 80 per cent of the Primary teachers and over 70 per cent of the secondary teachers are women in sharp contrast to the national average of about 50. This sums up succinctly the efforts that went into promoting girls' education in Goa much earlier than many others whose benefits we are reaping even today for which reason there is hardly any difference in the school enrolment figures between boys and girls.

All in all there were many outstanding features in the school system that was once upon a time efficiently and effectively established and dedicatedly promoted by some of the Portuguese in the "Estado da India Portuguesa".

References

Afonso, John Correia. *The Impact of English on Goan Society*, in 'Goan Society through the Ages' (seminar papers) ed. B.S. Shastry, Goa University Publications, 1987.

Afonso, Propercia Correia Pereira. *Bases de reorganisacao do ensino publico primario na Primeiro Congresso Provincial da India Portugueza*, Imprensa Nacional, Nova Goa, 1916.

Amonkar, Sudha. *Development of Girls' Education* in Report on the Conference on The Development of Women's Education, Directorate of Education, Panaji, 1969.

Amor, Manuel Antunes. *Instruccao Primaria*. Typographia Rangel, Bastora, 1925.

Anuario da India Portugueza, Imprensa Nacional, Nova Goa, 2nd Series, 1929.

Anuario da India Portugueza, Imprensa Nacional, Nova Goa, 2nd Series, 1953.

Boletim do Governo do Estado da India, Extraordinario, Typographia Nacional, Nova Goa, 1841.

Boletim Oficial, Imprensa Nacional, Nova Goa, 1838, 1844, 1854, 1856, 1870, 1881, 1882, 1893, 1897, 1901, 1902, 1903, 1904, 1906, 1907, 1908, 1910, 1911, 1913, 1914, 1915, 1918, 1920, 1922, 1923, 1925, 1926, 1928, 1931, 1933, 1935, 1936, 1937, 1938, 1939, 1941, 1945, 1946, 1948, 1949, 1950, 1952, 1953, 1954, 1955, 1957, 1958, 1961.

Braganza e Cunha, Vicente. *Ensino Particular do Ingles* in 'Congress Provincial da India Portugueza', Vol. I, ed. By Antonio Maria da Cunha, Casa Luso-Francesa, Nova Goa, 1924.

Braganza, Luis de Menezes. *"A Educacao e O Ensino na India Portuguesa"* "A India Portuguesa" Vol. I and II, Imprensa Nacional, Nova Goa, 1922.

Coelho, Feliciano C. *Escolas de Primeiras Letras*, Nova Goa, 1931.

Cunha, Tristao de Braganza. *The Denationalization of Goans*, in Goa's Freedom Struggle, New Age Press, Bombay, 1961.

Da Cunha, A.M. *Educacao e Ensino*, in '*O Tempo*', Tip. Sadananda, Nova Goa, 1931.

De Barbuda, Claudio Lagrange Monteiro. *Instruccoes com que El-Rei D. Jose mandou passar ao Estado da India*, Imprensa Nacional, Nova Goa, 1908.

De Figuieredo, Propercia Correia Afonso. *Centenario da Fundacao das Escolas Primarias no Estado da India*, in *Escolas das Primeiras Letras*, Nova Goa, 1931.

—— *Instruccao e Educacao*, in 'Boletim Instituto Vasco da Gama', Vol. 8, Nova Goa, 1930.

Sampayo, Joao de Mello. *Breve Noticia da Origem dos Estudos Superiores em Goa por methodos europeus e em lingua Portugueza*, Imprensa Nacional, Nova Goa, 1905.

De Souza, Ubaldino Leonardo. *O Ensino de Inglez na India Portugues*, Tipographia Gomantak, Margao, 1936.

Couto, Joaquim Jose de Macedo. *Regulamento e instruccoes para o provimento das cadeiras de instruccao, primaria e secundaria no Estado da India Portugueza com os respectivos programmas*, Imprensa Nacional, Nova Goa, 1874.

Gomes, M. Ermelinda dos Stuarts Gomes, *O Ensino na India Antiga e Contemporanea*, in 'Escolas de Primeiras Letras', Nova Goa, 1931.

Gracias, J.A. Ismael. *Inspeccao superior do Ensino Publico na India Portuguesa*, 1846-1869 in 'O Oriente Portuguez', Dir., Imprensa Nacional, Nova Goa, Vol. XI, 1914.

Gracias, Pe. Roque de Piedade, *Ensino Primaria-Systema Metrico e Chorographia da India*, Tip. Rangel, Bastora, Goa, 1910.

Jorge, Rosario Octaviano. *Politica em Goa: Educacao e Instruccao*, Loutulim, Goa, 1926.

Legislacao do Estado da India, Imprensa Nacional, Nova Goa, 1936, 1946, 1950, 1952, 1953, 1954, 1955, 1957, 1958, 1961.

Lobo, Belarmino. *Our Portuguese Primary Schools, in* "A educacao e o ensino na India Portugueza", Imprensa Nacional, Nova Goa.

Lobo, Sertorio Crisologo. *Organizacao do Ensino na India desde o seculo XVI*, in *Memoria Historico-Eclesiastica da Arquidiocese de Goa*, Nova Goa, 1933.

Mascarenhas, Antonio. "*The Christian Nalanda*", in 'Goa Today', Panaji, September, 1984.

Mascarenhas, Constancio. *Reflexoes sobre a Instruccao em Goa*, Tip. Rangel, Bastora, 1979.

Mascarenhas, W.X. *Draft Plan, 1963-1966 on Education.* Government of Goa, Planning and Social Services Department, Secretariat, Panaji, 1966.

Menezes, Luis de. *A instrucao primaria nas escolas paroquias* in "Primeiro Congresso Provincial da India Portugueza", Imprensa Nacional, Nova Goa, 1916.

Pacheco, Antonio Caetano.*Plano Geral da Instruccao Publica nos Estados Portugueses da India*, Typograhia de Braga, Lisboa, 1848.

Pereira, Antonio Felix. *Escolas Primarias em Bardez, Pernem e Sanquelim*, in "O Oriente Portugues", April/July, No. 2 and 3, 1932.

Pereira, Elias Fernandes. *Guia dos examinations de Admissao*, Livraria Universal de Magalhaes e Moniz, Porto, 1879.

Pinto, Cristovam. *A Colonizacao Portugueza da India* in 'A India Portugueza', Imprensa Nacional, Nova Goa, 1923.

Priolkar, A.K. *Problemas Economicas e da Educacao*, Sessoes de Agosto e Outubro, Imprensa Nacional, Nova Goa, 1920.

Quexova Bandari, ed. *Em material de ensino por Prf. Venceslau Soares*, Composicao e Impressao de Typograhia "Rego", Nova Goa, 1944.

R.J. "A Inolvidavel Memoria de William Robert Lyons, Typographia Rangel, Bastora, 1926.

Saldanha, Marian. *A Luzitanizacao de Goa*, Imprensa Nacional, Lisboa, 1947.

Soares, Aloysius. "*Four Centuries of Education*" *in* "In the Mission Field", XCHR, The Times of India Press, Bombay, 1979.

—— Our *Portuguese Primary Schools*, in *Escolas de Primeiras Letras*, Nova Goa, 1931.

—— *Novas Tendencias do Ensino Primario*, Typographia Central, Nova Goa, 1935.

Telles, Ricardo Micael. *Os Franciscanos no Oriente e Seus Conventos*, Tipographia Rao e Irmaos, Nova Goa, 1922.

Terreiro, D.M. "*Fourth Annual Report*" *of Indo-Portuguese Association*, Calcutta, Howrah Printing Works, Calcutta, 1915.

Torrie, Joao Stuart da Fonseca. *Estatistica da India Portugueza*, Imprensa Nacional, Nova Goa, 1879.

Xavier, Jose Agostinho. *Repertorio Alphabetico e Remissivo das disposicoes contidas nos decretos e regulamentos sobre a Instruccao Primaria, Secundaria e Superior do Estado da India*, Imprensa Nacional, Nova Goa, 1897.

Secondary Sources

Altekar, Dr. A.S. *Education in Ancient India*, The Indian Bookshop, Benares, 1934.

Antonio Maria da Cunha. *Casa Luso-Francesca*, Nova Goa, 1924.

Azavedo, Lucio J. *Historia dos Cristaos Novos Portugueses*, Imprensa Nacional, Lisboa, 1921.

Bhatt, B.D. and Aggarwal J.C. *Educational Documents in India*. Arya Book Depot, New Delhi, 1987.

Boxer, C.R. *Four Centuries of Portuguese Expansion*, 1415-1825, Johannesburg, 1959.

——*Portuguese Society in the Tropics: The Municipal Councils of Goa, Macau, Bahia, Luanda*, 1510-1800, Wisconsin, Madison and Milwakee, 1965.

——*From Lisbon to Goa, (1500-1750)*, Variorum Reprints, London, 1984.

Carreira, Henrique Medina. *A Situacao Social em Portugal*, (1960-1995), organizacao de Antonio Barreto, Instituto de Ciencias Sociais, Universidade de Lisboa, 1996.

Chatterjee, Kalyan K. *English Education in India*, Macmillan Company of India Ltd., Delhi, 1976.

Chaube, Dr. S.P. *History of Indian Education*, Vinod Pustak Mandir, Agra,

Correia, Alberto Carlos Germano da Silva. *Historia Colonizacao Portuguesa na India*, 5 Vols., Agencia Geral do Ultramar, Lisboa, 1950-51.

Coutinho, Verissimo. *Education and Development in Goa*, ICSS, Rome, 1987.

D'Ayalla, Frederico Diniz. *Goa-Antiga e Moderna*, edicao II, Nova Goa, 1927.

Da Costa, Antonio Anastasio Bruto. *Goa sob a dominacao Portugueza*, Tipographia Ultramar, Margao, 1896.

Da Costa, J A J. *History of Goa*. Ramakant Printers, Mapuca, Goa, 1982.

Da Costa, P.J.Peregrino. *A Expansao do Goes pelo Mundo*, Reparticao Estatistica e Informacao, Pangim, 1956.

Da Cunha, A.M., *O tempo-educacao e ensino*, Tip. Sadananda, Nova Goa.

Da Cruz, A. *Goa: Men and Matters*, Ashok Printing Press, Vasco, 1974.

Da Fonseca, Jose Nicolau. *An Historical and Archaeological Sketch of the City of Goa*. Asian Educational Services, New Delhi, 1986.

Da Saldanha, M.J. Gabriel, *Historia de Goa (Politica e Arquelogica)*, Livraria Coelho, Nova Goa, 1925.

Da Silva. Dr. Francisco Antonio Wolfango. *A cultura da lingua Concani e o problema da educacao fundamental em Goa*, in "Boletim de Instituto Vasco da Gama", Imprensa Nacional, Nova Goa, Nov. 1933.

Danvers, Frederick Charles. *The Portuguese in India*, Vol. I and II, Asian Educational Services, New Delhi, 1988.

De Andrade, Antonio Alberto Banha. *A Reforma Pombalina dos Estudos Secundarias (1759-1771)*, Vol. I and II, Coimbra University, Coimbra, 1981.

De Kloguen, Denis L. Cottineau. *An Historical Sketch of Goa*. Asian Educational Services, New Delhi, 1995 (first published in 1831).

De Souza, Bento G. *Goan Society in Transition*, Bombay Popular Prakashan, 1975.

D'Costa, Adalyne. *Social Change in Goa*, D'Costa Publishers, Panjim, 1982.

Doshi, Sarayu (ed). *Goa: Cultural Patterns*, Marg Publications, Bombay, 1983.

Ferreira, Julio Albino. *Dicionario Ingles- Porttugues*. Avenida da Boa Vista, 28, Porto, Portugal, 1954.

Ghosh, Suresh Chandra. *History of Education in Modern India, 1757-1986*. Orient Longman, 1995.

Gomes, Benedito J. "*Um Prefacio Historico-Pedagogico*" in Anuario de Escolas Primarias, Director, Jaime Rangel, Tipografia Rangel, Bastora, 1927.

Gomes, Prof. Joaquim Manuel Aires. *Indo-Portuguese Historical Encyclopaedia*, Goa, India, 2000.

Gomes, Prof. Dr. Olivinho J.F., *The Religious Orders in Goa* (XVI-XVIII), Konkani Sorospot Prakashan, Chandor, Goa, 2003.

—— *Goa*, National Book Trust, New Delhi, 2002.

Gomes, Rena. Dissertation on *Primary Education in Goa* (1825-1925). University of Bombay, 1973.

Lello and Irmaos. Editors, *Dicionario Pratico illustrado*, Porto, 1960.

Lencaster, Joseph. *The Lencastrian System of Education*, Baltimore, 1821.

Livermore, H.V. *A New History of Portugal*, Cambridge University Press, London, 1969.

Lobo, Pythagoras da P. Editor, *O Indispensavel*. Typographia Rangel, Bastora, 1894.

Lopes, Maria de Jesus dos Martires. *Goa Setecentista-Tradicao e Modernidade*, Universidade Catolica Portugueza, Lisboa, 1996.

Marques, A.H. de Oliveira, *History of Portugal*, Imprensa Nacional- Casa de Moeda, Lisboa.

Mascarenhas, Antonio. *Goan Life and Outlook*, Lisbon, 1958.

Mascarenhas, Constancio. *A instrucao Publica na India Portugueza*, Sociedade de Geographia de Lisboa, 1959.

Mascarenhas, Myra Pinto. *The Pombaline Era in Goa (1750-1777),* A Thesis in History, Centre of Postgraduate Instruction and Research, Panjim, Goa, 1977.

Maxwell, Kenneth. *Pombal, Paradox of the Enlightenment*, Cambridge University Press, 1995.

Mendes, A. Lopes. *A India Portuguesa*. Imprensa Nacional, Lisboa, 1886.

Menezes, Braganca. Educacao e Ensino na India Portuguesa. Novo Goa, 1923.

Mhamai, S.K. *Goa: Educational Institutions through the Ages*, (Seminar papers) Directorate of Archives and Archaeology, Panaji, 2002.

Mitragotri, Dr. V.R. *Socio-Cultural History of Goa* (from the Bhojas to Vijayanagar), Instituto Menezes Braganza, Panaji, 1999.

Murthy Keshava B.R. "*Education in Portuguese Goa*" Surya Kumar Buyan Commemoration volume, Guwahati, 1966.

Naik, Gregory. *Jesuit Education in Western India*, Indian Missiological Review, Vol. IX, No. 4, Asian Trading Corporation, Bombay, 1987.

Naik, J.P. and Nurullah, Syed. *Students' History of Education in India, (1800-1973*). The Macmillan Company of India Ltd., Delhi, 1974.

Novo Michaelis. *Dicionario Illustrado*, Portuguese-English, 37th edition, Sao Paulo, Brazil, 1984.

Pereira, A.B. de Braganza, (ed). *Arquivo Portugues Oriental*, 10 Vols., Tipographia Rangel, Bastora, 1936-40.

Pinto, J.B. *Goan Emigration*, Boa Sorte, Goa, 1953.

Quadros, Amalia. *The Development of Primary Education in Goa from 1910 to 1961*, CPIR, University of Bombay, 1974.

Ramachandran, Padma and Ramkumar, Vasantha. *Education in India*, NBT, India, New Delhi, 2007.

Rao, R.P. *Portuguese Rule in Goa, 1510-1961*, Asia Printing House, Bombay, 1963.

Rivara, J.H. da Cunha, (ed). *Archivo Portugues Oriental*, 10 Vols., Imprensa Nacional, Nova Goa, 1857-1876.

Rodrigues, Maria Lourdes Bravo da Costa. *The System of Education in the Decade of the 1950s*, in 'Goa: Educational Institutions through the Ages', edited by S.K. Mhamai, Directorate of Archives and Archaeology, Panaji, 2002.

Serrao, Jose. Director, *Dicionario de Historia de Portugal*, Livraria Figuierinhas, Porto

Shastry, B.S. Ed. *Goan Society through the Ages* (Seminar papers), Goa University, Asian Publications Services, New Delhi, 1993.

Souza, Felipe Nery Thome Caetano do Rosario. *Noticia Historico e*

Legislacao da Instrucca Publica-Primaria, Secundaria e Superior na India Portugueza. Tip. Da Cruz, Rua de Ourem, No. 9, 1879.

Souza, Caetano Francisco de, *Instituicoes Portugueses de Educacao e Instruccao no Oriente*. Vol. I, Job Printing Press, Bombay, 1890.

Souza, Bento Graciano. *Goan Society in Transition* (A Study in Social Change), Popular Prakashan, Bombay, 1975.

Varde, P.S. *History of Education in Goa* (from 1510 to the present day). Goa Vidya Prathistan, Panaji, Goa, 1977.

Wagle and Coelho, George. *Goa: Continuity and Change*, Toronto, 1995.

Xavier, P.D. *Goa: A Social History (1510-1640)*, Rajhauns Vitaran, Panaji, 1993.

Index

OCCUPATIONAL HEALTH AND SAFETY OF CONSTRUCTION WORKERS

About the Authors

Dr. Pratibha Joshi is a Scientist in Agriculture Research Service (ARS), posted in Vivekanand Parvatiya Krishi Anusandhan Sansthan (ICAR), at Almora, Uttarakhand. She did her Ph.D. with ICAR-SRF (Senior Research Fellowship) from G.B.P.U. of Ag. & Tech. Pantnagar in the discipline of Family Resource Management in the year 2010 with the experience in Ergonomics.

Dr. Promila Sharma is Professor in the discipline of Family Resource Management, G.B.P.U.of Ag.& Tech. Pantnagar. She is having vast experience of research in Ergonomics field.

Dr. T.C. Thakur is a National Professor (ICAR) in the Deptt. of farm machinery and power engineering, G.B.P.U.of Ag.& Tech. Pantnagar having a great experience in the area of Agricultural Ergonomics. He is one of the recipients of the 'Awadh Samman Awards-2009' constituted by the Government of Uttar Pradesh, India as a Modern Agricultural Techniques Researchers for specialized work on agriculture.

Mr. Amit Khatter, is a Deputy Manager in Jindal Arc. Limited, Gurgaon, Haryana working in construction industry and sharing his experience and helping the poor workmanship of construction life.

Occupational Health and Safety of Construction Workers
Using Personal Protective Equipment

Pratibha Joshi
Promila Sharma,
T.C. Thakur
and
Amit Khatter

CONCEPT PUBLISHING COMPANY PVT. LTD.
NEW DELHI-110 059

ISBN-13 : 978-81-8069-913-9

First Published 2013

Published and Printed by

Concept Since 1974

Concept Publishing Company Pvt. Ltd.
A/15-16, Commercial Block, Mohan Garden
New Delhi-110059 (India)
T: 25351460, 25351794, *F*: 091-11-25357109
E: publishing@conceptpub.com, W: www.conceptpub.com
Editorial Office: H-13, Bali Nagar, New Delhi-110 015, India.

Cataloging in Publication Data--*Courtesy:* D.K. Agencies (P) Ltd. <docinfo@dkagencies.com>

Occupational health and safety of construction workers : using personal protective equipment / Pratibha Joshi ... [et al.].

p. cm.
Includes bibliographical references (p.) and index.
ISBN 9788180699139

1. Construction workers—Health and hygiene—India—Delhi. 2. Industrial hygiene—India—Delhi. 3. Industrial safety—India—Delhi. 4. Protective clothing India—Delhi. I. Joshi, Pratibha.

DDC 363.11962409545 6 23

G.B. Pant University of Agiculture and Technology
Pantnagar-263145, Distt. Udham Singh Nagar
(Uttarakhand) INDIA

Foreword

Construction is one of the important economic activity in India. It provides job opportunities to all categories of people either unskilled, semi-skilled or skilled. Construction workers face some of the most dangerous working conditions in the country on a daily basis. In urban sector increasing numbers of workers have taken up construction work as a means of immediate employment, which provides cash earnings at the end of the day. The rural masses migrate towards urban areas in search of job and being involved in this second largest occupation i.e., construction.

An attempt has been made to bring information regarding health and safety issues and provision of adequate protective supplies/equipment to the construction workers to ensure their safety. A comprehensive compilation in the form of book entitled "Occupational Health and Safety of Construction Workers: Using Personal Protective Equipment" is formulated to sensitizing PPE manufacturers, suppliers and safety management staff in a construction industry to manufacture and use the same for the health and safety of construction workers. This compilation consisted of identification of hazards, problems encountered, need for PPE, discomfort associated with existing PPE and suggest modifications in selected PPE.

I compliment Dr. Pratibha Joshi, Prof. Promila Sharma, National Prof. T.C. Thakur and Mr. Amit Khatter for their effort in publication of this important book.

I am sure that the scientific information contained in the form of various chapters on different aspects will be useful for the construction safety planners and managers, policy-makers, researchers and all those who are concerned in construction unit occupation. The valuable information in the book can also be used as a reference for students as well as for scientists and executives involved in the area of health and safety.

B.S. Bisht
Vice-Chancellor

Preface

Construction is one of the largest industries in India, which requires working at ever changing locations and work environments. Nearly 6.5 million people work at approximately 2,52,000 construction sites across the nation on any given day. Being as unorganised sector, the fatal injury rate for the construction industry is higher than the national average in this category for all industries. A variety of hazards exist in the construction sites. However, the risks associated with these hazards are greatly reduced or eliminated, if proper precautions and practices are used. PPE must be appropriate for the task to be completed and meet the challenges that a given occupational hazard can present. Correct fit increases effectiveness, wearer safety and wearer comfort.

In construction industry, workers may or may not be migrant workers but the fact is that they have maximum mobility and risk environment because of the nature of their occupation. They are always on move from one work site to another. Majority of all fatal on-the-job injuries occur in construction site. These hazards include mechanical, physical, chemical, biological, postural, electrical, thermal, vibration, noise and radiation.

This book highlights the demographic profile, occupational and medical history, anthropometric data, and physiological, psychological and postural ergonomic factors of construction workers. Along with environmental parameters, hazards presents in construction sites and problems encountered by construction workers with and without use of PPE and discomfort faced with the use of existing PPE while performing various construction activities viz. loading and unloading of materials, laser operations, gas cutting activity, powered tool operations, installation work and safety management and supervision were also be taken into consideration.

This book will help the construction site managers to identify the hazard present and risk associated with hazards in construction sites and to use ergonomic practices to minimize these hazards. This book is also useful for manufacturers who involve in manufacturing of PPE for reference of anthropometry of Indian men and industrial safety features to be incorporated for better quality and comfort of PPE. This book will also help the PPE users and construction workers to make them aware about the hazards and risks encountered at site and to know the prevention techniques to combat with the hazards.

Pratibha Joshi
Promila Sharma
T.C. Thakur
Amit Khatter

Acknowledgements

First of all, we express our deep sense of gratitude to God, the Almighty with whose grace, blessings and kindness, we have been able to light this humble piece of work.

With profound reverence, we express our deep sense of gratitude and indebtness to Dr. S.K. Rastogi, Professor and Head, Department of Veterinary Physiology, Dr. A.K. Shukla, Professor and Head, Department of Maths. Stat. and Computers, Dr. S.D. Samantray, Professor and Head, Depatment of Computer Engineering, and Dr. Gyanendra Sharma, Professor, Department of Agriculture Communication of G.B.P.U. of Ag. & Tech. for their constant inspiration, valuable suggestions, expert guidance and sustained interest during the course of investigation and preparation of book.

We would be failing in our duties if we don't mention our grateful thanks to Dr. D. Majumdar, Senior Scientist, Defence Institute of Physiology and Allied Sciences, Delhi and Dr. L.P. Gite, Project Coordinator, Central Institute of Agricultural Engineering, Bhopal for providing guidance and suggestions and timely help for accessing library in their respective institutes.

We can't ignore to thank Mr. K.N. Sen, Deputy General Manager, Larson & Toubro Limited and Mr. Siddarth Sarkar, Assistant Manager, DLF-Laing o' Rouke India Limited and construction workers, who cooperate with us.

Financial assistance in the form of Senior Research Fellowship by ICAR to Pratibha Joshi also fully acknowledged.

Though all others cannot be mentioned but none is forgotten.

Pantnagar

Dr. Pratibha Joshi
Dr. Promila Sharma
Dr. T. C. Thakur
Mr. Amit Khatter

Contents

List of Tables

List of Figures

List of Plates

1

Introduction

Construction is an industry that requires working at ever-changing locations and work environments. Nearly 6.5 million people work at approximately 2,52,000 construction sites across the nation on any given day (*The Hindu,* Sept. 9, 2006). Some of the main duties of general construction workers are to install various commercial, industrial and residential systems and to ensure that projects conform to building codes and regulations, and maintain various types of equipments and tools ensuring wellness and safety at the workplace. Construction is one of the important economic activities in India. It offers employment opportunities to all categories of people right from highly skilled to totally unskilled labourer. In urban sector, increasing numbers of workers have taken up construction work as a means of immediate employment, which provides cash earnings at the end of the day. The rural masses also migrate towards urban areas in search of job and being involved in this second largest occupation. In metropolitan cities, the construction work is predominantly a male dominated economic activity due to the arduous nature of work to be performed by the workers. The activities performed by workers in construction sites are basic construction work (working with mortar, cement, crushing stones, transportation of water, bricks etc.), loading/unloading of materials, cutting, grinding, welding, lifting, shuttering/formworks, scaffolding, reinforcement steel works, chipping/breaking, sawing/planning, installation, maintenance and management work. The type of workers involved in different types of tasks are unskilled construction labour and skilled labour performing operations as welding, chipping, handling power tools, helpers, supervisors and management staff.

Being an unorganized sector, the fatal injury rate for the construction industry is higher than the national average in this category of all the industries. A variety of hazards exist at the construction sites. However, the risks associated with these hazards are greatly reduced or eliminated, if proper precautions and practices are used. Some health and safety issues for construction workers are pain or injury from physical overexertion, repetitive manual tasks, or working in awkward positions, exposure to moulds, fungi or rodent droppings, exposure to lead, wood dust, asbestos, paints, solvents, and other toxic chemicals or materials, working in extreme temperatures and Ultra Violet (UV) radiation, working with hand tools, powered tools and heavy powered equipment, excess vibration of hands, arms or body from powered tools or equipment, confined spaces, noise, working at heights, electrical hazards, working with cranes, hoists, and other material handling equipment, falls, respiratory and fire hazards from wood dust, stress, shift work or extended work days. Excessive exposure to these hazards may result in acute injury, chronic illness, permanent disability or even death. Loss of concentration at work and fatigue arising from poor health conditions may increase the risk of accidents.

Construction work is featured by high labour turnover, constantly changing works environment and conditions on site, and different type of works being carried out simultaneously. All these factors caused by temporary nature of job create a high-risk environment.

Health hazards in the construction industry can be grouped under mechanical and non-mechanical hazards. Mechanical hazards including accidental issues from impact, penetration from scrap metal and sharp objects, crushing and physical hazards. However, non-mechanical sources of hazards include chemical, electrical, thermal and ergonomic hazards.

Physical hazards are noise, vibration, radiation, etc. Electrical hazards may include contact with power lines, cuts and burns, electric shocks and sparks etc., chemical hazards include splashing liquids, dusts, mists, fumes, vapours and penetration of chemicals. These chemicals from hazardous sources can affect the body via inhalation, ingestion, or skin absorption. Exposure to dusts for prolonged period may cause acute or chronic health effects. Any process involving breaking, crushing or grinding operations will generate dust. The workers at higher risk are operators of grinders, drillers, saw, cutters and masons.

Workers are also exposed to hand-transmitted vibrations in their workplace through the use of hand-held power tools from a small disc grinder to large driller. Continued usage of high magnitude vibration tools can result in Raynaud's Disease where the fingers become blanched (Mansfield, 2005), also known as vibration white finger, a part of Hand Arm Vibration Syndrome (HAVS) (Dong *et al.*, 2001; Wasserman, 1985). This disease affects the finger and the hands. In the long run, permanent damages to the nerves would result in a loss of sense of touch and dexterity. To prevent health hazards at workplace, all possible sources should be identified before commencement of construction work. Hazards at a construction site may come from hazardous substances used on site, and also environmental variables may create additional risks as heat and noise. When health hazards are identified, the first step is to try to eliminate them properly, either by doing the job in a different way or using a substitute. If prevention is not practicable, the next step is to try to control the risk as using water suppression to control dust emission. If, finally exposure of risk cannot be adequately controlled by any combination of measures, personal protective equipment should be provided.

Personal Protective Equipment (PPE) are designed to protect employees from serious injuries or illnesses due to workplace resulting from contact with chemical, radiological, physical, electrical, mechanical, or other workplace hazards. PPE is an item or items used to protect the eyes, face, head, body, arms, hands, legs and feet such as goggles, helmets, head covers, gloves, coveralls, vests, safety shoes, protective shields, earplugs and respirators. According to Occupational Safety and Health Administration (OSHA), PPE must be provided as a last resort, when other measures cannot provide enough protection. The employer is required to first make efforts to eliminate or minimize hazardous working conditions.

The best way to protect workers against hazards is to control problems at the source. OSHA stated that workers must have PPE that fits properly. Poorly fitted PPE may cause additional hazards. In the case of PPE, an effective training programme is required to ensure that the correct fit is achieved. Where occupational risk remains after application of engineering and work practice controls, Personal Protective Equipment should be worn. Although PPE may appear to be a relatively inexpensive and simple safeguard to counteract a risk yet its use is often far more expensive in terms of significant losses when not used properly. Therefore, as a routine task, PPE assessment should be made even if there are other means of risk control available. PPE must be appropriate for the task to be completed and meet the challenges that a given occupational hazard can present. Correct fit increases effectiveness, wearer safety, and wearer comfort. The greater the comfort, the greater the compliance by the worker and need to determine whether any hazard requires PPE.

The following points explain the need for PPE:

- When a hazard cannot be removed from the workplace, or when engineering controls are insufficient to control the hazard, PPE must be considered.
- PPE does not eliminate hazards from the workplace but places a barrier between the worker and the hazard. If the PPE fails or is not used properly, the worker will be exposed.
- The use of PPE by employees to minimize accidents, injuries, and illnesses that may be the result of exposure to hazards in the workplace.

The colour coding of safety equipment is important issue for visual identification of workers engaged in sites. For safety helmet general colour coding present is as White: for managers, supervisors, engineers; Green: for safety personnels; Blue: for sub-contractors; Yellow: for labourers; Black: for security personnels; Red: for signaller; Orange: for scaffolders; Grey: for drivers, DG's operator, plant technicians; Grey with Green strip along the periphery: for electricians. However, the jackets/vests are in Red: for signallers and Saffron Yellow (Green): for other workers (as per the company's policy).

In India, safety equipment should correspond to standards laid by Bureau of Indian Standards (BIS). A range of Indian standards which cover various types of personal protective equipments are as follows:

- Safety helmets conforming to IS: 2925-1984 should be used whenever, there is a risk of falling or suspended objects striking the head.
- Eye protection must confirm with IS: 5983-1980 which specifies the qualities of different types of protection as chemical, dust etc.
- Shoes or boots with steel toe-caps protects toes against crushing injuries from dropped objects or from injuries of impact or running over by heavy trolleys etc. Footwear may also incorporate steel mid sole plate to protect from penetrating injuries. Footwear should conform to IS: 5852-1996/IS: 11226-1993 (leather shoes with steel toe caps), IS: 12254-1993/IS: 13695-1993 (rubber/PVC knee boots/gum boots).
- Gloves of different types can be used to protect against a range of hazards such as extreme temperatures, corrosive materials, toxic chemicals, infection risks, sharp or abrasive materials, vibration, etc. Dexterity, grip, fit and comfort are important. Using the wrong size of glove diminishes performance and may cause danger.
- IS: 9473-1980 (dust respirator), IS: 1179-1967 for welding helmets, IS: 9973-1981 for visor are other relevant standards.

Rationale for the Study

The purpose of combining ergonomics in relation to construction workers and the use of PPE is to identify occupational health hazards of construction workers and make relevant strategies to reduce accidents to some extent by taking into consideration. The relationship between human body and design of PPE, physiological and psychological attributes may be estimated and the need is to validate ergonomically sound PPE to reduce occupational hazards. Quite a good number of studies have been conducted abroad on buildings and occupational health hazards but there is very limited information available in the literature on the use of PPE tools in the construction work. Therefore, there is a need to design ergonomically sound user's friendly PPE in terms of minimizing the occupational health hazards of users during work and to increase the efficiency of the worker.

Considering the above facts and ideas in mind, the present study entitled "Ergonomic Assessment of Personal Protective Equipment in Relation to Occupational Health and Safety of Construction Workers" was planned.

Objectives of the Study

- To study the demographic profile of construction workers.
- To assess existing conditions in terms of activity profile i.e., type of task, duration of task and frequency of performance and occupational health hazards of construction workers with and without the use of PPE.
- To study the physiological, psychological and situational attributes of construction workers.
- To validate PPE in terms of dimensions of anthropometric data of users, comfort and ease in use and redesigning of selected PPE through Computer Aided Designing (CAD) and supplying of information to manufacturers.

Hypotheses of the Study

- Action categories of REBA are independent of activities performed by construction workers.
- There is no significant difference in mean HR, and Energy Expenditure during performance of various construction activities.
- The average muscular grip strength of different workers with and without gloves is same.

Assumptions of the study

Ergonomically sound PPE tools designed on the basis of anthropometric measurements of construction workers can reduce occupational health hazards.

Limitations of the Study

- The study was conducted on 120 respondents only.
- The samples of the investigation were construction workers in metropolitan cities.
- The study was limited to male construction workers.

Delimitation

The sample was selected from various construction sites of Delhi.

2

Review of Literature

An extensive survey of all available past studies relevant to the field of investigation, is an essential condition for the formulation of hypotheses. According to Young (1996), a review of pertinent works and thinking by others helps to enlarge, enrich, and clarify one's own work and thinking.

The review of literature serves as a background for the present investigation and helps in understanding it in proper perspective. An exhaustive review of the studies relevant to the topic has been presented in the following sub-heads:

1. Anthropometric Measurements
2. Injuries and Accidents in Construction Work
3. Ensure Wellness in Workplace: Use of PPE
4. Selection Criteria and Standards of PPE
5. Discomfort Associated with PPE
6. Postural and Vibration Hazards
7. Salient Findings from Review

1. Anthropometric Measurements

The word 'anthropometry' is derived from the Greek words *anthropos* (Man) and *mentron* (measure), therefore, literal meaning of anthropometry is measurements of the human body. It involves systematic measurement of the physical characteristics of human body, primarily dimensional descriptors of body size and shape. The anthropometric data are used in ergonomics as reference data in planning ergonomic workplace layouts, to specify the physical dimensions of equipment, evaluating a wide range of products from clothing to spacecraft to "fit the task to the man" (Grandjean, 1980), thus enhancing operational ability, safety, convenience and comfort while performing tasks without augmenting work efficiency and reducing work cost (Verghese *et al.*, 1989).

Clauser *et al.* (1986) reported various categories of anthropometric measurements based upon area of application mentioned as basic body size descriptors, key dimensions for sizing and design of personal items, clothing and personal equipment pattern, dimensions used to develop manikins or test dummies, dimensions useful for the design and sizing of load carrying equipment, head and face dimensions for the designing of headgear, optical, and auditory devices, hand, finger, wrist and forearm measurements used in the design and sizing of gloves, foot and ankle dimensions needed for the design and sizing of shoes and boots, and dimensions recommended for use in standards.

Gite and Yadav (1989) reported that in Indian agriculture, hand tools, animal-drawn equipment and tractor/power operated machinery are extensively used for various operations. The equipment are either operated or controlled by human workers. Use of anthropometric data can help in the proper design of equipment for better efficiency and more human comfort. They identified 52 body dimensions for the design of the equipment and proposed that extensive surveys should be carried out in different regions of the country to generate the necessary data useful in farm machinery design.

The human geometry and the geometry of the product must be suitably fitted together (Kreifeldt, 1991) for safety as well as for functional reasons. Thus, appropriate anthropometric applications are necessary for a 'human compatible' designed product.

Anthropometry is the approach, which deals with the measurements of the human external body dimensions in static and dynamic conditions (Chakrabarti, 1997). Anthropometric data are fundamental to the design of safe and usable products (Norris and Wilson, 1997), and the benefits of using these data in designing process are widely recognized.

Thakur and Sharma (1998) ergonomically assessed various activities performed by women farmers. Anthropometric measurements of the women farmers in standing postures were taken to design and modify agricultural implements for the operations i.e., digging of land, levelling, weeding, hoeing, sowing and application of fertilizers. For harvesting improved sickle were designed taken into account the anthropometric measurements of hand and palm.

Anthropometry data sets are one way of bringing the physical dimensions of users into the designing process, however, there are limitations for design teams using these. Information sources are also fragmented making it difficult for the practicing designer to locate and compile relevant data (Porter *et al.*, 1999).

Dewangan (2005) conducted a survey of thirty-three anthropometric dimensions from 280 male farmers belonging to 7 states of eastern region. Range, mean, standard deviation, coefficient of variation, 5th, 50th, and 95th percentile for each anthropometric dimension were calculated for entire region. The anthropometric dimensions of farm youths of the North-Eastern Region were compared with those of the northern, eastern, southern and western regions of India. It was found that the people of the North-Eastern Region had most of the body dimensions lower than those from other regions except southern and eastern regions of India. It was also stated that for efficient designing of tools and machines for higher productivity, the anthropometric data of the operators are very essential.

Lili Du *et al.* (2006) conducted head-and-face anthropometric survey of Chinese workers and reported millions of workers in China rely on respirators and other personal protective equipment to reduce the risk of injury and occupational diseases. An anthropometric survey of Chinese civilian workers was conducted in 2006, with a total of 3000 subjects (2026 males and 974 females) between the ages of 18 and 66 years. Some representative indices as facial dimensions (face length, face width, nose protrusion, and nasal root breadth), height, weight, neck circumference, waist circumference and hip circumference were measured. Through comparison with the facial dimensions of American subjects, this study indicated that Chinese civilian workers have shorter face length, smaller nose protrusion, larger face width and longer lip length.

Dhyani (2007) cited in her research study that, anthropometry is an integral part of human limitations and capabilities and the fact that the anthropometric dimensions vary significantly from individual to individual. It is essential to consider the range of variability in general body size, gender, racial/ethnic differences while designing the tools and equipment.

2. Injuries and Accidents in Construction Work

Construction safety (the intermediate phase between a finished design and a completed building) is largely the responsibility of the contractors and other site professionals. Most construction accidents result from basic root causes such as lack of proper training, deficient enforcement of safety, unsafe equipment, unsafe methods or sequencing, unsafe site conditions, not using the safety equipment that was provided, and a poor attitude towards safety (Toole, 2002).

The construction industry stands out from other employments as having one of the highest worker injury and fatality rates. Construction comprises a very small percentage of the overall workforce. Yet, the incidence rate for non-fatal injuries and illnesses exceeds that of many other industries. The construction industry has the most fatalities of any other industry sector (Bureau of Labour Statistics, 2004).

Sokol (2004) reported that the construction industry is different from others in many respects. Employee turnover is high, employment terms are generally shorter, the industry contains a large number of small contractor and sub-contractor businesses, and noise levels on a typical construction site are often unpredictable and constantly changing. He also reported that construction workers are not comfortable on the job without their tool belts and various other gear, including their gloves, hard hats, steel-toed boots and other personal protective equipment. Responses indicated that between 2001 and 2004, nine of 10 Personal Protective Equipment (PPE) types (hard hats, safety shoes or boots, protective eyewear, gloves, fall protection, hearing protection, respirators, protective coveralls and face shields) showed increases in the percentages of workers in heavy construction who are wearing them when needed. According to the study, the safety vest was the only type of PPE that declined in use over three-year period. Hard hats, safety vests and safety shoes or boots continue to be the most commonly used types of PPE, with more than two-thirds of construction workers wearing them when needed, however, face shields, protective coveralls, and respirators are worn regularly when needed by the smallest percentages i.e., about 45 per cent each. However, those three PPE types all showed significant increases from the earlier studies. Some studies have shown that a fairly large percentage of construction accidents could have been eliminated, reduced, or avoided by making better choices in the design and planning stages of a project (Hecker *et al.*, 2005).

Stout *et al.* (2006) stated in National Institute for Occupational Safety and Health (NIOSH) science blog that research to practice programme 2006, conducted by NIOSH mentioned that construction workers suffer from injury, disability, and death from workplace incidents. Statistics shows that on an average, 16 workers died each day from traumatic injuries and overall, 5,840 workers died from an occupational injury and more than 4 million workers had a non-fatal injury or illness. Research to practice programme focused on the transfer and translation of effective prevention practices including PPE products to reduce illness and injuries and increased workplace use.

Construction is a high accident-prone industry. Accidents in construction are about three times more than that in manufacturing industries. The most common accident on a construction site is the fall of a person from heights. The general causes and approximate percentages of these accidents in a construction site are fall of workers from height (50%), fall of material on workers (10%), during transportation (10%), lifting equipment (5%), electricity shock, etc. (5%), underground excavation, earth or well sinking (5%), miscellaneous (drowning, building collapse etc.) were 15 per cent. The construction industry has several special features, which affect the safety and health of workers compared to those in regular manufacturing industries (*The Hindu*, Sept. 9, 2006).

Brent (2007) reported in his study, that 12 per cent of silicosis deaths in construction (1985–1999) and approximately 48,000 workers in construction were exposed over the NIOSH Recommended Exposure Limit (1993). He also found that sweating, heat stress with PPE (e.g. face shields, goggles, reflective vests), lack of comfort, fogging of face-piece and safety glasses, difficulty of wearing safety glasses with respirators and visual obstruction from respirator (hoods) were some of the health issues of construction workers.

Chol *et al.* (2007) discussed the workplace ergonomic issues in highway construction, and the safe work practices associated with the prevention of ergonomic-related injuries and illnesses in the construction field. In order to achieve the study objectives, a survey was designed and sent to Wisconsin based construction contractors. The survey results indicated that hand and finger injuries due to cutting operations and back injuries due to the manual handling of heavy materials to be the most frequent construction task/injury combination. All of the construction firms surveyed had a safety programme. However, most of the contractors did not have a site-specific ergonomics programme. The construction workers were usually walking/working on the ground, ladder and scaffold, and spent significant amount of time for the manual lifting or carrying heavy materials. The findings from this study may assist safety and health professionals in the construction industry in making effective changes for improving health and productivity.

Yingfeng and Yong (2008) reported construction zone safety has been a research focus in many countries for many decades. In the United States, highway construction zones remain a serious safety concern for government agencies, legislatures, and the highway industry. In this study, the fatal and injury accidents between 1992 and 2004 in Kansas highway construction zones were examined systematically and their major characteristics were compared. The results showed there is significant impact of fatal and injury accidents in the construction zones. The researchers found that head injuries was the dominant type for fatal accidents and a large percentage of fatal accidents was due to disregarded traffic control, alcohol consumption, avoidance of the use of personal protective clothing and unfavourable light conditions and complicated road geometries contributed to causing a larger percentage of fatal accidents. Based on the study results, practical safety counter measures targeted at different severity of accidents are recommended in terms of construction zone traffic control and public education.

3. Ensure Wellness in Workplace: Use of PPE

Engineering controls and good work practices should be used to minimize worker exposure to health hazards. Because of the variable exposure concentrations in the construction industry and the difficulty of monitoring a mobile workforce, PPE should be used whenever workers are potentially exposed to occupational health hazards (OSHA/NIOSH, 1991). The use of PPE should supplement the continued use of engineering controls and good work practices, NIOSH Alert (April, 1992).

According to Bill (2002), safety glasses, hardhats, fall protection, respirators, earplugs and other Personal Protective Equipment (PPE) go a long way towards eliminating avoidable accidents and occupational illnesses. He mentioned that appropriate PPE not only saves employees from pain, suffering and life-altering injuries but it also saves company money, protects overall productivity levels and safeguards profits. For such concerns every construction company require protective equipment easily accessible to employees at every job site. Along with the use of PPE, there is a need for trained service representative to visit each work site on a regular schedule and assessment of risk factors, review of injury history and overall safety needs. According to results from the 2002 Road Construction Market Investigation for ISEA, one of the most often cited reasons for not using Personal Protection Equipment (PPE) more regularly is "lack of style/comfort" (Koppes and Pearson, 2002).

Results from a new ISEA survey (2002) of safety leaders indicate that Personal Protective Equipment (PPE) used in the heavy construction industry is on the rise, but that hundreds of thousands of workers in dangerous jobs are still unprotected when they need to be. The survey also showed that the perceived importance of PPE is increasing in the heavy construction industry. When asked to rate the importance of the various types of PPE in minimizing risk of injury in construction, six types (hardhats, protective eyewear, safety shoes, hearing protection, face shields, and protective coveralls) showed increases in their importance from 2001 to 2002; one type (respiratory protection) showed no change; and three types (safety vests, fall protection and gloves) showed decreases.

Occupational Safety and Health Council (2002) reported that the use of personal protective equipment usually implies that the worker is expected to operate in a potentially hazardous environment with the protective equipment as one of the key means of preventing exposure. It is, therefore, vital that the effectiveness and reliability of the protective equipment is ensured. Unfortunately, personal protection is often seen as an inexpensive solution of controlling occupational hazards, and little consideration is given to the selection of suitable and effective devices, the maintenance of the devices and to the training of persons using the devices. A comprehensive survey was conducted to investigate the quality as well the standards of the PPE being sold and used in Hong Kong, and to determine the level of awareness, knowledge and attitude of storekeepers who sell PPE and workers who use PPE at work. A broad range of PPE was investigated, including safety helmets, dust masks, ear plugs, safety gloves and respirators. The findings reveal that a substantial percentage of PPE sold in the market did not bear any labels or marks indicating conformance to any standards.

Scott *et al.* (2002) reported that Personal Protective Equipment (PPE) are readily available and widely recommended, yet their usage among agricultural workers are largely unknown. In their investigation a mail survey of 2,483 farmers in six Mid-western states with telephone follow-up addressed PPE usage related to sun exposure, noise abatement, chain saw usage, welding and metal work, handling of large animals in and out of confinement facilities, feed handling, manure storage facilities, and mixing and applying chemicals. Summary statistics of survey responses were compiled. They found that with the exception of welding masks, PPE usage was low. Farmers were satisfied with availability of PPE through local hardware and farm cooperatives, but the decision to use PPE was personal and influenced little by outside parties.

Public Employees Occupational Safety and Health Programme (PEOSH, 2003) in New Jersey stated that, Personal Protective Equipment (PPE) should not be used as a substitute for engineering, work practice, and/or administrative controls. PPE should be used in conjunction with these controls to provide employee safety and health in the workplace. PPE includes all clothing and other work accessories designed to create a barrier against workplace hazards. The basic element of any management programme for PPE should be an in-depth evaluation of the equipment needed to protect against the hazards at the workplace. Management dedicated to the safety and health of employees should use that evaluation to set standard operating procedures for personnel. PPE includes devices for protecting the eyes, face, head and extremities. Protective clothing, respiratory devices, and protective shields and barriers are also included. The PPE must be used and maintained in a sanitary and reliable condition.

Personal Protective Programme in WCU (2004) covers the use of any Personal Protective Equipment used to protect the wearer from bodily contact with physical, biological and chemical hazards present in the workplace. Selection of Personal Protective Equipment should be on the basis of utilizing guidelines set forth in this PPE Programme and shall make that selection based upon the hazards to which the employees are likely to be exposed. Selection will also be based on the equipment's protective properties related to the specific conditions of the environment in which it will be used. Hazards potentially present at work sites and their relationship to the type of PPE to be used, stressing that the selection of PPE is based upon the hazards present.

New York Committee for Occupational Safety and Health (NYCOSH, 2005) observed that wearing PPE can be uncomfortable (especially in hot weather) or awkward, and many people complain that it gets in the way of doing the job. Although PPE cannot usually completely protect the wearer, people often get a false sense of security when they use it. Also, PPE protects only the person wearing it and many people may not be able to wear PPE due to certain types of medical conditions. Problems such as incorrect fit, use of the wrong PPE for the job, use of damaged or poorly maintained PPE or inconsistent PPE use, can all result in less than adequate protection. It is always preferable for the employer to remove or minimize hazards.

OSHA (2005) report for construction indicated that the OSHA standards most frequently included in the agency's citations (U.S. Department of Labour Occupational Safety and Health Administration) in 2004 were: scaffolding, fall protection (scope, application, definitions), ladders, head protection, excavations (requirements for protective systems), hazard communication, fall protection (training requirements), construction (general safety and health provisions), electrical (wiring methods, design and protection). For the construction industry, NIOSH and the Occupational Safety and Health Administration (OSHA) have recently recommended that exposure to lead dust and fumes be minimized by the use of engineering controls and work practices, and by the use of Personal Protective Equipment (PPE) including respirators for additional protection (OSHA/NIOSH 1991). Airborne lead concentrations and blood lead concentrations should be monitored to determine the effectiveness of controls and PPE.

Greenland *et al.* (2007) reported Personal Protection Equipment (PPE) is recommended for use during airway management of patients with highly contagious respiratory tract illness. While its use in chemical hazards and its effect on airway management was assessed and found significant. Eighteen workers at various level of training were asked to wear three different types of PPE while performing four different types of tracheal intubation activity. The PPE used included the eye shield, face shield and the "Dustmaster". A short questionnaire was used to examine participants' subjective experiences of wearing the various types of PPE. All subjects found that the face shield was uncomfortably hot to wear. Although, certain types of PPE may be uncomfortable to wear and noisy.

4. Selection Criteria and Standards of PPE

Mayer and Korhonen (1999) found in their investigation that the lack of scientific and technical knowledge in certain complex fields, together with schedule constraints, have led to adopt others standards insufficiently validated tests, relying sometimes on an empirical approach. Thus, even PPE with positive results in tests required by the standards can nevertheless prove to be unsatisfactory when used at work. Several research projects have already been carried out on equipment, fall arresting systems, protective clothing, and gloves by several health and safety institutes in Europe. The results would suggest practical solutions to improve the representativity of several European Committee for Standardization test methods and to focus more on informing and training workers on the manner of wearing PPE, in particular respiratory protective equipment or hearing protectors.

Szczecinska and Lezak (2000) conducted research study in the Central Institute for Labour Protection on ergonomic aspects of Personal Protective Equipment (PPE) design and use. Research was related to, among other things, a comparison of body strain and work time limitation for users wearing gas-tight and drill suits. Some other studies were connected with the biophysical properties of clothing materials for medical use. On the basis of the measurement results, a proposal of clothing construction with an optimum combination of protection and comfort was created. Research leading to the development of test methodology concerning automatic welding filters with switchable luminous transmittance is also conducted in CIOP. The article also brings up the subject of designing new PPE assuring a high level of comfort. A model of material to be used under tight protective clothing, an inflammable harness for working at a height, and a model of intelligent clothing that will assist human thermo-regulation processes during physical effort are examples of new PPE.

Anonymous (2007) said that the choice of Personal Protective Equipment (PPE) should be the last preventive measure to be taken for risk reduction. That means that the users of PPE should be those workers who are exposed to the technologically *unavoidable* higher risks (extreme conditions, high-risk specialized tasks, short-term temporary tasks etc.), which could be countered by the use of PPE. In the study, it further unveiled that employers and their staff also not made the right choice of standardized PPE. For a number of reasons i.e., an incomplete workplace risk assessment by the employer, failure to consult workers on the tasks performed, purely economic considerations disregarding the need for protection, or a lack of information from the PPE manufacturer, if a wrong PPE is chosen, it may not protect workers properly from specific hazards. It might also be unsuitable for other hazards, cause discomfort, stop other preventive equipment from doing its job, or add new risks inherent to its use and PPE often only represent the most 'achievable' compromise between safety and well-being.

Donna (2008) argued when it comes to PPE, the OSHA standard is unequivocal. OSHA requires the use of Personal Protective Equipment (PPE) to reduce employee exposure to hazards when engineering and administrative controls are not feasible or effective in reducing these exposures to acceptable levels. Despite the clarity of this requirement, the reality is, that non-compliance in the workplace continues to be a concern. Eighty-seven per cent of safety professionals surveyed at the National Safety Council (NSC) Congress in October 2007 said they had observed workers failing to wear PPE when they should have been. Eighty-five per cent of safety professionals answered yes to the same question in a similar survey undertaken at the 2006 NSC Congress. In an effort to understand the reasons for non-compliance, the 2007 survey asked why people failed to wear PPE when they should have been. The main reason cited was "discomfort," according to 62 per cent of respondents who had observed non-compliance in the workplace. Next was that the workers thinking PPE was not necessary for the task. These were followed by too hot, fit poorly, unattractive-looking, not easily accessible from the site of the work task. Therefore, PPE should be based on ergonomically proven standards.

5. Discomfort Associated with PPE

Paull and Rosenthal (1987) evaluated the effects of wearing PPE in hot conditions and found that the protective clothing caused physiological heat strain comparable to adding temperature between 34°C—41°C leading to uncomfortable use of PPE in hot weather. The complexities of using physiological data to interpret the effects of protective clothing were demonstrated by Holmer *et al.* (1992). The study showed that heart rate, O_2 consumption and temperature are all closely interrelated and considering one of these factors in isolation to determine the thermal impact of clothing can be misleading. PPE can increase the metabolic cost of work, both by adding weight and by restricting movement.

Akbar-Khanzadeh *et al.* (1995) reported that the degree of comfort of Personal Protective Equipment (PPE) was investigated in an automobile encapsulating plant. Up to 96.2 per cent of employees used one or a combination of PPE. Only 8 per cent of the workers felt their respirators were comfortable, 30 per cent tolerated their respirators, and 62 per cent rated them as uncomfortable. The percentage of employees who rated their PPE (other than a respirator) as comfortable ranged from 32 to 52 per cent. For comfort factor, coveralls/aprons rated 52 per cent, safety glasses 51 per cent, rubber gloves 42 per cent, and hearing protectors 36 per cent. PPE was tolerable (just acceptable) for about 30 per cent of the employees. To increase the effectiveness and safety of PPE, the human-factor aspects of PPE design should be emphasized more and quality improvement should cover the wearability of PPE.

Love *et al.* (1996) identified that any item of inadequate PPE which imposes a barrier between the surface of the body and the surrounding air is likely to interrupt evaporation and have an effect on heat transfer. In hot conditions, evaporation of sweat is normally the main avenue for heat transfer from the body to the environment and any barrier between the body and surrounding air, which prevents sweat evaporation may, therefore, increase heat accumulation.

Farhang (1998) interviewed 366 workers in a metal refining plant to investigate factors contributing to the discomfort or dissatisfaction of wearing Personal Protective Equipment (PPE). Up to 97.8 per cent of these individuals used one or more types of PPE. The percentages of employees who reported their hard hats and cooling vests as comfortable were 17 per cent and 19 per cent, respectively. Twenty-five per cent of workers felt their respirators and safety harnesses were comfortable. Safety glasses ranked at 50 per cent, gloves 53 per cent and safety shoes 54 per cent for comfort factor. The percentage of employees who tolerated their PPE (just acceptable) ranged from 27 per cent to 52 per cent. The most frequently cited factors contributing to discomfort or dissatisfaction of wearing PPE were related to the workers' beliefs that the PPE was not needed, created a new hazard, interfered with work, was too heavy, was hard to wear, prohibited breathing or communicating, irritated skin, put pressure on the body, and was of an undesirable type or model.

Hanson (1999) unveiled that in many industrial situations workers are required to wear Personal Protective Equipment (PPE) to protect them from hazards. Although offering protection, wearing some forms of PPE in hot climate may increase the risk of heat strain as most forms of PPE have a higher insulative value.

Donna (2007) observed that 85 per cent of the safety professionals surveyed by Kimberly-Clark Professional at the National Safety Council (NSC) Congress in November 2006 said they had observed people in their organizations failing to wear Personal Protective Equipment (PPE) when they should have been. Nearly half said this had happened on numerous occasions, while 38 per cent described these occurrences as infrequent. In addition to this, 66 per cent of safety professionals said PPE compliance was an issue within their organizations, 40 per cent described it as a "major concern" that they were attempting to correct and 57 per cent of respondents who observed PPE non-compliance in the workplace said the workers attributed this to poor fit or discomfort. The main reasons for non-compliance were lack of awareness of workplace hazards, lack of training on how to don, doff and use PPE, ill-fitting uncomfortable garments and lack of "breathability" and inadequate supplies.

The survey also polled safety professionals about safety issues. The top two workplace issues, selected from a list of choices, were insufficient management support and/or resources for health and safety functions and under-reporting of workplace injuries and illnesses.

The report of European Committee for Standardization (2007), mentioned Ergonomic Suitability Test for PPE. The aim of the ergonomic suitability test was to ensure that the end users should be comfortable with the PPE and that performance degradation could be limited. The EST study include general examination of size suitability of PPE as per body size of the employee in the environment to be operated, and inspection for sharp edges, rough surfaces, protruding ends and related faults and scoring done on four point scale *viz.*, 0, 1, 2, 3 for No problem; Slight problem of comfort or impediment; Problems of comfort or impediment and of fatigue or accuracy of movement; More severe problems of comfort and fatigue that would limit the duration of tolerable use of the PPE; A severe problem that makes the PPE unsafe, or hazardous to wear because of severe impediment to movements. Other related parameters as vision abstraction, sweating discomfort, fitting and adjustability of PPE, weight of PPE, putting on and taking-off of PPE, was assessed and sample pieces found significant and further recommended to wear in required occupations.

6. Postural and Vibration Hazards

Brantingham *et al.* (1970) reported that the primary occupational symptoms and diseases related to prolonged constrained standing are pain, discomfort, fatigue, swelling of the lower extremities and foot, due to blood pooling and varicosities of the lower extremities. There is pronounced effect of posture of an individual on the energy expenditure (Gross and Crandall, 1973).

Chaffin (1977) reported that the muscle fatigue starts with a feeling of discomfort, which is successively increased to a dull, burning pain that at least makes all further muscle activity impossible. A decreased muscle force characterizes the localized muscle fatigue on the one hand and by discomfort pain on the other hand. Chaffin (1977) also reported the character of localized muscle fatigue as given below:

***Grade I*:** A study of tightening or slight cramp in the muscle.

***Grade II*:** A sustained feeling of cramp, with a deep, intermittent burning pain.

***Grade III*:** A continuous burning pain with a wish to cease the muscle work.

***Grade IV*:** Impossibility to go on with the muscle activity.

Grandjean (1988) pointed out that static load is associated with a high risk of arthritis of joints, inflammation of the tendon and symptoms of chronic degeneration of the joints, painful muscle spasms and inter-vertebral disc troubles. Further Aaras and West Gaurd (1988), Keyserling *et al.* (1988), Ryan (1989) and Burdorf *et al.* (1991) supported the abovesaid facts by stating that poor body posture was the major cause of musculo-skeletal disorders. A good working posture reduces the physiological cost of work and fatigue to the minimum, whereas static muscular efforts and incorrect postures for long periods during performance of work can damage the inter-vertebral discs (Varghese *et al.*, 1989).

Genaidy and Karwowski (1993) investigated the discomfort associated with postures at joint, which deviated from the natural position. It was revealed that in standing position, lumber extension was perceived to be more uncomfortable than lateral lumber bending or rotation. In both standing and sitting posture, flexion of the back was least uncomfortable of the extreme postures.

Boocock *et al.* (1994) reported that tasks involving lumber extended postures (overhead work) are relatively common, may incur moderately high compressive loads on the lumber spine and are a potential source of occupationally related back pain. It has been demonstrated that simple ergonomic intervention at the workplace can result in a reduction of lumber extension required for overhead work. The values of such intervention, in terms of reducing load, remains to be determined.

De Looze *et al.* (1994) reported that different aspects of working body postures are related to specific injuries. For instance, the need to bend the torso is generally considered to be important factors in low back bending, repetitive or prolonged elevation of the arms above the shoulders resulting to shoulder injuries and knee injuries related to its repeated or prolong knee bending/flexion. If such injuries are to be prevented these particular postures should be avoided as much as possible.

Haslegrave (1994) pointed out that the good posture is important to the comfort of all people at work. A poor posture becomes a hazard to health and safety in two main situations; in tasks, which are static in nature and involve maintaining the posture for relatively long periods, and in tasks, which involve the exertion of force. In the first situation, the postural loads on muscles and joints can lead to muscular fatigue, pain and in long term to cumulative physiological changes and injury.

As studied by Oberg *et al.* (1994), the knowledge about muscle fatigue can be used in ergonomics for the design of workplaces and work tools. It can also be used to design and improve working methods.

According to Larson and Hannihen (1995) excessive musculo-skeletal stress at work, especially with static load, is believed to play a major role in low back pain, neck and shoulder disorders. Electromyographic recording during working conditions has been used to quantify muscular stresses, allowing better designing of work environment to reduce low back pain and neck shoulder tension.

Corlette *et al.* (1998) showed adoption of poor working postures in order to perform tasks, which could lead to postural stress, fatigue and pain and may in turn force the operator to stop working until the muscle recover.

Rio (1998) reported that those inadequate postures, as the extreme ones and the static ones, take to general or specific overloads of the musulo-skeletal system, being one of the main factors in the origin of musculo-skeletal disturbances related to the work.

A study conducted by Gangopadhyay and Bandopadhyaya (1999) in Bengali community of Calcutta revealed that there were symptoms of pain in different parts of musculo-skeletal system after completion of work. It was concluded from the study that postures and mode of work had a great effect on the development of musculo-skeletal disorders.

European Commission (2002) compiled in a report that there are differences in the levels of vibration generated by the same kind of tools. It was shown that time of usage in various types of tools as wrench, sander, polisher is long, but these tools emit low levels of vibration. However, hammer-drill, grinder, cutter generate high vibration. It was also reported that workers were not really aware that vibration transmission to their hand cause ill-effect (Cited in Margarita *et al.*, 2008).

Repetitive strain injury describes a range of conditions caused by the constant repetition of certain movements. There are injuries to muscles, tendons and nerves caused by over-use or misuse of muscles and tendons. They most commonly affect the hands, wrists, elbows, arms, shoulders, back or neck, unlike strains and sprains, which usually, result from a single incident called acute trauma, repetitive strain injuries develop slowly over time; thus they are also called cumulative trauma disorders or muscular skeletal disorders (*The Week,* 2004).

Hand Arm Vibration Syndrome (HAVS) is a disease that involves circulatory disorders as vibration white finger, sensory and motor disorders, and musculo-skeletal disorders, which may occur in workers who use vibrating handheld tools, in particular drillers, grinders, saws, and jackhammers (Weir and Lander, 2005).

Margarita *et al.* (2008) stated that the relevance of studying hand arm vibration in power tools for construction industry is highlighted by a statistical portrait revealing that 17 per cent of European workers report being exposed to vibration from handheld tools or machinery for at least half of their working time. It was also found approximately 13 per cent, 1 per cent of workers affected by muscular pain and cardiovascular diseases respectively, and vibration is a well-established risk factor for peripheral circulation impairment in the hands (the so-called 'vibration white finger').

The severity of the biological effects of hand-transmitted vibration in working conditions is influenced by, frequency and magnitude of vibration, duration of exposure per working day, direction of forces applied by the operator through hands to the tool or workplace, method of working and the operator's skill etc. Along with this certain factors may specifically affect the circulation changes caused by hand-arm vibration as climatic conditions, diseases which affect the circulation and noise ISO: 5349-1986 (E).

7. Salient Findings from Review

The perusal of the literature in this chapter thus revealed the following:

1. Anthropometric data is most critical factor in designing the tools and equipment and it is essential to consider the range of variability in general body size, gender, racial/ethnic differences while designing the tools and equipment.

2. Construction is a high accident-prone industry.
3. The construction workers suffered from injury, disability and death from workplace accidents.
4. For prevention of hazards at workplace, control measures should be applied. If, exposure of risk cannot be adequately controlled by any measures, proper PPE should be provided.
5. It is important to find out discomfort associated with Personal Protective Equipment (PPE).

It can be concluded from the literature cited on various aspects of anthropometric data, construction work injuries and illnesses, hazard prevention techniques and discomfort associated with PPE, that most of the studies were conducted on abroad and very little organized information available especially in Indian context. Scarcity of information on above-mentioned aspects provided a solid reason to assess the PPE in relation to occupational health and safety of construction workers as a research problem.

3

Materials and Methods

The methods and procedures applied in the selection of sample, identification of variables, their measurement and the statistical tools used for analyzing the data are important parts of any research venture. In many ways, the methodology of a study is important than the analysis.

A badly designed study can never be retrieved, whereas a poorly analyzed one can usually be re-analyzed. Consideration of design is also important because the design of a study will govern how the data are to be analyzed. In order to facilitate systematic presentation, it is divided into the following sections:

1. Research Design
2. Conceptual Framework
3. Selection of Variables
4. Operational Definitions
5. Selection, Construction and Description of Tools
6. Sampling Design
7. Data Collection Procedure
8. Data Processing and Analysis

1. Research Design

"A research design is the arrangement of conditions for collection and analysis of data in a manner that aims to combine relevance to research purpose with economy in procedure". In a study, research design is needed because it facilitates the smooth sailing of the various research operations in a systematic manner.

In the present study descriptive-cum-experimental research design was selected to find-out relationship between occupational health hazards and the use of PPE in construction industry, to validate ergonomically sound PPE in terms of dimensions of anthropometric measurements of users and discomfort associated with PPE.

2. Conceptual Framework

"Conceptual framework of the study represents the relation of the variables with respect to objectives of the study". It was proposed that if the ergonomically designed PPE tools will be used by construction workers, it may reduce the occurrence of accidents. Ergonomically designed PPE will be functionally sound for task performance. For this the anthropometric measurements of workers, health issues in construction sites, effect of environmental parameters etc. were recorded. Detail of conceptual framework is shown in the Fig. 3.1.

3. Selection of Variables

A variable is entity which can take different values. More specifically, variables are those attributes of objects, events, things and beings which vary and can be measured. In other words, variables are the characteristics or conditions that can be observed, manipulated or controlled by the researcher. Variables under study are categorized into three groups viz. dependent variables, constant and independent variables. The schematic representation of the interaction of variables used in study is given in Fig. 3.2.

Independent Variables (X)

Independent variables in an experiment are those which can be manipulated by the experimenter and predict and caused fluctuation in dependent variables. Independent variables

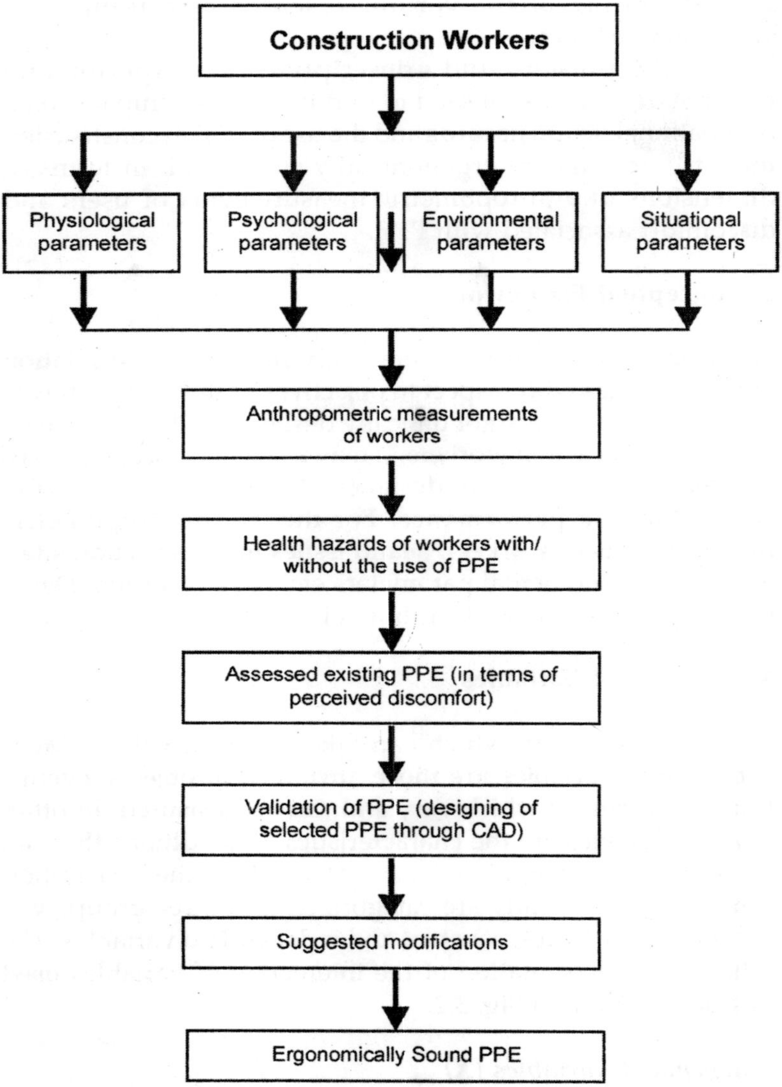

Fig. 3.1 : Conceptual framework of the study.

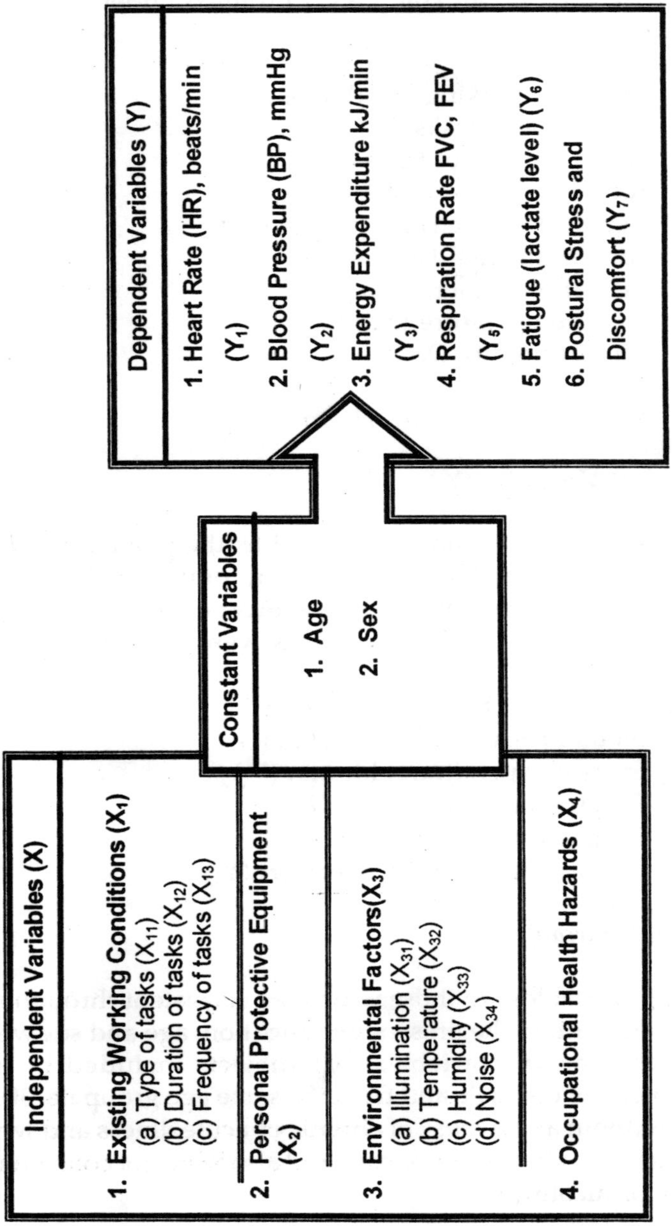

Fig. 3.2 : Schematic representation of interaction of variables.

relevant to the present study were grouped under following sub-categories.

(i) Existing Working Conditions (X_1)
   (a) Type of tasks (X_{11})
   (b) Duration of tasks (X_{12})
   (c) Frequency of tasks (X_{13})
(ii) Personal Protective Equipments(X_2)
(iii) Environmental Factors(X_3)
   (a) Illumination (X_{31})
   (b) Temperature (X_{32})
   (c) Humidity (X_{33})
   (d) Noise (X_{34})
(iv) Occupational Health Hazards (X_4)

Dependent Variables (Y)

Dependent variables may be defined as the phenomenon or characteristics hypothesized to be the outcome. These are measures to change imposed by the independent variables.

Following dependent variables were identified in the study.

1. Heart Rate (HR), beats/min (Y_1)
2. Blood Pressure (BP), mmHg (Y_2)
3. Energy Expenditure, kJ/min (Y_3)
4. Respiration Rate FVC, FEV (Y_4)
5. Fatigue (Lactate level) (Y_5)
6. Postural Stress and Discomfort (Y_6)

Constant variables

Constant variables are those which are consistent throughout the experiment. In the present investigation, age and sex were taken as constant variables. All subjects included in the experiments were male and from the same age group i.e. 30±5 years, without any history of chronic or acute illness and were not under any kind of medication and also were not consuming alcohol or nicotine stuff.

4. Operational Definitions

(i) ***Anthropometric Measurements*:** It is the measurements of human body, which includes body dimensions and the mechanical aspects of motion using anthropometric kit.

(ii) ***Blood Pressure*:** Flow of blood between heart and the active musculature during dynamic muscular effort, blood is squeezed out of the muscle due to contraction but flows back easily during the subsequent relaxation.

(a) ***Diastolic Pressure*:** It is the lower level of blood pressure. The period of relaxation of the heart during which the heart chamber fills with blood.

(b) ***Systolic Pressure*:** It is the upper level of blood pressure. The period of contraction during which heart pumps blood into the arteries.

(c) ***Mean Blood Pressure*:** At normal resting heart rates mean blood pressure can be approximated using the more easily measured systolic and diastolic pressures, SP and DP:

Mean Blood Pressure (mmHg)
= DP+ 1/3 (SP-DP) ....(3.1)

(iii) ***Construction Workers*:** Construction workers are those who work in construction sites. In present investigation construction workers include basic construction labourers (who were engaged in loading/de-loading of materials, concreting, mixing etc.), laser tool operators (doing welding and soldering), gas cutting, power tool operators, doing installation work, and safety management and supervision staff.

(iv) ***Heart Rate*:** It is defined as the number of hearts beats per minute.

(v) ***Measure of Energy Expenditure Rate*:** The normal heart rate and increased heart rate during performance of tasks are measured and then energy expenditure is calculated with the help of following formula:

Energy Expenditure Rate (kJ/min)
= 0.159 x Avg. working HR – 8.72 ......(3.2)

(vi) ***Perceived Exertion*:** It is the subjective evaluation of the exertion perceived by the subject on a scale rating 0 (no exertion) to 10 (maximum exertion).

(vii) ***Physiological Fatigue*:** A State in which the capacity of an individual to do work diminishes and in an advanced stage of fatigue, the individual may not be able to do any work. The fatigue is due to the accumulation of metabolic products, the exhaustion of energy yielding substances and other muscular, respiratory and circulatory phenomena.

(viii) ***Posture in Work*:** Posture means maintaining the normal curve of body while performing various activities. Posture in work means the whole centre of gravity remains as close as possible to that of normal standing/sitting erect condition.

(ix) ***Physical Fitness Index (PFI)*:** Physical fitness is the state of health of workers. To calculate PFI, the workers were asked to perform the exercise or step stool ergometer for 5 minute, then the heart rate, at the end of I, II and III minute of recovery and then PFI is assessed by using the following equation:

Physical Fitness Index (PFI) =

$$\frac{\text{Duration of activity/s}}{\text{Sum of I, II and III minute of recovery of HR}} \times 100 \quad ...(3.3)$$

Respondents ranked from poor to excellent on the basis of PFI are as follows:

(a) Up to 80—Poor physical fitness
(b) 81-100—Low average fitness
(c) 101-115—High average fitness
(d) 116-135—Good fitness
(e) 136-150—Very good fitness
(f) Beyond 150—Excellent fitness

(x) ***Rapid Entire Body Assessment* (*REBA*):** It is a whole body assessment tool which was initially designed to provide a pen and paper postural analysis tool to be used in the field by direct observations (Hignett and Atamney, 2000). In the present study, it was used to assess the type of unpredictable working postures found in construction industries. Data was collected about the body postures, force used, type of movement or action, repletion and coupling. A final REBA score is generated giving an indication about the level of risk and urgency with which action should be taken on a five-point action level scale of AL_0 to AL_4, from 'no action required' through to 'action necessary now'.

(a) AL_0—Scoring 1 (negligible risk level means no action is necessary)

(b) AL_1—Scoring 2 or 3 (low risk, further action may be needed)

(c) AL_2—Scoring 4 to 7 (medium risk level and change is required soon)

(d) AL_3—Scoring 8 to 10 (high risk and action necessary now)

(e) AL_4—Scoring 11+ (very high risk, action necessary now)

(xi) ***Stress in Work*:** Physical and mental stage when the ability or efficiency to work reduces.

(xii) ***Vibration*:** It is the mechanical hazard in which waves are emitted from the source.

(xiii) ***Hand Arm Vibration* (*HAV*):** It is vibration transmitted into worker's hands and arms when using hand-held power tools such as hammer drill, grinder, hand-drill machine, concrete breaker, chop-saw (cutter), wooden saw, etc., which exposes workers to high level of vibration.

Hand-arm vibration is defined as a 'local vibration' referring to vibration entering the body through the hand and palm areas (Griffin, 1990).

(xiv) ***Hand-Arm Vibration Syndrome* (*HAVS*):** It is the most common vibration-related problem which affects the hand and arms. It is the condition associated with the destruction of small blood vessels and nerve damage in the finger. The affect of HAVS ranges from mild short-term 'tingling' sensation in the fingers to severe pain and loss of dexterity. Common symptoms include 'vibration white finger' or 'dead finger'. Method of scoring the areas of digits affected by blanching, numbness, tingling in hands given by Griffin (1990) was adopted and described below:

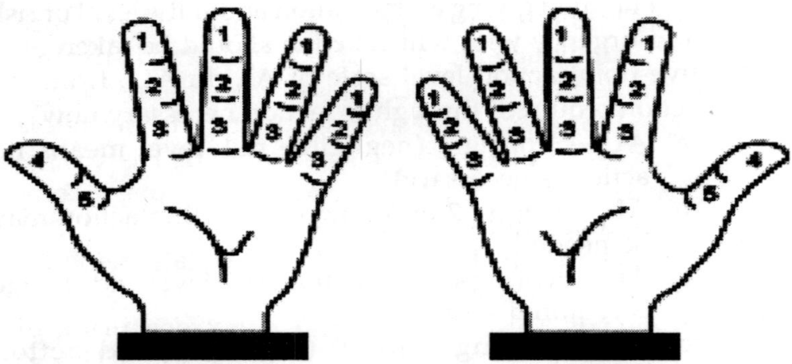

Left hand Right hand

If, score is 01366_{left} and 01300_{right}, then system of scoring corresponds to the areas of effect on the digits commencing with the thumb. On the fingers, a score of 1 is given for effect on the distal phalanx, a score of 2 for middle phalanx, and a score of 3 for proximal phalanx. On the thumbs, the scores are 4 for distal phalanx and 5 for the proximal phalanx. The problem scores may be based on statements from the affected person and visual observations.

(xv) ***RMS (Root Mean Square Value)*:** Square root of the average of the squared values of each momentary measured value during measurement time (range).

$$\text{Vrms} = \sqrt{\frac{I}{T}\int_{t1}^{t2} V(t)^2 dt} \qquad \text{...(3.4)}$$

(xvi) ***PEAK (Peak Value)*:** Maximum value in measurement time (range).

$$\text{Vpeak} = |V(t)| \text{ max} \qquad \text{...(3.5)}$$

(xvii) ***CF (Crest Factor)*:** The ratio of Peak value to RMS value is called as CF (Crest Factor).

$$CF = \frac{\text{Peak}}{\text{RMS}} \qquad ...(3.6)$$

(xviii) ***Lactate Level***: It is a measure of the amount of lactic acid in the blood. Lactate is a direct product of muscular work. During intense work, the muscle cells produce lactic acid, which rapidly diffuses into blood stream. Accumulation of lactic acid occurs when there is a high demand for energy but the supply of O_2 to the cell is limited, as in intense working condition. The unit of measurement is mmol/l i.e. milli-moles per litre of blood (Anonymous, 1986).

At rest the normal range for blood lactate is 0.5-2.2 mmol/l (Gollnick *et al.*, 1986).

(xix) ***Spirometry***: Spirometry meaning the measuring of breadth specifically, a type of pulmonary (lung) function test that measures the amount in (volume) and/or speed (flow) of air that can be inhaled and exhaled. Lung function indices include as following:

- ***Forced Vital Capacity (FVC)***: It is the volume of air that can forcibly be blown out after full inspiration and measured in litres. (Fig. 3.3)

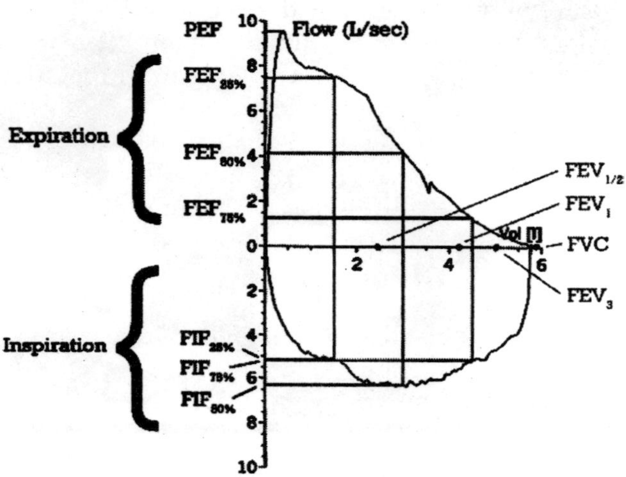

Fig. 3.3 : FVC graph.

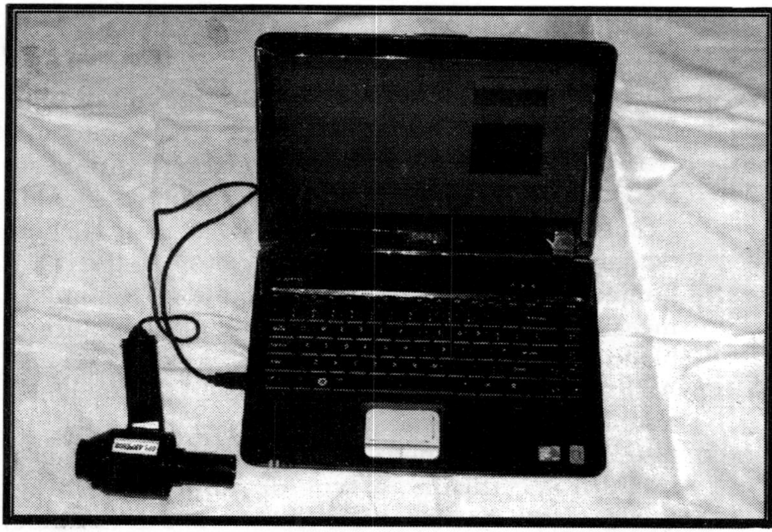

Plate 1: Spirometer.

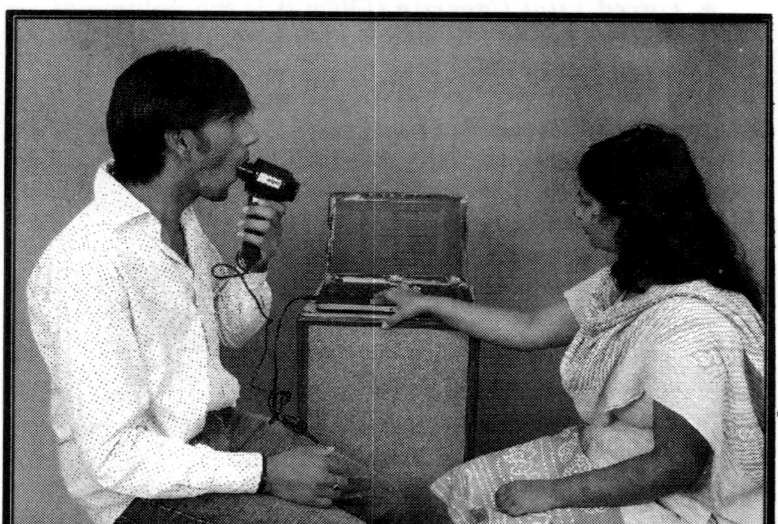

Plate 2: Measurement of Respiration Capacity.

- ***Forced Expiratory Volume* (*FEV*):** It is the volume of air that can be forced out while taking a deep breadth. It is an important measure of pulmonary function. The forced expiratory volume in the first second is FEV_1.
- **FEV_1/FVC:** This is the ratio of FEV_1 to FVC. In healthy adults this should be approximately 75—80 per cent.
- ***Peak Expiratory Flow* (*PEF*):** It is the speed of the air moving out of subject's lungs at the beginning of the expiration and measured in liters per second (l/s).

(xx) ***Relative Humidity*:** It refers to an index of amount of water vapours in the air or it is the water vapour pressure at a given temperature.

(xxi) ***Sound Level*:** It is the ability of respondents to hear clearly without stress and strain to ears. Sound is measured in decibel (dB).

5. Selection, Construction and Description of Tools

Selection of the tool

Different tools were used as an instrument for collecting data for research work.

1. ***Interview Schedule*:** The interview schedule was found to be appropriate tool, which would adequately gather information pertaining to the research work.
2. ***Checklist*:** Checklist was used to collect in-depth information about the hazards present in construction site and identification of useful PPE to prevent these hazards and for vibration analysis.
3. ***Data Table and Worksheet*:** For anthropometric data, environmental parameters, physiological responses and postural analysis, data table and worksheet were developed.
4. ***Discomfort Scale*:** A three point discomfort rating scale was developed for assessing discomfort associated with PPE use.

5. ***Borg General Scale* (1982)**: It was used for assessing the perceived exertion of subjects while performing various activities.
6. ***Experimental Tables***: These tables were developed to record the measurement of physical fitness of the workers, physiological cost of work and grip strength in different work settings.
7. ***Software***: Various software as DB-2004/master_cvndb1.mdb and BPL ARPEMIS were used for hand arm vibration and pulmonary lung function, respectively.

Construction and description of tools

Section 1

The pre-coded interview schedule was constructed in order to collect information about the background of construction workers. It contains data on personal, occupational and medical history of respondents.

Section 2

This section deals with the protocols for collecting the information regarding the anthropometric measurements of the respondents required for designing of Personal Protective Equipment (PPE).

Section 3

It is comprised of checklist for hazard assessment and risk involved with and without the use of PPE.

Section 4

This section includes checklist for identification of PPE for hazard prevention. The required information was recorded from mid-level of management in a construction industry including safety managers, site engineer and execution officials, to cross-check information obtained from general workers.

Section 5

This section adopts REBA Employee Assessment Worksheet developed by Hignett and Atamney (2000) for postural analysis of respondents.

Section 6

This section is comprised of vibration analysis checklist pertaining information on use of hand-held power tool and state of vibration hazard symptoms.

Section 7

This section deals with discomfort rating scale associated with the use of PPE. It was comprised of statements regarding the use of personal protective equipment, rated on three point Likert type scale.

Section 8

This section includes experimental tables and software used to record information of physical fitness index, environmental parameters in record period, spirometry, vibration, etc.

The instrument prepared initially was distributed to a panel of judges for establishing its content validity. They were requested to judge the clarity and relevance of the instrument. The judges were experts from various colleges and departments i.e., College of Agriculture (Department of Agriculture Communication), College of Basic Sciences and Humanities (Department of Maths, Stats., and Computer), College of Vety. Sciences (Department of Physiology), College of Technology (Department of Farm Power and Machinery and Department of Computer Engg.) of Govind Ballabh Pant University of Agriculture and Technology, Pantnagar. Some questions were modified and added as suggested by the judges.

Development of Discomfort Rating Scale

The best way to protect workers against hazards is to control problems at the source. OSHA stated that workers must have PPE that fits properly. Poorly fitted PPE may cause additional hazards. Where occupational risk remains after application of engineering and work practice controls, PPE should be worn. Considering this, a three-point rating scale was developed to measure comfort or discomfort by the use of PPE.

(i) Item Collection

A number of items which could contribute towards the comfort/discomfort derived from the use of Personal Protective Equipment (PPE) were collected from the literature available and concerned experts in the field. Items relevant to study, on various areas was collected and thoroughly screened and cited in order to make them more simple, clear and meaningful to elicit maximum information.

(ii) Establishment of content validity of tool

- **(a) Test of validity**: Validity is the most critical criterion and indicates the degree to which an instrument measures what it is supposed to measure. In other words, validity is the extent to which differences found with a measuring instrument reflect true differences among those being tested.
- **(b) Content validity of discomfort scale:** Content validity is the extent to which a measuring instrument provides adequate coverage of the topic under study. Its determination is primarily judgmental and intuitive. It is determined by using a panel of persons, who judges the measuring instrument and found it should meet the standards.

  For establishing the content validity of discomfort scale in present study, the statements were formulated relating to structural/dimensional discomfort, material related discomfort etc. This was judged by a panel of experts of various colleges of G.B.P.U. of Agriculture and Technology, Pantnagar. For this a score sheet was prepared for the judges and screening of statements was done on the basis of following criteria:

(a) Those statements, selected by 70 per cent or more judges on relevance were retained in the scale.

(b) Those statements, which were not clear by 70 per cent or more judges, were reformed to make them more clear and meaningful.

(c) ***Pre-testing and establishment of reliability of scale:*** A pilot study was conducted to establish the feasibility of the instrument on a sample of 33 construction workers. The responses of construction workers on each statement of scale was quantified by assigning score as given below:

Minor changes were made in the instrument on the basis of pilot study which was then utilized for the final data collection.

Reliability is the level of internal consistency or stability of the measuring devices. The reliability, therefore, refers to the **test consistency.** The reliability of the scale was tested with the application of split-half technique. The zero order correlation between even and odd numbered items was worked out as a measure of reliability. The coefficient of reliability was computed with the help of Spearmen Brown Prophecy Formula as given below:

$$r = \frac{(\Sigma xy)}{\sqrt{(\Sigma x)^2.(\Sigma y)^2}} \quad ...(3.7)$$

Following equation was used to understand reliability coefficient of the scales:

$$r_{11} = \frac{2r_{½}I/II}{1 + r_{½}I/II} \quad ...(3.8)$$

where,

r_{11} = reliability coefficient of whole test

$r_{1/2}I/II$ = reliability coefficient of half test

The reliability coefficient of the discomfort scale was computed as 0.78.

6. Sampling Design

For selection of the study area, purposive sampling and for respondents election simple random sampling without replacement was used.

Selection of locale

Delhi/NCR construction sites were purposively selected for the present investigation. Purposive sampling was adopted which involves deliberate selection of particular unit of the universe on convenience basis.

Sample size

A sample size a definite plan for obtaining sample from a given population keeping in view the nature of universe, nature of study, type of sampling technique, availability of finance, size of population and time available etc. An exhaustive list of construction sites employees were taken from their respective administrative department, then from the list, 120 construction workers performing group of activities as basic construction activities (loading/de-loading of materials, working with mortar, cement, crushing stones, transportation of water, bricks etc.), laser tool operations, gas-cutting, using power tools, installation, management and supervision work were selected purposively. Broadly two types of labour category i.e., unskilled (performing basic construction work and installation), skilled labour (involved in laser operations, handling power tool, cutting etc.) and safety management and supervision staff were selected. From each sub-category 20 respondents were selected for field survey and 5 respondents were selected for field experiment, thus making 120 samples for survey and 30 samples for control group. The details of the sampling design are shown in Figure 3.4.

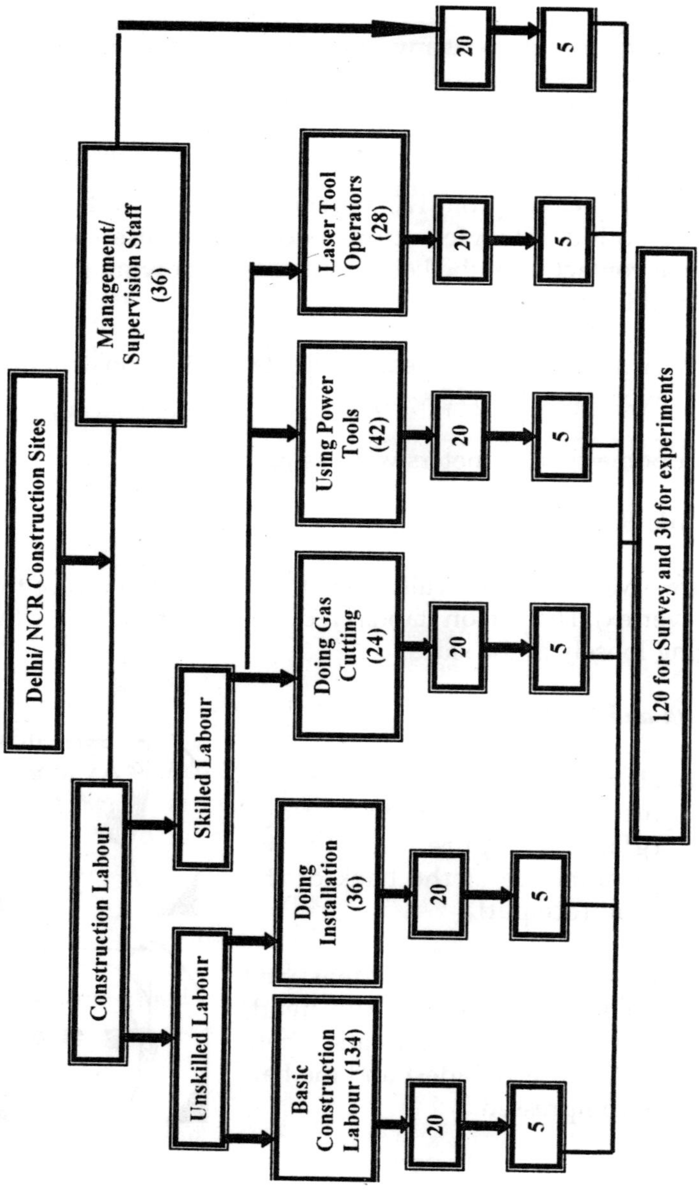

Fig. 3.4 : Schematic representation of sampling design.

7. Data Collection Procedure

The data for the present investigation was collected in two different phases in the following order:

Phase 1

The descriptive data from 120 workers was collected by using the pre-coded interview-cum-record schedule through personal contact from the key informants. Following protocol was used for this phase:

- Anthropometric measurements of the construction workers from 120 samples.

Anthropometric parameters were as given below:

1. Whole Body

Stature—Measured vertically from the floor to the top of the head (vertex). The person stands erect, looking ahead, the arms hanging loosely at the sides.

2. *Head and Neck*

(i) ***Head length***—The length measured from the brow ridge (glabella Figure 3.5) to the prominence at the back of the head (occiput).

(ii) ***Head breadth***—Measured horizontally across the head, above and behind the ears, where the head is broadest and the hair is compressed.

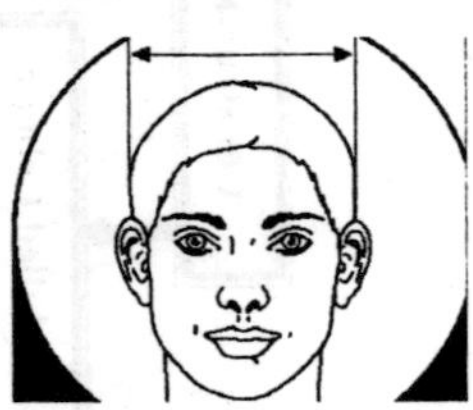

(iii) ***Head height***—Measured vertically from the bony tip of the chin (menton) to the top of the head (vertex).

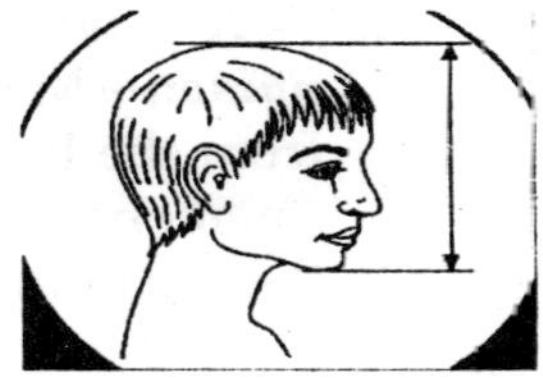

(iv) ***Head circumference***—Measured around the maximum circumference of the head, just above the brow ridges at the front and the most protruding portion of the back of the head (occiput). Hair should be compressed.

(v) ***Bitragion arc length***—Measured from the tragion of one ear vertically over the top of the head to the tragion of the other ear with sufficient tape tension to flatten the hair.

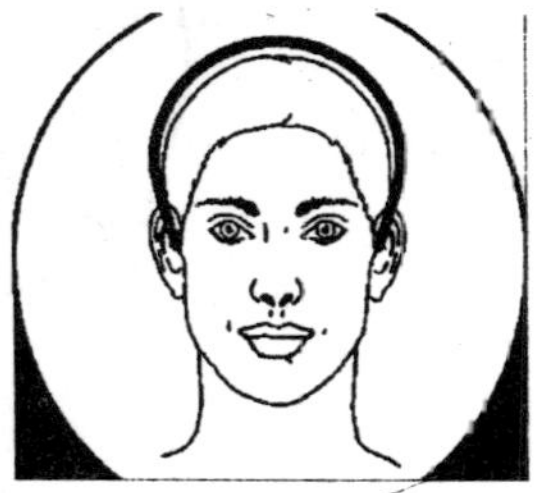

(vi) ***Sagittal arc length***—Measured along the surface from the brow ridge (glabella) to the prominence at the back of the head (occiput).

3. *Face*

(i) ***Face length-menton to brow***—Measured vertically from the bony tip of the chin (menton) to the brow ridge (glabella).

(ii) ***Face length—menton to naison***—Measured vertically from the bony tip of the chin (menton) to the depression at the top of the nose (naison).

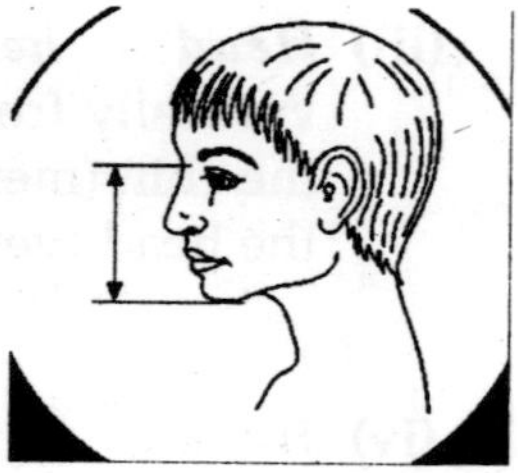

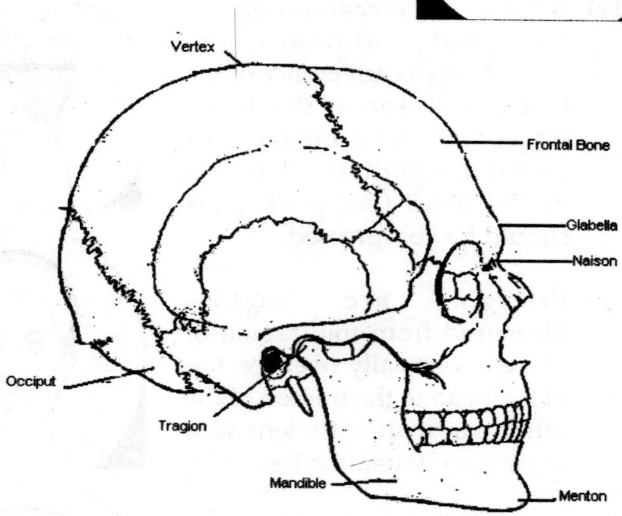

Fig. 3.5 : Landmark of human skull.

(iii) ***Face breadth***—Measured horizontally between the broadest portion of the cheekbones, between the eyes and ears.

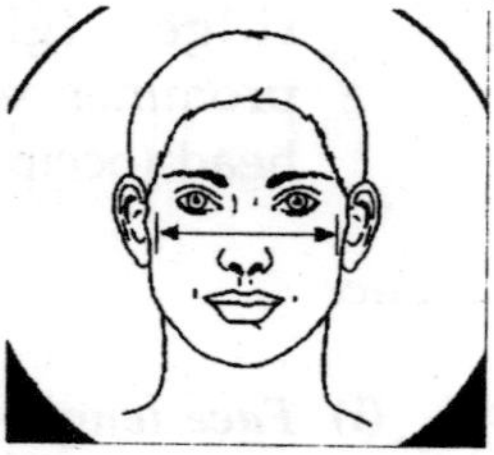

(iv) ***Jaw width***—Measured horizontally between the outer angles of the jawbone.

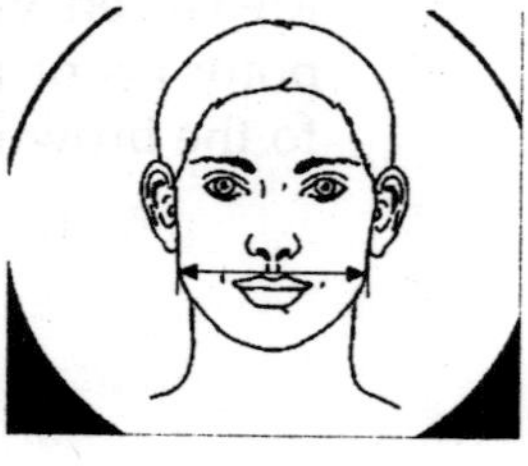

4. Hand

(i) ***Hand length***—Measured from the wrist crease directly below the pad of the muscle at the base of the thumb (thenar eminence) to the tip of the middle finger. The hand and fingers should be held straight and flat, palm upper-most.

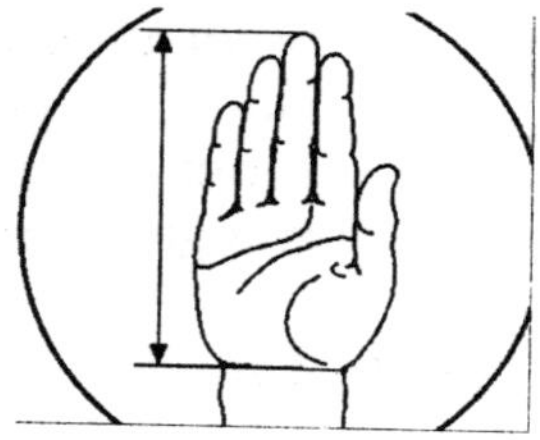

(ii) ***Palm breadth***—Measured at the widest aspect between metacarpal-phalangeal joints II (index finger) and V (little finger). Hand and fingers held straight and the thumb held away (abducted) from the palm.

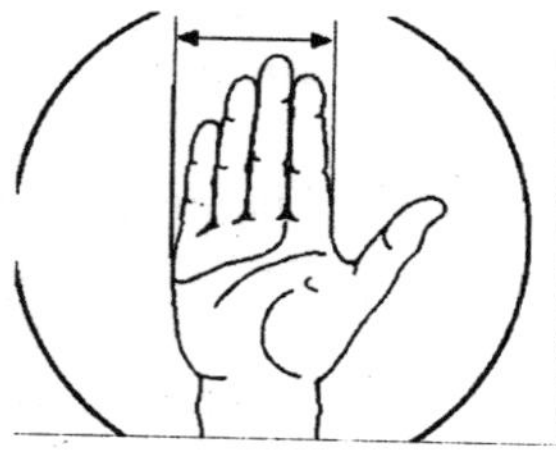

(iii) ***Palm breadth-max***—Measured across the palm of the hand at the level of the base of the thumb, including the joint at the base of the thumb.

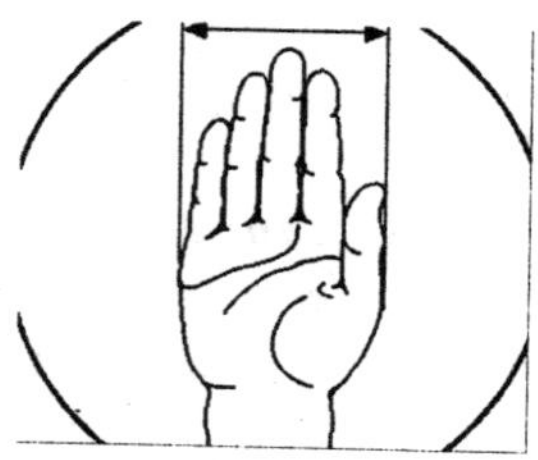

(iv) ***Palm length***—Measured from the baseline (wrist crease) to the crease between the middle finger and the palm. Hand and fingers held straight and flat. The thumb held away (abducted) from the palm.

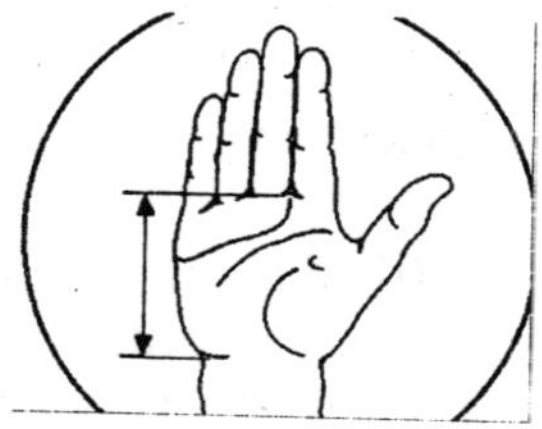

(v) ***Hand thickness***—Measured from the pad of muscle at the base of the thumb to the back of the hand. Hand and fingers held straight, with the thumb aligned along the side of the palm. (A maximum measure of flat hand thickness).

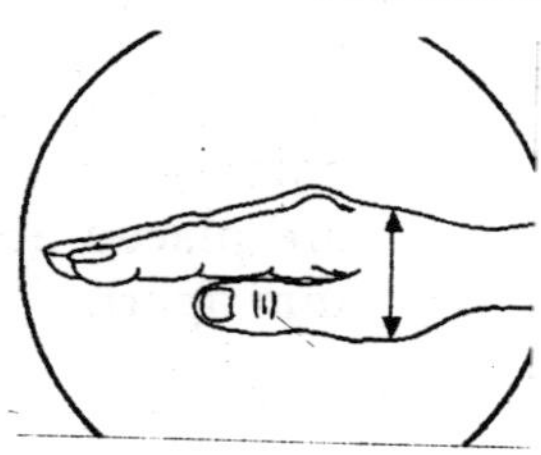

(vi) ***Thumb length***—Measured from the tip of the thumb to the base of the thumb at the level of the skin web between it and the index finger. Thumb held straight out from palm.

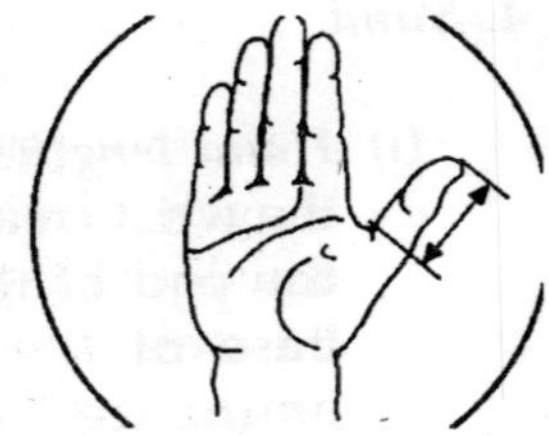

(vii) ***Thumb width***—Measured across the broadest part of the thumb joint. Thumb held straight.

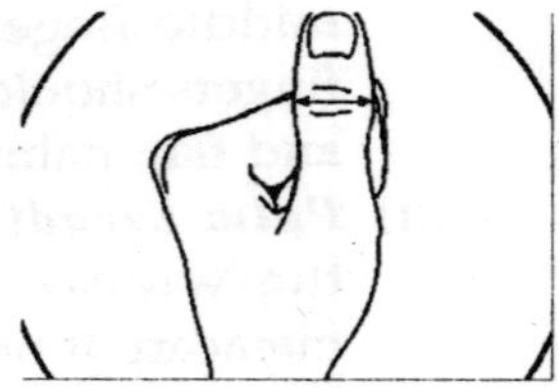

(viii) ***Finger length***—Measured from the tip of the middle finger to the skin crease at the base of the finger, parallel to its long axis. The hands and fingers should be held straight and flat, palm uppermost.

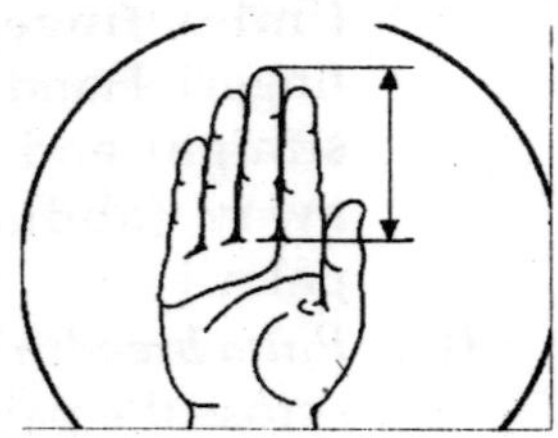

(ix) ***Finger width***—Measured across the broadest part of the middle joint (proximal joint) of the middle finger. Finger held straight.

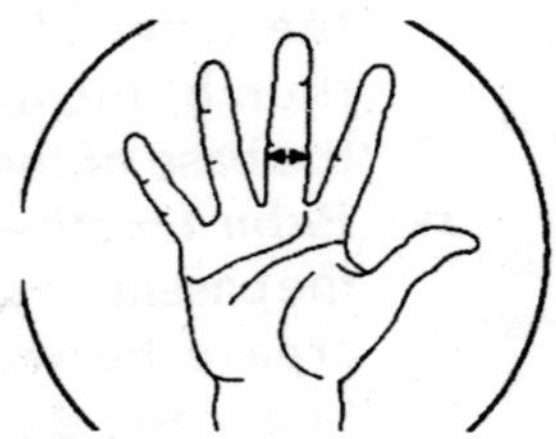

5. Foot

(i) ***Foot length***—Measured horizontally from the tip of the longest toe to the back of the heel. The person stands erect with his weight evenly balanced on both feet, which are placed approximately 100 mm apart.

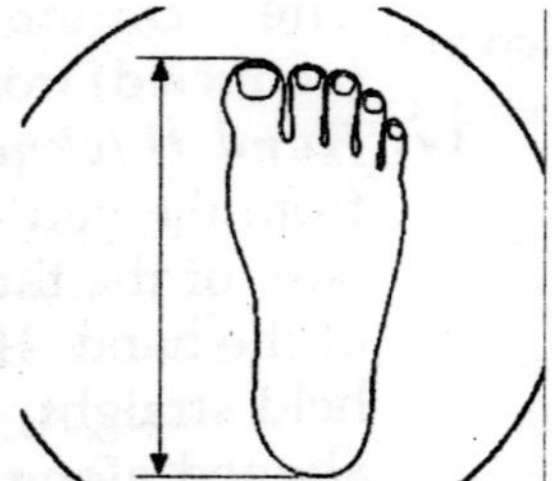

(ii) ***Foot breadth***—Measured horizontally across widest part of the foot, perpendicular to the length of the foot. This is usually at the medial point of the meta tarsal phalangeal joint (where the toes begin). Subject stands with feet approximately 100 mm apart.

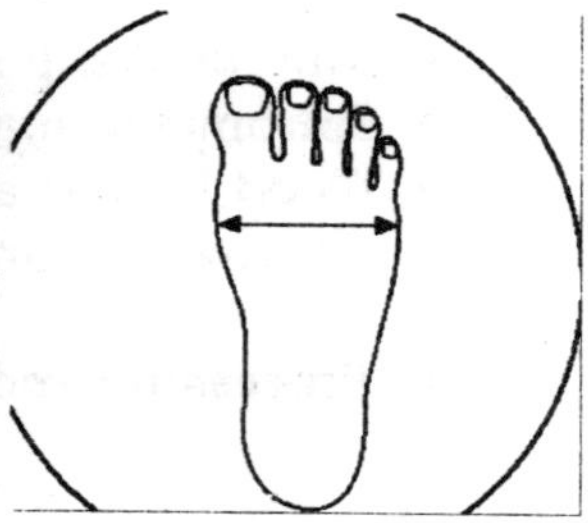

- Hazard analysis in construction site from sample respondents.
- Postural assessment of construction workers.
- Physical fitness index of construction workers.
- Identification of PPE for hazard prevention from 20 managerial and supervision staff to verify the hazard present in construction site and required PPE to prevent them.
- Perceived discomfort associated with PPE was taken from sample respondents.
- Vibration analysis of power tool users (20 samples) at construction site.

Phase 2

Before the collection of experimental data physical fitness index were calculated and 5 respondents from each group (basic construction worker, laser tool operators, gas cutting, handling power tools, performing installation work, management and supervision staff) who were physically fit and without any chronic illness, performing their activities were selected for experiments.

Environmental parameters in workshop and construction site were also recorded.

Following test parameters were measured from experiments:

- Physiological cost of work in terms of B.P., H.R. energy expenditure rate of 30 construction workers (5 respondents from each group).

- Muscular grip strength of control group.
- Spirometry analysis of workers.
- Blood Lactate analysis of basic construction workers.
- Hand-arm vibration analysis from power tools.

8. Data Processing and Analysis

Categorization

For the analysis, the variables were categorized as given below:

(i) ***Age***: Age was measured in terms of numbers of full years the respondents completed at the time of interview. It was categorized as follows:

1. 20—25 years
2. 26—30 years
3. 31—35 years
4. 36—40 years
5. ≥ 41 years

(ii) ***Educational qualification***: Operationally, education referred as the formal education attained by the respondents. It was categorized as:

1. Illiterate
2. Primary School
3. Middle School
4. High School
5. Intermediate
6. Graduate

(iii) ***Native place***: Essentially, it is the place from where the subject originally belongs to, and categorized as:

1. U.P. East
2. Bihar
3. Jharkhand
4. West Bengal
5. Delhi

(iv) ***Income (Rs. per month)***: It refers to the monthly income in terms of money accrued from their occupation and was categorized as:

1. <5000
2. 5000 – 7500
3. 7500-10,000
4. 10,000 – 15,000
5. ≥ 15,000

v. **Occupational history** : It involves the type of activities performed by the construction workers and categorized as:

1. Basic construction activities
2. Laser operations
3. Gas cutting
4. Using power tools
5. Installation
6. Safety management and supervision

Coding and tabulation of data

The information collected was coded into the coding sheets and then transferred into tabular form.

Statistical analysis

(i) Frequency and percentage were computed for analyzing the personal profile, occupational history, medical profile, nicotine and alcohol consumption habit, hazard analysis, discomfort associated with PPE, postural and vibration analysis, etc.

(ii) In the present investigation mean, standard deviation and percentile (5th, 95th percentile) were calculated to analyze anthropometric data.

(iii) For relational statistics Chi-square, ANOVA were computed.

4

Results and Discussion

The facts and findings of the investigation emerged from statistical treatment of the collected data have been presented in this chapter. The findings of the study were produced through composite summary tables and pictorial graphs which are in concurrence with the said objectives. They are described under different sub-heads as follows:

1. Demographic profile of construction workers.
2. Occupational history of construction workers.
3. Medical history of respondents.
4. Nicotine and alcohol consumption habit.
5. Physical Fitness Index (PFI) of construction workers.
6. Rating of Perceived Exertion (RPE) of construction workers.
7. Anthropometric measurements of construction workers.
8. Comparative analysis of hazard identification with and without the use of PPE.
9. Identification of PPE for hazard prevention.
10. Rapid Entire Body Assessment (REBA) analysis for postural assessment of construction workers.
11. Perceived discomfort associated with the use of PPE.
12. Vibration analysis of power tool users in construction industry.
13. Environmental conditions during field experiments.
14. Physiological cost of work of subjects during experiments.

15. Grip strength of subjects during experiments.
16. Spirometry analysis of subjects.
17. Vibration analysis of power tool operators during experiments.
18. Blood Lactate analysis of subjects involved in loading/un-loading activities during experiments.
19. Design development of helmet and gloves through CAD.
20. Comparison between the dimensions of existing PPE and ergonomically designed PPE.
21. Testing of Hypothesis.
22. Action Plan.

1. Demographic Profile of Construction Workers

Table 4.1 shows the demographic profile of construction workers of Delhi/NCR which is described as follows:

Age

The age of the construction workers ranged from 20 to above 40 years. About 42.5 per cent of the total workers fall under the age group of 31-35 years followed by 24.17 per cent in the age group of 20-25 years. A handsome proportion of workers i.e., 2.5 per cent were in the category of ≥ 41 years. The mean age of basic construction workers, respondents engaged in laser operations, gas cutting, installation, power tool users and, safety managers and supervisors were 27 ±2.47, 28.95 ±3.17, 30.9 ±2.41, 30.2 ±1.78, 33.95 ±2.17 and 29.9 ±1.57 years, respectively.

Educational qualification

Education is an important variable which may influence the division of labour. The educational level of respondents in the present study varied from illiterate to graduation. Literacy level among the construction workers was very low and majority of them i.e., 41.67 per cent were illiterate. About 23.33 and 7.5 per cent of construction workers were educated up to primary and middle school, respectively. It was further revealed from the investigation that very few proportion of respondents were studied up to intermediate (5%) and graduation level (19.17%). As individual observations were analyzed it was found that majority of basic construction workers (70%) were illiterate followed by 60 per cent power tool operators, 45 per cent respondents involved in gas cutting, 40 per cent in laser operations and 35 per cent in installation work. However, all safety managers and supervisors were educated up to graduation level or more. One of the main reasons for high proportion of illiterate basic construction workers was because of the fact that these people were migrant from other states.

Native place

The data regarding native place of respondents shows that a large proportion of respondents as 23.33, 26.67, 5.83 and 36.67 per cent belonged to U.P. (Uttar Predesh) East, Bihar, Jharkhand and West Bengal, respectively. It was further unveiled that only 7.5 per cent people originally belonged to Delhi who were engaged in construction work. Majority of basic construction workers (60%) were migrated from U.P. East followed by 35, 20, 15, 5 and 5 per cent workers who engaged in laser operations, gas cutting, installation, handling power tools, and safety managers and supervisors. However, 35 and 10 per cent safety managers and supervisory staff and respondents involved in cutting operations were belonged to Delhi only.

Income (Rs. per month)

Income of respondents was also important variable in the study. If the economic condition of the workers is better, they can enjoy the good physical and mental health. Income category in the present study ranged from <5000 to ≥ 15,000 per month. A large proportion of respondents i.e., 42.5 per cent were earning less than Rs. 5000 per month. However, approximately 19 per cent and 14 per cent of workers were getting income in the range of Rs. 5000 to 7500 and Rs. 7500 to

10,000 per month. Only a few proportion of respondents i.e. 7.5 per cent were in the earning category of Rs. 10,000 to 15,000 per month and 16.8 per cent of construction workers were getting ≥ 15,000 Rs. per month.

As category-wise data was analysed and it was found from investigation that the mean income of basic construction workers, persons involved in laser operations, gas cutting, handling power tools, installation and, safety management and supervision were 4,480 ±3.52, 4,750 ±2.74, 4,075 ±3.16, 7,450 ±2.56, 4,375 ±7.35 and 18,850 ±3.85 Rs. per month.

On the whole, it was observed from abovestated parameters that major proportion of selected construction workers were in the age group of 31-35 years and illiterate. The income detail revealed that majority of respondents i.e., 42.5 per cent were earning less than Rs. 5000 per month. It was also evident that a commendable proportion of workers (92.50%) were migrated from U.P. East, Bihar, Jharkhand and West Bengal.

Table 4.1: Demographic profile of respondents

(N=120)

Personal characteristics	*Categories*	*Total*	*B.C. W.*	*L.O.*	*G.C.*	*P.T. O.*	*Ins.*	*S.M. S.*
Respondent's information								
Age (years)	20–25	29 (24.17)	11 (55)	8 (40)	5 (25)	4 (20)	1 (5)	—
	26–30	20 (16.18)	6 (30)	2 (10)	—	1 (5)	4 (20)	7 (35)
	31–35	51 (42.5)	1 (5)	9 (45)	12 (60)	1 (5)	15 (75)	13 (65)
	36–40	17 (14.18)	2 (10)	1 (5)	3 (15)	11 (55)	—	—
	≥ 41	3 (2.5)	—	—	—	3 (15)	—	—
	Mean Age		27 ±2.47	28.95 ±3.17	30.9 ±2.41	33.95 ±2.17	30.2 ±1.78	29.9 ±1.57
Educational qualification	Illiterate	50 (41.67)	14 (70)	8 (40)	9 (45)	12 (60)	7 (35)	—
	Primary School	28 (23.33)	4 (20)	7 (35)	8 (40)	6 (30)	3 (15)	—

Table 4.1 (*contd.*)

Personal characteristics	*Categories*	*Total*	*B.C. W.*	*L.O.*	*G.C.*	*P.T. O.*	*Ins.*	*S.M. S.*
Respondent's information								
	Middle School	9 (7.5)	2 (10)	1 (5)	1 (5)	—	5 (25)	—
	High School	4 (3.33)	—	1 (5)	1 (5)	—	2 (10)	—
	Intermediate	6 (5)	—	2 (10)	1 (5)	—	3 (15)	—
	Graduate and Above	23 (19.17)	—	1 (5)	—	2 (10)	—	20 (100)
Native place	U.P. East	28 (23.33)	12 (60)	7 (35)	4 (20)	1 (5)	3 (15)	1 (5)
	Bihar	32 (26.67)	6 (30)	5 (25)	6 (30)	7 (35)	4 (20)	4 (20)
	Jharkhand	7 (5.83)	—	3 (15)	1 (5)	2 (10)	1 (5)	—
	West Bengal	44 (36.67)	2 (10)	5 (25)	7 (35)	10 (50)	12 (60)	8 (40)
	Delhi	9 (7.5)	—	—	2 (10)	—	—	7 (35)
Income (Rs. per month)	<5000	50 (42.5)	12 (60)	9 (45)	11 (55)	2 (10)	16 (80)	—
	5000-7500	24 (19.17)	8 (40)	8 (40)	5 (25)	3 (15)	—	—
	7500-10,000	17 (14.17)	—	3 (15)	4 (20)	8 (40)	2 (10)	—
	10,000-15,000	9 (7.5)	—	—	—	7 (35)	2 (10)	—
	≥ 15,000	20 (16.18)	—	—	—	—	—	20 (100)
	Mean Income		4,480 ±3.52	4,750 ±2.74	4,075 ±3.16	7,450 ±2.56	4,375 ±7.35	18,850 ±3.85

Note: Figures in parentheses indicate the percentage values.
B.C.W. = Basic Construction Work; L.O. = Laser Operations; G.C. = Gas Cutting; P.T.O. = Power Tool Operations; S.M.S. = Safety Management and Supervision.

2. Occupational History of Construction Workers

The construction industry is the most dangerous land based civilian work sector. Construction work is not only the process of building, but also involves many other type of side activities from basic construction work to management. The data pertaining to the occupational profile of selected respondents is presented in Table 4.2. It was observed that multiple responses were found in case of activities performed by workers as 45 and 20 per cent of workers engaged in either basic construction activities (loading/unloading of materials, mixing, concreting, scaffolding, etc.) and installation work, respectively. However, skilled construction labourers were engaged in laser operations (16.67%), gas cutting (16.67%) and power tool operations (18.33%). Approximately 16 per cent of skilled workers were belonging to safety management and supervision group.

Table 4.2: Occupational history

(N=120)

Type of activity	*Workers Involved*	*Duration of task*	*Frequency of task*
Basic construction activities as loading/unloading of materials	54*(45)	Long	Sometimes
Laser operations as welding, soldering	20(16.67)	Moderate	Sometimes
Gas cutting	20**(16.67)	Moderate	Sometimes
Power tool operations	22**(18.33)	Long	Always
Installation	20*(16.67)	Long	Sometimes
Safety management and supervision	20(16.67)	Long	Always

Note: 1. Figures in parentheses indicate the percentage values.
2. Duration: Short (< 15 min), Moderate (15 min- 1 h), Long (> 1 h)
* multiple response, ** multiple response by skilled workers

As far as duration of activity is concerned, it was found from the study that basic construction work, power tool operations, installation and management were long duration task because these were performed for more than 1 h daily. Therefore, laser operations and gas cutting was performed for 15 min to 1 h in each trial daily and categorized as moderate task. As frequency of task characterized as never, sometimes and always, and it was noticed that basic construction activities, laser operations, gas cutting and installation were performed by workers sometimes, but power tool operations and, management and supervision work were performed, always by construction workers.

3. Medical History of Respondents

Table 4.3 shows the medical profile of selected construction workers of Delhi/NCR construction sites during the last one year and the data regarding various illnesses are mentioned below:

Common illnesses

It was found that about 45 per cent of respondents suffered from cough, cold and fever which was reported temporary in nature (in 21.67% from the job and in 14.16% from other sources). However, continuous occurrence of cough, cold and fever were also reported by few respondents i.e., 5.83 per cent (from the job) and 3.33 per cent (from other sources).

Occurrence of headache, bodyache, irritation in eyes were also reported by commendable proportion (70%, 75.83% and 91.67%) of respondents, respectively which were predominantly reported as temporary (from the job) in nature.

Chronic illnesses

Various type of chronic illnesses such as diabetes mellitus, heart problem, B.P. (Blood Pressure) problem as well as occupation induced illnesses like respiratory problem, stiffness in hand joints, cuts and wounds, numbness in body and tingling in hand were also reported by respondents.

The incidence rate of diabetes mellitus was found only in 4.16 per cent of respondents. Heart and B. P. problems were reported by 30 and 25.83 per cent of people which was temporary in nature. A commendable proportion of construction workers i.e., 63.33 per cent, 57.5 per cent, 80 per cent, 79.87 per cent and 83.33 per cent complained that they suffered from respiratory problem, stiffness in hand joint, cuts and wounds, numbness in body and tingling in hand, respectively which arise from the job and temporary in concern by majority of respondents. The reason for high incident rate of chronic illness (which was temporary in nature) might be because the construction workmen were engaged in most risky and vulnerable environment coupled with exposure to dust, fumes, flying objects, vibration, heat etc.

Table 4.3: Medical history of construction workers during the last one year

(N=120)

Sl. No.	*Illness/ symptoms*	*Occurrence*		*Types of illness*			
		Yes	*No*	*Temporary*		*Continuous*	
				From the job	*From other sources*	*From the job*	*From other sources*
	Common illness						
1.	Cough, Cold, Fever	54 (45)	66 (55)	26 (21.67)	17 (14.16)	7 (5.83)	4 (3.33)
2.	Headache	84 (70)	36 (30)	29 (24.17)	18 (15)	11 (9.17)	26 (21.67)
3.	Bodyache	91 (75.83)	29 (24.17)	24 (20)	18 (15)	23 (19.16)	26 (21.67)
4.	Irritation in eyes	110 (91.67)	10 (8.33)	34 (28.33)	26 (21.67)	19 (15.83)	31 (25.83)
5.	Digestive problem	79 (65.83)	41 (34.17)	28 (23.33)	19 (15.83)	32 (26.66)	—
	Chronic illness						
6.	Diabetes Mellitus	5 (4.16)	115 (95.84)	—	—	—	5 (4.16)
7.	Heart problem	36 (30)	84 (70)	8 (6.66)	28 (23.33)	—	—
8.	B.P. problem	31 (25.83)	89 (74.17)	11 (9.17)	20 (16.63)	—	—
9.	Respiratory problem	76 (63.33)	44 (36.67)	48 (40)	—	28 (23.33)	—
10.	Stiffness in hand joint	69 (57.5)	51 (42.5)	50 (41.66)	—	19 (15.83)	—
11.	Cuts and wounds	96 (80)	24 (20)	84 (70)	—	12 (10)	—
12.	Numbness in body	95 (79.87)	25 (20.83)	44 (36.67)	17 (14.16)	27 (22.5)	7 (5.83)
13.	Tingling in hand	100 (83.33)	20 (16.67)	43 (35.83)	18 (15)	36 (30)	3 (2.5)

Note: Figures in parentheses indicate the percentage values.

4. Nicotine and Alcohol Consumption Habit

The data pertaining to nicotine and alcohol consumption are presented in Table 4.4 and Figure 4.1.

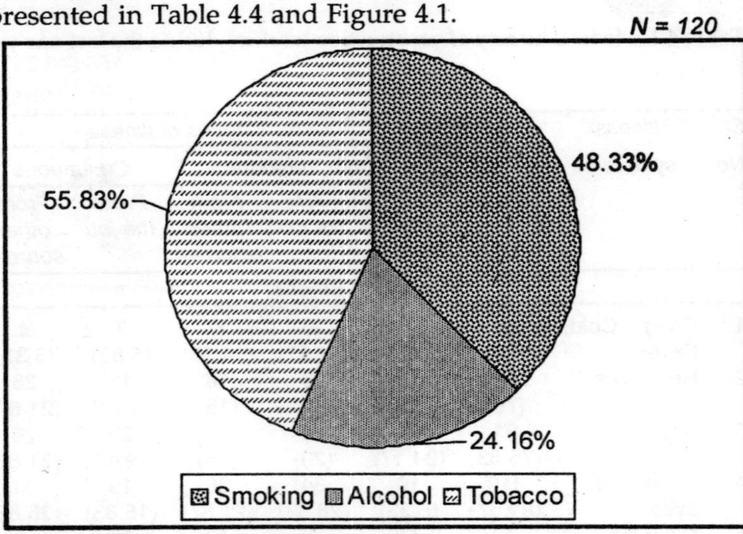

Fig. 4.1 : Nicotine and alcohol consumption by construction workers.

Figure 4.1 unveils that 48.33 per cent and 24.16 per cent of respondents were engaged in smoking (bidis and/or cigarettes) and alcohol consumption. However, 55.83 per cent of respondents were found snuffing/chewing tobacco.

Smoking habit

It is evident that nearly half of the sample respondents were indulged in smoking and 25.83 per cent were smoking cigarettes or bidis regularly. It was also found that 15.83, 13.33 and 10.0 per cent were consuming cigarettes/bidis from 2-4, 5-7 and 8-11 years, whereas 9.17 per cent respondents were consuming cigarettes from ≥12 years. As far as the consumption amount is concerned, it was found from the investigation that 23.33 per cent of construction workers were taking 1-3 cigarettes/day followed by 20.83 and 4.17 per cent who were consuming 4-6 and ≥ 7 cigarettes/day, respectively.

Table 4.4: Distribution of respondents as per nicotine and alcohol consumption

(N=120)

Parameters	*No. of respondents*		
Smoking habit		Yes	58 (48.33)
		No	62 (51.67)
Years of consumption	2-4 years		19 (15.83)
	5-7 years		16 (13.33)
	8-11 years		12 (10)
	≥12 years		11 (9.17)
Smoke regularly	Yes		31 (25.83)
	No		27 (22.5)
Consumption amount (no. of Cigarettes per day)	1-3		28 (23.33)
	4-6		25 (20.83)
	≥ 7		5 (4.17)
Tobacco consumption		Yes	67 (55.83)
		No	53 (44.17)
Years of consumption	2-4 years		18 (15)
	5-7 years		11 (9.17)
	8-11 years		21 (17.5)
	≥ 12 years		17 (14.17)
Snuff or chew regularly	Yes		58 (48.33)
	No		9 (7.5)
Consumption amount (no. of times per day)	1-3		22 (18.33)
	4-6		34 (28.33)
	≥ 7		11 (9.17)
Alcohol consumption		Yes	29 (24.16)
		No	91 (75.83)
Years of consumption	2-4 years		3 (2.5)
	5-7 years		7 (5.83)
	8-11 years		7 (5.83)
	≥ 12 years		12 (10)
Drinking regularly	Yes		18 (15)
	No		11 (9.17)
Consumption amount (no. of peg per day)	1-3		13 (10.83)
	4-6		12 (10)
	≥ 7		4 (3.33)

Note: Figures in parentheses indicate the percentage values.

Tobacco consumption

More than half of respondents were consuming tobacco and 48.33 per cent were snuffing or chewing it regularly. The year of consumption varied from 2-4 to ≥12 years. It was found that 17.5 per cent were consuming from 8-11 years followed by 15,

14.17 and 9.17 per cent who were snuffing/chewing it from 2-4, ≥ 12 and 5-7 years, respectively. The consumption amount ranged from 1-3 to ≥ 7 times per day.

Alcohol consumption

A large proportion i.e., 24.16 per cent of construction workmen were consuming alcohol and approximately 15 per cent were drinking regularly. Year of consumption in case of alcohol consumption also varied from 2-4 to ≥12 years. Approximately 10.83 and 10.0 per cent were drinking 1-3 and 4-6 glass/peg per day. However, pocket some proportion of respondents i.e., 3.33 per cent were consuming ≥ 7 peg/day. Kulkarni (2007) reported that the associated addiction with alcohol, tobacco and smoking contributes to illness and suffering to construction workers.

5. Physical Fitness Index (PFI) of Construction Workers

The physical fitness is a term which denotes individual's ability to accomplish a given task in a given time period. Subjects should be healthy and should not have respiratory problems, and should be given at least 15 minutes of rest before the start of measurement. Table 4.5 and Figure 4.2 depict the physical fitness index of construction workers. The data has been described on the basis of activity profile of construction workers.

Good PFI score was found in 55 per cent for basic construction workers, 70 per cent for laser tool operators, 35 per cent in those who involved in gas cutting activity, 60 per cent in power tool users, 45 per cent in workers involved in installation and 30 per cent in safety managers and supervision staff. In totality about 49.17 per cent of construction workers have good PFI score. About 10 per cent of workers were having excellent physical fitness level and only 3.33 fell under the category of low average physical fitness. A good proportion of respondents as 20 and 17.5 per cent were having high average and very good physical fitness level, respectively and none of the respondents were in the category of poor

Table 4.5: Physical fitness index of construction workers

Sl. No.	Physical Fitness Index(PFI)	Frequency (Construction Workers Job)						
		Basic construction work n=20	Laser operations n=20	Gas cutting n=20	Power tool operations n=20	Installation n=20	Safety management and supervision n=20	Total N=120
1.	Poor (up to 80)	—	—	—	—	—	—	—
2.	Low average (81-100)	—	—	1 (5)	—	1 (5)	2 (10)	4 (3.33)
3.	High average (101-115)	3 (15)	1 (5)	4 (20)	1 (5)	7 (35)	8 (40)	24 (20)
4.	Good (116-135)	11 (55)	14 (70)	7 (35)	12 (60)	9 (45)	6 (30)	59 (49.17)
5.	Very Good (136-150)	4 (20)	3 (15)	5 (25)	4 (20)	2 (10)	3 (15)	21 (17.5)
6.	Excellent (Beyond 150)	2 (10)	2 (10)	3 (15)	3 (15)	1 (5)	1 (5)	12 (10)

Note: Figures in parentheses indicate the percentage values.
N= Sample size.

$$\text{PFI} = \frac{\text{Duration of activity (minute)}}{\text{Sum of 1st, 2nd and 3rd minute recovery heart rate (beats/min)}} \times 100$$

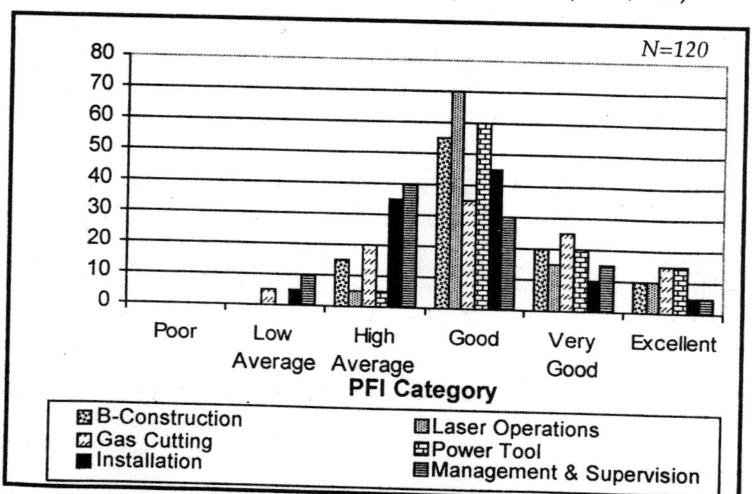

Fig. 4.2 : Distribution of respondents on the basis of Physical Fitness Index.

physical fitness level. It could, therefore be concluded that most of them were having high average to very good level of physical fitness.

6. Rating of Perceived Exertion (RPE) of Construction Workers

To study the effect of various construction activities on the subject's perception of exertion, they were asked to give ratings on a 10 point scale after completion of task. Table 4.6 and Figure 4.3 envisaged the mean exertion perceived by construction workers. It was found that the mean rating of perceived exertion ranged from 3.77 to 5.8 on the basis of verbal expression of fatigue. It was further found from the study that workers involved in handling power tools felt weak to extremely strong exertion with mean rating of 5.8, followed by slightly low i.e., mean RPE 5.7 in case of basic construction activities. It was also noticed that mean RPE score was almost equal in case of gas cutting (5.1) and installation activities (5.2). However, safety managers and supervision staff felt somewhat

Table 4.6: Rating of perceived exertion during various activities performed by construction workers

(N=120)

Activities	*RPE Score*												
	0.0	*0.5*	*1.0*	*2.0*	*3.0*	*4.0*	*5.0*	*6.0*	*7.0*	*8.0*	*9.0*	*10.0*	*Mean*
Basic construction work (n = 20)	—	—	3	—	1	1	2	4	2	7	—	—	5.70
Laser operations (n = 20)	—	1	4	3	2	4	1	-	2	3	—	—	3.77
Gas cutting (n = 20)	—	—	—	2	4	3	1	3	6	—	1	—	5.1
Power tool operations (n = 20)	—	—	—	2	—	3	4	2	4	5	—	—	5.8
Installation (n = 20)	—	—	—	3	2	1	2	7	4	1	—	—	5.2
Safety management and supervision (n = 20)	1	3	—	—	2	—	4	6	3	1	—	—	4.62

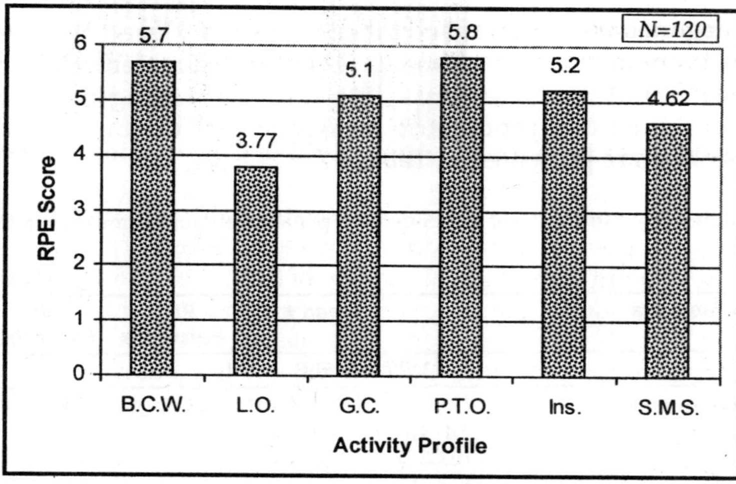

Fig. 4.3 : Mean RPE score of construction workers.

strong to heavy exertion on the basis of mean RPE score (4.62). Least exertion was found in case of laser tool operations activity might be because these activities were not performed in continuation.

It was concluded from the above results that the high RPE score of 8.8 was found during power tool operations, whereas the lowest score of 3.77 was found during laser tool operations.

7. Anthropometric Measurements of Construction Workers

Bone, muscle and other minute dimensions of anatomy are mostly referred for medical and other necessities, but for designing and/or assessing products for human use, the anthropometric measurements has to be considered. The anthropometric data is used as reference data in planning, designing and evaluating ergonomically sound user's friendly products and layouts. The study of anthropometry is not just about body measurements, it is about how to employ required body measurements efficiently while designing individual items or products. Anthropometry includes measurements of body dimensions. Hence, in present study, a total of 24 body measurements were taken, which were grouped under five categories viz. 2 whole body measurements, 7 head and neck anthropometric measurements, 4 face measurements, 9 hand and 2 foot measurements. The data pertaining to above mentioned anthropometric measurements of construction workers are presented in Table 4.7.

Table 4.7: Distribution of respondents as per anthropometric measurements

(N=120)

Parameters			*Mean ± SD*	*95th Percentile*	*5th Percentile*
			Whole Body		
Stature (cm)			165.13 ± 3.57	171.02	159.24
Weight (kg)	40-50	18 (15)	57.36 ± 7.39	69.55	45.17
	50-60	64 (53.33)			
	60-70	33 (27.5)			
	≥ 70	5 (4.16)			
			Head and Neck		
Head length (cm)			18.19 ± .55	19.1	17.3
Head breadth (cm)			14.46 ± .86	15.87	13.04
Head height (cm)			16.95 ± .49	17.76	16.14
Head circumference (cm)			54.53 ± 2.0	57.83	51.23
Bitragion arc length (cm)			33.79 ± 1.65	36.51	31.07
Sagital arc length (cm)			34.44 ± 1.16	36.35	32.52
Sub mandibular arc (cm)			26.28 ± 1.58	28.88	23.67
			Face		
Face measurement–menton to brow (cm)			10.95 ± 0.4	11.61	10.29
Face measurement–menton to naison (cm)			10.12 ± 0.41	10.79	9.44
Face breadth (cm)			11.62 ± 0.31	12.13	11.11
Jaw width (cm)			9.98 ± 0.55	10.88	9.07
			Hand Measurements		
Hand length (cm)			18.62 ± 0.24	19.02	17.69
Palm breadth (cm)			9.35 ± 0.27	9.79	8.90
Palm breadth-max (cm)			10.67 ± 0.16	10.93	10.41
Palm length (cm)			10.43 ± 0.18	10.73	10.13
Thumb length (cm)			6.68 ± 0.19	6.99	6.36
Thumb width (cm)			2.29 ± 0.21	2.63	1.94
Finger length (middle finger) (cm)			7.95 ± 0.35	8.5	7.45
Finger width (middle finger) (cm)			2.28 ± 0.09	2.43	2.13
Hand thickness (cm)			3.16 ± 0.35	3.74	2.6
			Foot Measurements		
Foot length (cm)			24.24 ± 0.92	25.75	22.72
Foot breadth (cm)			11.69 ± 0.38	12.32	11.06

Whole body measurements

This includes the stature and weight of the respondents. As shown in Table 4.7, it was found that mean height of construction workers was 165.13 cm with standard deviation of ± 3.57. The 95th and 5th percentiles were found to be 171.02 and 159.24 cm, respectively. It was further revealed from the study that weight ranged from 40 kg to ≥ 70 kg and average weight was 57.36 kg. The 95th and 5th percentile of weight were calculated as 69.55 and 45.17 kg. The findings are in-line with the study conducted by (Ghosh and Iqbal, 2002), who also found that the average height of male was 168.2 cm with standard deviation of ± 6.22 and average weight was 59.80 kg with standard deviation of ± 10.6.

Head and neck measurements

Head and neck measurements are crucial parameters for functional designing of helmet, and visor. The measurements include head length, head breadth, head height, head circumference, bi-tragion arc length, sagital arc length and sub-mandibular arc. It is also evident from the Table 4.7 and Figure 4.4 that the mean values of head length, head breadth, head

(N = 120)

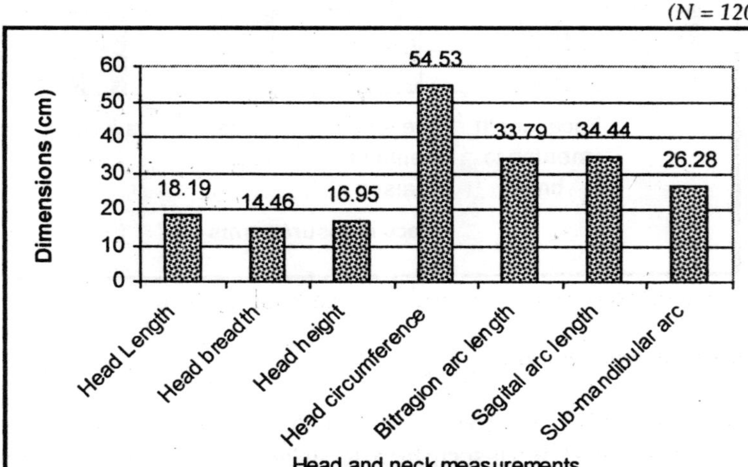

Fig. 4.4 : Head and neck anthropometry of construction workers.

height, head circumference, bi-tragion arc length, sagital arc length and sub-mandibular arc of construction workers were 18.19 ± .55, 14.46 ± .86, 16.95 ± .49, 54.53 ± 2.0, 33.79 ± 1.65, 34.44 ± 1.16 and 26.28 ± 1.58 cm, respectively.

Face Measurements

Face measurements are important parameters for designing face masks and respirators. It is clear from the Table 4.7 and Figure 4.5 that the average face length-menton to brow and face length-menton to naison were 10.95 ± 0.4 cm (11.61 cm 95th percentile and 10.29 cm 5th Percentile) and 10.12 ± 0.41 cm (10.79 cm 95th percentile and 9.44 cm 5th percentile, respectively. However, face breadth and jaw width were 11.62 ± 0.31 cm and 9.98 ± 0.55 cm, respectively. The 95th and 5th percentile of face breadth were 12.13 cm and 11.11 cm and that of jaw width were 10.88 cm and 9.07 cm, respectively.

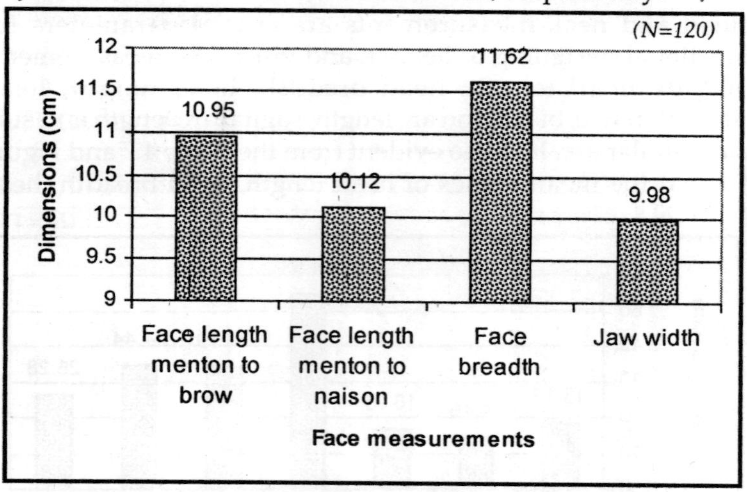

Fig. 4.5: Face anthropometric dimensions of construction workers.

Hand measurements

The assessment of physical dimensions of the human hand provides a metric description to ascertain human machine compatibility (Fraser, 1980).

The anthropometric measurements of hand were taken with straight and flat hand. As regards the measurement landmark and positioning of the hand, it has been noted that the dimensions of a straight and flat hand are significantly longer than those of the relaxed hand (Garrett, 1971). In the relaxed hand, there is a likely unconscious tendency to curl the hand leading to wrong measurements.

Hand anthropometry is required for designing and sizing of gloves. Selected hand parameters such as hand length, palm breadth, palm breadth-max, palm length, thumb length, thumb width, finger length (middle finger), finger width (middle finger) and hand thickness were measured and are presented in Table 4.7 and Figure 4.6. It was observed that mean values of all the above-mentioned measurements were found as hand length (18.62 ± 0.24 cm), palm breadth (9.35 ± 0.27 cm), palm breadth-max (10.67 ± 0.16 cm), palm length (10.43 ± 0.18 cm), thumb length (6.68 ± 0.19 cm), thumb width (2.29 ± 0.21 cm), finger length-middle finger (7.95 ± 0.35 cm), finger width - middle finger (2.28 ± 0.09 cm) and hand thickness (3.16 ± 0.35 cm).

(N=120)

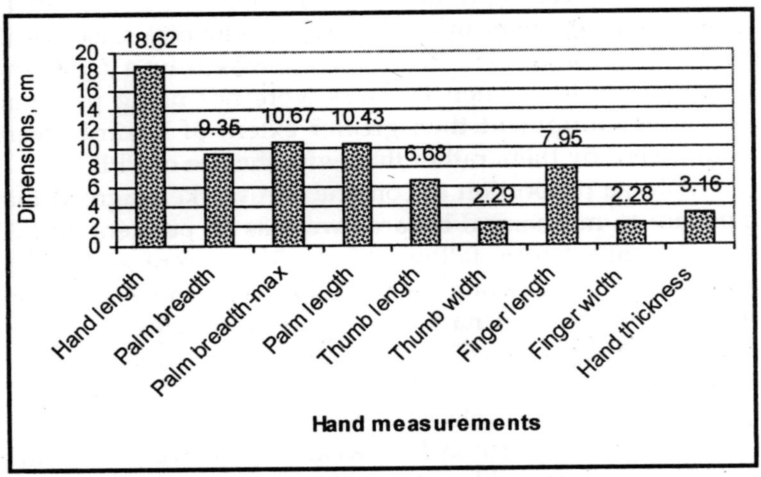

Fig. 4.6: Hand anthropometry of construction workers.

Foot measurements

Foot dimensions are required for designing and sizing of shoes and boots. The data is presented in Table 4.7. It is evident from the investigation, that the 5th, 50th and 95th percentile of foot length were calculated as 22.72, 24.24 and 25.75 cm. However, the average foot breadth and 95th and 5th percentile were found to be 11.69 ± 0.38 cm, and 12.32 and 11.06 cm, respectively.

8. Comparative Analysis of Hazard Identification with and without the Use of PPE

The problem regarding construction industry is not that the hazards and risks are unknown, but it is very difficult to accurately identify in a constantly changing work environment. To prevent health hazards at work, all possible hazards that may be encountered should be identified in advance. Table 4.8 indicates that various types of hazards present in construction areas include impact from falling objects, parts and tools, penetration with nails, scrap metal and sharp objects, chemical hazards as splashing liquids (oils, paints, acids etc.), dust/mists, fumes/vapours and penetration of chemicals, electrical, thermal, postural, vibration etc. It was found from the investigation that when workers were not using personal protective equipment then greater extent of hazards were encountered by them rather than with the use of PPE.

A large proportion of construction workers agreed that exposure to mechanical hazards were as 85 per cent and 35 per cent impact from falling objects, 70 per cent and 17 per cent impact from falling parts, 76 per cent and 36 per cent penetration through nails and penetration through scrap metal/sharp objects as 65 per cent and 35 per cent were felt by without and with the use of PPE, respectively. Non-mechanical hazards like chemical, electrical, thermal, heat and water were also more in case of non-PPE wearer. However, very little variations were found in postural hazards such as 53 per cent and 51 per cent (force), 55 per cent and 48 per cent (repetition), 45 per cent and 35 per cent (load) and 50 per cent and 51 per cent (awkward posture) perceived by non-PPE and PPE users, respectively, revealing. Therefore, that PPE is not greatly effective in relation to preventing postural hazards.

In addition to it, other hazards such as working in height, vibration, and noise and radiation exposure were less countered to PPE users as 21 per cent, 11 per cent, 18 per cent and 21 per cent, respectively.

Table 4.8: Opinion of construction labourers as per hazard present at construction sites

(N=100)

Type of hazard	*Sources of hazard*	*Identification of hazard*	*Without PPE*	*With PPE*
Mechanical Hazard	Impact	Falling object	85 (85)	35 (35)
		Falling parts/tools	70 (70)	17 (17)
	Penetration	Nails	76 (76)	36 (36)
		Scrap metal, Sharp objects	65 (65)	35 (35)
	Crushing	Rolling objects	45 (45)	40 (40)
		Cart/vehicles	51 (51)	23 (23)
	Chemical	Splashing liquids (oils, paints, acids etc.)	70 (70)	18 (18)
		Dust, Mists	56 (56)	21 (21)
		Fumes, vapours	51 (51)	20 (20)
		Penetration of chemicals	56 (56)	15 (15)
Non-mechanical hazards	Electrical	Contact with power lines	28 (28)	18 (18)
		Cuts and burns	66 (66)	13 (13)
		Electric shocks	51 (51)	16 (16)
		Sparks	53 (53)	12 (20)
	Thermal	Exposure to heat	50 (50)	21 (21)
		Exposure to cold	56 (56)	11 (11)
	Heat	Flying sparks	60 (60)	16 (16)
	Water	Slipping/Tripping	50 (50)	20 (20)
Non-Mechanical Hazards	Postural	Force	53 (53)	51 (51)
		Repetition	55 (55)	48 (48)
		Load	45 (45)	35 (35)
		Awkward posture	50 (50)	51 (51)
	Working in height	Falling from height	58 (58)	21 (21)
	Confined space	Suffocation	47 (47)	33 (33)
		Restricted movements	46 (46)	50 (50)
	Other hazards	Exposed to vibration	51 (51)	11 (11)
		Exposed to Noise	56 (56)	18 (18)
		Exposed to radiation	65 (65)	21 (21)

Note: Figures in parentheses indicate the percentage values.

9. Identification of PPE for Hazard Prevention

A cross-analysis was performed with 20 safety managers and supervisor staff from construction sector regarding hazard identification and required PPE to prevent occupation injuries and accidents. Data regarding such phenomena has been outlined in Table 4.9. Workplace injuries are a leading cause of eye and face trauma, vision loss and disability. It was found that eye and face were affected by cutting, drilling, welding and soldering type of work activities with work related exposure to dust, dirt, UV radiation, flying particles, hazardous liquid chemical mists, glare or high intensity light, hot sparks and other laser operations accounted for more than 60 per cent.

The results were supported by findings of Adams *et al.* (2007), as most of visible hazards for eye and face are airborne dust, sand particles, filling due to grinders, laser/infrared or UV radiation amongst others.

It was further found that most of the respondents agreed that hazards present in construction sites could not be eliminated without the use of PPE and various kinds of PPE that might be used for the workers in construction industry to protect their eyes and face against occupational injuries and infections i.e., safety glasses, dust tight goggles, impact goggles, chemical goggles, welding helmet, laser goggles etc.

Adams *et al.* (2007) also reported that welding goggles and shields can be used to prevent eye damage that might be caused by bright lights and heat as well as from arc welding.

According to National Library of Medicine (2008), millions of people sustain head and brain injuries through blows and pressure on head. Head injuries are common in construction set-up due to the types of activities that take place on daily basis. More than 60 per cent of respondents replied that head injuries could occur due to impact from beams, pipes, exposed electrical wiring or component, falling or fixed objects and machine parts. Adams *et al.* (2007) further added that head injuries could be caused by activities such as falling objects, spillage and debris from conveyer belts, electric shocks and head bumping.

Table 4.9: Identification of PPE for hazard prevention

N=20

Body Parts	*Work activities*	*Work related exposure*			*Hazard eliminated without the use of PPE*		*Required PPE*
		Parameter	*Yes*	*No*	*Yes*	*No*	
Eyes and Face	• Cutting • Drilling	Dust	18 (90)	2 (10)	2 (10)	18 (90)	Safety Glasses
	• Welding	Dirt	20 (100)	—	1 (5)	19 (95)	Dust Tight Goggles
	• Soldering	UV	20 (100)	—	—	20 (100)	Safety Goggles
		Flying particles/ Objects	17 (85)	3 (15)	3 (15)	17 (85)	Impact Goggles
		Hazardous liquid chemicals mists	12 (60)	8 (40)	8 (40)	12 (60)	Chemical Goggles
		Glare/high intensity lights	15 (75)	5 (25)	5 (25)	15 (75)	Safety Glasses
		Laser operations	18 (90)	2 (10)	3 (15)	17 (85)	Welding Helmet/Laser Goggles
		Hot sparks	17 (85)	3 (15)	2 (10)	16 (80)	Safety Glasses
Head	• Loading/Deloading	Beams	20 (100)	—	—	20 (100)	Protective helmet
	• Gas cutting	Pipes	12 (60)	8 (40)	9 (45)	11 (55)	-do-
	• Welding	Exposed electrical wiring or components	17 (85)	3 (15)	6 (30)	14 (70)	Protective helmet • Type A • Type B
	• Use of power tool	Falling objects	20 (100)	—	3 (15)	17 (85)	Safety helmet
	• Installation	Fixed object	15 (75)	5 (25)	9 (45)	11 (55)	-do-
		Machine parts	11 (55)	9 (45)	10 (50)	10 (50)	-do-
Hands and Arms	• Material handling	Irritating chemicals	18 (90)	2 (10)	5 (25)	15 (75)	Chemical resistant gloves
	• Grinding	Tools or materials that could scrape, bruise, or cut	20 (100)	—	7 (35)	13 (65)	Abrasion/cut resistant gloves

(*Contd.*)

Table 4.9 (*Contd.*)

Body Parts	*Work activities*	*Work related exposure*			*Hazard eliminated without the use of PPE*		*Required PPE*
		Parameter	*Yes*	*No*	*Yes*	*No*	
	• Welding • Hammering • Working with glass	Extreme heat/ cold	12 (60)	8 (40)	9 (45)	11 (55)	Temperature resistant gloves
		Electric shock	17 (85)	3 (15)	8 (40)	12 (60)	Shock resistant gloves
		Vibration	20 20	—	4 (20)	16 (80)	Anti-vibration
		Sharp injury	18 (90)	2 (10)	7 (35)	13 (65)	Protective sleeves
Feet or Legs	• Building maintenance • Construction • Use of highly flammable materials • Welding	• Exposed electrical wiring or components	12 (60)	8 (40)	9 (45)	11 (55)	Safety shoes or boots with electrical protection
		• Heavy equipment	20 (100)	— —	4 (20)	16 (80)	Safety shoes with toe protection
		• Slippery surfaces	18 (90)	2 (10)	4 (20)	16 (80)	Anti-slip soles
		• Impact from Objects	20 (100)	—	7 (35)	13 (65)	Safety shoes with toe protection and steel plate
		• Crushing	20 (100)	—	5 (25)	15 (75)	Safety shoes with toe protection
		Sharp injury	17 (85)	3 (15)	4 (20)	16 (80)	Foot-Leg guards
		Chemical penetration	20 (100)	—	6 (30)	14 (70)	Chemical resistance shoes
		Extreme heat/ cold	16 (80)	4 (20)	8 (40)	12 (60)	Heat/cold protection (Padded shoes)
Body/ Skin	• Construction activities • Fibreglass installation • Welding	Working in heights	18 (90)	2 (10)	4 (20)	16 (80)	Safety harness
		Impact from flying objects	20 (100)	—	12 (60)	8 (40)	Body suit
		Chemical splashes	16 (80)	4 (20)	5 (25)	15 (75)	Coveralls, Apron
		Extreme heat/ cold	14 (70)	6 (30)	7 (35)	13 (65)	Insulated jacket
		Sharp or rough edges	17 (85)	3 (15)	5 (25)	15 (75)	Abrasion/cut resistance suit

(*Contd.*)

Table 4.9 (*Contd.*)

Body Parts	*Work activities*	*Work related exposure*			*Hazard eliminated without the use of PPE*		*Required PPE*
		Parameter	*Yes*	*No*	*Yes*	*No*	
Lungs/ Respiratory	• Painting • Fibre-glass installation • Confined space work • Construction work	Dust or particulate	20 (100)	—	(10) (10)	(90) (90)	Dust mask
		Toxic gas/ vapour	18 (90)	2 (10)	4 (20)	16 (80)	Disposable particulate
		Chemical irritants (acids)	18 (90)	2 (10)	3 (15)	17 (85)	Replaceable filter particulate
		Welding fume	20 (100)	—	7 (35)	13 (65)	Dust mask
		Paint spray	17 (85)	3 (15)	6 (30)	14 (70)	Dust mask
Ears/ Hearing	• Basic construction work • Use of power tool • Installation	• Loud work environment	20 (100)	—	—	20 (100)	Ear plugs
		• Noisy machines	20 (100)	—	3 (15)	17 (85)	Ear muffs

Notes: 1. Type 'A' helmet-Low voltage; Type 'B' helmet-High voltage.
2. Figures in parentheses indicate the percentage values.

Severe head injuries can lead to permanent brain damage or death. It, therefore, becomes important to protect workers against these head injuries which are sometimes fatal or life threatening. To protect head, PPE has to be used at all times when performing duties that could expose the workers to any possible type of head injuries which protect the wearer against falling objects, bumps, and knocks against stationary or moving objects.

Unfortunately, hands are the most vulnerable parts of human body as they are prone to injuries and infections. It was also further revealed from observation that hand and arms related injuries occur greatly (>90%) with irritating chemicals and with materials that could scrap, bruise or cut, 60 per cent with thermal effect, 85 per cent with electrical shock etc. For such reasons it becomes vital for workers to protect their hands from occupational injuries and other forms of danger.

Schoemen and Schroder (1994) also stated that hands should be protected against potential agents such as chemical substances including infecting agents, mechanical injuries, bruises, abrasions, extreme temperature, electrical shock, falling or sharp objects, and many more risks that workers could expose to. There should be various types of hand protective devices to cater for different hazards, for example chemical resistant, abrasion/cut resistant, anti-vibration gloves and protective sleeves. Since, the construction industry has activities that can pose as a danger to workers lower extremities, safety measures need to be taken to protect them from all types of trauma. More than 60 per cent managerial staff agreed that feet and legs could be injured with exposed electrical wiring, heavy equipments, slippery surfaces, impact from objects and crushing, sharp injuries, chemical penetration etc. To safeguard the workers feet, most of respondents agree that there can be different types of PPE as safety boots or shoes with steel toe-caps, and sole plate built into them. In addition to it, there can be metatarsal and toe guards, which protect the instep area and toes from impact and compression hazards.

It was further found that body/skin could be affected if the persons were engaged in fibreglass installation, welding, working in height and exposed to flying objects, chemical splashes and sharp and rough edges. However, respondents who involved in painting, fibreglass installation, confined space work and other dangerous environment were more prone to lung and respiratory diseases. It was further observed that >85 per cent respondents exposed to dust and particulate, toxic gas/vapours, chemical irritants, welding fumes and paint spray.

As far as hearing is concerned, it was found that construction labour, power tool users and installation personnels were exposed to loud work environment and noisy machines. Noise induced hearing loss occurs if workers persist to work in a noisy area in excess of noise at a level of 80 dB (A) at a distance of one metre without wearing ear muffs or ear plugs (Hattingh and Accut, 2003).

10. Rapid Entire Body Assessment (REBA) Analysis for Postural Assessment of Construction Workers

The construction workers face some of the most dangerous working conditions on a daily basis. The accurate measurement of workers exposure to the risk assessment as WMSDs has been of vital importance. Musculo-skeletal system primarily with the dimensions, compositions and the mass properties of body segments and the work related musculo-skeletal disorders caused due to frequent bending, pulling or pushing of muscles, overexertion, adoption of asymmetric and awkward postures and unsupported positions used for task completion. Such postural hazards which are due to operations performed mainly for a long period can cause a pain for lifetime and disability. Therefore, present investigation is intent to provide an objective measure of the postural risk of construction workers and to evaluate a job's level of risk with the application of REBA (Rapid Entire Body Assessment) technique.

The results regarding subjective assessment of postural risk with the help of REBA and observation technique furnished information of risk factors and work postures were assessed and enclosed in Table 4.10 and Figure 4.7. Various postures of neck, trunk and leg in group A (plus load/force), upper arms, lower arms and wrists in group B (plus coupling) along with activity score were observed and analyzed. It was found that a sum total of 31.67 per cent construction workers were in AL_2 which interprets medium risk level and change is required soon followed by 28.33 per cent workers in AL_3 (high risk and action necessary now), 21.66 per cent in AL_1(low risk, further action may be needed). However, only 14.16 per cent of workers were found to be in AL_0 indicating 'negligible' risk level, means no action is necessary i.e., acceptable posture.

Table 4.10: REBA analysis for postural assessment of construction workers

Activity Profile	*REBA Action Category*				
	AL_0	*AL_1*	*AL_2*	*AL_3*	*AL_4*
Basic Construction Work (n = 20)	2 (10)	2 (10)	4 (20)	10 (50)	2 (10)
Laser Operations (n = 20)	6 (30)	3 (15)	3 (15)	7 (35)	1 (5)
Gas Cutting (n = 20)	2 (10)	9 (45)	4 (20)	5 (25)	0 (0)
Installation (n = 20)	4 (20)	3 (15)	9 (45)	4 (20)	0 (0)
Power Tool Operations (n = 20)	(1) (5)	4 (20)	8 (40)	5 (25)	2 (10)
Safety Management and Supervision (n = 20)	2 (10)	5 (25)	10 (50)	3 (15)	0 (0)
Total (N=120)	17 (14.16)	26 (21.66)	38 (31.62)	34 (28.33)	5 (4.17)

Note: Figures in parentheses indicate the percentage values.

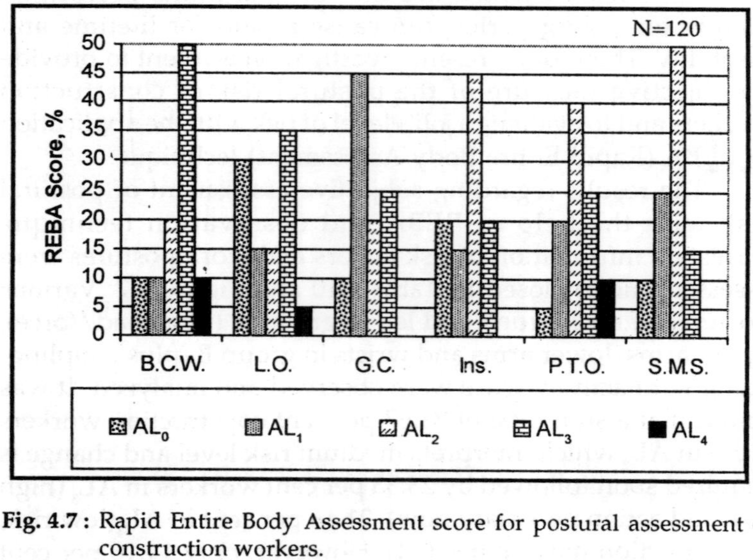

Fig. 4.7 : Rapid Entire Body Assessment score for postural assessment of construction workers.

When the activities were analyzed individually, it was observed that majority of workers who involved in basic construction activities (50%) were in the zone of AL_3 (high risk and action necessary now) followed by laser operations (35%), handling power tool (25%), gas cutting (25%), installation (20%), and, safety management and supervision (15%), respectively.

It was further observed that in the periphery of AL_2, major proportion of safety management and supervision (50%), installation (45%), respondents involved in gas cutting (20%), basic construction activities (20%), laser operations (15%) and power tool operations (40%) were found indicating medium risk level. However, in AL_4 (very high risk, action necessary now) there were mainly basic construction workers (10%), power tool operators (10%) and laser tool operators (5%). As an interesting issue of very few respondents in AL_0 corresponding to the fact that few subjects worked in construction sites in an acceptable posture are really a matter of concern.

According to Phesant (1991), "Postures which are initially adopted for occupational reasons may become habitual outside the working context and finally become irreversible owing to the shortening and fibrous contraction of muscles and soft tissues." Thus, asymmetric postures and unsupported positions can increase the load on spine. Postural stress can increase the physiological cost and fatigue while performing the task and may also lead to pain and injuries to vertebral column in the long run.

11. Perceived Discomfort Associated with the Use of PPE

Although PPE help to protect employees against work related injuries and illness, it was found from investigation that employees were reluctant to spontaneously use these. According to Guild *et al.* (2001) various problems that workers encounter in their regular use of PPE were as uncomfortable and of improper size. Workers were often removing their gloves, helmet and hearing aid when feeling uncomfortable.

Data pertaining to associated discomfort with PPE use are outlined in Table 4.11. It is clearly evident from the table that a large population of respondents agreed about poor fit of PPE (55.66%), helmet requiring adjustment to fit properly

(36.66%) and helmet blocking the evaporation of sweat (63.33%) resulting from problems in design level. However, due to problem in material, approximately 52 per cent, 45 per cent and 42 per cent of respondents experienced irritation in skin, skin got red and insulated PPE encourages heat accumulation in body, respectively. Ill fitting gloves may interfere with workers' performance as they slip-off easily, thus increasing the operational time thereof.

Cornell High Energy Synchrotron Source (2007) indicated that one of the problems with gloves is that they can be caught between parts, especially if they do not fit snugly, resulting in serious injuries to the workers. This is supported by Safe and Healthy Working (2007), in the explanation of potential danger of entanglement during drilling if one is wearing loose fitting gloves.

It can be further envisaged from Table 4.11 that at the functional level, perceived discomfort were as restricting movement (13.33%), restricting visibility due to helmet (28.33%), more items of PPE causing discomfort (21.67%), gloves reducing grip strength (35%), gloves limiting movements of fingers (20%), frequent breathing is required when wearing full face mask (6.67%), glare in eyes due to laser operations (20%), and no provision of individual alteration to clothing (36.66%).

According to Adams *et al.* (2007), eye protecting PPE also accumulate condensation, which makes it difficult for workers to see well through the mist and its (eye protecting equipment) surface may easily scratch resulting in a field of vision being affected. Other problem encountered by respondents with the use of PPE was indicated as fungal and bacterial infection in foot (45%), swelling in toes (30%) and goggles accumulated dust in its surface (26.67%). The results were in-line with study conducted by Robinson (2001) who found that certain problems which were caused by poorly fitted footwear causing severe aching feet, fallen arches (flat feet), malformation of toes and sprains. Further, it was supported by Guild *et al.* (2001) that humid environment inside the foot, PPE can predispose workers to skin maceration, irritation and can result in fungal and bacterial infection and malodors of the feet.

Table 4.11: Perceived discomfort associated with the use of PPE

(N=120)

Sl. No.	*Para-meters*	*Problems due to PPE use*	*Opinion of respondents*			*Weighted mean Score*
			Agree	*Undecided*	*Disagree*	
1	Design Level	Not properly fit (helmet, gloves)	68 (56.67)	14 (11.66)	38 (31.66)	1.45
		Requiring adjustments (helmet)	44 (36.66)	16 (13.33)	60 (50.00)	1.23
		Blocking the evaporation of sweat (helmet)	76 (63.33)	6 (5)	38 (31.66)	1.58
2	Due to material	Causing irritation in skin	62 (51.67)	24 (20)	34 (28.33)	1.32
		Skin go red (gloves)	54 (45)	26 (21.66)	40 (33.33)	1.23
		Insulated PPE encourages heat accumulation in body	50 (41.67)	24 (20)	46 (38.33)	1.22
3	Functional level	Restricting movement	16 (13.33)	46 (38.33)	58 (48.33)	0.75
		Restricting visibility (helmet)	34 (28.33)	28 (23.33)	58 (48.33)	1.05
		More items of PPE creating discomfort	26 (21.66)	42 (35.00)	52 (43.33)	0.86
		Gloves reducing grip strength	42 (35.00)	16 (13.33)	62 (51.67)	1.22
		Gloves limiting movements of fingers	24 (20)	30 (25)	66 (55)	0.95
		Frequent breathing is required when wearing full face mask-helmet	8 (6.67)	44 (36.66)	68 (56.67)	0.70
		Glare in eyes while performing laser operations (visor)	24 (20)	34 (28.33)	62 (51.67)	0.92
		No provision of individual alteration to clothing	44 (36.66)	18 (15.00)	58 (48.33)	1.22
4	Others	Fungal and bacterial infection in foot	54 (45)	26 (21.67)	40 (33.33)	1.23
		Swelling in toes due to regular use of shoes	36 (30)	46 (38.33)	38 (31.66)	0.92
		Goggles accumulate dirt in its surface	32 (26.67)	26 (21.67)	62 (51.67)	1.05

Note: Figures in parentheses indicate the percentage values.

In the nutshell, it can be concluded that if PPE does not fit properly, it may not provide the desired protection and also, discourage employees from using it.

12. Vibration Analysis of Power Tool Users in Construction Industry

Intensive vibration can be transmitted to the hands and arms of power tool operators at construction sites from vibration tools. Depending on the type and place of work, vibration can enter one arm only or both arms simultaneously, and may be transmitted through the hands' arm to the shoulder. The perceived vibration is the source of discomfort and possibly reduced proficiency.

In order to ensure occupational safety the data regarding vibration hazard is outlined in Tables 4.12 and 4.13.

Table 4.12: Vibration analysis of power tool users in construction industry

(N=20)

S. No.	*Parameters and sub-categories*		*No. of respondents*
1.	Dominant hand	Left	4 (20)
		Right	16 (80)
2.	Time in present job	≤ 5 years	3 (15)
		6-10 years	13 (65)
		11-15 years	4 (20)
3.	Tools used	Cutter	12 (60)
		Sander/Polisher	11 (55)
		Breaker/Driller	8 (40)
		Hammer drill	9 (45)
		Saw	7 (35)
		Grinder	5 (25)

Note: Figures in parentheses indicate the percentage values.

It was found from investigation that majority of power tool users (65%) were working with vibrating tools from 6-10 years followed by 11-15 years (20%) and ≤ 5 years. The dominant hand of operating power tool or exposure to vibration was right hand as reported by 80 per cent of workers. Variety of tools used by workers at construction sites were cutter, sander and/or polisher, breaker/driller, hammer drill, saw and grinder.

The continued and habitual use of vibrating tools have been found to be connected with various diseases affecting the blood vessels, nerves, bones, joints, muscles or connective tissues of the hands and arms. It was further observed from Table 4.13 that major proportion of vibrating tool users were

Table 4.13: Analysis of vibration hazard symptoms

(N=20)

Sl. No.	*Symptoms*		*Respondents' distribution*
		White finger	
1.	Colour changes		11 (55)
2.	Description of change in colour	Blue	5 (25)
		Red	3 (15)
		White	3 (15)
3.	White finger, clearly de-markable	2 (10)	
4.	Last episode of colour changes	< 8 months ago	4 (20)
		8-12 months ago	5 (25)
		> 1 year ago	2 (10)
5.	Seasonal effect (white colour)	Winter	3 (15)
		Summer	—
		Both	—
6.	Other triggering factors	While handling vibrating tools	2 (10)
		After work	7 (35)
		Night	11 (55)
		Tingling	
7.	Ever experienced	Yes	13 (65)
		No	7 (35)
8.	Triggering factors	While handling vibrating tools	1 (5)
		After work	4 (20)
		After exposure to cold	8 (40)
		During white finger	2 (10)
		After white finger	7 (35)
		At night time	6 (30)
		Numbness	
9.	Ever experienced	Yes	11 (55)
		No	9 (45)
10.	Triggering factors	While handling vibrating tools	2 (10)
		After work	6 (30)
		After exposure to cold	5 (25)
		During white finger	2 (10)
		After white finger	1 (5)
		At night time	8 (40)

Note: Figures in parentheses indicate the percentage values.

experiencing vibration hazard syndrome in form of changing colour of fingers, tingling in hands and numbness reported by 55 per cent, 65 per cent and 55 per cent of respondents, respectively.

Since the colour change were reported by 55 per cent of power tool users as blue (25%), red (15%) and white (15%) with clearly demarkable white finger in 10 per cent of respondents. The episodes of white colour was further accelerated in winter reported by all respondents and major triggering factor for elevating problem was recognized as handling power tools for long hours.

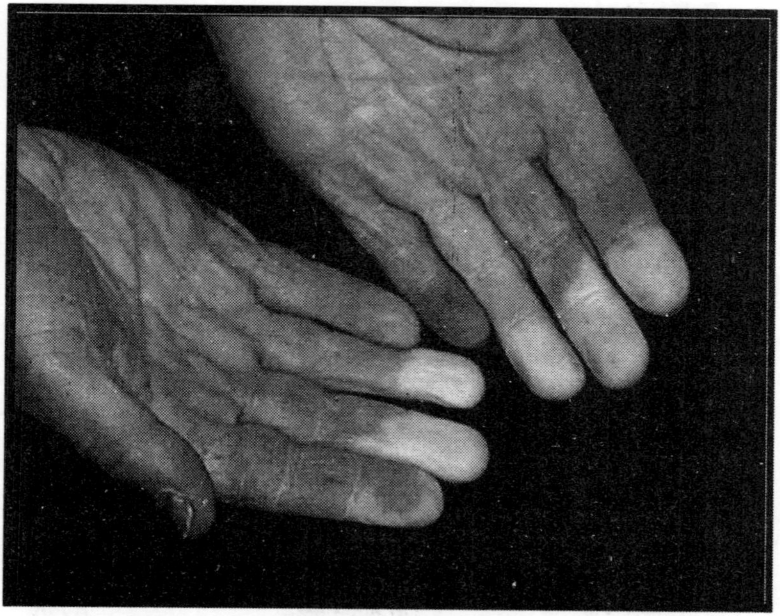

Plate 3: Vibration Induced White Finger.

Tingling in hands was reported in 5 per cent (while handling power tools), 20 per cent (after work), 40 per cent (after exposure to cold), and in 10 per cent and 30 per cent of subjects during and after white finger, respectively. In night time, the sensation of tingling and numbness were aggravated. However, 55 per cent of respondents experienced numbness in hands and associative factors which trigger the condition such as exposure to cold, use of power tools for long hours and white finger.

13. Environmental Conditions during Field Experiments

As weather has a profound effect on human health and some of such factors include temperature, humidity, illumination, noise, heat, sunshine, solar radiation, etc. The magnitude of activity is greatly influenced by such environmental variables. Table 4.14 depicts the environmental condition during the experimental phase.

Environmental parameters were recorded in area viz. construction site and workshop where basic construction and pre-fabrication activities are performed. Some pre-fabrication activities include welding, gas cutting, sawing, reinforcement work as performed in workshop. The maximum and minimum temperature were 38.7°C and 28.9°C, 37.2°C and 32.5°C at construction site and workshop, respectively. The humidity ranged from 50 to 70 per cent at construction site and 42 to 67 per cent at workshop. However, noise level was 88 dB(A) and 76.8 dB(A) at site and workshop, respectively. It was further found that illumination was more at site (1086 lux) as compared to workshop (692 lux) indicating more visibility around construction area.

Table 4.14: Environmental parameters during record period

Activity Areas	*Temperature °C*		*Humidity*		*Noise*	*Light*
	Max	*Min*	*Max*	*Min*	*dB*	*(lux)*
Basic Construction Site	38.7°C	28.9°C	70 per cent	50 per cent	88	1086
Workshop	37.2°C	32.5°C	67 per cent	42 per cent	76.8	692

The noise is known to distract, confuse and make mental concentration more difficult. Depending on the individual, the noise intensity and the length of exposure, may affect hearing in long run. It is recommended as per IS : 12207 (1999) that maximum ambient noise at operator's ear level should not exceed 90 dB (A) for 8 h duration. But it was further conceded that 40 h of exposure per week of noise of 90 dB (A) or greater will result in hearing loss.

It can be concluded that all the measured environmental variables were more at construction site as hot climate (temperature), humid, increased noise level (nearly upper limit of exposure) and adequate illumination.

14. Physiological Cost of Work of Subjects during Experiments

Tables 4.15 to 4.17 and Figures 4.8 and 4.9 show the effect of activities performed on physiological cost of work. A total of 5 replications were conducted to observe physiological cost of work in terms of Heart Rate (HR) and Energy Expenditure Rate (EER).

Physiological cost of work in terms of heart rate

The results of experiments conducted on various workers (as per activity profile) were analyzed and presented in Table 4.15 for mean HR and per cent increase in heart rate from its resting level.

Table 4.15: Physiological cost of work of construction worker in terms of heart rate (beats/min)

(N=30)

Sl. No.	*Activity Profile*	*Mean Heart Rate (beats/min)*			*Per cent increase in HR (Recovery Period)*
		Resting	*During Work*	*Recovery*	
1.	Basic Construction Work	83	127.8	98	18.07
2.	Laser Operations	81.8	124	95	16.14
3.	Gas Cutting	84	122.8	93	10.71
4.	Power Tool Operations	82	118	94.8	15.61
5.	Installation	85	124	97	14.12
6.	Safety Management and Supervision	84.8	120	92	8.49

$$\text{Per cent increase} = \frac{\text{After activity} - \text{Before activity}}{\text{Before activity}} \times 100$$

Exerting human energy during performance of activities resulting an increase of heart rate. The mean resting heart rate ranged as 82 to 85 beats/minute for various activities. The variations of such responses for different activities are described in succeeding section.

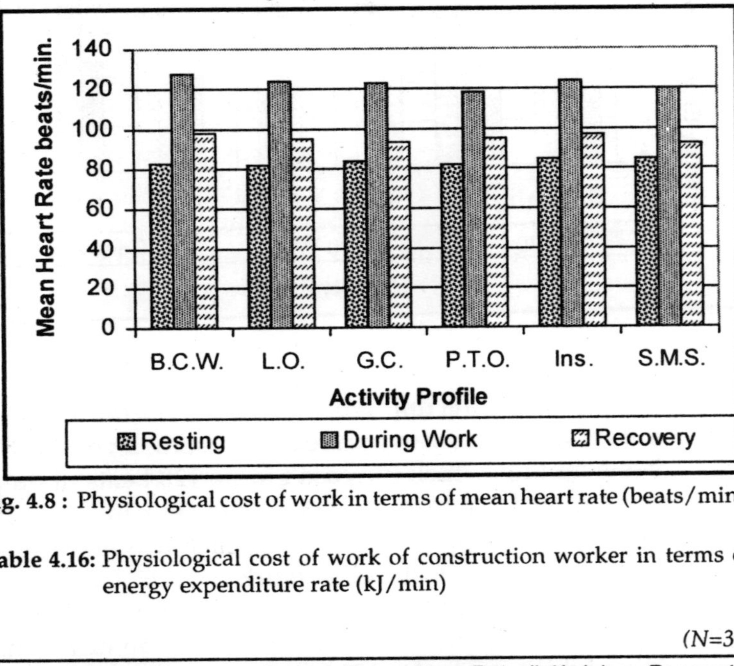

Fig. 4.8 : Physiological cost of work in terms of mean heart rate (beats/min).

Table 4.16: Physiological cost of work of construction worker in terms of energy expenditure rate (kJ/min)

(N=30)

Sl. No.	*Activity Profile*	*Energy Expenditure Rate (kJ/min)*			*Per cent increase in EER (Recovery Period)*
		Before Work	*During Work*	*After Work*	
1.	Basic Construction Work	4.48	11.60	6.68	49.11
2.	Laser Operations	4.29	11	6.39	48.95
3.	Gas Cutting	4.64	10.81	6.07	30.82
4.	Power Tool Operations	4.32	10.04	6.35	46.99
5.	Installation	4.80	11	6.70	39.58
6.	Safety Management and Supervision	4.76	10.36	5.91	24.16

$$\text{Per cent increase} = \frac{\text{After activity} - \text{Before activity}}{\text{Before activity}} \times 100$$

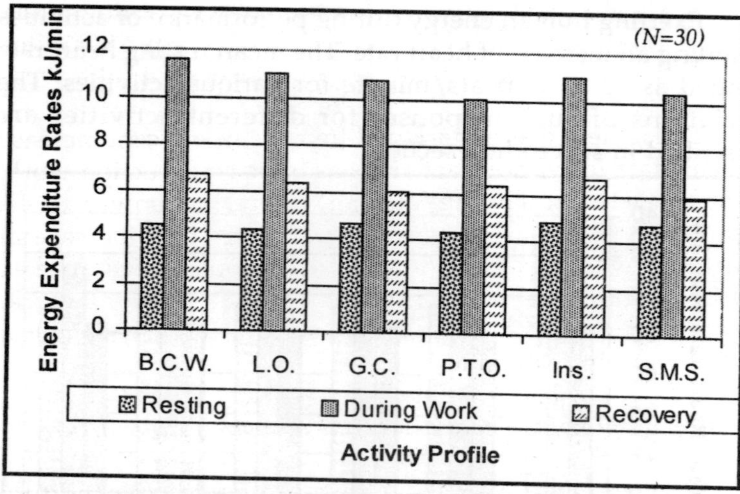

Fig. 4.9: Physiological cost of work in terms of energy expenditure (kJ/min).

- ***Basic Construction Work (loading/unloading of materials)***: The mean heart rate at resting level was 83 beats/minute, which increased up to 128 beats/minute during performance. Whereas, per cent increase in heart rate was found to be 18.07, which was maximum in case of basic construction work.
- ***Laser Tool Operations***: For laser operations, it was found that mean HR was 82 beats/minute at resting level, which reached to 124 beats/min during work with per cent increase of 16.14.
- ***Gas Cutting***: The mean heart rate during work was recorded as 123 beats/min and per cent increase in heart rate was 10.71 from its resting level.
- ***Handling Power Tools***: The mean Heart Rate (HR) before work, during work and recovery period was 82, 118, 95 beats/min, respectively and per cent increase in heart rate was 15.61 which was also high.
- When installation work was performed, the mean heart rate increased up to 124 beats/min (during activity) from its resting level (85 beats/min) and per cent increase was found to be 14.12.

- For management and supervision staff resting, work and recovery HR was found to be 85, 120 and 92 beats/min, respectively with per cent increase of 8.49.

Thus, there was a marked difference in per cent increase in heart rate for various activities as basic construction work, laser operations, sawing/cutting, operating power tools, installation and management work. The per cent increase in heart rate was maximum in basic construction activity i.e., loading/unloading and minimum in management work. Figure 4.8 summarizes the information regarding physiological cost of work in relation to heart rate.

Physiological cost of work in terms of energy expenditure

Table 4.16 and Figure 4.9 show the mean Energy Expenditure Rate (EER) kJ/min and increase in EER from its resting level for various types of activities performed by selected construction workers.

- While loading/unloading activity (i.e. basic construction work), the energy expenditure rate before work was 4.48 kJ/min which increased up to 11.60 kJ/min (during work), with per cent increase of 49.11.
- For laser operations (welding) EER at resting, work and recovery period was 4.29, 11 and 6.39 (kJ/min), respectively with per cent increase of 48.95.
- In case of power tool operators per cent increase in EER found to be 46.99, followed by installation, gas cutting and, safety management and supervision work as 39.58, 30.82 and 24.16, respectively.

In the nutshell, it can be concluded that on the basis of energy expenditure, basic construction work (loading/unloading) was found to be most strenuous activity, however, safety management and supervision was least exhaustive one.

Physiological cost of work in terms of blood pressure and pulse rate

The data pertaining to information regarding average blood pressure and pulse count are presented in Table 4.17.

- In basic construction activity (loading/unloading), the resting mean blood pressure (B.P. mmHg) was 87 which increased up to 106 (during activity), with a change in pulse rate from 83 to 105.
- For laser operations, mean blood pressure and pulse rate (before activity) were 89 and 76 mmHg which may increased up to 107 and 98 mmHg, respectively.
- In case of gas cutting activity, the mean blood pressure recorded was 91.33 mmHg (before work) and 104.93 mmHg (during work) with a change in mean pulse rate from 79.4 to 99.8.
- Handling power tool was most strenuous activity after loading/unloading with a change in blood pressure 89 to 105.53 mmHg and in pulse rate 77 to 102.4 per minute, before and after activity, respectively.

Table 4.17: Physiological cost of work of construction worker in terms of Blood Pressure (mmHg) and Pulse Rate (per min)

(N=30)

Activity Profile	*Resting (mean value)*		*During Work (mean value)*		*Per cent Increase (During Work)*	
	Mean B.P. (mmHg)	*Pulse Rate/min*	*Mean B.P. (mmHg)*	*Pulse Rate/min*	*B.P.*	*Pulse Rate*
Basic Construction Work	86.67	83.4	105.90	104.8	22.18	25.65
Laser Operations	88.67	75.8	107.00	98	20.67	29.28
Gas Cutting	91.33	79.4	104.93	99.8	14.89	25.69
Power Tool Operations	89.00	77.0	105.53	102.4	18.57	32.98
Installation	87.00	79.8	103.86	98.8	19.38	23.80
Safety Management and Supervision	90.87	74.0	103.27	98.4	13.64	32.97

- When installation work was performed, the mean B.P. and pulse rate was 87 mmHg and 79.8 per min (before activity), 103.86 mmHg and 98.8 per minute (after work), respectively.

- For safety management and supervision work, average B.P. and pulse count ranged from 91 to 103.5 mmHg and 74 to 98.4 per minute.

Thus, it is evident from the data that on the basis of blood pressure and pulse rate, basic construction work was most demanding activity and safety management and supervision was least tiring.

15. Grip Strength of Subjects During Experiments

It was measured for checking the power in the hands of construction workers. The results of experiment showed decline in muscular grip strength after completion of activity. The results further revealed that the accommodation of personal protective equipment reduces the grip strength.

Table 4.18 and Figure 4.10 indicate per cent change in grip strength of right hand with and without the use of PPE

Table 4.18: Grip strength of construction workers

(N=30)

Sl. No.		*Activities*	*Average muscular grip strength (kg.)*					
			Resting		*After work*		*% change in grip strength*	
			Left	*Right*	*Left*	*Right*	*Left*	*Right*
1.	Basic Construction Work	Without PPE (Gloves)	23	24.5	21.5	22.5	6.52	8.16
		With PPE(Gloves)	20.5	24	19.5	22	4.88	8.33
2.	Laser Operations	Without PPE(Gloves)	24.5	26.5	22	23.5	10.20	11.32
		With PPE(Gloves)	21	24	19.5	21.5	7.14	10.42
3.	Gas Cutting	Without PPE(Gloves)	24	26.5	22	23.5	8.33	11.32
		With PPE(Gloves)	22.5	25	20.5	23	8.89	8.00
4.	Power Tool Operations	Without PPE(Gloves)	23.5	24.5	21.5	20	8.51	18.37
		With PPE(Gloves)	22	23	19.5	19.5	13.64	15.22
5.	Installation	Without PPE(Gloves)	22.5	24.5	20	20.5	11.11	16.33
		With PPE(Gloves)	21	23	19	20	9.52	13.04
6.	Safety Management and Supervision	Without PPE(Gloves)	23.5	25	22	23.5	6.38	6.00
		With PPE(Gloves)	21	22.5	20	21	4.76	6.67

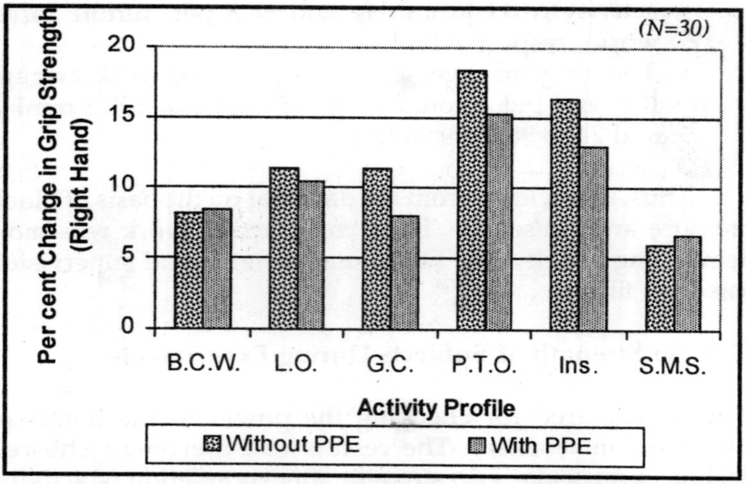

Fig. 4.10 : Per cent change in grip strength (Right hand).

for basic construction workers (8.33 and 8.16 kg), laser operations (10.42 and 11.32 kg), gas cutting (8.0 and 11.32 kg), handling power tools (15.22 and 18.32 kg), installation (13.04 and 16.33 kg), safety management and supervision (6.67 and 6.0 kg), respectively. It was further observed that maximum decline in grip strength for right hand was in case of handling power tools followed by installation, laser tool operations, gas cutting, basic construction work and management and supervision work. Besides right hand, the data regarding left hand's muscular grip strength also reduced after work performance as indicated in Figure 4.11.

It is concluded that muscular grip strength was condensed in performing all the activities. In addition, owing to the use of gloves, per cent change in grip strength was showing more reduction.

16. Spirometry Analysis of Subjects

Spirometery is the most common of the pulmonary function tests. The spirometery test is performed using a device called a spirometer. Spirometers are widely applied by the healthcare professionals to assess lung function. This medical equipment

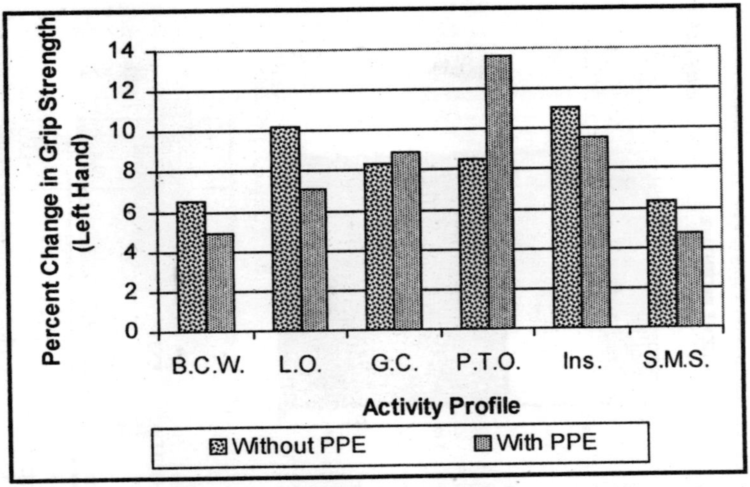

Fig. 4.11 : Per cent change in grip strength (Left hand).

measures the volume of air inspired and expired by the lungs. Spirometer is a precision differential pressure transducer for the measurements of respiration flow rates. The spirometers record the amount of air and the rate of air that is breathed in and out over a specified time. The output produced by a spirometer is called a kymograph trace. To use spirometer, a person breathes into a mouthpiece. The doctor may ask the person to breathe normally or to take a deep breath and blow the air quickly out of the lungs, like blowing up a balloon. A recording device measures the amount of air inhaled or exhaled and the time taken each breath took. These measurements can help to find out if a person has a lung problem. In the present investigation Pc-based spirometer was used, which is directly connected to the serial port turns any computer into a spirometer that allows user to manage lung function screening in a simple and quick way.

The respiration rate was measured before entering into construction site and after 8 hours work performance as pre- and post-analysis (Fig. 4.12). On the basis of documented history of respondents as age, height, weight and smoking habit the predicted values of FVC, $FEV_{0.5}$, FEV_1, FEV_1/FVC per cent and PEF were documented, and pre- and post-values were

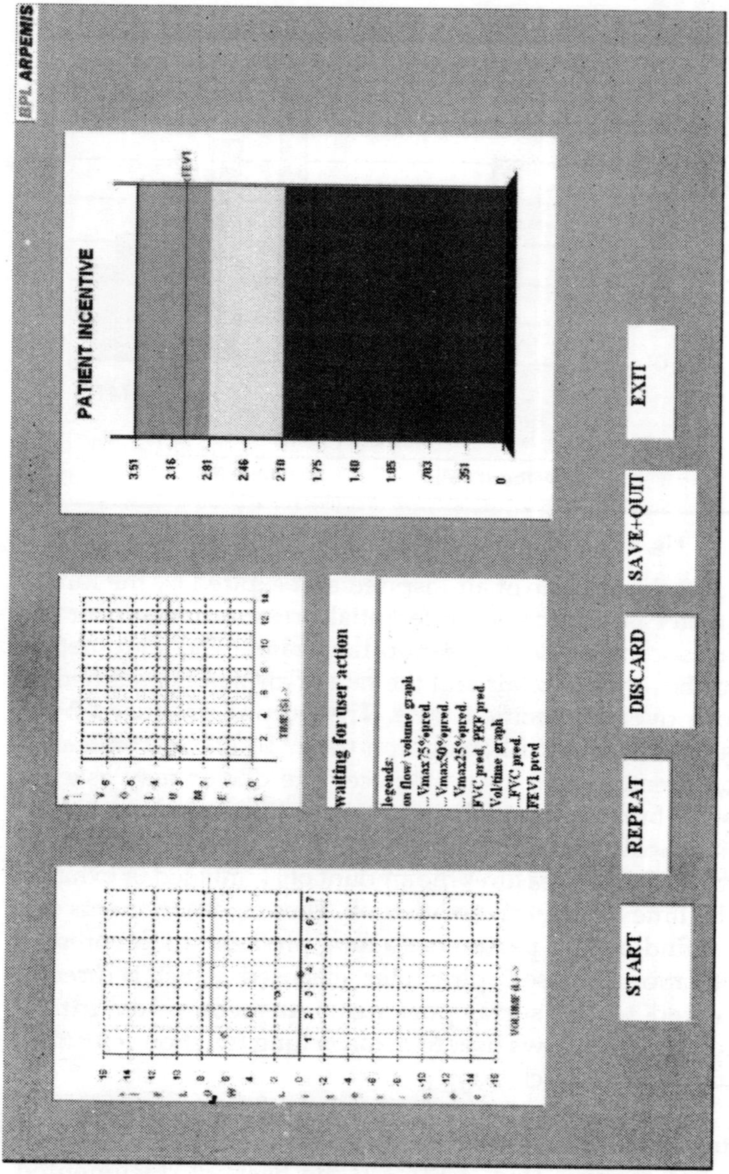

Fig. 4.12 : Test protocol for respiration rate.

PULMONARY FUNCTION TEST REPORT

ID No. :1
Patient Name :RAM
Age(yrs.) : 23 Sex:M Weight(Kg): 65
Indications :
Comments :
History of Smoking : Non - Smoker

Report Date: 21-11-2009
Eth. Corr.(%): 80
Height(cm): 162 BSA(m^2): 1.69

FVC GRAPHS

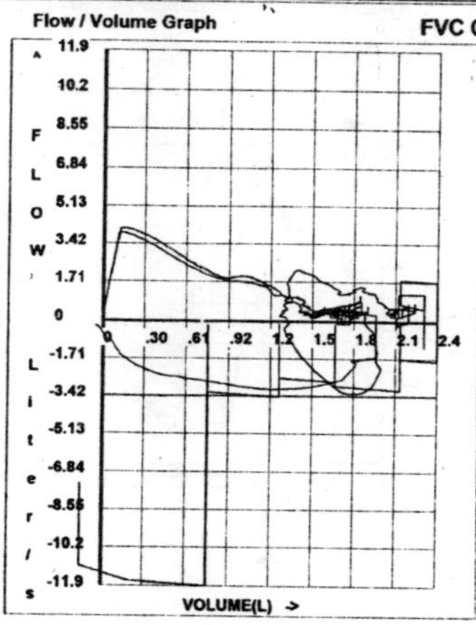

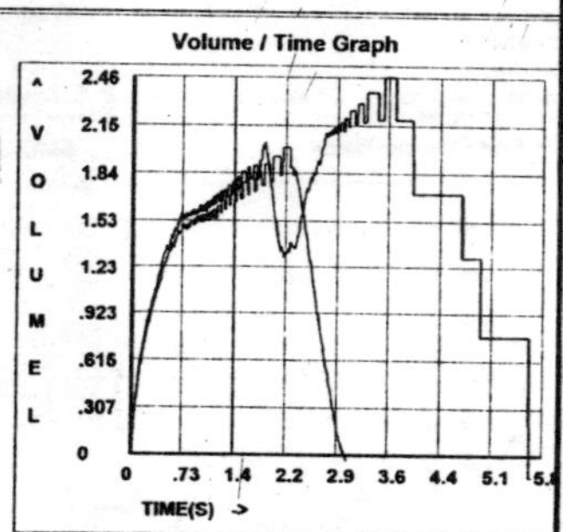

TEST RESULTS

Date of Test ->	21/11/2009			21/11/2009			
Time of Test ->	22:38:49			22:40:53			
Parameter (U)	Pred.#	Pre	%Pred.	Post	%Pre	%Pred.	%Change
FVC (L)	3.558	2.01	56.49	2.462	122.4	70.04	22.48
FEV0.5 (L)		1.261		1.344	106.5		6.582
FEV1 (L)	3.01	1.57	52.15	1.594	101.5	52.31	1.528
FEV1/FVC %	81.45	78.10	95.89	64.73	82.87	77.92	-17.1
PEF (L/s)	7.222	3.886	53.80	4.124	106.1	56.60	6.124
PIF (L/s)		3.172		11.97	377.5		277.5
FEF25-75% (L/s)	3.651	1.524	41.74	0.825	54.13	21.24	-45.8
Vmax25% (L/s)	6.176	3.093	50.08	3.013	97.41	48.85	-2.58
Vmax50% (L/s)	3.99	1.745	43.73	1.665	95.41	40.99	-4.58
Vmax75% (L/s)	1.749	0.317	18.12	0.397	125.2	21.67	25.23
FET100% (s)		2.26		3.76	166.3		66.37

INTERPRETATION: PRE: MODERATE OBS
POST: SEVERE

#Predicted Equations : ERS93

BPL ARPEMIS Page #1/1

Fig. 4.13 : Spirometry analysis (sample respondent 1).

PULMONARY FUNCTION TEST REPORT

ID No. :2

Patient Name :RAMESH Eth. Corr.(%): 80

Age(yrs.) : 32 Sex:M Weight(Kg): 55 Height(cm): 167 BSA(m^2): 1.61

Indications :

Comments :

History of Smoking : Smoker for 3 Years @ 5 Cigarettes/Day

FVC GRAPHS

Flow / Volume Graph

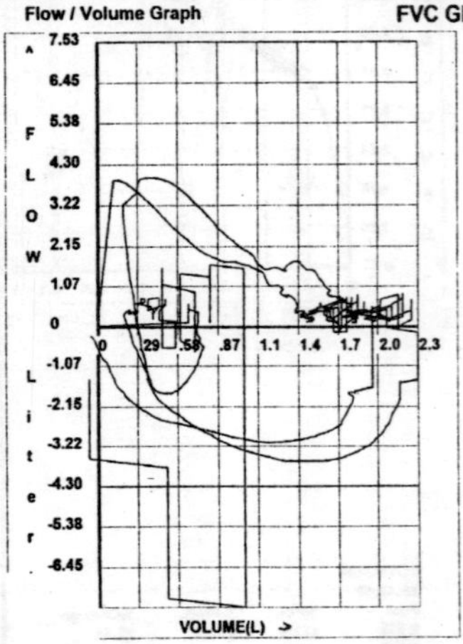

Volume / Time Graph

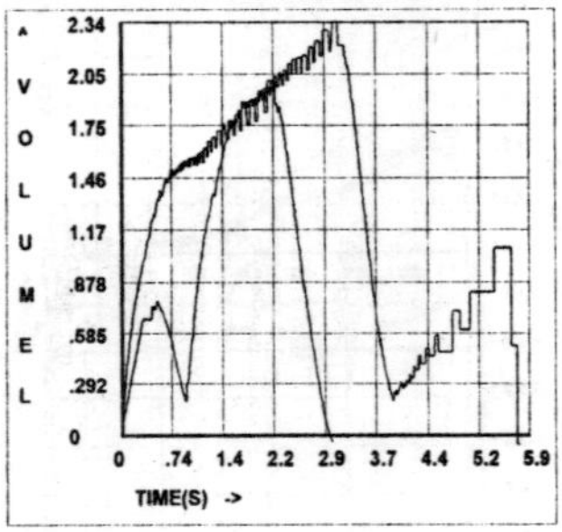

TEST RESULTS

Date of Test ->

Time of Test ->

Parameter (U)	Pred.#	Pre	%Pred.	Post	%Pre	%Pred.	%Change
FVC (L)	3.558	2.343	65.85	2.01	85.78	56.49	-14.2
FEV0.5 (L)		0.726		1.261	173.6		73.69
FEV1 (L)	3.01	0.345	11.46	1.57	455.0	52.15	355.0
FEV1/FVC %	81.45	14.72	18.07	78.10	530.5	95.89	430.5
PEF (L/s)	7.222	4.203	58.19	3.886	92.45	53.80	-7.54
PIF (L/s)		7.534		3.172	42.10		-57.8
FEF25-75% (L/s)	3.651	1.596	43.71	1.524	95.48	41.74	-4.51
Vmax25% (L/s)	6.176	3.965	64.20	3.093	78.00	50.08	-21.9
Vmax50% (L/s)	3.99	1.983	49.69	1.745	87.99	43.73	-12.0
Vmax75% (L/s)	1.749	0.714	40.82	0.317	44.39	18.12	-55.6
FET100% (s)		3.18		2.26	71.06		-28.9

INTERPRETATION: PRE: MILD
POST: SEVERE

#Predicted Equations : ERS93

BPL ARPEMIS Page #1/1

Fig. 4.14 : Spirometry analysis (sample respondent 2).

PULMONARY FUNCTION TEST REPORT

ID No. :3

Patient Name :CHANDU — Eth. Corr.(%): 80

Age(yrs.) : 26 — Sex:M — Weight(Kg): 54 — Height(cm): 158 — BSA(m^2): 1.54

Indications :

Comments :

History of Smoking : Non - Smoker

FVC GRAPHS

Flow / Volume Graph

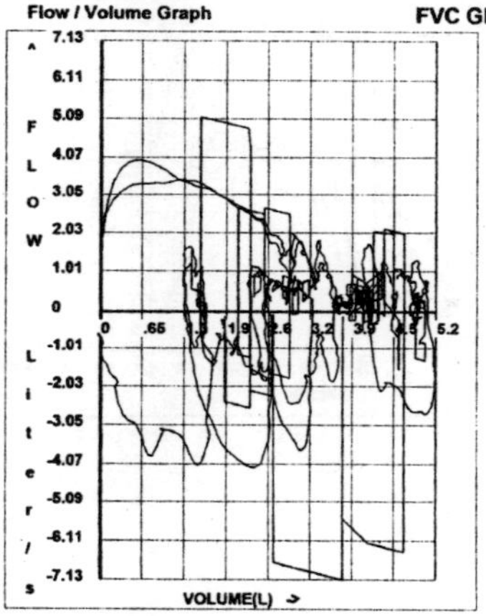

Volume / Time Graph

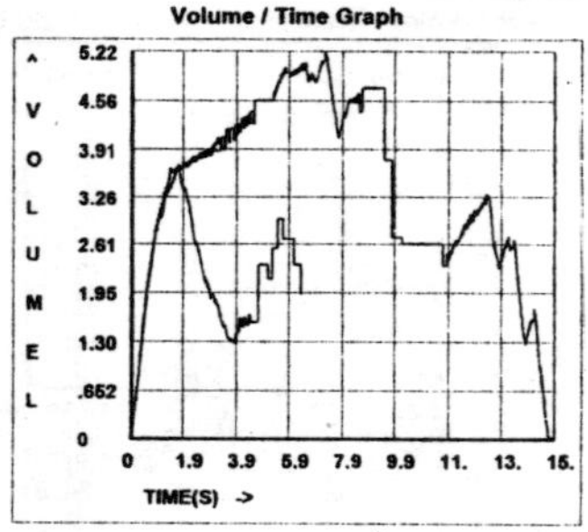

TEST RESULTS

	Pred.#	Pre	%Pred.	Post	%Pre	%Pred.	%Change
FVC (L)	3.268	3.711	113.5	5.222	140.7	159.7	40.71
FEV0.5 (L)		1.511		1.582	104.6		4.698
FEV1 (L)	2.84	2.795	98.41	2.891	103.4	101.7	3.434
FEV1/FVC %	82.53	75.32	91.26	55.35	73.48	67.07	-26.5
PEF (L/s)	6.987	5.155	73.77	4.044	78.44	57.87	-21.5
PIF (L/s)		2.617		7.137	272.7		172.7
FEF25-75% (L/s)	3.718	2.877	77.38	1.108	38.51	29.80	-61.4
Vmax25% (L/s)	5.922	3.41	57.58	3.489	102.3	58.91	2.316
Vmax50% (L/s)	3.866	3.172	82.04	2.379	75	61.53	-25
Vmax75% (L/s)	1.686	1.824	108.1	0.476	26.09	28.23	-73.9
FET100% (s)		1.8		7.33	407.2		307.2

INTERPRETATION

PRE: NORMAL
POST: MILD

#Predicted Equations : ERS93

BPL ARPEMIS — Page #1/1

Fig. 4.15 : Spirometry analysis (sample respondent 3).

PULMONARY FUNCTION TEST REPORT

ID No. :4
Patient Name :ATEEK
Eth. Corr.(%): 80
Age(yrs.) : 34 Sex:M Weight(Kg): 56 Height(cm): 163 BSA(m^2): 1.6
Indications :
Comments :
History of Smoking : Non - Smoker

Flow / Volume Graph

FVC GRAPHS

Volume / Time Graph

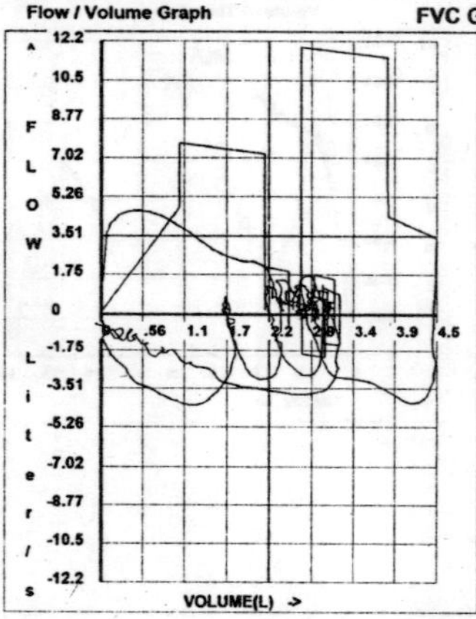

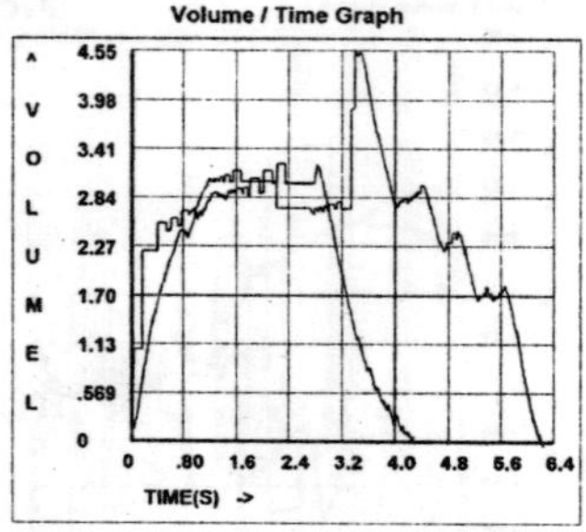

TEST RESULTS

	Pred.#	Pre	%Pred.	Post	%Pre	%Pred.	%Change
FVC (L)	3.332	4.556	136.7	3.236	71.02	97.11	-28.9
FEV0.5 (L)		2.546		1.868	73.36		-26.6
FEV1 (L)	2.826	2.724	96.39	2.665	97.83	94.30	-2.16
FEV1/FVC %	81.09	59.79	73.73	82.35	137.7	101.5	37.73
PEF (L/s)	6.957	12.29	176.6	4.679	38.06	67.25	-61.9
PIF (L/s)		4.362		3.807	87.27		-12.7
FEF25-75% (L/s)	3.52	1.159	32.92	2.864	247.1	81.36	147.1
Vmax25% (L/s)	5.955	7.692	129.1	4.6	59.80	77.24	-40.1
Vmax50% (L/s)	3.819	2.141	56.06	2.855	133.3	74.75	33.34
Vmax75% (L/s)	1.624	12.05	742.2	0.872	7.234	53.69	-92.7
FET100% (s)		3.43		2.85	83.09		-16.9

INTERPRETATION:

PRE: BO DERLINE
POST; MILD

#Predicted Equations : ERS93

BPL ARPEMIS

Page #1/1

Fig. 4.16 : Spirometry analysis (sample respondent 4).

PULMONARY FUNCTION TEST REPORT

ID No. :5

Patient Name :MOHD. AHMED Eth. Corr.(%): 80

Age(yrs.) : 36 Sex:M Weight(Kg): 62 Height(cm): 170 BSA(m^2): 1.72

Indications :

Comments :

History of Smoking : Non - Smoker

FVC GRAPHS

Flow / Volume Graph

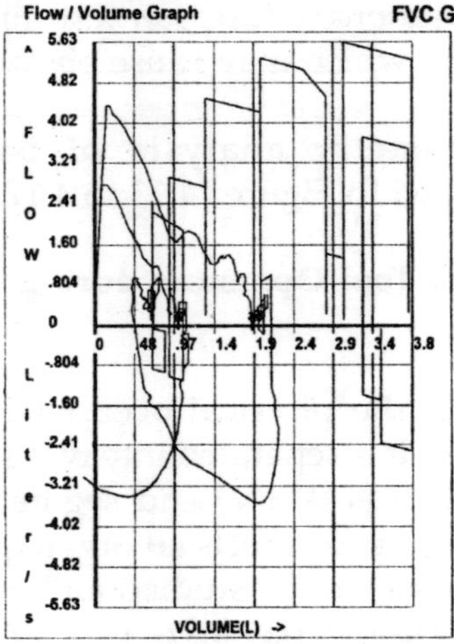

Volume / Time Graph

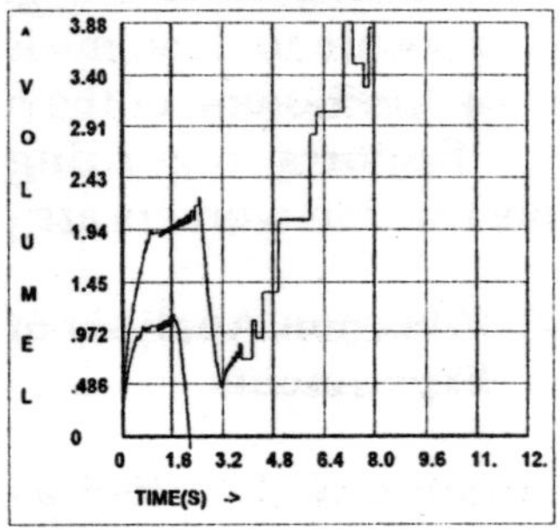

TEST RESULTS

Date of Test ->	21/11/2009			21/11/2009			
			Pred.	[illegible]			%Change
[illegible]	[illegible]	[illegible]	107.6	[illegible]	[illegible]	31.60	-70.6
FEV0.5 (L)		1.38		0.94	68.11		-31.8
FEV1 (L)	3.021	1.927	63.78	0.987	51.21	32.67	-48.7
FEV1/FVC %	80.73	49.54	61.36	86.45	174.5	107.0	74.51
PEF (L/s)	7.232	5.63	77.84	2.776	49.30	38.38	-50.6
PIF (L/s)		3.569		3.489	97.75		-2.24
FEF25-75% (L/s)	3.56	1.13	31.74	1.549	137.0	43.51	37.07
Vmax25% (L/s)	6.214	1.745	28.08	2.776	159.0	44.67	59.08
Vmax50% (L/s)	3.982	0.079	1.983	1.665	2107.	41.81	2007.
Vmax75% (L/s)	1.729	1.427	82.53	0.714	50.03	41.29	-49.9
FET100% (s)		7.39		1.7	23.00		-76.9

INTERPRETATION: Moderate Obs ESA Obs

PRE: MILD
POST: MODERATE

#Predicted Equations : ERS93

BPL ARPEMIS Page #1/1

Fig. 4.17 : Spirometry analysis (sample respondent 5).

measured after test performance. Test results varied from borderline obstacles to severe obstacles.

For sample respondents 1, 2, 3, 4, 5 the test report of pulmonary function test before work were moderate obstacles, mild obstacles, normal spirometry, borderline obstacles, and mild obstacles which was changed as severe, severe, mild, mild and moderate after 8 hrs. of work in above-mentioned cases. The reason behind change in pulmonary function test might be exposure to dust, mists, fumes which may cause obstacles in the functioning of the lung.

Reports regarding spirometry analysis of basic construction workers are presented in Figures 4.13 to 4.17.

17. Vibration Analysis of Power Tool Operators during Experiments

Vibration is classified as one of the physical occupational hygiene hazards in the workplace. It is separated into two sub-categories i.e., Whole-Body Vibration (WBV) and segmental vibration. Segmental vibration exposure affects an organ, part or "segment" of the body. The most widely studied and most common type of segmental vibration exposure is Hand-Arm Vibration (HAV) exposure, which affects the hands and arms. Workers may be exposed to HAV when operating hand-held power tools. Exposure may result in a range of health effects collectively known as Hand-Arm Vibration Syndrome (HAVS). The most well-known health effect is vibration white finger, but other effects include damage to sensory nerves, muscles and joints in the hands and arms.

Vibration hazards pose both acute and chronic health problems. Daily exposure to hand and arm vibration by workers who use vibrating tools powered by electricity can cause physical damage to the hands and arms. This study considers the use of hand-held power tools at construction site and measurement of vibration levels in terms of velocity, displacement, acceleration and enveloped acceleration (E_3) with the help of vibration equipment (CardVibro Neo and pocket PC).

FFT and waveform analysis of hand-held power tools

Table 4.19 depict the FFT (Fast Fourier Transform) and waveform analysis. It can be observed from the data that two high values of velocity (mm/s) of different hand-held power tools were measured at vertical, horizontal and axial direction. Axial velocity (opposite to force direction) was more than vertical and horizontal directions. The two high values of velocity (mm/s) in vertical direction were grinder (17.87 and 12.22), polisher (16.34 and 13.97), sander (5.855 and 5.504), breaker (4 and 13.97), hammer drill (3.048 and 2.491), saw (1.246 and 0.665) and cutter (1.246 and .665). The high 2 values of velocity in horizontal direction were hammer drill (4.202 and 3.922), saw (15.58 and 4.741), cutter (4.673 and 1.278), polisher (4.326 and 2.607), breaker (2.695 and 1.451), grinder (0.024 and 0.022), and sander (4.326 and 2.607).

ISO Vibration Evaluation Standard for Velocity—Vibration Evaluation Standard by Vibration Severity

Vibration evaluation standard for machine operating with rotational speed between 600 ~12,000 RPM. The standard vibration is the vibration generating on machine surface or bearing. The frequency range is limited to 10 ~1,000 Hz.

Appendix A
Vibration Severity

Class I	Small machine
Class II	Medium size machine
Class III	Large machine
Class IV	Turbo machine

Ranges of Vibration Severity		Example of quality judgment for separate classes of machine			
Range	RMS-velocity (mm/s) at the range limits	Class I	Class II	Class III	Class IV
0.28					
0.45	0.28	A			
0.71	0.45		A	A	
1.12	0.71				A
1.8	1.12	B			
2.8	1.8		B		
4.5	2.8	C		B	
7.1	4.5		C		B
11.2	7.1			C	
18	11.2				C
28	18	D	D		
45	28			D	
71	45				D

Where, A=Good; B=Fair; C=Caution; D=Danger

Bearing Evaluation—for enveloped acceleration E_3 measurement

General guidelines for setting enveloped acceleration measurement alarms for bearing monitoring were established using statistical analysis of existing databases. The figures in this chart are provided as general guidelines only.

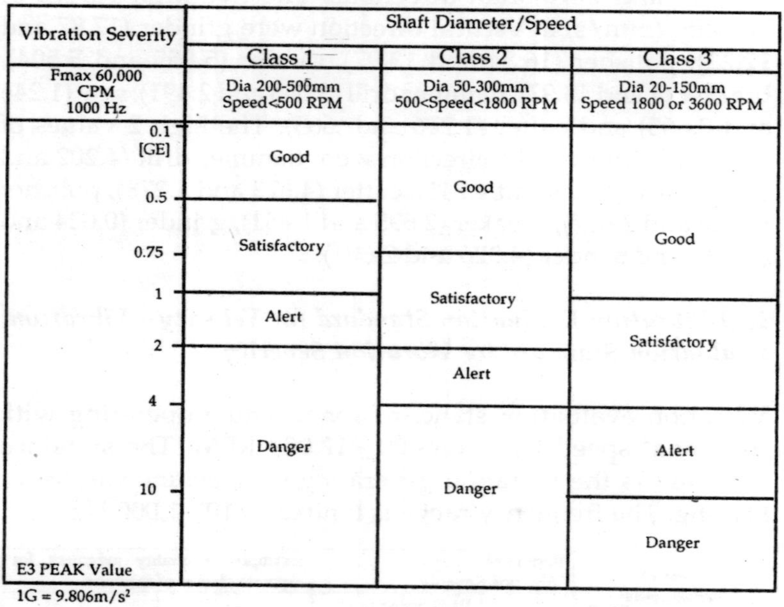

High two values of velocity in axial region were 4.005 and 1.433 for hammer drill, 106.6 and 12.21 for saw, 2.698 and 1.935 for cutter, 15.58 and 4.741 for polisher, 4.005 and 1.433 for breaker, 14.84 and 8.483 for grinder and 106.6 and 12.21 for sander.

Measurement of OA (overall value) vibration of power tools

Table 4.20 shows the overall value of vibration in terms of displacement, acceleration, enveloped acceleration (E_3), and velocity. The measuring parameters for acceleration, enveloped

Table 4.19: FFT analysis of power tools used at construction sites

Parameters ↓ / Power Tool →			Hammer drill			Saw			Cutter			Polisher		
			V	H	A	V	H	A	V	H	A	V	H	A
High	**X_1**	**Freq., Hz**	42.50	8.750	26.25	42.50	17.81	77.81	80.00	453.8	456.3	16.88	27.19	17.81
two		**Vel., mm/s**	3.048	4.202	4.005	1.246	15.58	106.6	42.28	4.673	2.698	16.34	4.326	15.58
values		**Freq., Hz**	8.750	7.500	158.1	455.0	78.44	155.9	161.3	42.50	42.50	74.69	54.69	78.44
	X_2	**Vel., mm/s**	2.491	3.922	1.433	0.665	4.741	12.21	16.24	1.278	1.935	13.97	2.607	4.741

Parameters ↓ / Power Tool →			Breaker			Grinder			Sander		
			V	H	A	V	H	A	V	H	A
High	**X_1**	**Freq., Hz**	26.56	25.94	26.56	87.50	45.63	88.75	54.69	27.19	77.81
two		**Vel., mm/s**	4.76	2.695	4.005	17.87	0.024	14.84	5.855	4.326	106.6
values	**X_2**	**Freq., Hz**	79.69	78.13	158.1	175.0	8.125	355.0	27.19	54.69	155.9
		Vel., mm/s	2.06	1.451	1.433	5.646	0.022	8.483	5.504	2.607	12.21

Table 4.20: Measurement of OA (overall value) vibration of power tools (on axial region)

Parameters	*Power Tools*	*Hammer Drill*	*Saw*	*Cutter*	*Polisher*	*Breaker*	*Grinder*	*Sander*
Acceleration (m/s^2)	**RMS**	17.22	50.01	69.18	37.49	42.14	47.14	36.87
	Peak	45.83	111.0	127.7	79.49	227.5	135.8	94.81
	C.F.	2.662	2.219	1.846	2.121	5.399	2.881	2.572
Velocity mm/s	**RMS**	8.193	17.12	32.86	78.83	17.56	30.91	38.63
	Peak	21.20	38.56	76.93	138.9	49.41	97.09	92.00
	C.F.	2.588	2.252	2.341	1.762	2.815	3.141	2.382
	Judgment (vibration severity)	Danger	Danger	Danger	Danger	Danger	Danger	Danger
E_3(m/s^2)	**RMS**	10.72	23.83	28.44	3.204	53.08	26.96	19.91
	PEAK	30.10	50.84	52.67	11.10	131.0	72.11	67.69
	C.F.	2.807	2.134	1.852	3.465	2.467	2.674	3.4
	Judgment (vibration severity)	Satisfactory	Alert	Alert	Satisfactory	Danger	Alert	Alert
Displacement μm – (Peak to Peak)	**PEAK**	83.17	121.1	259.3	745.6	220.6	922.5	217.3

acceleration (E_3), and velocity were RMS, peak, and C.F. however; displacement can be measured in terms of peak. Maximum acceleration (m/s^2) was found (in terms of RMS) for cutter (69.18) followed by saw, grinder, breaker, polisher, sander and hammer drill as 50.01, 47.14, 42.14, 37.49, 36.87, and 17.22. Root Mean Square velocity (mm/s) in Z-axis (axial direction) was 8.193 for hammer drill, 17.12 for saw, 17.56 for breaker, 30.91 for grinder 32.86 for cutter, 38.63 for sander and 78.83 for polisher. Measured values of RMS velocity were compared with ISO vibration evaluation standard (Appendix-A, see page No. 121) with machine type and vibration severity was in range of danger for all power tools. Enveloped acceleration (m/s^2) in terms of peak value were 11.10 for polisher, 30.10 for hammer drill, 50.84 for saw, 52.67 for cutter, 67.69 for sander, 72.11 for grinder, and 131.0 for breaker. Measured values of E_3 (enveloped acceleration) was compared with bearing evaluation and vibration severity varied from satisfactory to danger criteria as hammer drill (satisfactory), saw (alert), cutter (alert), polisher (satisfactory), breaker (danger), grinder (alert), and sander (alert). Displacement from peak to peak was found maximum in case of grinder with 922.5 μm, followed by polisher, cutter, breaker, sander, saw and hammer drill as 745.6, 259.3, 220.6, 217.3, 121.1, and 83.17 respectively.

18. Blood Lactate Analysis of Subjects Involved in Loading/ Unloading Activity during Experiments

Lactate is known as a fatigue inducing agent. Insufficient washout of Lactate that induces intracellular acidity impairs the excitation, contraction and metabolic processes, thus may depress the maximal power output and ends-up with muscle fatigue. Lactate produced under light to moderate exercise is removed by liver, heart and non-active skeletal muscle. Aerobic metabolism matches the energy demand and Lactate is shuttled to non-active tissue to oxidise the Lactate formed. At rest the lactic acid mechanism is just 'ticking over' so the blood level of Lactate is low at about 0.5 to 1.6 mmol/l (millimoles per litre of blood) but as the intensity of exercise increases, the blood level of Lactate also rises. Eventually exhaustion occurs at which time the Lactate level might be 10 or 20 times the resting level. It is referred to as the 'Lactate threshold' at a level of about 3.5-4.0 mmol/l. During intense or prolonged work, lactic acid builds up due to the reason that fatigue occurs.

Data pertaining to blood Lactate level is presented in Table 4.21 and Figure 4.18. It is evident from the data that before the activity mean blood Lactate level was 3.54 mmol/l, which rose up to 11.12 mmol/l after 8 h. When the individual data is considered, it was found that in all the cases blood Lactate concentrations increased significantly indicating fatigue level.

Table 4.21: Blood Lactate (mmol/l) Concentration of Basic Construction Workers

(N=5)

Sample No.	*Parameter*	*Before activity*	*After activity*
1.	Blood Lactate	2.3	8.5
2.	Concentration	2.8	7.4
3.	(mmol/l)	4.3	20.3
4.		2.6	6.2
5.		5.7	13.2
	Mean	**3.54**	**11.12**

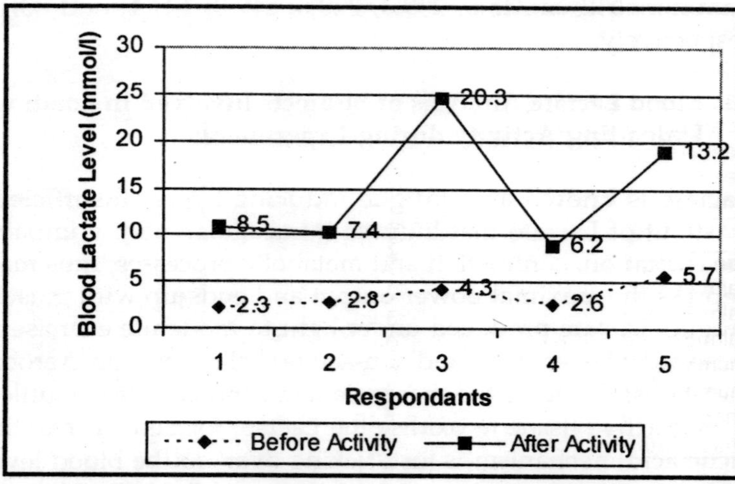

Fig. 4.18 : Blood Lactate concentration in basic construction workers.

Although, Lactate is a great predictor of performance capacity and tremendously important muscle fuel during sustained activity, yet if it begins piling up in the blood at fairly low speeds the muscles must have a poor capacity for utilizing a key source of energy, thus, work output will be slightly low and fatigue will occur relatively early.

19. Design Development of Helmet and Gloves through CAD

All the anthropometric dimensions of construction workers were analyzed and on the basis of that, the final dimensions (shown in Table 4.22) were used for the design development of helmet and gloves for construction workers.

As the ratchet arrangement is adjustable, the dimensions used for ratchet was 95th percentile of head circumference. Other dimensions used for helmet were 95th percentile head length and head breadth. For proper fitting of helmet at head, design dimension was used as bitragion arc –40 mm, head circumference + 20 mm.

Table 4.22: Dimensions for designing of helmet and gloves for construction workers

Measurements	*5th Percentile*	*50th Percentile*	*95th Percentile*
	For Helmet		
Head Circumference	51.23	54.5	57.83
Head Length	17.3	18.19	19.1
Head Breadth	13.04	14.46	15.87
Bitragion arc	31.07	33.79	36.51
	For Hand Gloves		
Hand Length	17.6	18.62	19.02
Palm Length	10.13	10.43	10.73
Palm Breadth	8.90	9.35	9.79
Palm Breadth (Max)	10.41	10.67	10.93
Thumb Length	6.36	6.68	6.99
Thumb Width	1.94	2.29	2.63
Finger Length	7.45	7.95	8.5
Finger Width	2.13	2.28	2.43

Percentile of Hand anthropometry was important for sizing of gloves as 5th percentile for small size, 50th percentile for medium size and 95th percentile for large size.

20. Comparison between the Dimensions of Existing PPE and Ergonomically Designed PPE

When the dimension of existing PPE (helmet and gloves), and ergonomically sound PPE were calculated for comparison then it was found (Table 4.23) that there was a measurable difference in dimensions. Where it was also calculated statistically, then significant difference was found in all the dimensions of existing PPE and ergonomically designed PPE.

Table 4.23: Comparison between the dimensions of existing PPE and ergonomically designed PPE

Measurements	*Dimensions of Ergonomically Designed PPE (cm)*	*Dimensions of Existing PPE (cm)*
	Helmet	
Head Circumference	60 (95th percentile + 2 cm)	68
Head Length	19.1 (95th percentile)	20
Head Breadth	15.9 (95th percentile)	16.5
Bitragion Arc	32.5 (95th percentile – 4 cm)	33
	Hand Gloves (Small Size)	
Hand Length	17.6 (5th percentile)	18
Palm Length	10.15 (5th percentile)	11
Palm Breadth	8.9 (5th percentile)	10
Palm Breadth (Max)	10.4 (5th percentile)	12
Thumb Length	6.36 (5th percentile)	7
Thumb Width	1.94 (5th percentile)	3
Finger Length (Middle Finger)	7.45 (5th percentile)	7.5
Finger Width	2.13 (5th percentile)	3
	Hand Gloves (Medium Size)	
Hand Length	18.62 (50th percentile)	20
Palm Length	10.5 (50th percentile)	12
Palm Breadth	9.36 (50th percentile)	11
Palm Breadth (Max)	10.67 (50th percentile)	12.5
Thumb Length	6.68 (50th percentile)	7.5
Thumb Width	2.29 (50th percentile)	3.5
Finger Length (Middle Finger)	8.1 (50th percentile)	8
Finger Width	2.28 (50th percentile)	3
	Hand Gloves (Large Size)	
Hand Length	19.2 (95th percentile)	23
Palm Length	10.7 (95th percentile)	13.5
Palm Breadth	9.79 (95th percentile)	12.5
Palm Breadth (Max)	10.93 (95th percentile)	13.5
Thumb Length	6.99 (95th percentile)	80
Thumb Width	2.63 (95th percentile)	3.5
Finger Length	8.5 (95th percentile)	9.5
Finger Width	2.43 (95th percentile)	3.5

As the existing helmet and gloves were not properly fitted (Table 4.11) therefore, employees were reluctant to use them regularly.

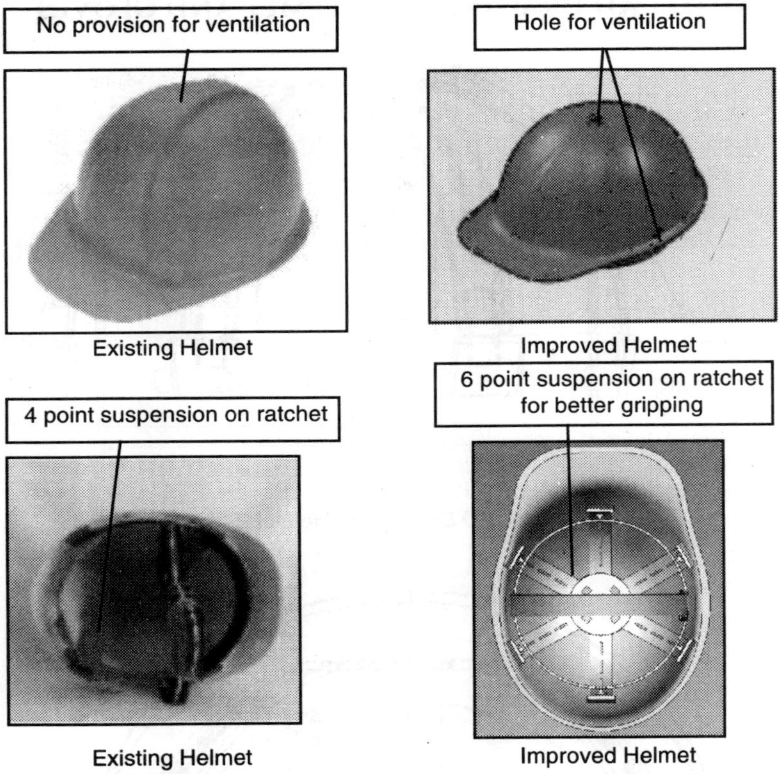

Plate 4: Difference between Existing and Ergonomically Designed Helmet.

In the present investigation design development of helmet and gloves was done on the basis of anthropometric data of users' which need to be tested on the basis of relevant standards.

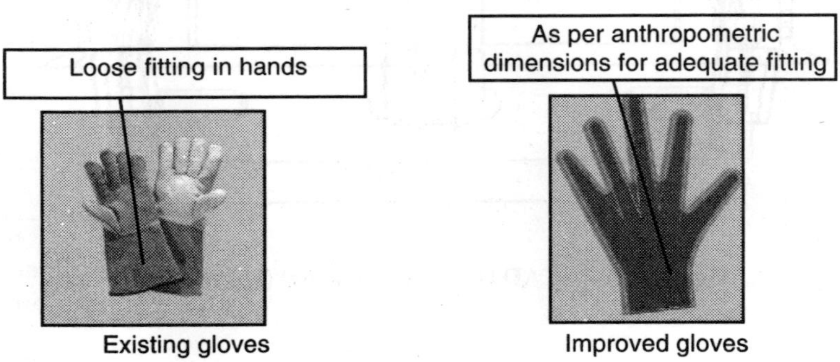

Plate 5: Difference between Existing and Ergonomically Designed Gloves.

AUTO CAD DRAWINGS OF HELMET AND GLOVES

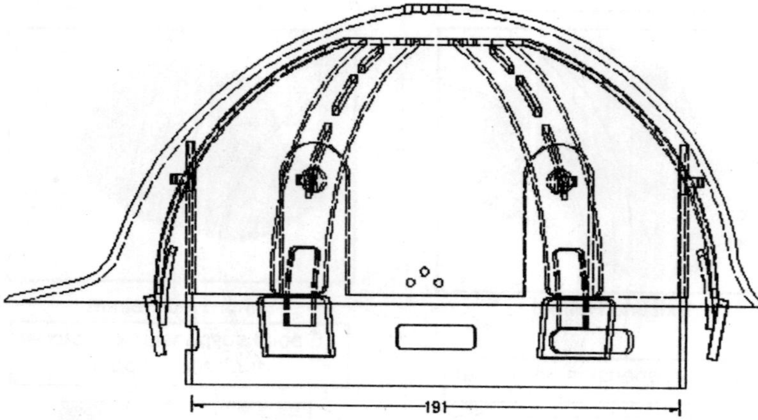

Fig. 4.19: Auto CAD Drawing of Helmet (Side View).

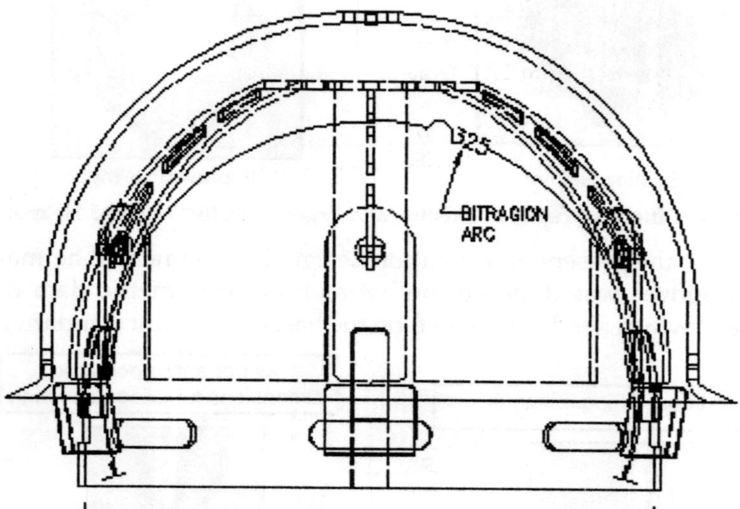

Fig. 4.20: Auto CAD Drawing of Helmet (Front View).

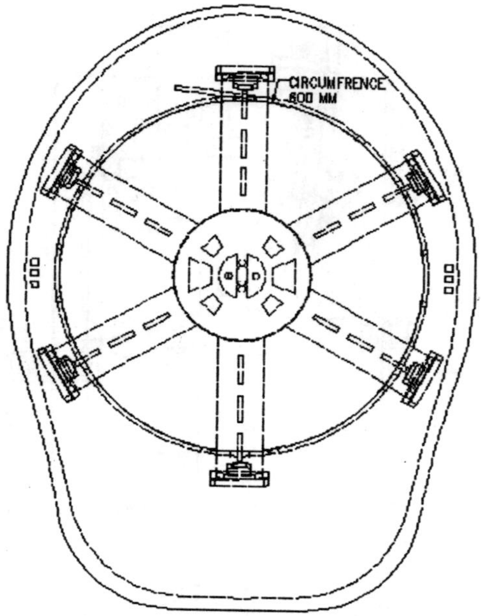

Fig. 4.21: Auto CAD Drawing of Helmet (Inner View).

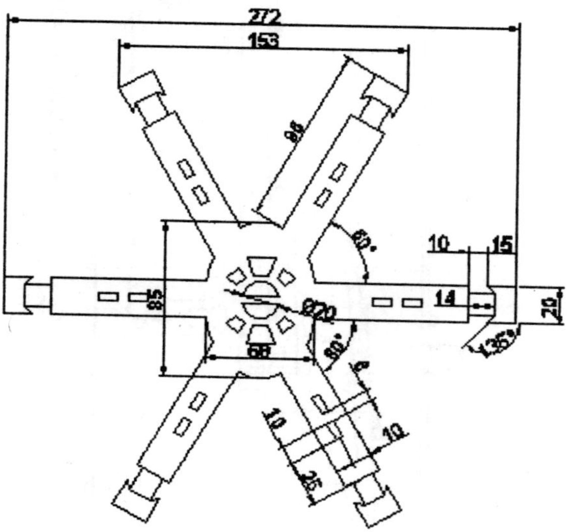

Fig. 4.22: Auto CAD Drawing of Helmet Suspension.

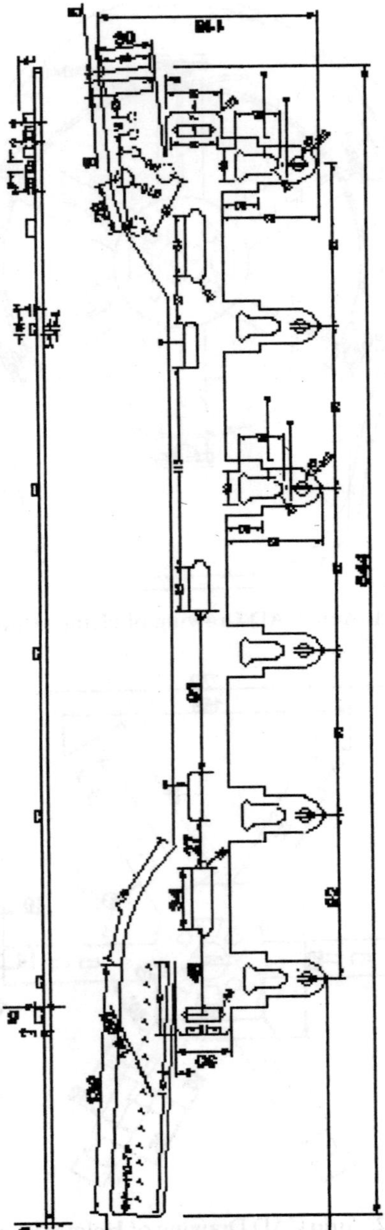

Fig. 4.23: Auto CAD Drawing of Helmet Ratchet.

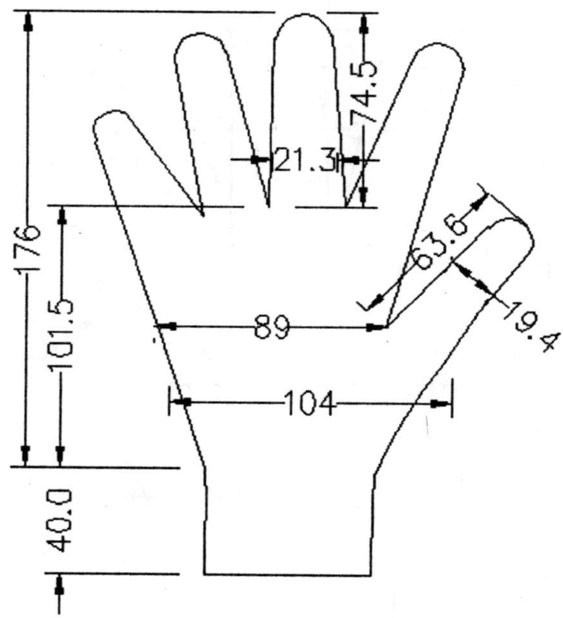

Fig. 4.24: Auto CAD Drawing of Hand Gloves (Small Size).

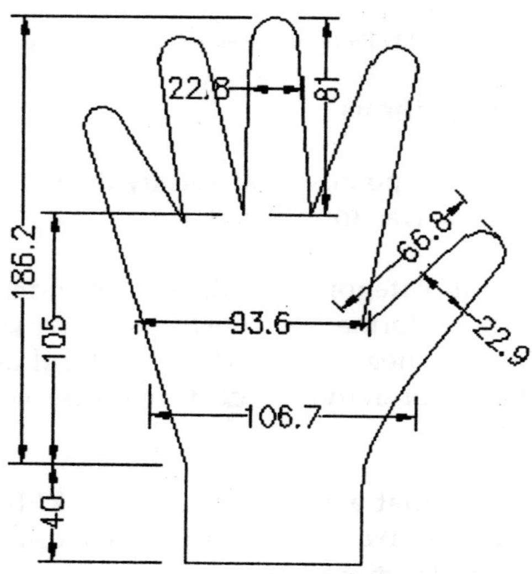

Fig. 4.25: Auto CAD Drawing of Hand Gloves (Medium Size).

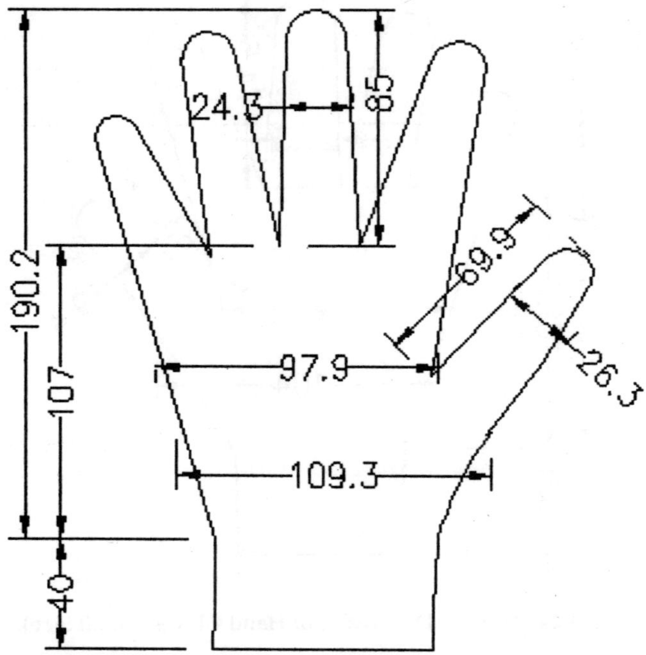

Fig. 4.26: Auto CAD Drawing of Hand Gloves (Large Size).

21. Testing of Hypothesis

In order to test the hypothesis statistically the null hypothesis as presented below was formulated.

1. H_0: Action categories of REBA are independent of activities performed by construction workers.
   H_1: Action categories of REBA postural analysis are dependent of activities performed by construction workers.

It was found that action categories of REBA postural analysis technique are dependent on various activities performed by construction workers.

Table 4.24: Test of significance for REBA analysis

Activity Profile	*REBA Action Category*					*Chi-square value*
	AL_0	AL_1	AL_2	AL_3	AL_4	
Basic construction work	2	2	4	10	2	15.05*
Laser operations	6	3	3	7	1	
Cutting	2	9	4	5	0	
Installation	4	3	9	4	0	
Power tool Operations	1	4	8	5	2	
Safety management and supervision	2	5	10	3	0	

* Significant at 5% level of significance (c^2 value was calculated after merging some classes of activity profile as expected frequency is less than 5).

2. H_0: There is no significant difference in mean Heart Rate (HR), and Energy Expenditure Rate during performance of various construction activities.

H_1: Significant difference exists in mean HR and Energy Expenditure Rate during performance of various construction activities.

ANOVA technique is applied to compare various activities and mean heart rate (during activity). The results of ANOVA technique are presented in Table 4.25. The results were found to be significant at $P<0.05$, indicating average Heart Rate and EER were significantly higher in case of basic construction workers i.e. 127.8 beats/min and 11.60 kJ/min, respectively as compared to other groups.

Table 4.25: Analysis of variance for HR and EER

Activities	*Mean HR (During Work)*	*F value*	*Mean E.E.R (During Work)*	*F value*
Basic construction work (n=5)	127.8	4.201787*	11.60	5.48896*
Laser operations (n=5)	124		11.00	
Gas cutting (n=5)	122.8		10.81	
Power tool operations (n=5)	118		10.04	
Installation (n=5)	124		11.00	
Safety management and supervision (n=5)	120		10.36	
	SEM = 1.6723 C.D. 5% = 4.488 C.V. = 3.045		SEM = .34523 C.D. = .9634 C.V. = 3.34	

* Significant at 5% Level of significance.

Table 4.26: Analysis of variance for muscular grip strength of hands (with and without gloves)

Activities	*Grip Strength Left Hand (Without Gloves)*	*F value*	*Grip Strength Left Hand (With-Gloves)*	*F value*	*Grip Strength Right Hand (Without Gloves)*	*F value*	*Grip Strength Right Hand (With-Gloves)*	*F value*
Basic construction Work (n=5)	21.5	6.102301*	19.5	6.189352*	22.5	5.808100*	22.0	4.635961*
Laser operations (n=5)	22.0		19.5		23.5		21.5	
Gas cutting (n=5)	22.0		20.5		23.5		23.0	
Power tool operations (n=5)	21.5		19.5		20.0		19.5	
Installation (n=5)	20.0		19.0		20.5		20.0	
Safety management and supervision (n=5)	20.0		20.0		23.5		21.0	
	SEM = .31356 C.D. 5% = .9152 C.V. = 3.2611		SEM = .20901 C.D. 5% = .61241 C.V. = 2.3872		SEM = .65939 C.D. 5% = 1.9246 C.V. = 6.6356		SEM = .59578 C.D. 5% = 1.73895 C.V. = 6.2958	

* Significant at 5% Level.

3. H_0: The average muscular grip strength of construction workers is same (with and without gloves).
   H_1: The average muscular grip strength of construction workers is not same (with and without gloves).

The results of ANOVA technique for average muscular grip strength (both hands, with and without gloves) are presented in Table 4.26. The results were found to be significant at $P<0.05$. In case of left hand average grip strength was significantly reduced for basic construction workers and power tool operators as compared to other groups. In case of right hand average grip strength was further significantly reduced for basic construction workers and power tool operators as compared to other groups.

22. Action Plan

• ***Action Plan 1—Suggestive Measures***

Modernization and industrialization have paved a good way to the construction industry. Expanding and fast growing construction sector, and in general, lack of greater employment opportunity elsewhere, has drawn large number of workers in this sector. It is commonly known that accidents have serious implications to the construction industry both in financial and humanitarian terms. Construction accidents may cause many problems such as de-motivation of workers, disruption of site activities, delay of project progress, and adversely affecting the overall cost, productivity and reputation of the construction industry (Mohamed, 1999). Construction industry accounts for the highest number of worker fatalities of any industry. Hazards posed by construction sites include exposure to noise, dust and other chemicals, working from high elevations and in confined spaces, working with power tools and other mechanical equipment, exposure to electricity, and performing excavations. Most of the construction accidents result from basic root causes such as lack of proper training, deficient enforcement of safety, unsafe equipment, unsafe methods or sequencing, unsafe site conditions, not using the safety equipment that was provided, and a poor attitude towards safety. In the present section, the suggestive measures are given under three sections:

1. For construction site managers/safety managers.
2. For PPE manufacturers.
3. For users.

(a) Suggestive Measures for Construction Site Managers/ Safety Managers

Considering the adverse impacts of accidents, construction safety management is of genuine concern to all stakeholders in the construction industry especially for personnel involved in safety management. Addressing construction safety, hazard identification and risk management is important concern. Hazard identification is fundamental to construction safety management, unidentified hazards present the most unmanageable risks. Three processes are important for construction managers such as "Find", "Assess" and "Fix". Hazard identification is the process used to identify all the possible situations in the workplace where people may be exposed to injury, illness or disease (Process 1: Find). Risk assessment is the process used to determine the likelihood that people may be exposed to injury, illness or disease in the workplace arising from any situation identified during the hazard identification process (Process 2: Assessment). Risk control is the process used to identify all practicable measures for eliminating or reducing the likelihood of injury, illness or disease in the workplace, to implement the measures and to continually review the measures in order to ensure their effectiveness (Process 3: Fix). To determine the best control measure, consideration must be made of the "hierarchy of controls" as follows:

- Eliminate the hazard wherever possible.
- Minimize the risk either by substitute, modify or introduce engineering controls.

- Back-up controls as administration of implement administrative controls and safe working practices—the use of written procedures or require Personal Protective Equipment (PPE).

Recommendations

Before work starts on site

Health and safety should be designed into constructions, before, during and after the building phase. It is cheaper and easier to control the risks to workers in construction before work starts on site, for example by:

- Putting in place a purchasing policy for machinery and work equipment (for example, buying tools with low noise and vibration emissions);
- Setting health and safety requirements in tender specifications (meeting national legislation as a minimum);
- Planning the work process to minimize the number of workers who could be harmed (for example, schedule noisy work when the least number of workers are likely to be exposed);
- Starting your control activities before getting to site (for example, by planning, training, site induction and maintenance activities);
- Setting down the procedures for effective consultation and participation of workers on OSH issues;
- Ensuring all persons, including managers, are trained and able to carry out their work without risk to the safety or health of themselves or other workers.

Management on site

Employers, with project supervisors, must cooperate and protect workers' health and safety. This can be achieved by:

- Conducting a walk-through of the area to identify sources of hazards to workers. Consider basic hazard categories such as fall, struck, caught, contact, and routes of entry for hazardous substances.
- Observing hazard sources i.e., motion, extreme temperatures, chemical sources and states, harmful dust, strong light radiation, falling or sharp objects, pinch points, electrical sources, workplace lay-out and location of work stations to determine possible exposure.
- Avoiding risks to all workers.
- Evaluating risks that cannot be avoided.
- Combating risks at source.
- Using collective measures to protect workers.
- Determining what PPE is available and what protection it offers.
- Obtaining advice on proper selection.
- Instituting workplace trials.
- Evaluating cost considerations of PPE usage.
- Ensuring PPE meets standards/certification.
- Selecting protective equipment that ensures a level of protection greater than the minimum required to protect workers from the hazards.
- Considering comfort and fit carefully.
- Reappraising PPE regularly to determine if the equipment provides adequate protection. Seeking worker input on any selected PPE.
- Establishing emergency procedures.
- Informing workers of the risks present and the necessary control measures.
- Ensuring appropriate training.

The control measures should be put in place and checks made to ensure that they are working and are meeting legal requirements.

(b) Suggestive Measures for PPE (Personal Protective Equipment) Manufacturers

The anthropometric data is used as reference data in planning ergonomic workplace lay-outs, in evaluating specification in determining dimensions for ergonomically sound product, thus enhancing operational ability, safety, convenience and comfort while performing tasks besides augmenting work efficiency and reducing work cost (Verghese, *et al.*, 1989).

Anthropometric data should be utilized in the design process on the basis of the behavioural aspects. To design a machine/workstation/tool for a single individual's need, his own body dimensions may be considered directly, but to design a machine or workstation for mass use and for mass production, proper percentile selections of the data and appropriate clearance allowances should be made. Percentiles are the statistical values of a distribution of variables transferred into a hundred scales. If 100 men lined up from least to greatest in any respect, percentiles are values corresponding to each man. In other words 5th man makes 5th percentile value, 50th man makes 50th percentile value and 95th man makes 95th percentile value and so on.

- Beside, using only one dimension for helmet designing as head circumference, head breadth, sub-mandibular arc and bitragion arc should be considered.
- The inner harness can be formed with adjustable head band with four/six or eight point textile tape suspension (instead of plastic) arrangement for better gripping. The head band shall have adjustable nape strap with lower extension to prevent dislodging.
- The helmet shall be made of ABS (Acrylo-Nitrile Butadine Styrene) grade material and light weight. The material which safety helmets are made of does deteriorate with age, therefore, it must be replaced after three years or earlier, if it has been subjected to an impact or other damage.

- The sweat band is made of brushed cloth provided over foam for absorption of sweat.
- The helmet shall have smooth finished surface and free from burrs and sharp edges with adjustable chin strap to prevent the helmet coming-off, if the wearer falls.
- The helmet shall have four vent holes at highest point on either sides to facilitate the flow of air for improved comfort and have provision for fitment of ear muff on either sides.
- Appropriate head clearance should be provided.
- Multi-positions for printing the company's logo can be provided.
- Percentile values of face measurements should be taken for designing eye and face protective equipment.
- Percentile values of hand and foot measurements should be considered for designing and sizing of hand gloves and boots.
- All PPE should be manufactured as per the appropriate industrial standards

Aspects Considered for Advising the Manufacture

- Anthropometric data
- Ergonomic design
- Convenience and comfort during use
- Quality and reliability, and
- Suitability under tropical conditions.

(c) Suggestive Measures for Users

It is recommended that consumers should use ergonomically sound user friendly protective equipments and should have adequate knowledge about when PPE is necessary; what PPE is necessary; how to properly put-on, take-off, adjust, and wear PPE; the limitations of the PPE, and the proper care, maintenance, useful life and disposal of the PPE.

Action Plan 2

Guidelines for Manufacturers involved in Pre-manufacturing

As Personal Protective Equipment (PPE) help to protect employees against work related injuries and illness, there are various problems that construction workers encountering in their regular use of PPE are as uncomfortable, and of improper size leads to many body related problems. Workers were often removing their gloves, helmet and hearing aid when feeling uncomfortable.

Taking above into consideration there is a need to develop ergonomically sound helmets and gloves for construction labours. For this first of all, the anthropometric measurements required for designing helmet and hand gloves should be taken with the appropriate instruments, so that the PPE will be accurately fitted to these people. The instruments should be used as:

- Anthropometric kit
- Sliding caliper
- Spreading caliper

Pictures of Instruments

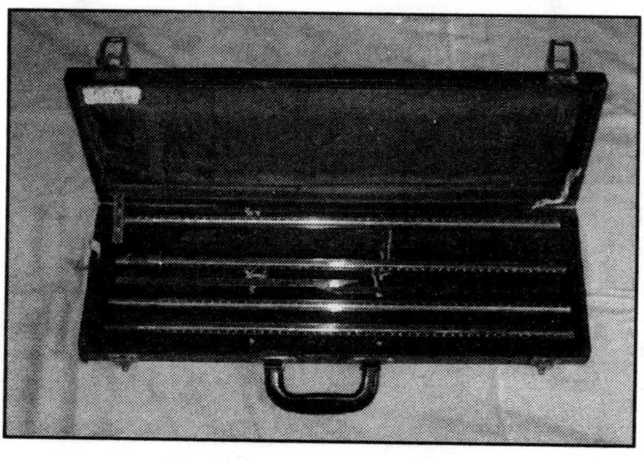

Plate 6: Anthropometric Kit.

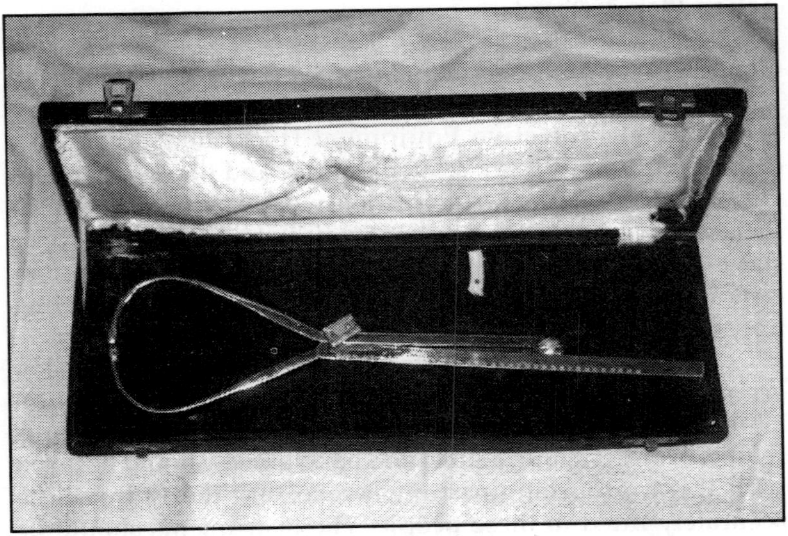

Plate 7: Spreading Caliper.

Plate 8: Sliding Caliper.

Pictures of Measurements for Helmet

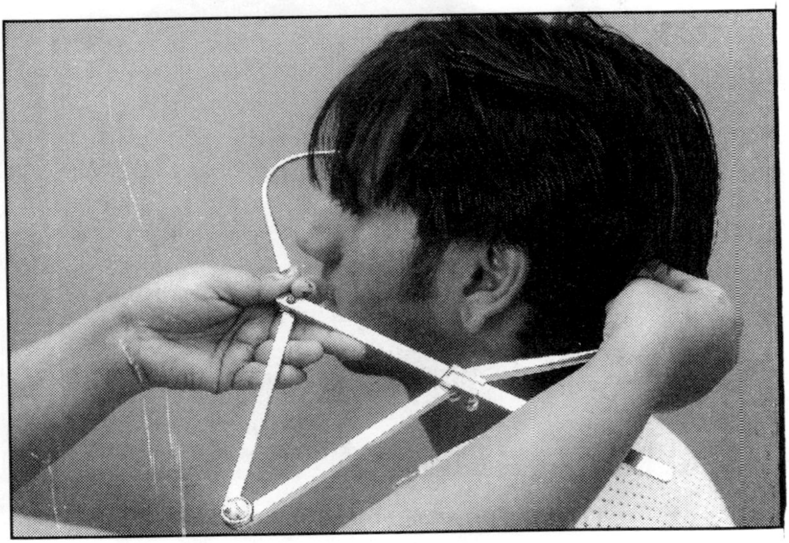

Plate 9: Measuring Head Length.

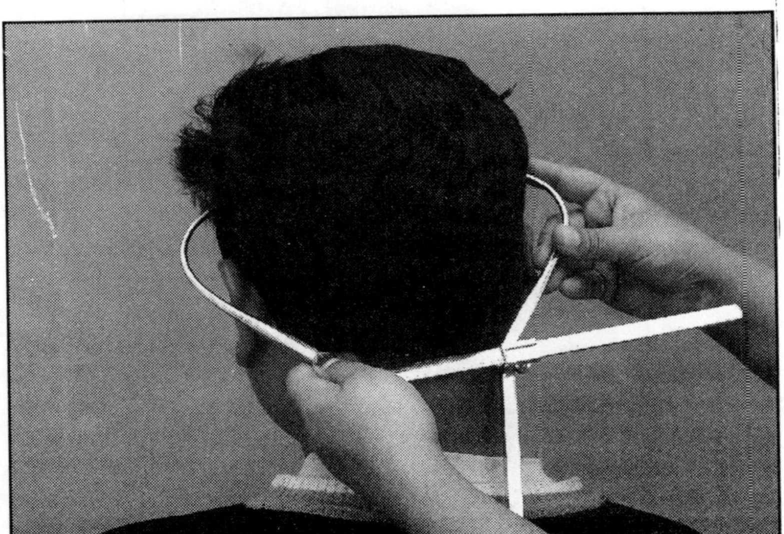

Plate 10: Measuring Head Breadth.

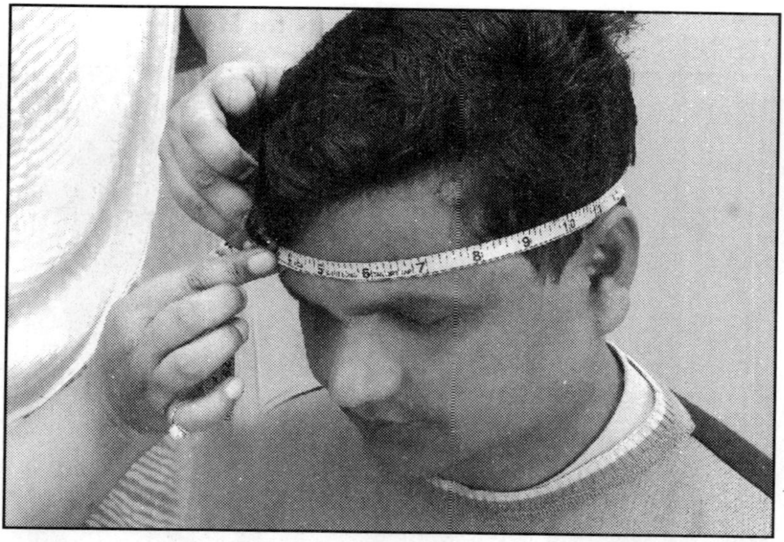

Plate 11: Measuring Head Circumference.

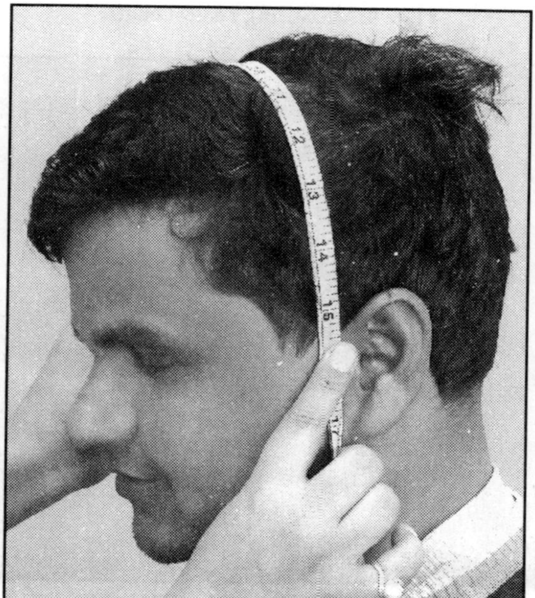

Plate 12: Measuring Bitragion Arc Length.

Pictures of Measurement for Hand Gloves

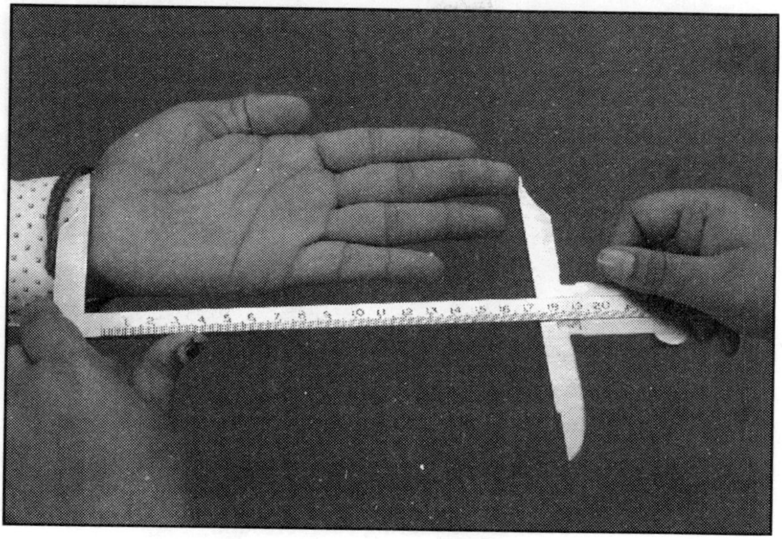

Plate 13: Measuring Hand Length.

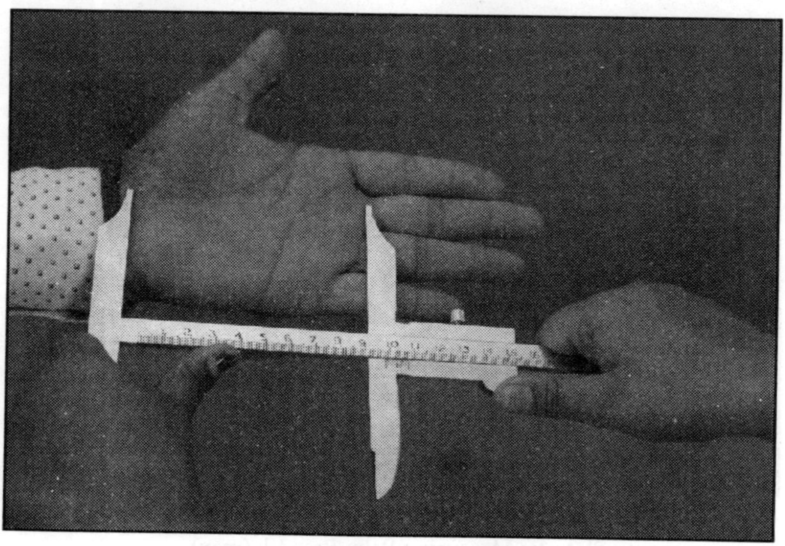

Plate 14: Measuring Palm Length.

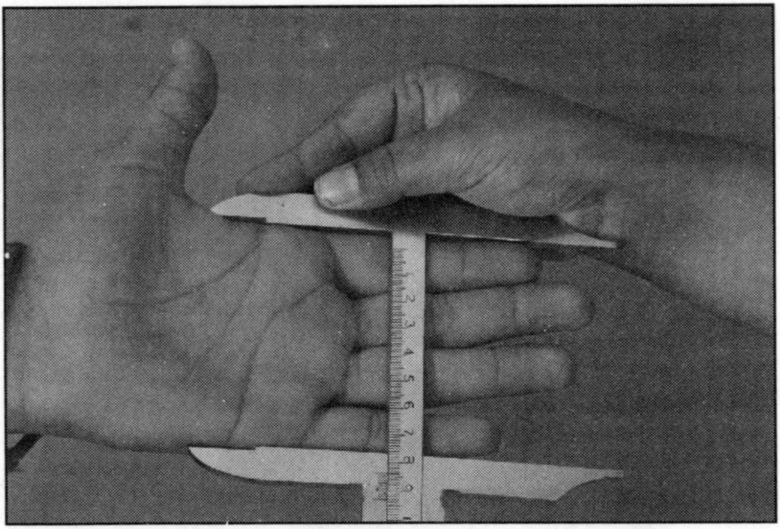

Plate 15: Measuring Palm Breadth.

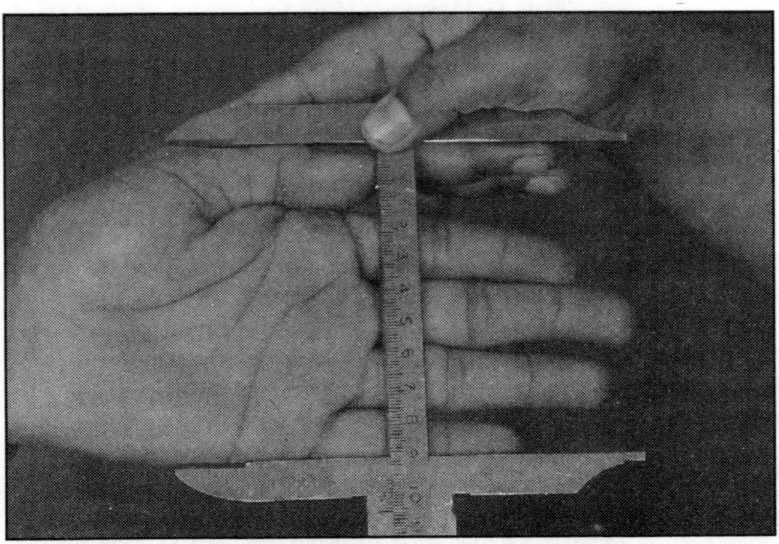

Plate 16: Measuring Palm Breadth (max).

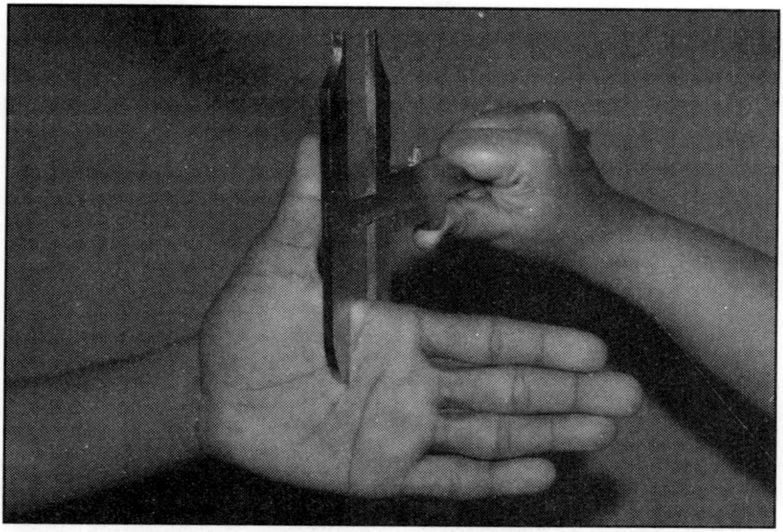

Plate 17: Measuring Hand Thickness.

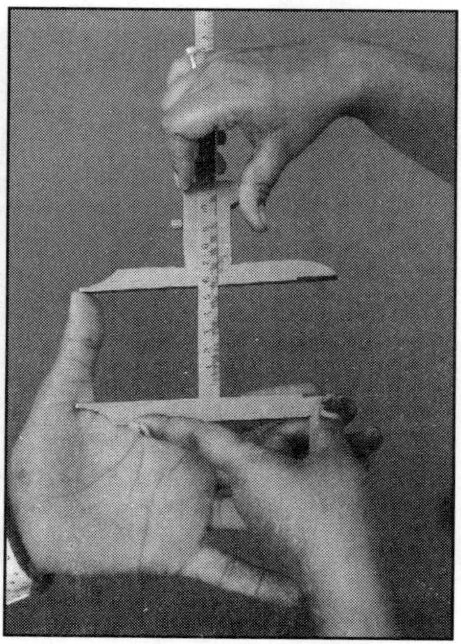

Plate 18: Measuring Thumb Length.

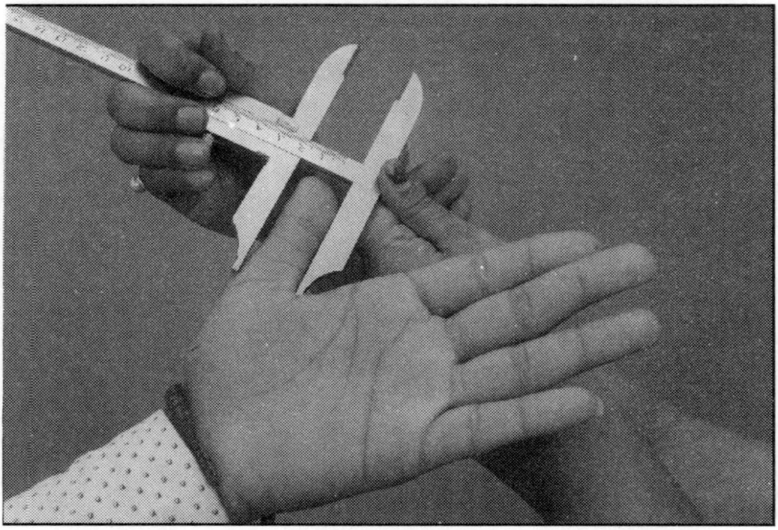

Plate 19: Measuring Thumb Width.

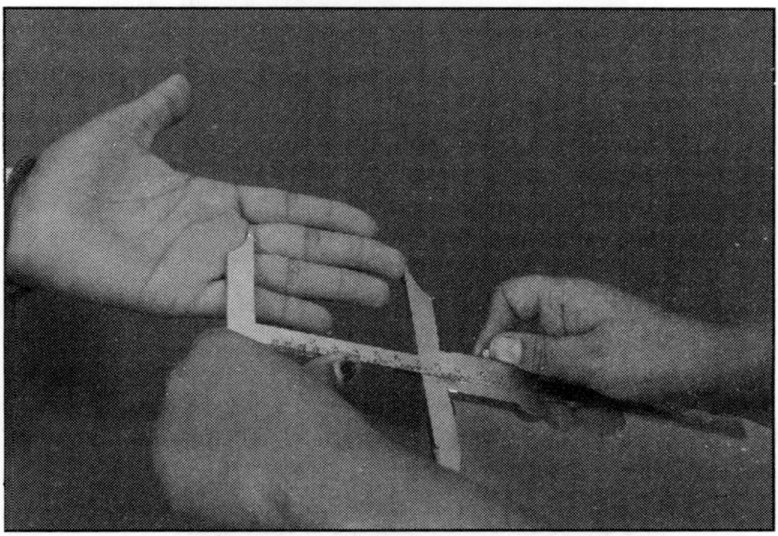

Plate 20: Measuring Finger Length.

Plate 21: Measuring Finger Width.

Percentile Values used for Designing

Measurement	*5th Percentile*	*50th Percentile*	*95th Percentile*
	For Helmet		
Head Length (For adjustable ratchet)			√
Head Breadth (For adjustable ratchet)			√
Bitragion Arc-40mm (For PVC net)			√
Head circumference (For adjustable ratchet)			√
	For Hand Gloves		
Size of Gloves	*Small*	*Medium*	*Large*
Hand Length	√	√	√
Palm Length	√	√	√
Palm Breadth	√	√	√
Palm Breadth (Max)	√	√	√
Thumb Length	√	√	√
Thumb Width	√	√	√
Finger Length	√	√	√
Finger Width	√	√	√

Method of Calculating Percentile

Calculation for 5th percentile: It is used to measure the minimum requirement with regard to dimension.
Calculation for 50th percentile: It is used to measure the average requirement with regard to dimension.
Calculation for 95th percentile: It is used to measure the maximum requirement with regard to dimension.

Formula for calculation:

$$Pp = \frac{L + PN - F}{Fp} \times i$$

where,

Pp = Required percentile rank.
L = Lowest value of the class interval where Pp falls.
PN = Cumulative frequency in relation to the Pp point.
F = Cumulative frequency below the lowest value of Pp class.
Fp = Actual frequency of Pp class.
i = Class interval.

Design Development through CAD

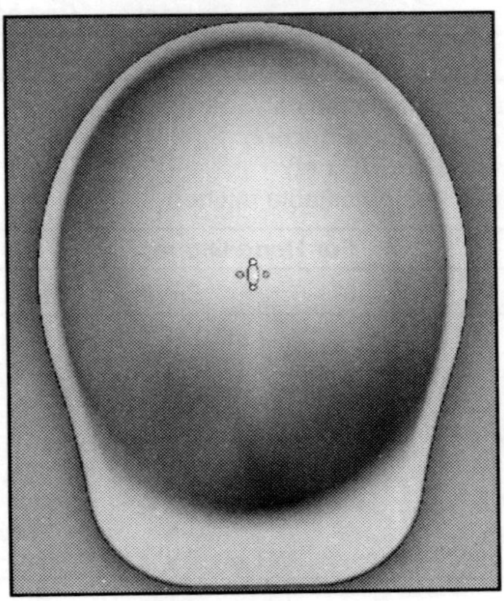

Plate 22: Top View of Helmet.

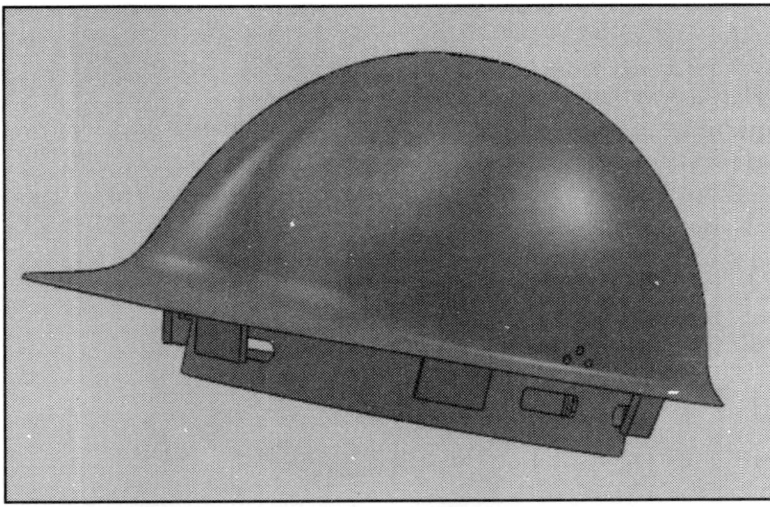

Plate 23: Side View of Helmet.

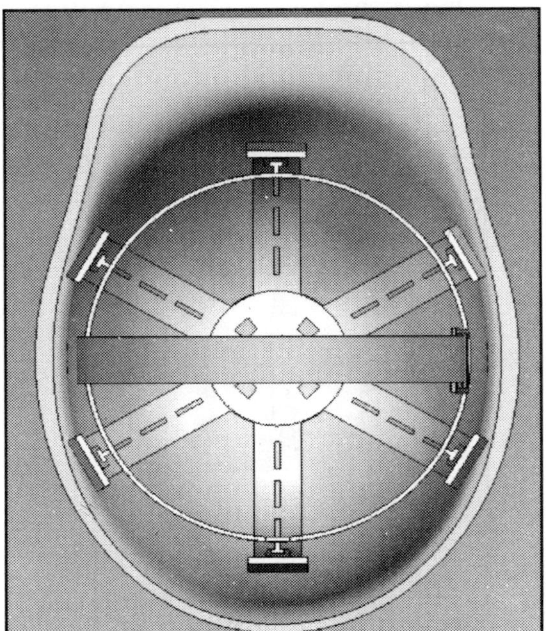

Plate 24: Internal View of Helmet.

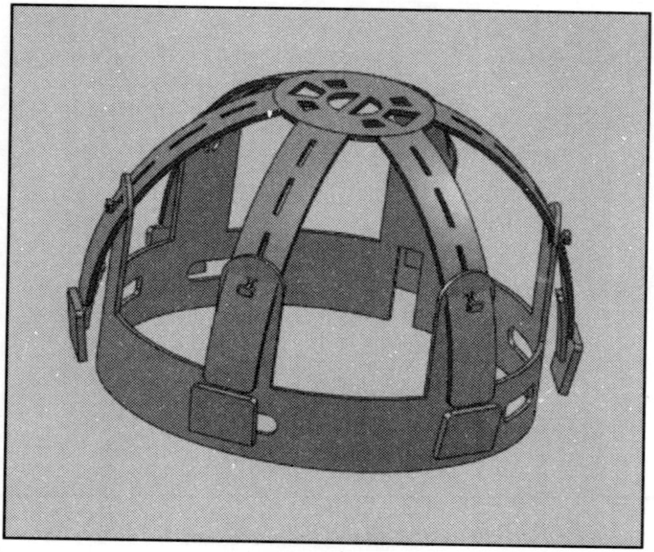

Plate 25: Ratchet with Suspension.

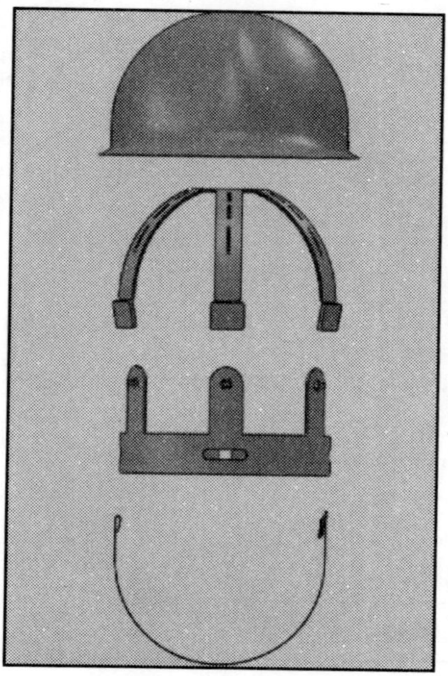

Plate 26: Loose Parts of Helmet.

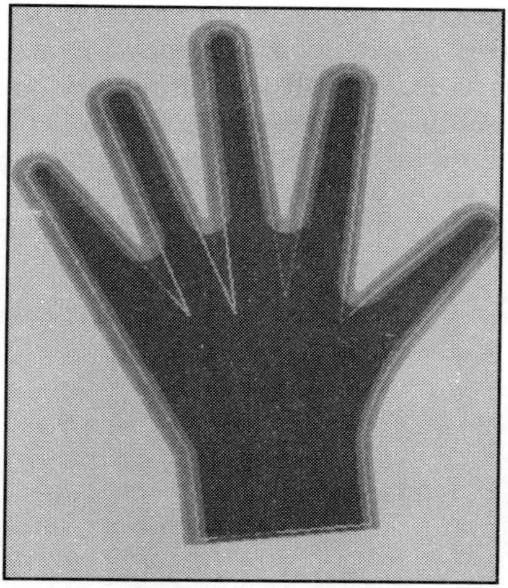

Plate 27: Isometric View of Hand Glove.

Action Plan 3

Safe Zone: Use PPE in Construction Industry Guide for Safety Managers

Being an unorganized sector, the fatal injury rate for the construction industry is higher than the national average in this category for all industries. A variety of hazards exist in the construction sites. The risks associated with these hazards are greatly reduced or eliminated, if proper precautions and practices are used. Some health and safety issues for construction workers are pain or injury from physical overexertion, repetitive manual tasks, or working in awkward positions, exposure to moulds, fungi or rodent droppings, exposure to lead, wood dust, asbestos, paints, solvents, and other toxic chemicals or materials, working in extreme temperatures and UV radiation, working with hand tools, powered tools and heavy powered equipment, excess vibration in the hands, arms or body from powered tools or equipment, confined spaces, noise, working at heights, electrical hazards, working with cranes, hoists, and other material handling equipment, falls, respiratory and fire hazards from wood dust, stress, shift work or extended work days. Excessive exposure to these hazards may result in acute injury, chronic illness, permanent disability or even death. Loss of concentration at work and fatigue arising from poor health conditions may increase the risk of accidents.

Plate 28: Construction Industry Guide for Safety Managers.

Hazard identification

Hazard can be defined as a physical or chemical characteristic that has the potential to cause harm to people, property and to the environment.

To prevent health hazards at work, all possible sources should be identified before commencement of construction work. Hazards at a construction site may come from hazardous substances used on site, and environmental variables may create additional risks as heat and noise.

Steps for prevention

Level 1: Eliminate the hazard wherever possible

Level 2: Minimize the Risk

- Substitute for something safer.
- Modify the plant, equipment, chemical or other items.
- Introduce engineering controls.

Level 3: Back-up controls

- Implement administrative controls and safe working practices—the use of written procedures.
- Require Personal Protective Equipment (PPE) to be used.

Whichever method of risk control is determined, ensure that the control does not contribute to the existing hazard or introduce a new hazard to the area. Also, after a period of time review the effectiveness of the control measure.

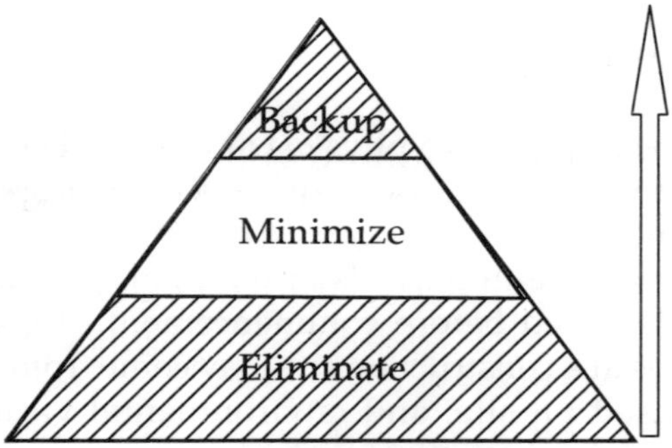

Steps for prevention.

Medical Surveillance

Medical surveillance is basically a system of monitoring the health status of workers engaged in hazardous occupations. The objective is to detect early signs of illness so that intervention may be taken to prevent permanent health damage. This is particularly useful for occupational illness with long latent period.

The examination should be done by a medical practitioner with sound knowledge in occupational medicine. It is recommended that in the construction industry should undertake pre-employment and periodic medical examination because they may have prolonged exposure to a high

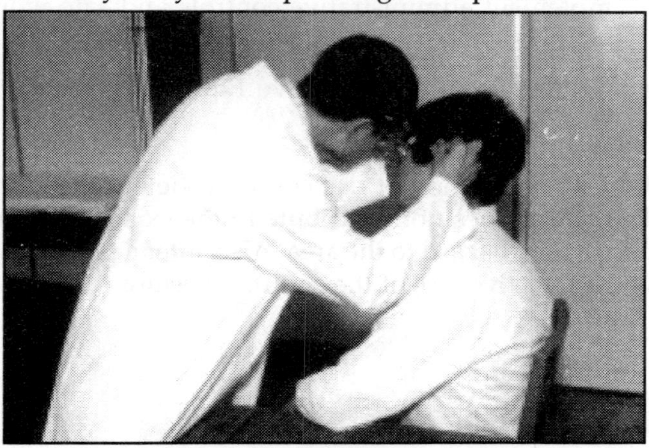

Plate 29: Medical Surveillance.

concentration/level of hazardous substances and/or physical agents.

Personal Protective Equipment (PPE)

PPE is an item or items used to protect the eyes, face, head, body, arms, hands, legs and feet such as goggles, helmets, head covers, gloves, coveralls, vests, safety shoes, protective shields, earplugs and respirators.

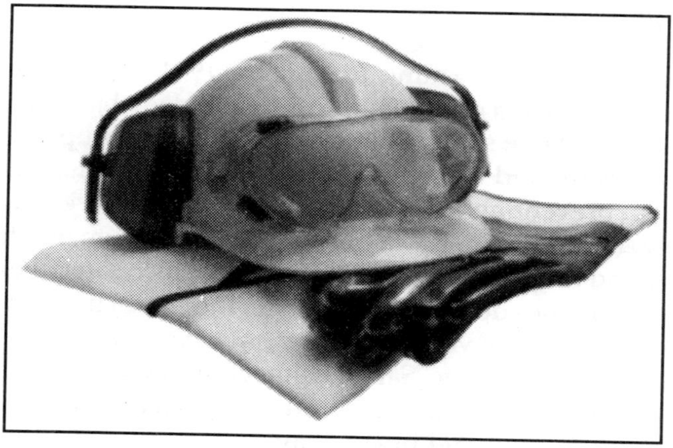

Plate 30: Personal Protective Equipments.

PPE must be provided as a last resort, when other measures cannot provide enough protection.

Selection of PPE

Where risk assessment has identified the need for PPE, the nature of the hazard predominantly influences the type of PPE to be chosen. Other factors which must be considered are:

- The environment in which it must be used,
- The length of time it will be used for,
- Any possible adverse effects on safety, for example, reduced hearing, limited peripheral vision, restricted movement,

- The characteristics of the individuals who will need to use it,
- Arrangements to support the use of PPE, e.g. adequate storage space, training, inspection, records, replacements, and the time and financial resources needed to do it properly.

Types and Standards (PPE)

Head protection

Safety helmets conforming to IS: 2925-1984 should be used whenever there is a risk of falling or suspended objects striking the head. Suitable safety helmets must be of appropriate size for the wearer and have adjustable headband. A chin strap is useful in preventing the helmet coming off if the wearer falls. However, welding helmets and welding hand shield should correspond to IS: 1179 -1967. The material which safety helmets are made of does deteriorate with age, therefore, they must be replaced after three years or if they have been subjected to an impact or other damage. Safety helmets should be stored away from direct sunlight, chemicals and extreme temperatures, and should not be modified in any way.

Plate 31: Head Protection.

Safety footwear

Shoes or boots with steel toecaps protect toes against crushing injuries from dropped objects or from injuries from impact or running over by heavy trolleys, etc. Footwear may also incorporate steel mid sole plate to protect from penetrating injuries.

Footwear should conform to IS: 5852-1996/IS: 11226-1993 (leather shoes with steel toe caps), IS: 12254-1993/IS: 13695-1993 (rubber/PVC knee boots/gum boots). In some circumstances footwear with slip resistant soles or waterproofing may be needed.

Plate 32: Safety Footwear.

Eye and face protection

Visors, face shields or safety glasses or goggles are used to protect against flying material causing injury Eye protection must confirm with IS: 5983-1980 which specifies the qualities of different types of protection as chemical, dust, mists etc.

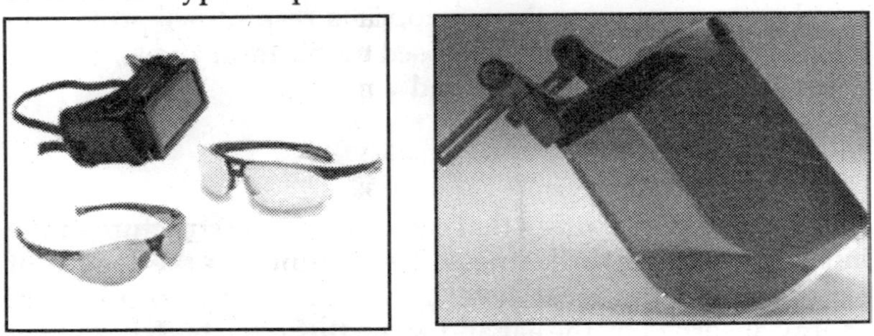

Plate 33: Eyes and Face Protection.

Hand protection

Gloves of different types can be used to protect against a range of hazards such as extreme temperatures, corrosive materials, toxic chemicals, infection risks, sharp or abrasive materials, solvents and even tools which generate excessive vibration. The risk assessment should specify what type/s of glove is necessary and the assessor must also consider the needs of the wearer in the activities which are hazardous. Dexterity, grip, fit and comfort are important.

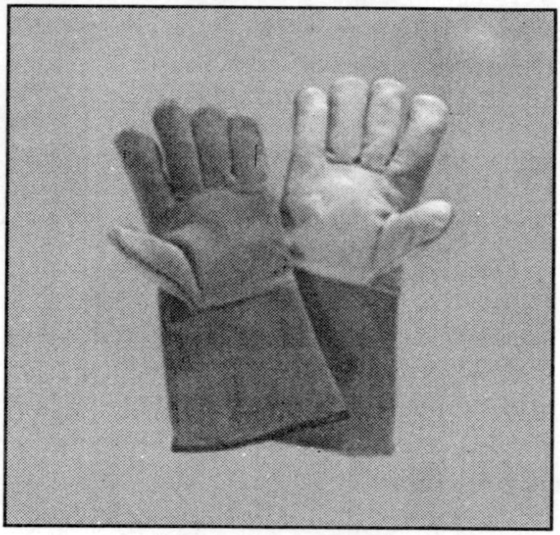

Plate 34: Hand Protection.

Respiratory protection

Employees must wear the appropriate respiratory protection when employees may be exposed to harmful dusts, fumes, gases, mists, smokes, sprays and vapours.

Hearing protection

Noise is a form of energy that can damage the structure of the inner ear leading to deafness. The product of the length of exposure and the noise level gives the amount of physical energy absorbed by the ear and when this is too high it is likely that cumulative damage will occur. Employees must provide and ensure that employees wear the appropriate hearing protection when noise levels in various workplaces exceed 85dB (A) there is a significant risk of noise induced hearing loss over a period of time. Ear muffs (re-usable) and ear plugs-disposable (with manufactures specifications against the type of noise) can be used.

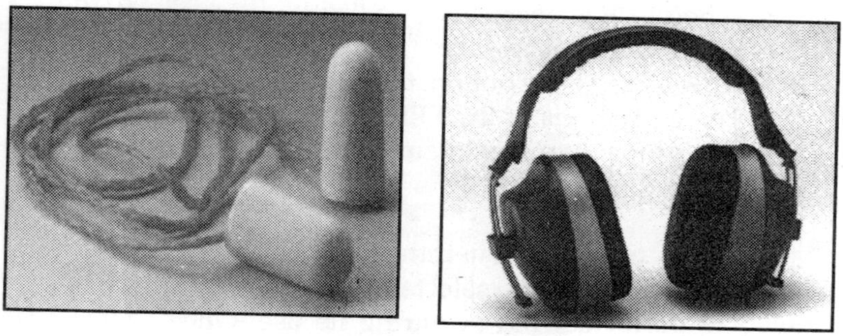

Plate 35: Hearing Protection.

Fall Protection

For fall protection safety harness must be used.

Plate 36: Fall Protection.

Training

The employer shall provide training to each employee who is required to use PPE. Each such employee shall be trained to know at least the following:

- When PPE is necessary
- What PPE is necessary
- How to properly put on, take off, adjust, and wear PPE
- The limitations of the PPE, and
- The proper care, maintenance, useful life and disposal of the PPE.

Workers must demonstrate that they understand and have the ability to use the selected PPE properly before being allowed to perform work requiring its use. Once training is accomplished, the employer shall verify that each affected employee has received and understood the required training.

5

Summary and Conclusion

Construction is one of the largest industry in India, employing over 7.6 million workers, or about 5 per cent of the Indian work-force. In construction industry, workers may or may not be migrant workers but the fact is that they have maximum mobility because of the nature of their occupation. They are always on move from one work-site to another after the construction work at a site is over. Majority of all fatal on-the-job injuries occur in construction.

Construction workers face some of the most dangerous working conditions in the country on a daily basis. Although there are regulations, statutes, ordinances and industry standards that mandate employers to provide a reasonably safe working environment, thus, the construction workers suffer from serious injuries at an alarming rate. The sheer number of hazards on a construction site makes it virtually impossible to prevent all injuries from occurring. These hazards include falls from scaffolds and other elevations, being struck by moving or falling machinery, electrocution, health hazards resulting from exposure to asbestos and chemicals, injuries caused by defective or unsafe equipment, and lifting and repetitive motion injuries. Construction industry accounts for the highest number of workers' fatalities of any industry. Other hazards posed by construction sites include exposure to noise, dust and other chemicals, working from high elevations and in confined spaces, working with power tools and other mechanical equipment, exposure to electricity and performing excavations. Moreover, the companies are not ready to compensate with employees having partial and full injuries, and are not covered by life insurance. Adequate accident relief equipment like helmets, hand gloves and shoes, safety belts, protection eye wear etc, safety materials and equipment should be provided to the construction workers.

The present study indicates the plight of the construction workers in Delhi/NCR. Majority of construction workers are migrated labourer from different regions from India. Migration from different states to other states in India has now become so rampant that its impact is felt in every aspect of life. Migration becomes a way of life to many, who are unskilled and semi-skilled and find it difficult to get better jobs in their native places. These migrant workers are spread across the width and length of the country. Construction workers are labourers who are migrated from different regions and states leaving their native villages in search of daily job. These people in general are nomadic in their life and usually do not return to their birthplace or natives. They work under very hazardous conditions. The working conditions and the facilities provided at the sites are far from satisfactory. Safety conditions and measurers are hardly met. Certain research oriented questions like weather, hazard present in site, postural assessment of construction workers, identification of suitable PPE for hazard prevention, discomfort from PPE use, noise, illumination, vibration and respiratory hazards in construction area etc. Therefore, in quest to seek answers to some of these queries the present study was envisaged on the topic entitled, "Ergonomic Assessment of Personal Protective Equipment in Relation to Occupational Health and Safety of Construction Workers" was undertaken with the following specific objectives:

- To study the demographic profile of construction workers.
- To assess existing conditions in terms of activity profile i.e., type of task, duration of task and frequency of performance, and occupational health hazards of construction workers with and without the use of PPE.
- To study physiological, psychological and situational attributes of construction workers.

- To validate PPE in terms of dimensions of anthropometric data of users, comfort and ease in use and redesigning of selected PPE through CAD and supplying of information to manufacturers.

In the present study descriptive-cum-experimental research design was chosen. Various tools like interview schedule, checklist, experimental table, worksheets, discomfort rating scale, Borg General Scale (1982), Software: DB-2004/ master_cvndb1.mdb and BPL ARPEMIS, and various instruments such as anthropometric kit, lactate instrument, vibration meter, noise level meter, thermohygrometer, spirometer, lux meter, weighing machine, REBA worksheet were used for data collection.

A list of employees was taken from corresponding administrative department of the company. A total of 300 construction workers were present at construction site including basic construction work, laser operations, power tool operations, involvement in gas cutting, installation work, and safety management and supervision staff. The random sampling technique without replacement was chosen. The data were collected in two different phases, i.e. in Phase-I, the descriptive data using interview schedule, checklist and REBA worksheet and in Phase-II, the experimental data was collected. Twenty respondents from each worker category for field survey and 5 from each category for field experiments were taken, thus making a total of 120 samples for descriptive data and 30 (25%) for experimental purpose.

All the responses received on the data sheet were categorized and analyzed using both descriptive (frequency, percentage, average, percentile, standard deviation, and weighted mean score) and the relational statistics (Chi-square and ANOVA) were computed.

Results of the study

The mean age of basic construction workers, respondents engaged in laser operations, gas cutting, installation, power tool users and, safety managers and supervisors were 27 ±2.47 years, 28.95 ±3.17 years, 30.9 ±2.41 years, 30.2 ±1.78 years, 33.95 ±2.17 years and 29.9 ±1.57 years, respectively. In case of educational qualification construction workers were very low literacy rate and majority of them i.e., 41.67 per cent were illiterate. About 23.33 per cent and 14.17 per cent of construction workers were educated up to primary and middle school, respectively and very few respondents had studied up to intermediate (5.83%) and graduation level (7.5%). However, all safety managers and supervisors were educated up to graduation level or more. When income of construction workers was estimated, it was found that 42.5 per cent were earning less than Rs. 5,000 per month and approximately 19 per cent and 14 per cent of workers were getting income in the range of Rs. 5,000—7,500 and Rs. 7,500—10,000 per month. Only a few proportion of respondents i.e., 7.5 per cent were in the earning category of Rs. 10,000—15,000 per month and 16.8 per cent of construction workers were getting ≥ Rs. 15,000 per month.

As far as native place of respondents were concerned, it was evident that a commendable proportion of workers (92.50%) were migrated from U.P. East, Bihar, Jharkhand and West Bengal.

The occupational detail revealed that multiple activities are performed by workers as 45 per cent and 20 per cent of workers were engaged in either basic construction activities (loading/unloading of materials, mixing, concreting, scaffolding etc.) and installation work, respectively. However, skilled construction labourers were engaged in laser operations such as welding and soldering (16.67%), cutting and sawing (16.67%) and power tool operations (18.33%). Approximately 16 per cent of skilled workers belonged to supervisory and management group. Regarding duration of activity, it was found from the study that basic construction work, power tool operations, installation and management were long duration task because these were performed for more than 1 hr. daily, and welding and cutting was performed for 15 min to 1 hr. in each trial daily and categorized as moderate task.

About 45 per cent of respondents were suffered from common illnesses as cough, cold and fever which was reported temporary in nature. However, continuous occurrence of cough, cold and fever were also reported by few respondents. Occurrence of headache, bodyache, irritation in eyes were also reported as 70 per cent, 75.83 per cent and 91.67 per cent of respondents, respectively which were predominantly reported as temporary in nature.

Data related to chronic illnesses as diabetes mellitus, heart problem, B.P. problem and occupation induced illnesses such as respiratory problem, stiffness in hand joint, cuts and wounds, numbness in body and tingling in hands were also reported by respondents.

Data regarding nicotine consumption revealed that 55.83, 48.33 and 24.16 per cent of respondents were engaged in snuffing/chewing tobacco, smoking (beedies and/or cigarettes) and alcohol consumption, respectively.

PFI score indicated that good PFI in 55 per cent basic construction workers, 70 per cent laser operators, 35 per cent in those who involved in cutting/sawing, 60 per cent in power tool users, 45 per cent in workers involved in installation and 30 per cent in management staff. It could, therefore, be concluded that most of them were having high average to very good level of physical fitness.

The mean rating of perceived exertion ranged from 3.77 to 5.8 on the basis of verbal expression of fatigue. High RPE score of 8.8 was found during power tool operations whereas the lowest score of 3.77 was found during welding activity.

The mean height of construction workers was 165.13 cm and average weight was 57.36 kg. Mean values of head length, head breadth, head height, head circumference, bitragion arc length, sagital arc length and sub-mandibular arc of construction workers were 18.19, 14.46, 16.95, 54.53, 33.79, 34.44 and 26.28 cm, respectively. The average face length-menton to brow, face length-menton to naison, face breadth and jaw width were 10.95, 10.12, 11.62 and 9.98 cm, respectively. Hand anthropometry is essential for designing and sizing of gloves. Mean values of hand anthropometric dimensions (cm) were found as hand length (18.62), palm breadth (9.35), palm breadth-max (10.67), palm length (10.43), thumb length (6.68), thumb width (2.29), finger length-middle finger (7.95), finger width-middle finger (2.28) and hand thickness (3.16) cm. Feet dimensions i.e. mean foot length and foot breadth were found to be 24.24 cm and 11.69 cm, respectively.

As far as mechanical and non-mechanical hazards are concerned, it was found that most of the construction workers (non-PPE users) agreed that they are exposed to mechanical hazards such as impact from falling objects and falling parts, penetration through nails and scrap metal/sharp objects. Non-mechanical hazards such as chemical, electrical, thermal, heat and water were also more in case of non-PPE wearer. In addition to it, other hazards such as working at height, vibration and noise, and radiation exposure were less encountered to PPE users as 21 per cent, 11 per cent, 18 per cent and 21 per cent only. It was further found that most of the respondents agreed that hazards present in construction sites could not be eliminated without the use of PPE that might be used by the workers in construction industry to protect them from occupational injuries and infections.

Results of REBA postural analysis show that, a sum total of 31.16 per cent construction workers were in AL_2 (medium risk level and change is required soon) followed by 28.33 per cent workers in AL_3 (high risk and action necessary now), 21.66 per cent in AL_1 (low risk, further action may be needed), and only 14.16 per cent of workers were in AL_0 indicating 'negligible' risk level means no action is necessary (acceptable posture).

The discomfort felt with PPE was due to poor fit (55.66%), blocking the evaporation of sweat (63.33%), irritation in skin (52%), skin got red (45%) and insulated PPE encourage heat accumulation in body (42%). Other perceived discomfort were restricting movement (13.33%), restricting visibility due to helmet (28.33%), gloves reducing grip strength (35%), gloves limiting movements of fingers (20%), glare in eyes due to laser operations (20%), and no provision of individual alteration to clothing (36.66%).

As far as vibration analysis of power tool operators in construction industry is concerned, it was found that majority of power tool operators (65%) were working with vibrating tools from 6-10 years. The tools present at site were cutter, sander and/or polisher, breaker/driller, hammer drill, saw and grinder. The workers experiencing vibration hazard syndrome in form of changing colour of fingers, tingling in hands and numbness were reported by 55 per cent, 65 per cent and 55 per cent of respondents, respectively.

All the measured environmental variables such as hot climate (temperature), humidity, increased noise level (nearly upper limit of exposure) and adequate illumination were higher at construction site.

Data regarding physiological cost of work showed per cent increase in heart rate, energy expenditure rate and blood pressure were maximum in basic construction activity i.e., loading/unloading and minimum in management work. Both left and right hand's muscular grip strength was reduced after work performance. In addition to it, owing to the use of gloves, per cent change in grip strength was showing more reduction. Further, spirometry analysis of basic construction workers showed borderline obstacles to severe obstacles in respiratory tract.

For vibration severity FFT and waveform analysis (on vertical, horizontal and axial region) and OA values on axial direction (velocity, acceleration, displacement and E_3) were calculated. The results regarding velocity and enveloped acceleration (E_3) were evaluated on the basis of ISO vibration evaluation standards and bearing evaluation resulting danger (velocity basis), and satisfactory to danger level (E_3).

Lactate analysis report of basic construction workers showed marked increase in blood lactate level from resting to after activity, indicating lactic acid accumulation in blood leading to fatigue.

Conclusion

On the basis of findings of this investigation, the following conclusions were drawn:

(i) The mean age of basic construction workers, respondents engaged in laser operations, gas cutting, installation, power tool users and, safety managers and supervisors were 27 ±2.47, 28.95 ±3.17, 30.9 ±2.41, 30.2 ±1.78, 33.95 ±2.17 and 29.9 ±1.57 years, respectively.

(ii) The income details revealed that the mean income of basic construction workers, persons involved in laser operations, gas cutting, handling power tools, and installation and, safety management and supervision were 4,480 ±3.52 Rs., 4,750 ±2.74 Rs., 4,075 ±3.16 Rs., 7,450 ±2.56 Rs., 4,375 ±7.35 Rs. and 18,850 ±3.85 Rs. per month.

(iii) Most of the workers were migrated from East U.P., Bihar, Jharkhand and West Bengal.

(iv) Basic construction activities, laser operations, gas cutting, power tool operations, installation, and safety management and supervision work were performed by workers at site.

(v) Although, most of the construction workers were engaged in snuffing/chewing tobacco, smoking (beedies and/or cigarettes) and alcohol consumption, yet most of them were having high average to very good level of physical fitness.

(vi) On the basis of rate of perceived exertion, high RPE score was found during power tool operations, whereas the lowest score was found during laser operations.

(vii) Various mechanical and non-mechanical hazards exposure as impact from falling objects and falling parts, penetration through nails and scrap metal/sharp objects, chemical, electrical, thermal, heat and water were present at site with higher intensity in case of non-PPE wearer.

(viii) It was further found that most of the respondents agreed that hazards present at construction sites could not be eliminated without the proper use of PPE.

(ix) As per REBA postural analysis, most of the construction workers were in AL_2 (medium risk level and change is required soon).

(x) The problems with regular use of PPE associated discomfort was poor fit, blocking the evaporation of sweat, irritation in skin, skin got red, insulated PPE encourages heat accumulation in body, restricting movement, restricting visibility, reduced grip strength, limiting movements of fingers, glare in eyes etc.

(xi) Majority of power tool operators (65%) were working with vibrating tools from 6-10 years. The tools present at site were cutter, sander and/or polisher, breaker/driller, hammer drill, saw and grinder.

(xii) Most of the workers experienced vibration hazard syndrome in the form of changing colour of fingers, tingling in hands and numbness.

(xiii) Per cent increase in heart rate, energy expenditure rate and blood pressure were maximum in basic construction activity i.e., loading/unloading and minimum in management work.

(xiv) Both left and right hand's muscular grip strength was reduced after work performance. Moreover, owing to the use of gloves, per cent change in grip strength showed higher reduction.

(xv) Spirometry analysis of basic construction workers showed borderline obstacles to severe obstacles in respiratory tract.

(xvi) FFT and waveform analysis showed maximum velocity on Z-axis and OA (overall) values on axial direction were in the range of satisfactory to danger level (E_3), and velocity on danger category.

(xvii) Lactate analysis report of basic construction workers showed marked increase in blood lactate level from resting to after activity, indicating lactic acid accumulation in blood resulting in fatigue.

(xviii) The anthropometric measurements related to designing and sizing of PPE tools were taken. On the basis of such measurements selected PPE (helmet and gloves) were designed through CAD.

The study brought out a number of important implications such as:

(i) ***For Safety Managers*****:** This study will help the safety managers who are involved in planning, controlling and executing work on construction sites.

(ii) ***For Manufacturers*****:** The findings of the study may provide some useful data for those who are manufacturing protective equipment for industrial safety about kind of features to be incorporated for better quality and comfort.

(iii) ***For Users*****:** This study will also help the users to make them aware about hazards and risk encountered at site and to know prevention technique to combat with the hazards.

Scope for Future Research

1. The recommendations of present study can be further tested with large sample size for better feasibility and reliability of results.
2. A similar study can be conducted on female construction workers for designing PPE for them.
3. Subjective feelings of stress and psychological problems can also be included.
4. Experimental structures of protective equipment as per the recommendations of present study can be built and subjects can be studied under controlled conditions for better reliability and implication of results.
5. Study can be conducted to find out extra features that can be incorporated to enhance its comfortability.

Bibliography

Aaras, A. and Westgaurd, R.H. (1988). "The effect of improved workplace design on the environment of work-related musculo-skeletal illness." *Applied Ergonomics,* 16: 91-97.

Adams, D.; Plessis, A.G.; Gumbie, A. and Willis, R.P.H. (2007). *Introduction to Safety Practice in South African Mines.* Braamfontien. Creda Communication. *e-reference.*http://www.answers.com/topic/protective-clothing?cat= health. (Retrieved on 27th August, 2007)

Akbar-Khanzadeh, F.; Bisesi, M. S.; Rivas, R.D. (1995). "Comfort of personal protective equipment." *Appl Ergon.* Jun, 26(3):195-8. PubMedresult.mht. (Retrieved on 26th November, 2008)

Anonymous (1986). "Lactic acid evaluation in energy contribution." *Br Jnl Sp Med,* 10, 197-201.

Anonymous (2007). "Improving the procedures for the selection and use of PPE at work." *e-reference.* workzonesafety_org. mht. (Retrieved on 12th July, 2007)

Bill, M. (2002). *Safety Equipment companies strive to make PPE accessible at job sites,* published in ISEA newsletter-protection update Fall-2002. North Moore Street Arlington, USA.

Boocock, M.G.; Jackson, J.A.; Burton, A.K. and Tillotson, K.M. (1994). "Continuous measurement of lumber spinal posture using flexible electrogonionmetres." *Ergonomics,* 37: 175-85.

Brantingham, C.R.; Beekman, B.E.; Moos, C.N. and Gordon, R.B. (1970). "Enhanced venous pump activities as a result of standing on a varied terrain floor surface." *J. Occupational Med,* 12: 164-69.

Brent Doney (2007). *Health concerns and Personal Protective Equipment (PPE) use in roadway construction,* paper presentation in Work Zone Conferences-2007. *e-reference* workzonesafety_org.mht. (Retrieved on 23rd March, 2008).

Burdorf, A.; Derksen, J.; Naaktgeboren, B. and Riel, M.V. (1991). "Measurement of trunck bending during work by direct observation and continuous measurement." *Appl Ergonomics,* 23(4): 263-67.

Bureau of Labour Statistics, U.S. Department of Labour, 2004.

Chaffin, D. B. (1977). "Localized muscle fatigue definition and measurement." *J. Occupational Med,* 15: 346-54.

Chakrabarti, D. (1997). "Ergonomics of the design of products, equipments and accessories." *Indian Journal of Indus Med,* 20 (2): 49-63.

Chol, Sang D.; Hudson, L.; Kangas, P.; Brett, J.; Maple, J.; and Bowen, C. (2007). "Personal Protective Equipment use in heavy construction." *e-reference.* workzonesafety_org/ppeclothing.mht. (Retrieved on 12th April, 2007).

Corelette, E.N.; Haslegrave, C.M. and Tracy, M.F. (1998). "Force exertion in awkward working postures." *Ergonomics,* 41: 1335-62.

Cornell High Energy Synchrotron Source (2007). *Personal Protective Equipment.* Cornell University. *e-reference.* http www.chess.cornell.edu/safety/manual/chptr5/prtclthg.htm. (Retrieved on 18th July, 2007).

De Looze, M.P.; Toussaint, H.M.; Ensink, J. and Mangus, C. (1994). "The validity of visual observation to assess posture in laboratory-stimulated manual material handling task." *Ergonomics,* 37: 1335-43.

Dewangan, K.N.; Prasanakumar, G.V.; Sujap, L.; and Chaudhary, M.D. (2005). "Anthropometric dimensions of farm youth of the north eastern region of India." *International Journal of Industrial Ergonomics,* 11: 979-989.

Dhyani, V. (2007). *Ergonomic studies on modes of carrying load by hill women.* Ph.D. Thesis, G.B. Pant University of Agriculture and Technology, Pantnagar, India.

Dong, R.G.; Rakheja, S.; Schopper, A.W.; Han, B. and Smutz, W.R. (2001). "Hand-transmitted vibration and biodynamic response of the human hand arm: a critical review." *Critical Reviews in Engineering,* 29 (4), 393-439.

Donna, McPherson (2007). *Top workplace safety issues and accidents in construction, safetyknowledgenetwork@kcc. com. e-reference* (Retrieved on 12th April, 2007)

Donna, McPherson (2008). *PPE compliance in the workplace: A continuing concern. safetyknowledgenetwork@kcc.com. e-reference* (Retrieved on 28th July, 2007).

European Commission (2002). "Work and health in EU. A statistical portrait. Data 1994-2004, European Commission." Cited in Margarita, V.; Joaquin, L.S.; Pablo, R. and Antonio, P.G. (2008). "Hand transmitted vibration in power tools: Accomplishment of standards and user's perception." *International Journal of Industrial Ergonomics,* 38: 652-660.

European Committee for Standardization Report (2007). "Personal Protective Equipment (PPE)—Test and evaluation" Ref. No.:CWA 15756:2007 D/E/F Management Centre: rue de Stassart, 36 B-1050 Brussels.

Farhang, A.K. (1998). "Factors contributing to discomfort or dissatisfaction as a result of wearing personal protective equipment," *Journal of human ergology*, 27, nº1-2, 70-75.

Fraser, T.M. (1980). "Ergonomic principles in the design of hand tools. Occup Safety and Health Series No. 44." Geneva: *International Labour Office*, p. 93.

Gangopadhyay, S. and Bandopadhyay, T. (1999). "Ergonomic study on analysis of normal activities of Indian women in kitchen." *Calcutta Univ. Calcutta Biomedicine*, 19: 123-28.

Garrett, J.W. (1971). "The adult human hand: some anthropo-metric and biomechanical considerations." *Hum Factors*, 13: 117-31.

Genaidy, A.M. and Karwowski, W. (1993). "The effect of neutral posture deviations on perceived joint discomfort rating in sitting and standing postures." *Ergonomic*, 36: 785-92.

Gite, L.P. and Yadav, B.G. (1989). "Anthropometric survey for agricultural machinery design: An Indian case study." *Applied Ergonomics*, 20 (3):191-196.

Grandjean, E. (1980). *Fitting the task to the man—an ergonomic approach.* Taylor and Francis Ltd., London, 77-81.

Grandjean, E. (ed.) (1988). *Fitting the Task to the Man—A textbook of Occupational Ergonomics*. Taylor and Francis Inc., London 35-36.

Greenland, K.B.; Tsui, D.; Goodyear, P.; Irwin, M.G. (2007). "Personal protection equipment for biological hazards: does it affect tracheal intubation performance?" *Resuscitatio*, Jul; 74(1):119-26.

Griffin, M.J. (1990). *Handbook of human vibration*. Academic Press Limited, London, 39-46.

Gross, I.H. and Crandall, E.W. (1973). *Management for modern families.* 3rd ed. Century Crafts, New York.

Guild, R.; Enrich, R.L.; Johnston, J.C.; and Ross, M.H. (2001). *SIMRAC: Handbook of occupational health practice in the South African mining industry*. Braamfontien. SIMRAC: Lippincott.

Hanson, M.A. (1999). "Development of a draft British standard: the assessment of heat strain for workers wearing Personal Protective Equipment." *Ann. Occup. Hyg.*, Vol. 43, No. 5, 309-319.

Haslegrave, C.M. (1994). "What do we mean by a working posture?" *Ergonomics*, 37(4): 781-99.

Hattingh, S.P. and Accut, J. (2003). *Occupational health management and practice for health practitioners.* Landadowe: Juta.

Hecker, S.; Gambatese, J.; and Weinstein, M. (2005). "Designing for Worker Safety," *Professional Safety*, September, 32-44.

Hignett, McAtamney (2000). "Rapid Entire Body Assessment (REBA)." *Applied Ergonomics*, 31, 201-205.

Holmer, I.; Nilsson, H.; Rissanen, S.; Hirata, K.; and Smolander, J. (1992). "Quantification of heat balance during work in three types of asbestos-protective clothing." *Int. Arch. Occup. Environ. Health,* 64, 243-249.

ISEA Report (2002). *Working to prevent injuries and save lives in road construction. e-reference.* ISEA.workzonesafety_org. mht. (Retrieved on 23rd Nov., 2007).

Keyserling, W.M.; Armstrong, T.J. and Puneet, L. (1988). "Ergonomic job analysis: a structure approach for identifying risk factors associated with overexertion injuries." *Applied Occup Envir Hyg,* 6: 253-63.

Koppes, B. and Pearson, G.(2002). *Is Your high-visibility apparel working for you,* published in ISEA newsletter-protection update Fall-2002. North Moore Street Arlington, USA.

Kreifeldt, J.G. (1991). "Application of ergonomics in product designing." *Proc. International Symposium on Ergonomics,* Occupational Health Safety and Environment, held at 1st Dec. IIT, Bombay, India.

Larson, D. and Hannihen (1995). "Surface electromyography: research clinical and sports applications." *Indian J. Physio Allied Sci.,* 49: 5-9.

Love, R.G.; Johnstone, J.G.; Crawford, J.; Tesh, K.M.; Graveling, R.A.; Ritchie, P.J.; Hutchison, P.A. and Wetherill, G.Z. (1996). *Study of the physiological effects of wearing breathing apparatus.* Home Office, London, (FRDG Publication No. 13/96).

Mansfield, N.J. (2006). "Filling the gap between manufacturers' declared values and hand-arm vibration emission under real working conditions." *Proceedings of the Institute of Acoustics,* 28(3), 346-352.

Margarita, V.; Joaquin, L.S.; Pablo, R. and Antonio, P.G. (2008). "Hand transmitted vibration in power tools: Accomplishment of standards and user's perception." *International Journal of Industrial Ergonomics,* 38: 652-660.

Mayer, A. and Korhonen, E. (1999). "Assessment of the protection efficiency and comfort of personal protective equipment in real conditions of use." *Int J. Occup Saf Ergon,* 5(3):347-60. PubMed Result.mht. (Retrieved on 12th Aug, 2008)

Mohamed, S. (2002). "Safety climate in construction site environments." *Journal of Construction Engineering and Management,* 128 (5): 375–383.

National Library of Medicine (2008). *e-reference.* http://www.nlm.nih.gov/medlineplus/headand braininjuries. html. (Retrieved on 18th July, 2007)

New York Committee for Occupational Safety and Health (NYCOSH) report (2005). *Use of PPE tool. e-reference.* http://www.nycosh.org. (Retrieved on 13th Jan, 2007)

NIOSH Alert (April 1992). DHHS (NIOSH) Publication No. 91-116a *e-reference.* Workzone.safety/NIOSHalert.org (Retrieved on 13th Jan, 2007).

Norris, B.J. and Wilson, J.R.(1997). *Designing safety into products making ergonomics evaluation a part of the design process.* The University of Nottingham, Nottingham, U.K.

Oberg, T. (1994). "Subjective and objective evaluation of shoulder muscle fatigue." *Ergonomics,* 37(8): 1323-33.

Occupational Safety and Health Council (1994). *The study of the quality of eye protector devices used in Hong,* cited in Occupational Safety and Health Council 2002, A survey on usage of Personal Protective Equipment in Hong Kong. *e-reference.* OSHC_SurveyUsageProtectiveEquip.pdf (Retrieved on 13th Jan, 2007)

Occupational Safety and Health Council (2002). *A survey on usage of Personal Protective Equipment in Hong Kong. e-reference.* OSHC_ Survey Usage ProtectiveEquip.pdf. (Retrieved on 13th Jan, 2007)

OSHA Report (2005). *Preventing lead poisoning in construction workers. e-reference* http://www.OSHA.org. (Retrieved on 13/Jan/2007)

Paull, J.M. and Rosenthal, F.S. (1987). "Heat strain and heat stress for workers wearing protective suits at a hazardous waste site." *American Industrial Hygiene Association Journal,* 48: 458-462.

Pheasant, S. (1991). *Ergonomics, Work and Health,* 98-107. Macmillan Press, Hampshire.

Porter, J.M.; Case, K. and Freer, M.T. (1999). "Computer aided design and human models." In: Karwowaski, W. (eds.). *Handbook of Occupational Ergonomics.* CRC Press LLC, Florida, 479-500.

Public Employees Occupational Safety and Health (PEOSH) Programme (2003). New Jersey Department of Health and Senior Services "Personal Protective Equipment" Publication: OSHA 3077.

Rio, R.P. (1998). *Musculoskeletal stress and health. e-reference.* www.ergo.huma. cornell.edu/guide-net.html. (Retrieved on 12th Oct, 2008)

Robinson, E. (2001). *Personal Protective Equipment. Foot protection. e-reference.* http://www.esf..uvm.edu/sirippt/footprotect/index.htm. (Retrieved on 23rd Feb., 2007)

Ryan, G.A. (1989). "Musculo-skeletal symptoms in supermarket workers." *Ergonomics,* 32(3): 359-71.

Safe and healthy working (2007). *Healthy and safety information: Personal Protective Equipment at work. e-reference.* http://www.satiw.co.uk/main-section/workplace-topic/personalprotective-equipment.cfm. (Retrieved on 3rd July, 2007)

Schoeman, J.J. and Schroder, H.H.E. (1994). "Vibration and white finger effect." *Occupational Hygiene,* Cape Town: Juta.

Scott, W.; Barbara, C.L.; Paul, D.G. and Dean, T.S. (2002). "Assessment of personal protective equipment use among Midwestern farmers." *Am. J. Ind. Med*, 42:236-247.

Shanthakumar, A.R. (2006). "Safety cover for construction workers, Department of Civil Engineering, IIT Madras;" published in *The Hindu*, Sep 9, 2006.

Sokol, B. (2004). "Safety equipment use trends upward in heavy construction." Published in ISEA newsletter-protection update Fall-2004.North Moore Street Arlington, USA.

Stout, Nancy Ed. D. and Pizatella, M.S. Tim (2006). "NIOSH science blog, research to practice for injury prevention, department of health and human services, centre for disease control and prevention." *e-reference.* http://www.NIOSH.org. (Retrieved on 22rd April, 2007).

Szczecińska, K. and Lezak, K. (2000). "Review of research studies of ergonomic aspects of selected personal protective equipment." *Int J. Occup Saf Ergon*, Spec No:143-51.

Thakur, T.C. and Sharma, P. (1998). "Ergonomic assessment of various activities performed by women farmers in farm households of hill region of U. P." Report of *ad hoc* Research Project. I.C.A.R., New Delhi.

The Week (2004). *Ergonomics—How to make your workplace comfortable?* p. 32.

Toole, T. (2002). "Construction site safety rules." *Journal of Construction Engineering and Management*, May-June, 203-210.

Verghese, M.A.; Chatterjee, L.; Atreya, N. and Bhatnagar, A. (1989). *Ergonomics in kitchen design*. UGC Report 10. Deptt. of Family Resource Management SNDT, Bombay, India.

W.C.U. (2004). *Personal Protective Programme in West Chester University of Pennsylvania. e-reference.* www.wcu.edu/safety.html . (Retrieved on 23rd July, 2008)

Wasserman, D.E. (1985). "Raynaud phenomenon as it relates to hand-tool vibration in the workplace." *American Industrial Hygiene Association Journal*, 46 (12), B10.

Weir, E. and Lander, L. (2005). "Hand arm vibration syndrome." *Canadian Medical Association Journal*, 172 (8): 1001-1002.

Yingfeng, Li. and Yong, B. (2008). "Comparison of characteristics between fatal and injury accidents in the highway construction zones", *Safety Science*, vol. 46. *e-reference.* workzonesafety_org.mht. (Retrieved on 13rd Jan, 2007)

Young, P.V. (1996). *Scientific social survey and research.* Prentice-Hall of India Pvt. Ltd., New Delhi.

Index